The Oxford Diocesan Calendar And Clergy List

Church of England. Diocese of Oxford

CHRIST CHURCH CATHEDRAL, OXFORD.

(Printed for the Oxford Diocesan Calendar.)

THE

Oxford

Diocesan Calendar

AND CLERGY LIST,

FOR THE YEAR OF OUR LORD

1859.

Containing,

A Calendar, with the Daily Lessons;

INFORMATION RELATING TO THE CHURCH,

THE UNIVERSITIES, AND THE STATE;

WITH A COMPLETE LIST OF THE PARISHES AND CLERGY

IN THE DIOCESE OF OXFORD,

THE DIOCESAN SOCIETIES, SCHOOLS, &c.;

AND GENERAL COUNTY INFORMATION.

SECOND YEAR OF ISSUE.

OXFORD AND LONDON:

JOHN HENRY AND JAMES PARKER.

AND SOLD BY ALL BOOKSELLERS.

M DCCC LIX.

PRINTED BY MESSRS. PARKER, CORNMARKET, OXFORD.

TO

THE RIGHT REVEREND

THE LORD BISHOP OF OXFORD,

THIS ATTEMPT

TO PLACE WITHIN THE REACH OF

CHURCHMEN

IN THE THREE COUNTIES OF BERKS., BUCKS., AND OXON,

A SUCCINCT ACCOUNT OF THE STATE AND PROGRESS OF THE CHURCH

IN THEIR DIOCESE,

IS,

WITH HIS LORDSHIP'S PERMISSION,

RESPECTFULLY DEDICATED

BY

THE PUBLISHERS.

PREFACE.

THIS Calendar consists of two Parts. The First Part has been published separately for some years, under the name of "PARKER'S CHURCH CALENDAR."

The same kind of information which the First Part affords with regard to the Church at large, is given far more fully, in the Second Part, respecting the individual Diocese of Oxford.

The cordial reception given to the first year's issue warrants the Publishers in anticipating a still larger measure of patronage for the present issue of the DIOCESAN CALENDAR.

By the information here afforded respecting the various CHURCH INSTITUTIONS in the diocese, the reader is enabled to see the works that are being carried on, and where most his aid and sympathy are required.

The complete list of the ARCHDEACONS, Rural Deans, Rectors, Vicars, and Curates in the diocese, with the districts or cures over which they severally preside, enables persons to realize the actual position of the Church in the diocese; while by the arrangement of each Deanery being complete in itself, with indices both to names and places, the address of every Clergyman in the diocese is always at hand, and intercommunication is facilitated.

By information respecting the SCHOOLS in the diocese, parents are enabled to select with greater independence the one most suitable to their requirements.

In the RECORD of the diocese most Churchmen will find matter of considerable interest, and the narrative of the works in one parish may lead to stimulate other parishes to active exertion; and, at the least, it cannot but be satisfactory to Churchmen to see what progress is being made around them.

CONTENTS.—PART I.

PART II.

GENERAL INDEX.

NOTES FOR THE YEAR 1859.

The Golden Number, XVII.
The Epact . . 26
The Sunday Letter . B.

Septuagesima Sunday . . Feb. 20	Whit-Sunday . . . June 12
Easter-day . . . . April 24	Trinity Sunday . . . „ 19
Rogation Sunday . . . May 29	Advent Sunday . . Nov. 27

The Feasts that are to be observed in the Church of England throughout the year.

ALL SUNDAYS.	*S. John Baptist* . . . June 24
The Circumcision . . . Jan. 1	S. Peter . . . „ 29
The Epiphany . . „ 6	S. James . . . July 25
The Conversion of S. Paul . „ 25	S. Bartholomew . . . Aug. 24
The Purification . . . Feb. 2	*S. Matthew* . . . Sept. 21
S. Matthias . . . „ 24	S. Michael . . . „ 29
The Annunciation . . Mar. 25	S. Luke . . . Oct. 18
Easter-Monday . . April 25	*S. Simon and S. Jude* . . „ 28
Easter-Tuesday . . „ 26	All Saints . . . Nov. 1
S. Mark . . . „ 25	S. Andrew . . . „ 30
S. Philip and S. James . . May 1	S. Thomas . . . Dec. 21
Ascension-day . . June 2	The NATIVITY of our LORD . „ 25
S. Barnabas . . „ 11	S. Stephen . . . „ 26
Whit-Monday . . „ 13	S. John the Evangelist . „ 27
Whit-Tuesday . . „ 14	The Holy Innocents . . „ 28

Those printed in Italic fall this year on fast-days, or days of abstinence.

The Vigils, Fasts, and days of abstinence throughout the year.

ALL THE FRIDAYS IN THE YEAR.	The Eve of S. John Baptist . June 23
The Eve of the Purification . Feb. 1	„ S. Peter . „ 28
Eve of S. Matthias . . . Feb. 23	„ *S. James* . July 23
THE FORTY DAYS OF LENT—Mar. 9 to	„ S. Bartholomew . Aug. 23
April 23 (except Sundays).	„ S. Matthew . Sept. 20
The Ember Days ⎫ W. . Mar. 16	The Ember Days ⎫ W. . „ 21
after ⎬ F. . „ 18	after ⎬ F. . „ 23
1st Sun. in Lent ⎭ S. . „ 19	Sept. 14 ⎭ S. . „ 24
The Eve of the Annunc. . „ 24	The Eve of S. Simon ⎫
Easter-even . . . April 23	and S. Jude ⎬ . Oct. 27
Rogation Days, M. . May 30	The Eve of All Saints . „ 31
„ „ T. . „ 31	„ S. Andrew . Nov. 29
„ „ W. . June 1	The Ember Days ⎫ W. . Dec. 14
The Eve of the Ascension-day „ 1	after ⎬ F. . „ 16
„ Pentecost . „ 11	Dec. 13. ⎭ S. . „ 17
The Ember Days ⎫ W. . „ 15	The Eve of S. Thomas . „ 20
after ⎬ F. . „ 17	„ the Nativity . . „ 24
Feast of Pent. ⎭ S. . „ 18	

Those Vigils printed in Italic are kept on the Saturday, the Holy-Day falling on a Monday.

NOTA BENE.—In the following Calendar all those days printed in Old English characters have a Proper Collect, Epistle, and Gospel appointed.
On all other days the Collect of the previous Sunday is to be said.
Where the mark ✝ occurs, the Collect for a previous day is appointed.
Where the mark ☉ occurs, the Collect for the morrow is to be used at even.
Where there is an asterisk, a reference is given at the foot of the page to such changes in the Services as are appointed in the Prayer-book.

| 31 Days. | JANUARY. | 1859. |

SUN.	1st	13th	25th	MOON.			
				New.	First Qr.	Full.	Last Qr.
Rises.	h. m. 8 8	h. m. 8 3	h. m. 7 51	Jan. h.m. 4 5 26 am.	Jan. h.m. 12 7 32 am.	Jan. h.m. 18 11 49 pm.	Jan. h.m. 25 8 45 pm.
Sets.	4 0	4 14	4 35				

Days.			Morn. Lessons.		Even. Lessons.	
1	S	*The Circumcision. *Feast.*	Gen. 17	Rom. 2	Deut 10 ver. 12	Colos. 2
2	B	*ii Sunday after Christmas. [†*Feast.*	Isa. 41	Matt. 1	Isa. 43	Rom. 1
3	M		Gen. 3	2	Gen. 4	2
4	Tu		5	3	6	3
5	W		7	4	8	4
		Epiphany.				
6	Th	*Epiphany. Twelfth day. Old [Christmas-Day. *Feast.*	Isa. 60	Luke 3 to v. 23	Isa. 49	John 2 to v. 12
7	F	*Abst.*	Gen. 9	Matt. 5	Gen. 12	Rom. 5
8	S	Lucian, P. and M. (A.D. 290). ☉	13	6	14	6
9	B	i Sunday after Epiphany. *Feast.*	Isa. 44	Matt. 7	Isa. 46	Rom. 7
10	M		Gen. 17	8	Gen. 18	8
11	Tu	Hilary Law Term begins.	19	9	20	9
12	W		21	10	22	10
13	Th	Hilary, B. & C. (368) Cam. Ter. beg.	23	11	24	11
14	F	Oxford Term begins. *Abst.*	25	12	26	12
15	S	☉	27	13	28	13
16	B	ii Sunday after Epiphany. *Feast.*	Isa. 51	Mat. 14	Isa. 53	Rom 14
17	M		Gen. 31	15	Gen. 32	15
18	Tu	Prisca, Rom. V. & M. (suf. A.D. 275).	33	16	34	16
19	W	*	35	17	37	1 Cor. 1
20	Th	Fabian, B. of Rome & M. (A.D. 250)	38	18	39	2
21	F	Agnes, Rom. V. & M. (A.D. 304). *Abst.*	40	19	41	3
22	S	Vincent, Span. D. & M. (A.D. 304). ☉	42	20	43	4
23	B	iii Sunday after Epiphany. *Feast.*	Isa. 55	Mat. 21	Isa. 56	1 Cor 5
24	M		Gen. 46	22	Gen. 47	6
25	Tu	Conversion of St. Paul, (A.D. 31; [suff. 68.) *Feast.*	Wisd. 5	Acts 22 to v. 22	Wisd. 6	Acts 26
26	W		Gen. 48	Mat. 23	Gen. 49	1 Cor. 7
27	Th		50	24	Exod. 1	8
28	F	*Abst.*	Exod. 2	25	3	9
29	S	☉	4	26	5	10
30	B	*iv Sunday after Epiphany. King Charles, Mart., 1649. *Feast.*	Isa. 57	Mat. 27	Isa. 58	1 Cor 11
31	M	*Hilary Law Term ends.	Exod. 8	28	Exod. 9	12

MEMORANDA.—1. The Circumcision. *Proper Coll., Epist. and Gosp.,* to serve for every day unto Epiphany. *Proper Preface* for Christmas-Day at Communion.
2. 2 Sunday after Christmas. *Collect, Epistle and Gospel* for the Circuncision.
6. The Epiphany. *Athanasian Creed.*   19. *Venite* in Psalms for the day.
30. K. Charles, Mart. to be kept the day following.   31. *Particular Service* for K. Charles, Mart. *Proper Hymn* instead of *Venite. Proper Psalms:* Morn., 9, 10, 11; Even., 79, 94, 85. *Proper Lessons:* Morn., 2 Sam. 1, Matt. 27; Even., Jer. 12, or Dan. 9, to ver. 22, Heb. 11, ver. 32, and 12, to ver. 7.

28 Days.	FEBRUARY.	1859.

SUN.	1st	13th	25th	MOON.			
				New	First Qr.	Full.	Last Qr.
Rises.	h. m. 7 41	h. m. 7 20	h. m. 6 56	Feb. h.m.	Feb. h.m.	Feb. h.m.	Feb. h.m.
Sets.	4 47	5 8	5 30	3 1 4am.	10 7 40 pm.	17 10 42am.	24 2 21 pm.

Days.			Morn. Lessons.		Even. Lessons.	
1	Tu	☉ *Vigil.*	Ex. 10	Mark 1	Ex. 11	1 Cor 13
2	W	Purif. of St. Mary the Virgin.	Wisd.9	2	Wis. 12	14
		[Candlemas-day. *Feast.*				
3	Th	Blasius, Bp. and Mar. (of Sebaste,	Ex. 12	3	Ex. 13	15
		[suffered A.D. 316).				
4	F	*Abst.*	14	4	15	16
5	S	Agatha, Virgin and Martyr (of Pa-	16	5	17	2 Cor. 1
		[lermo, suffered A.D. 253).☉				
6	B	5 Sunday after Epiphany. *Feast.*	Isa. 59	Mark 6	Isa. 64	2 Cor. 2
7	M		Ex. 20	7	Ex. 21	3
8	Tu		22	8	23	4
9	W		24	9	32	5
10	Th		33	10	34	6
11	F	*Abst.*	Lev. 18	11	Lev. 19	7
12	S	☉	20	12	26	8
13	B	6 Sunday after Epiphany. *Feast.*	Isa. 65	Mar.13	Isa. 66	2 Cor.9
14	M	Valentine, B. & M. (suf. A.D. 270).	Nu. 13	14	Nu. 14	10
15	Tu		16	15	17	11
16	W		20	16	21	12
17	Th		22	Luke 1	23	13
				to v. 39		
18	F	*Abst.*	24	1 v. 39	25	Gal. 1
19	S	*	☉ 27	2	30	2
20	B	Septuagesima Sunday. *Feast.*	Gen. 1	Luke 3	Gen. 2	Gal. 3
21	M		Nu. 35	4	Nu. 36	4
22	Tu		Deut. 1	5	Deut. 2	5
23	W	☉ *Vigil.*	3	6	4	6
24	Th	*St. Matthias, Apostle. *Feast.*	Wis. 19	7	Eclus 1	Eph. 1
25	F	*Abst.*	Deut. 5	8	Deut. 6	2
26	S	☉	7	9	8	3
27	B	Sexagesima Sunday. *Feast.*	Gen. 3	Luk.10	Gen. 6	Eph. 4
28	M	Cambridge Term div. noon.	Deu.11	11	Deu.12	5

MEMORANDA.

19. *Venite* in Psalms for the day.
24. St. Matthias. *Athanasian Creed.*

31 Days.	MARCH.	1859.

SUN.	1st	13th	25th	MOON.			
Rises.	h. m. 6 48	h. m. 6 21	h. m. 5 54	New.	First Qr.	Full.	Last Qr.
Sets.	5 38	5 59	6 18	Mar. h.m. 4 7 11 pm.	Mar. h.m. 12 4 39 am.	Mar. h.m. 18 9 45 pm.	Mar. h.m. 26 9 27 am.

Days.			Morn. Lessons.		Even. Lessons.	
1	Tu	DAVID, Archbp. of Menevia, (d. 544).	Deu.15	Luk.12	Deu.16	Eph. 6
2	W	CHAD, Bp. of Lichfield, (A.D. 673).	17	13	18	Phil. 1
3	Th		19	14	20	2
4	F	*Abst.*	21	15	22	3
5	S	☉	24	16	25	4
6	☉	Quinquagesima Sunday. *Feast.*	Gen. 9 to v. 20	Luk.17	Gen.12	Colos.1
7	M	PERPETUA, Maurit. M. (suf. A.D. 203).	Deu.28	18	Deu.29	2
8	Tu	Shrove-Tuesday.	30	19	31	3
		Lent.				
9	W	*Ash-Wednesday. *Fast.*	32	20	33	4
10	Th	†*Fast.*	34	21	Josh. 1	1Thes1
11	F	†*Fast.*	Josh. 2	22	3	2
12	S	GREGORY, B. of Rome and C. A.D. [(604). ☉†*Fast.*	4	23	5	3
13	☉	i Sunday in Lent. †*Feast.*	Gen.19 to v. 30	Luk.24	Gen.22	1Thes4
14	M	†*Fast.*	Josh. 8	John 1	Josh. 9	5
15	Tu	†*Fast.*	10	2	23	2Thes1
16	W	Ember-day. †*Fast.*	24	3	Judg. 1	2
17	Th	†*Fast.*	Judg. 2	4	3	3
18	F	EDWARD, King of West Sax.(A.D.978.) [*Ember-day.* †*Fast.*	4	5	5	1Tim.1
19	S	* Ember-day ☉†*Fast.*	6	6	7	2, 3
20	☉	ii Sunday in Lent. †*Feast.*	Gen.27	John 7	Gen.34	1Tim.4
21	M	BENEDICT, Abbot (A.D. 543). †*Fast.*	Jud. 10	8	Jud. 11	5
22	Tu	†*Fast.*	12	9	13	6
23	W	†*Fast.*	14	10	15	2Tim.1
24	Th	☉†*Fast. Vigil.*	16	11	17	2
25	F	Annunc. of the blessed V. M. †*Fast.*	Eclus2	12	Eclus3	3
26	S	☉†*Fast.*	Jud. 18	13	Jud. 19	4
27	☉	iii Sunday in Lent. †*Feast.*	Gen.39	John14	Gen.42	Titus 1
28	M	†*Fast.*	Ruth 1	15	Ruth 2	2, 3
29	Tu	†*Fast.*	3	16	4	Philem
30	W	†*Fast.*	1Sam 1	17	1Sam 2	Heb. 1
31	Th	†*Fast.*	3	18	4	2

MEMORANDA.—9. ASH-WEDNESDAY. *Proper Psalms:* Morn., 6, 32, 38 ; Even., 102, 130, 143. *Commination.* The *Collect* to be read throughout Lent after the Collect for the day. 19. *Venite* in Psalms for the day.

30 Days.			APRIL.				1859.

SUN.	1st	13th	25th	MOON.			
Rises.	h. m. 5 38	h. m. 5 11	h. m. 4 47	New.	First Qr.	Full.	Last Qr.
Sets.	6 31	6 50	7 11	Apr. h.m. 3 10 18am	Apr. h.m. 10 11 21am	Apr. h.m. 17 9 6 am	Apr. h.m. 25 4 45 am.

Days.				Morn. Lessons.		Even. Lessons.	
1	F		†*Fast.*	1 Sa. 5	John 19	1 Sa. 6	Heb. 3
2	S		☉ †*Fast.*	7	20	8	4
3	𝕭	ᵗⁱᵇ Sunday in Lent. RICHARD, Bp. [of Chichester, (A.D. 1253.) †*Feast.*		Gen. 43	John 21	Gen. 45	Heb. 5
4	M	S. AMBROSE, Bp. of Milan (A.D. 397). [†*Fast.*		1 Sa. 11	Acts 1	1 Sa. 12	6
5	Tu		†*Fast.*	13	2	14	7
6	W		†*Fast.*	15	3	16	8
7	Th		†*Fast.*	17	4	18	9
8	F		†*Fast.*	19	5	20	10
9	S		☉ †*Fast.*	21	6	22	11
10	𝕭	ᵇ Sunday in Lent.	†*Feast.*	Exod. 3	Acts 7	Exod. 5	Heb. 12
11	M		†*Fast.*	1 Sa. 25	8	1 Sa. 26	13
12	Tu		†*Fast.*	27	9	28	James 1
13	W		†*Fast.*	29	10	30	2
14	Th		†*Fast.*	31	11	2 Sa. 1	3
15	F	Cambridge Term ends.	†*Fast.*	2 Sam 2	12	3	4
16	S	Oxford Term ends.	☉ †*Fast.*	4	13	5	5
17	𝕭	Sunday next before Easter. [Palm-Sunday. †*Feast.*		Exod. 9	Mat. 26	Ex. 10	Heb. 5 to v. 11
18	M	Monday before Easter. †*Fast.*		2 Sa. 8	Acts 15	2 Sa. 9	1 Pet. 2
19	Tu	•Tuesday before Easter. ALPHEGE, [Abp. of Cant., (stoned 1012). †*Fast.*		10	16	11	3
20	W	Wednesday before Easter. †*Fast.*		Hos. 13	John 11 v. 45	Hos. 14	4
21	Th	Thursday before Easter. †*Fast.*		Dan. 9	John 13	Jer. 31	5
22	F	•Good Friday. †*Fast.*		Gen. 22 to v. 20	18	Isa. 53	2
23	S	Easter=Eben. ST. GEORGE, Mar. [(suff. A.D. 290). ☉ †*Fast.* *Vigil.*		Zech. 9	Luk. 23 v. 50	Ex. 13	Heb. 4
		Easter.					
24	𝕭	•Easter=Day. *Feast.*		Ex. 12	Rom. 6	Ex. 14	Acts 2 ver. 22
25	M	• Monday in Easter=Week. St. [Mark. *Feast.*		16	Mat. 28	17	3
26	Tu	•Tuesday in Easter=Week. *Feast.*		20	Luk. 24 to v. 13	32	1 Cor 15
27	W			2 Sa. 24	Acts 24	1 Kgs. 1	1 John 3
28	Th			1 Kgs. 2	25	3	4
29	F		*Abst.*	4	26	5	5
30	S		☉	6	27	7	2 3 Joh

MEMORANDA.—19. *Venite* in Psalms for the day.   22. GOOD FRIDAY. *Proper Psalms:* Morn., 22, 40, 54; Even., 69, 88.   24. EASTER-DAY. *Anthems* instead of *Venite. Proper Psalms:* Morn., 2, 57, 111; Even., 113, 114, 118. *Athanasian Creed. Proper Preface.* 25, 26. *Proper Preface* for Easter-day.

31 Days.		MAY.			1859.

SUN.	1st	13th	25th	MOON.			
				New	First Qr.	Full.	Last Qr.
Rises.	h. m. 4 35	h. m. 4 14	h. m. 3 58	May h. m.	May h. m.	May h. m.	May h. m.
Sets.	7 21	7 39	7 56	2 10 4 pm.	9 4 59 pm.	16 9 7pm.	24 10 49 pm.

Days.			Morn. Lessons.		Even. Lessons.	
1	B	*i Sunday after Easter. St. Philip [and St. James. *Feast.*	Eclus 7	John 1 ver. 43	Eclus 9	Jude
2	M		1 Kgs. 8	Acts 28	1 Kgs. 9	Rom. 1
3	Tu	Invent. of the Cross, (A.D. 326.)	10	Matt. 1	11	2
4	W	Oxf. and Camb. Terms begin.	12	2	13	3
5	Th		14	3	15	4
6	F	St. John, Ev. ante Port. Lat. *Abst.*	16	4	17	5
7	S	⊙	18	5	19	6
8	B	ii Sunday after Easter. *Feast.*	Nu. 23 and 24	Matt. 6	Nu. 25	Rom. 7
9	M		1 Kg 22	7	2 Kgs. 1	8
10	Tu		2 Kgs. 2	8	3	9
11	W		4	9	5	10
12	Th	Easter Term ends.	6	10	7	11
13	F	*Abst.*	8	11	9	12
14	S	⊙	10	12	11	13
15	B	iii Sunday after Easter. *Feast.*	Deu. 4	Mat. 13	Deut. 5	Ro. 14
16	M		2 Kg 14	14	2 Kg 15	15
17	Tu		16	15	17	16
18	W		18	16	19	1 Cor. 1
19	Th	*Dunstan, Abp. of Cant. (A.D. 988.)	20	17	21	2
20	F	*Abst.*	22	18	23	3
21	S	⊙	24	19	25	4
22	B	iv Sunday after Easter. *Feast.*	Deu. 6	Mat. 20	Deut. 7	1 Cor. 5
23	M		Ezra 4	21	Ezra 5	6
24	Tu		6	22	7	7
25	W		9	23	Neh. 1	8
26	Th	Augustine, first Abp. of Cant. (604).	Neh. 2	24	4	9
27	F	Ven. Bede, Pt. (A.D. 735). *Abst.*	5	25	6	10
28	S	⊙	8	26	9	11
29	B	*v Sunday after Easter. Rog. S. *Feast.* [King Charles II. Rest. 1660.	Deut. 8	Mat. 27	Deut. 9	1 Cor 12
30	M	*Rogation-day.*	Esth. 1	28	Esth. 2	13
31	Tu	*Rogation-day.*	3	Mark 1	4	14

MEMORANDA.—1. i. Sunday after Easter. *Proper Preface* for Easter-day. Lessons for the Sunday: Morn., Numb. 16; Even., Numb. 22.
19. *Venite* in Psalms for the day.
29. King Charles Restored. *Particular Service: Proper Hymn* instead of *Venite. Proper Psalms:* 124, 126, 129, 118. 1st Less. 2 Sam. 19, v. 9, or Numb. 16; 2nd Less., Epistle of St. Jude.

30 Days.	JUNE.	1859.

Sun rises.	h. m. 3 51	h. m. 3 45	h. m. 3 46	New Moon.	First Qr.	Full.	Last Qr.
Sets.	8 4	8 15	8 18	June h.m. { 1 7 10am. { 30 2 41pm.	June h.m. } 7 10 48pm.	June h.m. 15 10 18am.	June h.m. 23 2 32 pm.

Days.			Morn. Lessons.		Even. Lessons.	
1	W	NICOMEDE, Pr. & M. *Rog.-d.* ⊙ *Vigil.*	Esth. 5	Mark 2	Esth. 6	1Cor15
2	Th	*Ascension=Day. *Feast.*	Deu.10	Luk.24 ver. 44	2Kgs.2	Eph. 4 to v. 17
3	F	*Abst.*	Esth. 9	Mark 4	Job 1	2 Cor. 1
4	S	⊙	Job 2	5	3	2
5	B	*Sunday after Ascension=Day. *Feast.* [BONIFACE, Bp. (suff.,755).	Deu.12	Mark 6	Deu 13	2 Cor. 3
6	M		Job 6	7	Job 7	4
7	Tu		8	8	9	5
8	W		10	9	11	6
9	Th		12	10	13	7
10	F	Oxford Term ends. *Abst.*	14	11	15	8
11	S	St. Barnabas, Apostle. ⊙ *Vigil.*	Eclu10	Acts14	Eclu12	Acts 15 to v. 36
		Whitsuntide.				
12	B	*Whit=Sunday. *Feast.*	Deu.16 to v. 18	Acts10 ver. 34	Isa. 11	Acts 19 to v. 21
13	M	*Monday in Whitsun=Week. *Feast.*	Gen.11 to v. 10	1Co.12	Nu11v 16 to 30	1Cor14 to v. 26
14	Tu	*Tuesday in Whitsun=Week. *Feast.*	1Sa. 19 ver. 18	1Thes5 v.12to24	Deu 30	1 Jhn.4 to ver.14
15	W	Oxford Term begins. *Ember-day.*	Job 23	Mar.15	Jb.24,5	2Cor12
16	Th	Trinity Law Term ends.	26, 27	16	28	13
17	F	St. ALBAN, Martyr. *Ember-day.*	29	Luke 1	30	Gal. 1
18	S	⊙ *Ember-day.*	31	2	32	2
19	B	*Trinity Sunday. *Feast.*	Gen. 1	Matt. 3	Gen.18	1John5
20	M	*TRANS. OF KING EDW. (A.D. 1001). [ACC. OF QUEEN VICTORIA, 1837.	Job 35	Luke 4	Job 36	Gal. 4
21	Tu		37	5	38	5
22	W		39	6	40	6
23	Th	⊙ *Vigil.*	41	7	42	Eph. 1
24	F	*St. John Baptist. Midsummer-day.	Mal. 3	Matt. 3	Mal. 4	Matt14 to v. 13
25	S	⊙	Prov. 1	Luke 8	Prov. 2	Eph. 2
26	B	1 Sunday after Trinity. *Feast.*	Josh 10	Luke 9	Josh 23	Eph. 3
27	M		Prov. 5	10	Prov. 6	4
28	Tu	⊙ *Vigil.*	7	11	8	5
29	W	St. Peter, Apostle. *Feast.*	Eclu15	Acts 3	Eclu19	Acts 4
30	Th		Prov. 9	Luk12	Prov10	Eph. 6

MEMORANDA.—2. ASCENSION-DAY. *Proper Psalms :* Morn., 8, 15, 21; Even., 24, 47, 108. *Athan. Creed. Pr. Pref.* 5. SUNDAY AFTER ASCENSION. *Pr. Pref.* for Ascension-Day. 12. WHIT-SUNDAY. *Proper Psalms :* Morn. 48, 68 ; Even., 104, 145. *Athanasian Creed. Prop. Pref.* 13, 14. *Pr. Pref.* for Whit-Sunday. 19. TRINITY SUNDAY. *Venite* in Psalms for the day. *Athan. Creed. Pr. Pref.* 20. ACCESSION. *Particular Service.* 24. ST. JOHN BAPTIST. *Athan. Creed.*

31 Days.	JULY.	1859.

SUN.	1st	13th	25th	MOON.			
				First Qr.	Full.	Last Qr.	New.
Rises.	h. m. 3 49	h. m. 4 0	h. m. 4 14	July h.m. 7 5 54am.	July h.m. 14 12 53pm.	July h.m. 23 3 26am.	July h.m. 29 9 44pm.
Sets.	8 17	8 11	7 56				

Days.				Morn. Lessons.		Even. Lessons.	
1	F		Abst.	Prov 11	Luk.13	Prov12	Phil. 1
2	S	VISITATION OF THE B. V. MARY. ☉		13	14	14	2
3	B	ii Sunday after Trinity.	Feast.	Judg. 4	Luk.15	Judg. 5	Phil. 3
4	M	TRANSL. OF ST. MARTIN, B. and C.		Prov 17	16	Prov 18	4
5	Tu	Oxford Act and Camb. Com.		19	17	20	Colos.1
6	W			21	18	22	2
7	Th			23	19	24	3
8	F	Cambridge Term ends.	Abst.	25	20	26	4
9	S	Oxford Term ends.	☉	27	21	28	1Thes1
10	B	iii Sunday after Trinity.	Feast.	1 Sam 2	Luk.22	1 Sam 3	1Thes2
11	M			Ecles 1	23	Ecles 2	3
12	Tu			3	24	4	4
13	W			5	John 1	6	5
14	Th			7	2	8	2Thes1
15	F	SWITHUN, Bishop of Winch., Transl. [(A.D. 971).	Abst.	9	3	10	2
16	S		☉	11	4	12	3
17	B	iv Sunday after Trinity.	Feast.	1 Sa.12	John 5	1 Sa. 13	1Tim.1
18	M			Jer. 3	6	Jer. 4	2, 3
19	Tu	*		5	7	6	4
20	W	MARGARET, V. and M. at Antioch. [(A.D. 278).		7	8	8	5
21	Th	ST. MARY MAGDALEN.		9	9	10	6
22	F		Abst.	11	10	12	2Tim.1
23	S	☉ Vigil.		13	11	14	2
24	B	v Sunday after Trinity.	☉ Feast.	1 Sa.15	John12	1 Sa. 17	2Tim.3
25	M	*ST. JAMES, Apostle.	Feast.	Eclu21	13	Eclu22	4
26	Tu	ST. ANNE, Mother of the B. V. Mary.		Jer. 17	14	Jer. 18	Titus 1
27	W			19	15	20	2, 3
28	Th			21	16	22	Philem
29	F		Abst.	23	17	24	Heb. 1
30	S		☉	25	18	26	2
31	B	vi Sunday after Trinity.	Feast.	2 Sa.12	John19	2Sa.19	Heb. 3

MEMORANDA.—19. *Venite* in Psalms for the day.
25. ST. JAMES. *Athanasian Creed.*

31 Days.	AUGUST.	1859.

SUN.	1st	13th	25th	MOON.			
	h. m.	h. m.	h. m.	First Qr.	Full.	Last Qr.	New.
Rises.	4 25	4 44	5 2	Aug. h.m.	Aug. h.m.	Aug. h.m.	Aug. h.m.
Sets.	7 46	7 25	7 1	5 3 22pm.	13 4 34pm.	21 1 46pm.	28 5 14 am.

Days.			Morn. Lessons.		Even. Lessons.	
1	M	LAMMAS-DAY.	Jer. 29	John 20	Jer. 30	Heb. 4
2	Tu		31	21	32	5
3	W		33	Acts 1	34	6
4	Th		35	2	36	7
5	F	*Abst.*	37	3	38	8
6	S	TRANSFIGUR. OF OUR LORD. ⊙	39	4	40	9
7	𝔅	bii Sunday after Trinity. NAME OF [JESUS. *Feast*	2 Sa. 21	Acts 5	2 Sa. 24	Heb 10
8	M		Jer. 43	6	Jer. 44	11
9	Tu		45, 46	7	47	12
10	W	ST. LAWRENCE, Archd. of Rome and [M. (A.D. 258.)	48	8	49	13
11	Th		50	9	51	Jas. 1
12	F	*Abst.*	52	10	Lam. 1	2
13	S	⊙	Lam. 2	11	3	3
14	𝔅	biii Sunday after Trinity. *Feast*	1 Kg 13	Acts 12	1 Kg 17	Jas. 4
15	M		Ezek. 2	13	Ezek. 3	5
16	Tu		6	14	7	1 Pet. 1
17	W		13	15	14	2
18	Th		18	16	33	3
19	F	* *Abst.*	34	17	Dan. 1	4
20	S	⊙	Dan. 2	18	3	5
21	𝔅	ix Sunday after Trinity. *Feast*	1 Kg 18	Acts 19	1 Kg 19	2 Pet. 1
22	M		Dan. 6	20	Dan. 7	2
23	Tu	⊙ *Vigil.*	8	21	9	3
24	W	*St. Bartholomew, Apostle. *Feast*	Eclu 24	22	Eclu 29	1 John 1
25	Th		Dan. 10	23	Dan 11	2
26	F	*Abst.*	12	24	Hos. 1	3
27	S	⊙	Hos 2,3	25	4	4
28	𝔅	x Sunday after Trinity. ST. AUGUS- [TIN, Bishop of Hippo, C. and D. [(A.D. 430). *Feast*	1 Kg 21	Acts 26	1 Kg 22	1 John 5
29	M	Beheading of ST. JOHN BAPT.	Hos. 8	27	Hos. 9	2, 3 Jo.
30	Tu		10	28	11	Jude
31	W		12	Matt. 1	13	Rom. 1

MEMORANDA.—19. *Venite* in Psalms for the day.
24. ST. BARTHOLOMEW. *Athanasian Creed.*

SEPTEMBER.

30 Days.   **SEPTEMBER.**   **1859.**

SUN.	1st	13th	25th	MOON.			
	h. m.	h. m.	h. m.	First Qr.	Full.	Last Qr.	New.
Rises.	5 13	5 32	5 51	Sept. h.m.	Sept. h.m.	Sept. h.m.	Sept. h.m.
Sets.	6 46	6 18	5 52	4 4 5 am.	12 8 31am.	19 10 14pm.	26 1 56pm.

Days.			Morn. Lessons.		Even. Lessons.	
1	Th	GILES, ABBOT, (died A.D. 725.)	Hos. 14	Mat. 2	Joel 1	Rom. 2
2	F	*Abst.*	Joel 2	3	3	3
3	S	☉	Amos 1	4	Amos 2	4
4	B	xi Sunday after Trinity. *Feast.*	2 Kgs. 5	Mat. 5	2 Kgs. 9	Rom. 5
5	M		Amos 5	6	Amos 6	6
6	Tu		7	7	8	7
7	W	ENURCHUS, Bp. (d. A.D. 340).	9	8	Obadi.	8
8	Th	NATIVITY OF THE B.V. MARY.	Jonah 1	9	Jo. 2, 3	9
9	F	*Abst.*	4	10	Mica. 1	10
10	S	☉	Mica. 2	11	3	11
11	B	xii Sunday after Trinity. *Feast.*	2 Kg 10	Mat. 12	2 Kg 18	Rom 12
12	M		Mica. 6	13	Mica. 7	13
13	Tu		Nah. 1	14	Nah. 2	14
14	W	HOLY CROSS DAY, (recov. A.D. 335).	3	15	Hab. 1	15
15	Th		Hab. 2	16	3	16
16	F	*Abst.*	Zeph. 1	17	Zeph. 2	1 Cor. 1
17	S	LAMBERT, Bp. (of Maestricht; ap- [pointed A.D. 709) & M. ☉	3	18	Hag. 1	2
18	B	xiii Sunday after Trinity. *Feast.*	2 Kg 19	Mat. 19	2 Kg 23	1 Cor. 3
19	M		Zec 2,3	20	Zec 4,5	4
20	Tu	☉ *Vigil.*	6	21	7	5
21	W	St. Matthew. *Ember-day.*	Eclu 35	22	Eclu 38	6
22	Th		Zech. 8	23	Zech. 9	7
23	F	*Ember-day.* *Abst.*	10	24	11	8
24	S	*Ember-day.* ☉	12	25	13	9
25	B	xiv Sunday after Trinity. *Feast.*	Jerem 5	Mat. 26	Jer. 22	1 Cor 10
26	M	S. CYPRIAN, Abp. & M. (suff. 258).	Mal. 2	27	Mal. 3	11
27	Tu		4	28	Tobit 1	12
28	W		Tobit 2	Mark 1	3	13
29	Th	St. Michael and All Angels. [Michaelmas-day. *Feast.*	Gen. 32	Acts 12 to v. 20	Dan. 10 ver. 5.	Jude v.6 to 16
30	F	ST. JEROME, A.D. 420. *Abst.*	Tobit 4	Mark 3	Tobit 6	1 Cor 15

MEMORANDA.—19. *Venite* in Psalms for the day.
21. ST. MATTHEW. *Athanasian Creed.*

31 Days.	OCTOBER.	1859.

SUN.	1st	13th	25th	MOON.			
Rises.	h. m. 6 1	h. m. 6 22	h. m. 6 42	First Qr.	Full.	Last Qr.	New.
Sets.	5 40	5 10	4 45	Oct. h.m. 3 8 32 pm.	Oct. h.m. 11 11 51 pm.	Oct. h.m. 19 5 43 am.	Oct. h.m. 25 12 32 pm.

Days.		Morn. Lessons.		Even. Lessons.	
1	S	REMIGIUS, Bp. of Rheims, (d. 535). ☉	Tobit 7	Mark 4	Tobit 8	1 Cor 16
2	ℬ	xv Sunday after Trinity. *Feast.*	Jer. 35	Mark 5	Jer. 36	2 Cor. 1
3	M		Tob. 11	6	Tob. 12	2
4	Tu		13	7	14	3
5	W		Judth 1	8	Judth 2	4
6	Th	FAITH, Virgin and Martyr, (of Agen.; [suffered A.D. 290).	3	9	4	5
7	F	*Abst.*	5	10	6	6
8	S	☉	7	11	8	7
9	ℬ	xvi Sunday after Trinity. ST. DENYS, [B. and M. (A.D. 272). *Feast.*	Ezek. 2	Mar 12	Ezk. 13	2 Cor. 8
10	M	Oxford and Camb. Terms begin.	Judh 11	13	Judh 12	9
11	Tu		13	14	14	10
12	W		15	15	16	11
13	Th	Transl. of King Edward Conf. (died [1066; relics transl. 1163).	Wisd. 1	16	Wisd. 2	12
14	F	*Abst.*	3	Luke 1 to v. 39	4	13
15	S	☉	5	1 ver 39	6	Gal. 1
16	ℬ	xvii Sunday after Trinity. *Feast.*	Ezk. 14	Luke 2	Ezk. 18	Gal. 2
17	M	ETHELDREDA, Virgin, (died 670.)	Wisd. 9	3	Wis. 10	3
18	Tu	St. Luke, Evangelist. *Feast.*	Eclu 51	4	Job 1	4
19	W	*	Wis. 11	5	Wis. 12	5
20	Th		13	6	14	6
21	F	*Abst.*	15	7	16	Eph. 1
22	S	☉	17	8	18	2
23	ℬ	xviii Sunday after Trinity. *Feast.*	Ezk. 20	Luke 9	Ezk. 24	Eph. 3
24	M		Eclus 2	10	Eclus 3	4
25	Tu	CRISPIN, Martyr, (suffered 308).	4	11	5	5
26	W		6	12	7	6
27	Th	☉ *Vigil.*	8	13	9	Phil. 1
28	F	*St. Simon and St. Jude, Apostles.	Job 24 and 25	14	Job 42	2
29	S	☉	Eclu 10	15	Eclu 11	3
30	ℬ	xix Sunday after Trinity. *Feast.*	Dan. 3	Luk 16	Dan. 6	Phil. 4
31	M	☉ *Vigil.*	Eclu 14	17	Eclu 15	Colos. 1

MEMORANDA.
19. *Venite* in Psalms for the day.
28. ST. SIMON AND ST. JUDE. *Athanasian Creed.*

30 Days.   NOVEMBER.   1859.

SUN.	1st	13th	25th	MOON.			
	h. m.	h. m.	h. m.	First Qr.	Full.	Last Qr.	New.
Rises.	6 55	7 16	7 36	Nov. h.m.	Nov. h.m.	Nov. h.m.	Nov. h.m.
Sets.	4 33	4 14	3 58	2 4 19pm.	10 2 5pm.	17 1 6pm.	24 1 43pm.

Days.			Morn. Lessons.		Even. Lessons.	
1	Tu	All Saints' Day. *Feast.*	Wisd.3 to v.10	Heb 11 v.33, & 12to v.7.	Wisd.5 to v.17	Rev.19 to v.17
2	W	Mich. Law Term begins.	Eclu16	Luk 18	Eclu17	Colos 2
3	Th		18	19	19	3
4	F	*Abst.*	20	20	21	4
5	S	*Papists' Conspiracy, 1605. ☉	22	21	23	1Thes1
6	ⓑ	xx Sunday after Trinity. *Feast* [LEONARD, Confessor, (died 559).	Joel 2	Luk 22	Mica. 6	1Thes2
7	M		Eclu27	23	Eclu28	3
8	Tu		29	24	30tov.18	4
9	W		31	John 1	32	5
10	Th		33	2	34	2Thes1
11	F	S.Martin,Bp.(ofTours,d.397). *Abst.*	35	3	36	2
12	S	Camb. T. div. mid. ☉	37	4	38	3
13	ⓑ	xxi Sunday after Trinity. *Feast* [BRITIUS, Bp. (d. 444).	Hab. 2	John 5	Prov. 1	1Tim 1
14	M		41	6	42	2, 3
15	Tu	MACHUTUS, Bp. (of Alett, A.D. 564).	43	7	44	4
16	W		45	8	46tov.20	5
17	Th	HUGH, Bp. of Lincoln, (died 1200).	47	9	48	6
18	F	*Abst.*	49	10	50	2Tim 1
19	S	* ☉	51	11	Baru. 1	2
20	ⓑ	xxii Sunday after Trinity. *Feast* [EDMUND, King, (murd. A.D. 870).	Prov. 2	John12	Prov. 3	2Tim 3
21	M		Baru. 4	13	Baru. 5	4
22	Tu	CECILIA, V. & M. (suff. A.D. 230).	6	14	Susan.	Titus 1
23	W	St. CLEMENT, Bp. (of Rome; suffered [A.D. 100).	Bel&D	15	Isa. 1	2, 3
24	Th		Isa. 2	16	3	Philem
25	F	CATHARINE, V. & Mar. (suff. 307). [Mich. Law Term ends. *Abst.*	4	17	5	Heb. 1
26	S	☉	6	18	7	2
		Advent.				
27	ⓑ	Advent Sunday. *Feast*	Isa. 1	John19	Isa. 2	Heb. 3
28	M	†	10	20	11	4
29	Tu	☉ † *Vigil.*	12	21	13	5
30	W	*St. Andrew,Apostle. †*Feast*	Prov20	Acts 1	Prov21	6

MEMORANDA.

5. PAPISTS' CONSPIRACY: *Particular Service* appointed. *Proper Hymn* instead of *Venite. Proper Psalms :* 64, 124, 125. 1st Lesson, 2 Sam. 22 ; 2nd Lesson, Acts 23.
19. *Venite* in Psalms for the day.
30. ST. ANDREW. *Athanasian Creed.*

31 Days.	DECEMBER.		186

SUN.	1st	13th	25th	MOON.			
	h. m.	h. m.	h. m.	First Qr.	Full.	Last Qr.	New.
Rises.	7 46	8 0	8 7	Dec. h.m.	Dec. h.m.	Dec. h.m.	Dec. h.m.
Sets.	3 52	3 49	3 53	2 1 50pm.	10 3 13am.	16 9 15pm.	24 5 47am.

Days.				Morn. Lessons.		Even. Lessons.	
1	Th		†	Isa. 14	Acts 2	Isa. 15	Heb. 7
2	F		†Abst.	16	3	17	8
3	S		⊙ †	18	4	19	9
4	B	ii Sunday in Advent.	†Feast.	Isa. 5	Acts 5	Isa. 24	Heb.10
5	M		†	23	6	24	11
6	Tu	NICOLAS, Bishop of Myra in Lycia,		25	7tov.30	26	12
		[(died A.D. 326). †		27	7ver.30	28	13
7	W		†	27	7ver.30	28	13
8	Th	CONCEPT. OF THE B. V. MARY.	†	29	8	30	Jam. 1
9	F		†Abst.	31	9	32	2
10	S		⊙ †	33	10	34	3
11	B	iii Sunday in Advent.	†Feast.	Isa. 25	Acts11	Isa. 26	Jam. 4
12	M		†	37	12	38	5
13	Tu	LUCY, Virg. and Mart. (suf. A.D. 305).†		39	13	40	1 Pet. 1
14	W	Ember-day. †		41	14	42	2
15	Th		†	43	15	44	3
16	F	O SAPIENTIA. Ember-day. †		45	16	46	4
17	S	Oxford Term ends. Ember-day. ⊙ †		47	17	48	5
18	B	iv Sunday in Advent.	†Feast.	Isa. 30	Acts18	Isa. 32	2 Pet.1
19	M	*	†	51	19	52	2
20	Tu		⊙ † Vigil.	53	20	54	3
21	W	St. Thomas, Apostle.	†Feast.	Prov23	21	Prov24	1John1
22	Th		† Isa. 55	Isa. 55	22	Isa. 56	2
23	F		†Abst.	57	23	58	3
24	S		⊙Vigil.	59	24	60	4

Christmas.

25	B	*Christmas=Day.	Feast.	Isa. 9 to v. 8	Luke 2 to v. 15	Isa.7 v. 10 to17	Tit. 3 v. 4 to v 9
26	M	*St. Stephen, Martyr.	†Feast.	Prov28	Ac.6v8 7to v30	Ecles 4	Acts7v 30 to 55
27	Tu	*St. John, Apostle & Evang.	†Feast.	Ecles 5	Rev. 1	6	Rev.22
28	W	*Innocents' Day.	†Feast.	Jer. 31 to v. 18	Acts25	Wisd.1	1John5
29	Th			Isa. 61	26	Isa. 62	2 John
30	F		Abst.	63	27	64	3 John
31	S	SILVESTER, B. of Rome, (d. 335). ⊙		65	28	66	Jude

MEMORANDA.

19. *Venite* in Psalms for the day.
25. CHRISTMAS-DAY. *Proper Psalms:* Morn., 19, 45, 85; Even., 89, 110, 132. *Athanasian Creed. Proper Preface* in Communion Service.
26. ST. STEPHEN, 27. ST. JOHN, and 28. INNOCENTS' DAY. *Proper Preface* for Christmas-day.

MISCELLANEOUS NOTES FOR THE YEAR 1859.

Solar Cycle 20	Roman Indiction **2**
Jewish Era 5619-20	Julian Period 6572

Ramadan (month of abstinence with the Turks) commences April 4, 1859.
The year 1276 of the Mohammedan Era commences August 1, 1859.

ECLIPSES, 1859.

In the year 1859 there will be four Eclipses of the Sun, and two of the Moon—all invisible here.

1. A Partial Eclipse of the Sun on February 2, visible at Greenwich.

2. A Total Eclipse of the Moon, Feb. 16.
3. A Partial Eclipse of the Sun, Mar. 4.
4. A Partial Ecl. of the Sun, July 29.
5. A Total Eclipse of the Moon, Aug. 13.
6. A Partial Ecl. of the Sun, Aug. 27.

SEASONS, &c., 1859.

Spring Quar. com. Mar. 21, at 3.20 a.m. | Autumn Quar. com. Sep. 23, at 2.10 p.m.
Summer „ „ June 21, at 11.58 p.m. | Winter „ „ Dec. 22, at 8.3 a.m.

LAW TERMS, 1859.

Hilary Term	Begins Jan. 11.	Ends Jan. 31.
Easter „	„ Apr. 15.	„ May 12.
Trinity „	„ May 26.	„ June 16.
Michaelmas Term	„ Nov. 2.	„ Nov. 25.

UNIVERSITY TERMS, 1859.

Terms.	OXFORD.		CAMBRIDGE.		
	Begins.	Ends.	Begins.	Divides.	Ends.
Lent . . .	Jan. 14	Apr. 16	Jan. 13	Feb. 28, noon	Apr. 15
Easter . .	May 4	June 10	May 4	June 5, midnight	July 8
Trinity . .	June 15	July 9			
Michaelmas	Oct. 10	Dec. 17	Oct. 10	Nov. 12, midnight	Dec. 16

The Act, July 5 | The Commencement, July 5.

DAYS OF TRANSFER, DIVIDENDS, &c.

AT THE BANK OF ENGLAND.

Transfer Days in all the Stock and Annuity Offices are Tuesday, Wednesday, Thursday, and Friday.

Stock.	Divid. Due.	Stock.	Divid. Due.
3 per Cent. Consols		Bank Stock	
3 per Cent. 1726	Jan. 5, and July 5.	3 per Cent. Reduced..............	April 5, and Oct. 10.
New 5 per Cent. and annuities ending January, 1860		3½ per Cent. Long Annuities, and Annuities ending Oct.1859	

Hours for buying and selling Stock, 10 till 1 ; transferring, 11 till half-past 2 ; may be sold after 1, by paying 2s. 6d. for each transfer ; for accepting, 9 till 3 ; payment of dividends, 9 till 3.

AT THE EAST INDIA HOUSE.

India Stock, Tuesday, Thursday, and Saturday, January 5 and July 5.—India Bonds, March 31 and Sept. 30.—Transfers, 11 till 3 ; on Saturdays, 10 to 1 : dividends paid, 9 till 3.

HOLIDAYS KEPT AT THE PUBLIC OFFICES.

At the Banks and all Public Offices : Christmas-day and Good Friday.—Excise, Stamp, and Tax Offices : Good Friday, April 22 ; Day appointed to be kept as the Queen's Birthday ; Coronation-day, June 28 ; Prince of Wales' Birthday, Nov. 9 ; Christmas-day, December 25.

The Church.

THE ARCHBISHOPS AND BISHOPS OF
The English Church.

TOGETHER WITH THE
DEANS, ARCHDEACONS, AND PROCTORS
IN THE SEVERAL DIOCESES;
THE WHOLE FORMING THE
CONVOCATION*
IN THE TWO ECCLESIASTICAL PROVINCES OF ENGLAND.

Canterbury.

Rt. Hon. and Most Rev. JOHN BIRD SUMNER, D.D. 1848.
In room of HOWLEY, deceased. *Residence*, Lambeth-palace; Addington-park.
Secretary, F. Knyvett, Esq., Lambeth-pal. *Registrar*, W. H. Cullen, Esq., Canterbury. Income, £15,000. Jurisdiction: Most of the County of Kent. Population, 417,090. Acres, 914,170. Deaneries, 14. Benefices, 352. Curates—to Resident Incumbents, 100; to Non-Residents, 66. Church Sittings, 167,792.

Dean—Very Rev. H. ALFORD, B.D. 1857.
Archdeacon of Canterbury—Ven. James CROFT, M.A. 1825.
      „   *Maidstone*—Ven. Benjamin HARRISON, M.A. 1845.
Proctor for the Chapter—John RUSSELL, D.D.
Proctors for the Clergy—W. J. CHESSHYRE, M.A. A. OXENDEN, M.A.

York.

Rt. Hon. and Most Rev. THOMAS MUSGRAVE, D.D. 1847.
In room of HARCOURT, deceased. *Residence*, Bishopthorpe-palace; Belgrave-square, London. *Secretary*, C. A. Thiselton, Esq., York. *Registrar*, E. Vernon Harcourt, Esq. Income, £10,000. Jurisdiction: Yorkshire, except a part in the Diocese of Ripon. Population, 764,538. Acres, 2,261,493. Deaneries, 10. Benefices, 534. Curates—to Resident Incumbents, 122; to Non-Residents, 83. Church Sittings, 225,614.

Dean—The Hon. and Very Rev. Augustus DUNCOMBE, M.A. 1858.
Archdeacon of York—Ven. Stephen CREYKE, M.A. 1845.
      „   „   *East Riding*—Ven. Charles M. LONG, M.A. 1854.
      „   „   *Cleveland*—Ven. Edward CHURTON, M.A. 1846.
Proctors for the Chapter—Thos. H. CROFT, M.A. C. JOHNSTONE, M.A.
Proctors for the Clergy — William HEY, M.A. Thomas SALE, D.D.
    William L. PALMES, M.A. J. KING, M.A. C. CATOR, B.D.

London.

Rt. Hon. & Right Rev. ARCH. CAMPBELL TAIT, D.C.L. 1856.
In room of BLOMFIELD, deceased. *Residence*, London-house, St. James's-square.
Secretary, J. B. Lee, Esq. *Registrars*, John Shephard and J. B. Lee, Esqs. Income, £10,000. Jurisdiction: Middlesex, and a few Parishes in Essex, Kent, and Surrey. Population, 2,143,340. Acres, 246,157. Deanery, 1. Benefices, 324. Curates, 258. Church Sittings, 396,841.

Dean of St. Paul's—Very Rev. Henry Hart MILMAN, D.D. 1849.
      „   *Westminster*—Very Rev. R. C. TRENCH, D.D. 1856.
Archdeacon of London—Ven. William Hale HALE, M.A. 1842.
      „   *Middlesex*—Ven. John SINCLAIR, M.A. 1843.
      „   *Westminster*ᵇ—Ven. W. H. E. BENTINCK, M.A.
Proctor for Chapter of St. Paul's—Thos. DALE, M.A.
      „   „   *Westminster*—Christopher WORDSWORTH, D D.
Proctors for the Clergy—Robert G. BAKER, M.A. Alex. McCAUL, D.D.

ᵃ For further particulars, *vide* p. 27. ᵇ Of the Collegiate Chapter of Westminster.

Durham.

Right Rev. CHARLES THOMAS LONGLEY, D.D. 1856.

In room of MALTBY, resigned. *Residence*, Auckland-castle; 19, Bruton-street, London. *Secretaries*, Messrs. Burder and Dunning. *Registrar*, Hon. J. L. Barrington. Income, £8,000. Jurisdiction: Durham, Northumberland, and Hexhamshire. Population, 701,381. Acres, 1,906,835. Deaneries, 13. Benefices, 245. Curates —to Resident Incumbents, 85; to Non-Residents, 21. Church Sittings, 126,099.

Dean—Very Rev. George WADDINGTON, D.D. 1840.
Archdeacon of Durham—Ven. Charles THORP, D.D. 1831.
    „   *Northumberland*—Ven. George BLAND, M.A. 1844.
    „   *Lindisfarne*—Ven. R. C. COXE, M.A. 1853.
Proctor for the Chapter—Ven. Charles THORP, D.D.
Proctors for the Clergy—Hon. and Rev. F. GREY, M.A. T. L. STRONG, B.D. J. D. EADE, M.A. J. BESLEY, D.C.L. C. BIRD, M.A. W. DODD, M.A.

𝔚𝔦𝔫𝔠𝔥𝔢𝔰𝔱𝔢𝔯.

Right Rev. CHARLES RICHARD SUMNER, D.D. 1827.

In room of TOMLINE, deceased. *Residence*, Farnham-castle, Surrey; Winchesterhouse, St. James's-square. *Secretaries*, Messrs. Burder and Dunning. *Registrar*, Brownlow North, Esq. Income, £10,000. Jurisdiction: Hampshire and Surrey; also the Islands of Wight, Guernsey, Jersey, Alderney, and Sark. Population, 1,080,412. Acres, 1,598,568. Deaneries, 18. Benefices, 523. Curates—to Resident Incumbents, 229; to Non-Residents, 56. Church Sittings, 301,781.

Dean—Very Rev. Thomas GARNIER, D.C.L. 1840.
Archdeacon of Surrey—Ven. Charles J. HOARE, M.A. 1847.
    „   *Winchester*—Ven. Joseph C. WIGRAM, M.A. 1847.
Proctor for the Chapter—William WILSON, D.D.
    „   *Clergy of Winton*—Hon. and Rev. S. BEST.
    „   „   *Surrey*—John H. RANDOLPH, M.A.

𝔅𝔞𝔫𝔤𝔬𝔯.

Right Rev. CHRISTOPHER BETHELL, D.D. 1830.

In room of MAJENDIE, deceased. *Residence*, Bangor-palace. *Secretary*, H. B. Roberts, Esq. *Registrars*, H. B. Roberts and J. V. H. Williams. Income, varies. Jurisdiction: Anglesea, with parts of Carnarvonshire, Denbigh, Montgomery, and Merionethshire. Population, 192,964. Acres, 985,946. Deaneries, 13. Benefices, 132. Curates—to Resident Incumbents, 43; to Non-Residents, 17. Church Sittings, 52,426.

Dean—Very Rev. James Henry COTTON, B.C.L. 1838.
Archdeacon of Merioneth—Ven. Henry Weir WHITE, M.A. 1857.
    „   *Bangor*—Ven. John JONES, B.D. 1844.
Proctor for the Chapter—John William TREVOR, M.A.
Proctors for the Clergy—C. WILLIAMS, D.D. Jas. W. VINCENT, M.A.

𝔅𝔞𝔱𝔥 𝔞𝔫𝔡 𝔚𝔢𝔩𝔩𝔰.

Rt. Hon. & Rt. Rev. R. J. EDEN, D.D. (Lord AUCKLAND). 1854.

In room of BAGOT, deceased. *Residence*, Palace, Wells. *Secretary*, E. Davies, Esq. *Registrar*, W. F. Beadon, Esq. *Dep. Reg.*, W. Dore, Esq. Wells. Income, £5,000. Jurisdiction: County of Somerset, except Bedminster. Population, 424,492. Acres, 1,043,059. Deaneries, 13. Benefices, 462. Curates—to Resident Incumbents, 112; to Non-Residents, 101. Church Sittings, 179,132.

Dean of Wells—Very Rev. G. H. S. JOHNSON, M.A.
Archdeacon of Wells—Ven. Henry LAW, M.A. 1826.
    „   *Bath*—Ven. William GUNNING, B.C.L. 1852.
    „   *Taunton*—Ven. George A. DENISON, M.A. 1851.
Proctor for the Chapter—Hon. and Rev. W. J. BRODRICK, M.A.
Proctors for the Clergy—J. S. H. HORNER, M.A. E. A. OMMANNEY, M.A.

Carlisle.

Hon. and Right Rev. H. Montagu Villiers, D.D. 1856.

In room of Percy, deceased. *Residence*, Rose-castle, Cumberland. *Secretaries*, J. B. Lee, Esq., London; G. G. Mounsey, Esq., Carlisle. *Registrar*, Rev. Joseph Milner, M.A. Income, £4,500. Jurisdiction: Cumberland, except Alston, and Westmoreland, with Deanery of Furness, in Lancashire. Population, 277,911. Acres, 1,459,840. Deaneries, 7. Benefices, 262. Curates—to Resident Incumbents, 38; to Non-Residents, 9. Church Sittings, 48,472.

Dean—Very Rev. Francis Close, D.D. 1856.
Archdeacon of Carlisle—Ven. W. Jackson, D.D. 1855.
    ,,   *Westmoreland*—Ven. R. Wilson Evans, B.D. 1856.
Proctor for the Chapter—Henry Gipps, M.A.
Proctors for the Clergy—James Thwaites, M.A. Beilby Porteus, M.A. Robert Morewood, M.A. R. C. Hubbersty, M.A.

Chester.

Right Rev. John Graham, D.D. 1848.

In room of Sumner, translated. *Residence*, Palace, Chester. *Secretary*, Charles T. W. Parry, Esq., Chester. *Registrar*, H. Raikes, Esq. Income, £4,500. Jurisdiction: Cheshire, with parts of Lancashire. Population, 1,086,800. Acres, 1,072,200. Deaneries, 8. Benefices, 360. Curates—to Resident Incumbents, 180; to Non-Residents, 13; Church Sittings, 288,694.

Dean—Very Rev. Frederick Anson, D.D. 1839.
Archdeacon of Chester—Ven. Isaac Wood, M.A. 1847.
    ,,   *Liverpool*—Ven. J. Jones, M.A. 1855.
Proctor for the Chapter—James Slade, M.A.
Proctors for the Clergy—Rich. Greenall, M.A. Aug. Campbell, M.A. George Heron, M.A. Hugh McNeile, D.D.

Chichester.

Right Rev. Ashhurst Turner Gilbert, D.D. 1842.

In room of Shuttleworth, deceased. *Residence*, Palace, Chichester; 43, Queen Anne-street, London. *Secretary*, E. W. Johnson, Esq. *Registrars*, A. Otter, Esq.; and Rev. B. Phipps, M.A. *Deputy Registrars*, E. W. Johnson, and J. Hoper, Esqrs. Income, £4,200. Jurisdiction: County of Sussex. Population, 336,844. Acres, 934,851. Deaneries, 12. Benefices, 311. Curates—to Resident Incumbents, 75; to Non-Residents, 53. Church Sittings, 133,512.

Dean—Very Rev. George Chandler, D.C.L. 1830.
Archdeacon of Chichester—Ven. James Garbett, M.A. 1851.
    ,,   *Lewes*—Ven. W. B. Otter, M.A. 1855.
Proctor for the Chapter—Charles Pilkington, B.C.L.
    ,,   *Clergy of Chichester*—Frederick Vincent, M.A.
    ,,   ,,   *Lewes*—Sir H. Thompson, Bart.

Ely.

Right Rev. Thomas Turton, D.D. 1845.

In room of Allen, deceased. *Residence*, The Palace, Ely; Ely-house, Dover-street, London. *Secretaries*, Messrs. Burder and Dunning, London. *Registrar*, Rev. E. B. Sparke, M.A. Income, £5,500. Jurisdiction: Cambridgeshire, Bedfordshire, Huntingdonshire, and part of Suffolk. Population, 482,412. Acres, 1,357,765. Deaneries, 26. Benefices, 529. Curates—to Resident Incumbents, 97; to Non-Residents, 94. Church Sittings, 172,263.

Dean—
Archdeacon of Ely—
    ,,   *Sudbury*—Ven. George Glover, M.A. 1823.
    ,,   *Hunts*—Hon. and Ven. H. R. Yorke, M.A. 1856.
    ,,   *Bedfordshire*—Ven. Henry Tattam, D.D. 1844.
Proctor for the Chapter—William Selwyn, B.D.
Proctors for the Clergy—P. C. Claughton, M.A. James Fendall, M.A.

Exeter.
Right Rev. HENRY PHILLPOTTS, D.D. 1831.
In room of CAREY, translated. *Residence*, Palace, Exeter; Bishopstowe, Torquay. *Secretary*, R. Barnes, Esq., Exeter. *Registrar*, Rev. W. A. Walpole Keppel. Income, £5,000. Jurisdiction: Devonshire, Cornwall, and the Scilly Islands. Population, 922,656. Acres, 2,530,780. Deaneries, 32. Benefices, 657. Curates—to Resident Incumbents, 189; to Non-Residents, 77. Church Sittings, 323,037.

Dean—Very Rev. Thomas Hill LOWE, M.A. 1839.
Archdeacon of Exeter—Ven. John Moore STEVENS, M.A. 1820.
      ,,   *Totness*—Ven. R. H. FROUDE, M.A. 1820.
      ,,   *Cornwall*—Ven. W. J. PHILLPOTTS, M.A. 1845.
      ,,   *Barnstaple*—Ven. John BARTHOLOMEW, M.A. 1847.
Proctor for the Chapter—George MARTIN, M.A., *Chancellor.*
Proctors for the Clergy—E. H. BROWNE, B.D.   P. L. D. ACLAND, M.A.

Gloucester and Bristol.
Right Rev. CHARLES BARING, D.D. 1856.
In room of MONK, deceased. *Residence*, Rodborough-manor, Stroud. *Registrar of Gloucester, and Secretary*, T. Holt, Esq., Gloucester. *Registrar of Bristol*, Sir Thomas Beckett, Bart. *Dep. Reg. for Bristol*, C. S. Clarke, Esq., Bristol. Income, £5,000. Jurisdiction: Gloucestershire, City and Deanery of Bristol, Bedminster, and Abbot's Leigh, Somerset, Deaneries of Malmesbury and Cricklade, in Wiltshire. Population, 538,109. Acres, 1,000,503. Deaneries, 13. Benefices, 443. Curates—to Resident Incumbents, 121; to Non-Residents, 68. Church Sittings, 197,568.

Dean of Gloucester—Hon. and Very Rev. E. RICE, D.D. 1825.
  ,,   *Bristol*—Very Rev. Gilbert ELLIOTT, D.D. 1850.
Archdeacon of Gloucester—Ven. John TIMBRILL, D.D. 1825.
      ,,   *Bristol*—Ven. Thomas THORP, B.D. 1836.
Proctor for Chapter of Gloucester—Sir J. H. C. SEYMOUR, Bart., M.A.
Proctor for Chapter of Bristol—Edward BANKES, B.C.L.
Proctors for the Clergy—Sir G. PREVOST, Bt., M.A.   W. J. COPLESTON, M.A.

Hereford.
Right Rev. RENN DICKSON HAMPDEN, D.D. 1847.
In room of MUSGRAVE, translated. *Residence*, Palace, Hereford. *Secretary*, T. Evans, Esq., Hereford. *Registrar*, Rev. J. H. M. Luxmoore, M.A. Income, £4,200. Jurisdiction: Herefordshire, with parts of the Counties of Salop, Worcester, Radnor, and Montgomery. Population, 216,143. Acres, 986,244. Deaneries, 13. Benefices, 358. Curates—to Resident Incumbents, 45; to Non-Residents, 53. Church Sittings, 102,685.

Dean—Very Rev. Richard DAWES, M.A. 1850.
Archdeacon of Salop—Ven. William WARING, M.A. 1851.
      ,,   *Hereford*—Ven. Richard Lane FREER, D.D. 1852.
Proctor for the Chapter—Lord SAYE and SELE, D.C.L.
Proctors for the Clergy—John JEBB, M.A.   Jas. Wayland JOYCE, M.A.

Lichfield.
Right Rev. JOHN LONSDALE, D.D. 1843.
In room of BOWSTEAD, deceased. *Residence*, Eccleshall-castle, Stafford. *Secretary*, W. R. Hand, Esq., Stafford. *Registrar*, Rev. H. Mann. *Deputy Registrar*, Wm. Fell, Esq., Lichfield. Income, £4,500. Jurisdiction: Staffordshire, Derbyshire, and part of Salop. Population, 1,022,080. Acres, 1,740,607. Deaneries, 49. Benefices, 625. Curates—to Resident Incumbents, 178; to Non-Residents, 76. Church Sittings, 305,933.

Dean—Hon. and Very Rev. Henry E. J. HOWARD, D.D. 1833.
Archdeacon of Stafford—Ven. Henry MOORE, M.A. 1856.
      ,,   *Derby*—Ven. Thomas HILL, B.D. 1847.
      ,,   *Salop*—Ven. John ALLEN, M.A. 1847.
Proctor for the Chapter—John HUTCHINSON, M.A.
Proctors for the Clergy—Geo. Wm. MURRAY, M.A.   Hen. BURTON, M.A.

Lincoln.
Right Rev. JOHN JACKSON, D.D. 1853.

In room of KAYE, deceased. *Residence*, Riseholme, near Lincoln. *Secretary*, W. Moss, Esq., Lincoln. *Registrars*, R. Swan and R. Smith, Esqs. *Dep. Reg.*, Wm. Moss, Esq., Old Palace, Lincoln. Income, £5,000. Jurisdiction : Lincolnshire and Nottinghamshire. Population, 677,649. Acres, 2,302,814. Deaneries 30, subdivided into 59 Districts. Benefices, 796. Curates—to Resident Incumbents, 154 ; to Non-Residents, 156. Total number of Clergy, Incumbents and Curates, 877. Church Sittings, 238,831.

Dean—Very Rev. John Giffard WARD, M.A. 1845.
Archdeacon of Nottingham—Ven. George WILKINS, D.D. 1832.
    „   *Lincoln*—Ven. H. Kaye BONNEY, D.D. 1844.
    „   *Stowe*—Ven. W. B. STONEHOUSE, D.C.L. 1844.
Proctor for the Chapter—James A. JEREMIE, D.D.
Proctors for the Clergy—F. C. MASSINGBERD, M.A. H. MACKENZIE, M.A.

Llandaff.
Right Rev. ALFRED OLLIVANT, D.D. 1849.

In room of COPLESTON, deceased. *Residence*, Bishop's-court, Llandaff. *Secretaries*, Messrs. Burder and Dunning. *Registrars*, Josh. Huckwell and Simon Dunning, Esqs. Income, £4,200. Jurisdiction : Monmouthshire, and Glamorganshire, except Gower. Population, 337,526. Acres, 797,864. Deaneries, 6. Benefices, 230. Curates—to Resident Incumbents, 45 ; to Non-Residents, 44. Church Sittings, 64,268.

Dean—Very Rev. T. WILLIAMS, M.A. 1857.
Archdeacon of Llandaff—Ven. James Colquhoun CAMPBELL, M.A. 1857.
    „   *Monmouth*—Ven. William CRAWLEY, M.A. 1843.
Proctor for the Chapter—Ch. Augustus MORGAN, M.A.
Proctors for the Clergy—William PRICE, M.A. John HARDING, M.A.

Manchester.
Right Rev. JAMES PRINCE LEE, D.D. 1848.

Residence, Mauldeth-hall, near Manchester. *Sec. and Dep. Reg.*, J. Burder, Esq., Manchester. *Registrar*, T. D. Ryder, Esq. Income, £4,200. Jurisdiction : Deaneries of Amounderness, Tunstall, Blackburn, Manchester, and Leyland ; parish of Leigh, and such parishes in Deaneries of Kendal and Kirkby Lonsdale as are in Lancashire. Population, 1,405,870. Acres, 845,904. Deaneries. 15. Benefices, 339. Curates—to Resident Incumbents, 115 ; to Non-Residents, 25. Church Sittings, 259,393.

Dean—Very Rev. George Hull BOWERS, D.D. 1847.
Archdeacon of Manchester—Ven. R. M. MASTER, M.A. 1854.
    „   *Lancaster*—Vacant.
Proctor for the Chapter—Cecil D. WRAY, M.A.
Proctors for the Clergy — { Hugh STOWELL, M.A. / Richard DURNFORD, M.A. / John Owen PARR, M.A. } *double return.*

Norwich.
The Hon. and Rt. Rev. JOHN THOMAS PELHAM, D.D. 1857.

In room of HINDS, resigned. *Residence*, Palace, Norwich. *Secretary and Registrar*, J. Kitson, Esq., Norwich. *London Secretary*, J. B. Lee, Esq., Dean's-yard, Westminster. Income, £4,500. Jurisdiction : Norfolk, with the Eastern Division of the County of Suffolk. Population, 671,583. Acres, 1,994,525. Deaneries, 41. Benefices, 910. Curates—to Resident Incumbents, 187 ; to Non-Residents, 177. Church Sittings, 294,777.

Dean—Hon. and Very Rev. George PELLEW, D.D. 1828.
Archdeacon of Norwich—Ven. R. E. HANKINSON, M.A 1857.
    „   *Norfolk*—Ven. W. Arundell BOUVERIE, B.D. 1850.
    „   *Suffolk*—Ven. Thomas J. ORMEROD, M.A. 1846.
Proctor for the Chapter—Henry PHILPOTT, D.D.
Proctor for Clergy of Archd. of Norfolk—Augus. Macd. HOPPER, M.A.
    „   „   *Suffolk*—Thomas MILLS, M.A.

Oxford.

Right Rev. SAMUEL WILBERFORCE, D.D. 1845.

In room of BAGOT, translated. *Residence*, Cuddesdon-palace, Oxon. *Secretary and Deputy-Registrar*, J. M. Davenport, Esq., Oxford. Income, £5,000. Jurisdiction: Oxfordshire, Berkshire, and Buckinghamshire. Population, 503,042. Acres, 1,385,779. Rural Deaneries, 31. Benefices, 609. Curates—to Resident Incumbents, 130; to Non-Residents, 117. Church Sittings, 217,415.

Dean of Ch. Ch.—Very Rev. Henry George LIDDELL, D.D. 1855.
Archdeacon of Oxford—Ven. Charles Carr CLERKE, D.D. 1830.
      „   *Berks*—Ven. Jas. RANDALL, M.A. 1855.
      „   *Buckingham*—Ven. Edward BICKERSTETH, M.A. 1853.
Proctor for the Chapter—Richard W. JELF, D.D.
Proctors for the Clergy—Fran. K. LEIGHTON, D.D. Chas. LLOYD, B.A.

Peterborough.

Right Rev. GEORGE DAVYS, D.D. 1839.

In room of MARSH, deceased. *Residence*, Palace, Peterborough. *Secretary and Registrar*, H. P. Gates, Esq. Income, £4,500. Jurisdiction: Leicestershire, Northamptonshire, and Rutland. Population, 465,671. Acres, 1,240,327. Deaneries, 18. Benefices, 536. Curates—to Resident Incumbents, 92; to Non-Residents, 92. Church Sittings, 196,222.

Dean—Very Rev. Augustus P. SAUNDERS, D.D. 1853.
Archdeacon of Northampton—Ven. Owen DAVYS, M.A. 1842.
      „   *Leicester*—Ven. T. K. BONNEY, M.A. 1831.
Proctor for the Chapter—Marsham ARGLES, M.A.
Proctors for the Clergy—Lord A. COMPTON, M.A. G. E. GILLETT, M.A.

Ripon.

Right Rev. ROBERT BICKERSTETH, D.D. 1856.

In room of LONGLEY, translated. *Residence*, Palace, Ripon. *Secretaries*, S. Wise, Esq., Ripon; J. B. Lee, London. *Registrars*, J. B. Langhorne and S. Wise, Esqs. Income, £4,500. Jurisdiction: the Western and Northern parts of Yorkshire. Population, 1,120,000. Deaneries, 7. Benefices, 421. Curates—to Resident Incumbents, 114; to Non-Residents, 35. Church Sittings, 229,726.

Dean—Hon. and Very Rev. Henry D. ERSKINE, M.A. 1847.
Archdeacon of Richmond—Ven. C. DODGSON, M.A. 1854.
      „   *Craven*—Ven. Charles MUSGRAVE, D.D. 1836.
Proctor for the Chapter—Vacant.
Proctors for the Clergy—Thomas COLLINS, B.D. Lawrence OTTLEY, M.A. Samuel HOLMES, M.A. Thomas ALLBUTT, M.A.

Rochester.

Hon. and Right Rev. GEORGE MURRAY, D.D. 1827.

In room of PERCY, translated. *Residence*, Danbury-palace, Essex. *Secretaries*, Messrs. Burder and Dunning. *Registrars*, Ven. Archd. and Rev. J. King, M.A. Income, £5,000. Jurisdiction: City and Deanery of Rochester, Essex (except nine parishes), and Hertfordshire. Population, 577,298. Acres, 1,535,450. Deaneries, 36. Benefices, 564. Curates, 240. Church Sittings, 203,643.

Dean—Very Rev. Robert STEVENS, D.D. 1820.
Archdeacon of Rochester—Ven. Walker KING, M.A. 1827.
      „   *Essex*—Ven. Hugh Chambers JONES, M.A. 1823.
      „   *Colchester*—Ven. Charles Parr BURNEY, D.D. 1845.
      „   *St. Alban's*—Ven. Anthony GRANT, D.C.L. 1845.
Proctors for the Chapter—John GRIFFITH, D.D. Thos. ROBINSON, D.D.
Proctors for the Clergy—C. A. St. J. MILDMAY, M.A. G. B. BLOMFIELD, M.A.

Salisbury.
Right Rev. WALTER KERR HAMILTON, D.D. 1854.

In room of DENISON, deceased. *Residence*, Palace, Salisbury. *Secretary and Registrar*, F. Macdonald, Esq., The Close, Salisbury. Income, £5,000. Jurisdiction: greater part of Wiltshire, and whole of Dorsetshire. Population, 379,296. Acres, 1,309,617. Deaneries, 13. Benefices, 469. Curates—to Resident Incumbents, 150; to Non-Residents, 56. Church Sittings, about 155,000.

Dean—Very Rev. H. PARR HAMILTON, M.A. 1850.
Archdeacon of Wilts—Ven. William MACDONALD, M.A. 1828.
    ,,   *Dorset*—Ven. R. B. BUCKLE, M.A. 1836.
    ,,   *Sarum*—Ven. William E. HONY, B.D. 1846.
Proctor for the Chapter—Hon. and Rev. Samuel WALDEGRAVE, M.A.
Proctors for the Clergy—G. P. LOWTHER, M.A. Henry CASWALL, M.A.

St. Asaph.
Right Rev. THOMAS VOWLER SHORT, D.D. 1846.

In room of CAREY, deceased. *Residence*, Palace, St. Asaph. *Secs. and Dep. Reg.*, C. W. Wyatt and R. J. Sisson, Esqs. *Registrar*, Rev. J. F. Cleaver. Income, £4,200. Jurisdiction: Denbighshire and Flint, with parts of Montgomeryshire, Carnarvonshire, Merionethshire, and Salop. Population, 236,298. Acres, 1,067,583. Deaneries, 12. Benefices, 173. Curates—to Resident Incumbents, 41; to Non-Residents, 16. Church Sittings, 68,044.

Dean—Very Rev. C. Butler CLOUGH, M.A. 1854.
Archdeacon of St. Asaph—Ven. R. WICKHAM, M.A. 1854.
    ,,   *Montgomery*—Ven. William CLIVE, M.A. 1844.
Proctor for the Chapter—Henry GLYNNE, M.A.
Proctors for the Clergy—Richard BRISCOE, D.D. Robt. W. EYTON, M.A.

St. David's.
Right Rev. CONNOP THIRLWALL, D.D. 1840.

In room of JENKINSON, deceased. *Residence*, Abergwili-palace, Carmarthen. *Secretary*, J. Thirlwall, Esq. *Registrar*, Valentine Davis, Esq. Income, £4,500. Jurisdiction: Breconshire, Cardiganshire, Carmarthenshire, Pembrokeshire, Radnorshire, and Deaneries of East and West Gower, in Glamorganshire. Population, 407,758. Acres, 2,272,790. Deaneries, 18. Benefices, 411. Curates—to Resident Incumbents, 49; to Non-Residents, 67. Church Sittings, 118,877.

Dean of St. David's—Very Rev. Llewelyn LEWELLIN, D.C.L. 1840.
    ,,   *Ch. Ch., Brecon*—The BISHOP.
Archd. of St. David's—Ven. Thomas BEVAN, M.A., and Prebend of Mydrim.
    ,,   *Brecon*—Ven. R. DAVIES, M.A., and Prebend of Llanvaes.
    ,,   *Cardigan*—Ven. J. WILLIAMS, M.A., and Prebend of Llandyfriog.
    ,,   *Carmarthen*—Ven. John EVANS, B.D., and Prebend of Llanrhian.
Proctor for the Chapter of St. David's—
    ,,   ,,   *Brecon*—Vacant.
Proctors for the Clergy—Wm. Beach THOMAS, M.A. Joshua HUGHES, M.A.

Sodor and Man.
Hon. and Right Rev. HORATIO POWYS, D.D. 1854.

In room of EDEN, Lord AUCKLAND, translated. *Residence*, Bishop's-court, Isle of Man. *Secretary and Registrar*, Rev. Joseph Brown, M.A. Income, £2,000. Population, 52,387. Acres, 180,000. Benefices, 31. Curates, 14. Church Sittings, 17,210.

Archdeacon—Ven. Jos. Christian MOORE, M.A.
Proctor for the Clergy—Robt. DIXON, D.D.

𝔚orcester.

Right Rev. HENRY PEPYS, D.D. 1841.

In room of CARR, deceased. *Residence*, Hartlebury-castle, near Stourport. *Secretaries*, C. Evans, Esq., Worcester; and Messrs. Burder and Dunning, London. *Registrar*, Very Rev. T. H. Lowe, M.A. Income, £5,000. Jurisdiction: Worcestershire and Warwickshire, one parish in Gloucestershire, and three in Staffordshire. Population, 752,376. Acres, 1,037,451. Deaneries, 13. Benefices, 417. Curates— to Resident Incumbents, 134; to Non-Residents, 65. Church Sittings, 211,021.

Dean.—Very Rev. John PEEL, D.D. 1845.
Archdeacon of Worcester—Ven. Richard B. HONE, M.A. 1849.
„ *Coventry.*—Ven. John SANDFORD, B.D. 1851.
Proctor for the Chapter—Hon. and Rev. John FORTESCUE, M.A.
Proctors for the Clergy—H. A. WOODGATE, B.D. Rich. SEYMOUR, M.A.

RETIRED BISHOPS.

Right Rev. G. Trevor SPENCER, late Bishop of Madras, 1849.
Right Rev. Thomas CARR, late Bishop of Bombay, 1851.
Right Rev. E. MALTBY, late Bishop of Durham, 1856.
Right Rev. S. HINDS, late Bishop of Norwich, 1857.

STATISTICAL SUMMARY.

Total Population	18,070,735	Deaneries	472
„ Area in Acres	37,576,915	Benefices	12,023
„ Houses	3,299,794	Curates	4,879

FROM MR. HORACE MANN'S REPORT. 1851.

Province.	Population.	Places of Worship		Sittings.	
		Ch. of England.	Other Places.	Ch. of England.	Other Places.
Canterbury	12,785,048	11,626	15,231	4,153,896	3,469,014
York	5,285,687	2,526	5,338	1,196,948	1,497,333
Total	18,070,735	14,152	20,569	5,350,844	4,966,347

ADDITIONAL SEES IN ENGLAND AND WALES,
recommended by the Cathedral Commissioners.

ST. COLUMB (*for Cornwall*).
WESTMINSTER.
GLOUCESTER and BRISTOL (*to be again made independent Sees*).
SOUTHWELL.
BATH, from *Bath* and *Wells* and *Salisbury.*
BRECON, from *St. David's.*
COVENTRY, from *Worcester.*

CHELMSFORD, or COLCHESTER, from *Rochester.*
DERBY, from *Lichfield.*
IPSWICH, or BURY ST. EDMUND'S, from *Ely* and *Norwich.*
LIVERPOOL, from *Chester.*
NEWCASTLE, or HEXHAM, from *Durham.*

COADJUTOR BISHOPS.

The Cathedral Commissioners recommend—

"That a general statute should be framed, enabling her Majesty, after due inquiry by a commission specially appointed for that purpose, to recommend a person to be elected Coadjutor, *cum jure successionis*, to a Bishop, in case of such Bishop requiring such aid and relief, by reason of advanced age or protracted infirmity, and being ready to surrender a portion of his episcopal income in favour of such coadjutor."

Third and Final Report.

CONVOCATION [a].

The Province of Canterbury.

The Upper House.

THE ARCHBISHOP of Canterbury, *President.* 1

THE BISHOPS of

London.	Ely.	Lincoln.	Rochester.
Winchester.	Exeter.	Llandaff.	Salisbury.
Bangor.	Gloucester & Bristol.	Norwich.	St. Asaph.
Bath and Wells.	Hereford.	Oxford.	St. David's.
Chichester.	Lichfield.	Peterboro'.	Worcester.

} 20

Total Members, 21

The Lower House.

DEANS:—CANTERBURY—ST. PAUL'S, WESTMINSTER—WINCHESTER—BANGOR—WELLS—CHICHESTER—ELY—EXETER—GLOUCESTER, BRISTOL—HEREFORD—LICHFIELD—LINCOLN—LLANDAFF—NORWICH—OXFORD, (*Christ Church*)—PETERBOROUGH—ROCHESTER—SALISBURY—ST. ASAPH—ST. DAVID'S, BRECON (*Christ Church*)—WORCESTER 24

ARCHDEACONS. Vide pp. 19—26 58

PROCTORS for the Chapters. 25

PROCTORS for the Clergy 42

Total Members, 149

Prolocutor.—Very Rev. G. ELLIOTT, D.D. | *Actuary.*—GEORGE BURCHETT, Esq.
Vicar-General.—TRAVERS TWISS, D.C.L. | *Apparitor.*—FELIX KNYVETT, Esq.
Registrar.—FRANCIS HART DYKE, Esq. | *Door-Keeper.*—E. MANLEY CUMMINGS.

The Province of York.

The Upper House [b].

THE ARCHBISHOP of York, *President.* 1

THE BISHOPS of

Durham.	Chester.	Ripon.
Carlisle.	Manchester.	Sodor and Man.

} 6

Total Members of Upper House, 7

The Lower House.

DEANS:—YORK—DURHAM—CARLISLE—CHESTER—MANCHESTER—RIPON 6

ARCHDEACONS. Vide pp. 19—26 14

PROCTORS for the Chapters 7

PROCTORS for the Clergy 26

Total Members of Lower House, 53

Commissioners for the Archbishop.—The Dean, Precentor, Chancellor, and Canons Residentiary of York.

Prolocutor.—Unappointed. *Registrars.*—Messrs. HUDSON and J. BUCKLEY.

[a] The names of the several Bishops, Deans, Archdeacons, Proctors, &c. will be found beneath the respective Dioceses, pp. 19—26. The Dioceses, however, (with the exception of the five first,) are arranged for the sake of reference, in alphabetical order: but to distinguish the Provinces, those belonging to Canterbury are printed in Old English; those to York, in ordinary black type.

[b] In many Almanacks it is stated that in the Province of York there is but one house; this we have authority for stating is an error.

IRELAND.

Deaneries, 32.   **Benefices, 1,516.**   **Curates, 692.**

Armagh and Clogher.
Rt. Hon. and Most Rev. Lord J. G. Beresford, D.D. 1822.

ARMAGH.
Dean.—Very Rev. B.W.Disney, B.D.
Archdeacon.—Ven.J.W.Stokes,M.A.
Benefices 103.—Curates, 44.

CLOGHER.
Dean.—Hon. & V. Rev. R. Maude.
Archd.—Ven. J. A. Russell, M.A.
Benefices, 57.—Curates, 36.

Dublin and Kildare.
Rt. Hon. and Most Rev. Richard Whately, D.D. 1831.

DUBLIN and GLANDELAGH.
Dean.—Hon. H. Pakenham, D.D.
Archd. of Dublin.—Ven.J.West,D.D.
„ *Glandelagh.*—Vn.C.Strong,M.A.
Benefices, *Dublin*, 130.—Curates, 91.

KILDARE.
Dean.—VeryRev. J.Gregory, M.A.
Archdeacon.—Ven. J. Gregg, M.A.
Benefices, 43.—Curates, 23.

Meath.
Right Hon. and Most Rev. J. H. Singer, D.D. 1852.

Dean.—Very Rev. R. Butler, M.A.
Archdeacon.—Ven. E. A. Stopford.
Benefices 111
Curates 20

Cashel, Emly, Waterford, and Lismore.
Right Rev. Robert Daly, D.D.   1843.

CASHEL.
Dean.—Very Rev. G. O. Moore, M.A.
Archdeacon.—Ven. H. Cotton,LL.D.
Benefices, 40.—Curates, 11.

EMLY.
Dean.—Very Rev. D. Browne, M.A.
Archdeacon.—Ven. E. H. Brien, B.A.
Benefices, 21.—Curates, 4.

WATERFORD.
Dean.—V. Rev. E. N. Hoare, M.A.
Archdeacon.—Vn.RobertBell,M.A.
Benefices, 15.—Curates, 5.

LISMORE.
Dean.—Hn.&V.Rv.H.Browne,M.A.
Archd.—Ven. Ambrose Power,M.A.
Benefices, 54.—Curates, 17.

Cork, Cloyne, and Ross.
Right Rev. W. Fitzgerald, D.D. 1785.

CORK.
Dean.—VeryRv.H.T.Newman,M.A.
Archdeacon.—Ven.S.M.Kyle,LL.D.
Benefices, 70.—Curates, 49.

CLOYNE.
Dean.—Very Rev. J. Howie, M.A.

Archd.—Ven. William Ryder, M.A.
Benefices, 91.—Curates, 34.

ROSS.
Dean.—V. Rev. Jas. Stannus, M.A.
Archdeacon.—Vn.Alex.Stuart,M.A.
Benefices, 27.—Curates, 13.

Derry and Raphoe.
Right Rev. W. Higgin, D.D. 1853.

DERRY.
Dean.—VeryRev. T. B. Gough,M.A.
Archdeacon.—Vn. A.Edwards,M.A.
Benefices, 67.—Curates, 28.

RAPHOE.
Dean.—Lord E. Chichester, D.D.
Archdeacon.—Ven. F. Goold, M.A.
Benefices, 40.—Curates, 15.

Down, Connor, and Dromore.
Right Rev. ROBERT KNOX, D.D. 1849.

DOWN.
Dean.—V. Rev. T WOODWARD, M.A.
Archdn.—Ven. W. B. MANT, M.A.
Benefices, 48.—Curates, 17.

CONNOR.
Dean.—Very Rev. G. BULL, M.A.

Archdeacon.—J. SMITH, M.A.
Benefices, 70.—Curates, 32.

DROMORE.
Dean.—Very Rev. D. BAGOT, D.D.
Archdeacon.—Ven. J. SAURIN, M.A.
Benefices, 27.—Curates, 16.

Killaloe, Kilfenora, Clonfert, & Kilmacduagh.
Rt. Hon. & Rt. Rev. LUDLOW, Baron RIVERSDALE, D.D. 1839.

KILLALOE.
Dean.—Very Rev. J. HEAD, B.A.
Archdeacon.—Ven. E. KNOX, B.A.
Benefices, 70.—Curates, 16.

KILFENORA.
Dean.—V. Rev. M. J. KEATING, M.A.
Archdeacon.—Ven. J. WHITTY, M.A.
Benefices, 7.—Curate, 1.

CLONFERT.
Dean.—V. Rev. R. M. KENNEDY, M.A.
Archd.—Ven. J. H. G. BUTSON, M.A.
Benefices, 11.—Curates, 4.

KILMACDUAGH.
Dean.—V. Rev. J. A. BERMINGHAM.
Archd.—Hon. W. O'GRADY, M.A.
Benefices, 4.—Curates, 1.

Kilmore, Elphin, and Ardagh.
Right Rev. M. G. BERESFORD, D.D. 1854.

KILMORE.
Dean.—Rt. Hon. Lord FITZGERALD and VESEY, LL.D.
Archdn.—Hon. and Ven. J. AGAR.
Benefices, 46.—Curates, 37.

ELPHIN.
Dean.—Vy Rv. W. WARBURTON, D.D.

Archdeacon.—Ven. H. IRWIN, A.M.
Benefices, 43.—Curates, 12.

ARDAGH.
Dean.—Very Rev. H. U. TIGHE, B.A.
Archd.—Ven. J. C. MARTIN, D.D.
Benefices, 32.—Curates, 18.

Limerick, Ardfert, and Aghadoe.
Right Rev. HENRY GRIFFIN, M.A. 1853.

LIMERICK.
Dean.—Very Rev. A. L. KIRWAN, M.A.
Archd.—Ven. W. W. MAUNSELL, M.A.
Benefices, 63.—Curates, 14.

ARDFERT & AGHADOE.
Dean.—Very Rev. A. IRWIN, M.A.
Archd. of Ardf.-Vn. A. B. ROWAN, D.D.
Aghadoe.—J. W. FORSTER, LL.D.
Benefices, 48.—Curates, 20.

Ossory, Ferns, and Leighlin.
Right Rev. JAS. T. O'BRIEN, D.D. 1842.

OSSORY.
Dean.—V. Rev. C. VIGNOLES, D.D.
Archdeacon.—Ven. C. IRWIN, M.A.
Benefices, 69.—Curates, 36.

FERNS.
Dean.—Very Rev. H. NEWLAND, D.D.

Archd.—Ven. J. E. JOHNSON, D.D.
Benefices, 61.—Curates, 23.

LEIGHLIN.
Dean.—V. Rev. James LYSTER, M.A.
Archd.—H. & V. H. S. STOPFORD, M.A.
Benefices, 62.—Curates, 20.

Tuam, Killala, and Achonry.
Rt. Hon. and Rt. Rev. T. PLUNKET, D.D., Bar. of U. K. 1839.

TUAM.
Dean.—Hn. & V. Rv. R. PLUNKET, M.A.
Archdeacon.—Ven. J. CATHER, M.A.
Benefices, 33.—Curates, 25.

KILLALA.
Dean.—Very Rev. J. COLLINS, D.D.
Archdeacon.—Ven. W. JACKSON, M.A.

Benefices, 13.—Curates, 7.

ACHONRY.
Dean.—Very Rev. Lord Viscount MOUNTMORRES, LL.D.
Archd.—Ven. J. VERSCHOYLE, M.A.
Benefices, 10.—Curates, 3.

SCOTLAND.

TOTAL, in Scotland, (including Trinity College, Glenalmond).

Year.	Chs.&Chapls.	Clergy.	Parsonages.	Schools.	Daily Servs.
1851	12	130	38	57	...
1854	147	157	48	90	...
1855	151	162	49	104	36
1857	152	168	57	10?	31
1858	154	160	57	97	34

Edinburgh.

Right Rev. CHARLES H. TERROT, D.D. 1841. *Primus.*

Dean.—Very Rev. E. B. RAMSAY, M.A.
Synod Clerk.—Rev. John A. WHITE, M.A.
Registrar.—Hugh James ROLLO, W.S., Edinburgh.
Churches and Chapels, 23. Clergy, 26.
Parsonages, 5. Schools, 18. Daily Services, 4.

Aberdeen.

Right Rev. THOMAS GEORGE SUTHER, D.C.L. 1857.

Dean.—Very Rev. D. WILSON, M.A. | *Diocesan Clerk.*—Rev. A. RANKEN, M.A.
Churches and Chapels, 24. Clergy, 24.
Parsonages, 18. Schools, 20. Daily Services, 10.

Argyll and the Isles.

Right Rev. ALEXANDER EWING, D.D., D.C.L. 1847.

Dean.—Very Rev. S. HOOD. | *Synod Clerk.*—Rev. W. G. EATON.
Archdeacon of the Isles.—Ven D. AITCHISON, M.A.
„ *of Appin.*—Ven. W. D. IKIN.
Churches and Chapels, 15. Clergy, 14.
Parsonages, 5. Schools, 10. Daily Service, 1.

Brechin.

Right Rev. ALEXANDER P. FORBES, D.C.L. 1847.

Dean.—Very Rev. John MOIR, M.A.
Synod Clerk.—Rev. H. S. J. HOWARD, B.C.L.
Churches and Chapels, 14. Clergy, 16.
Parsonages, 9. Schools, 19. Daily Services, 5.

Glasgow and Galloway.

Right Rev. WALTER JOHN TROWER, D.D. 1848.

Dean.—Very Rev. W. S. WILSON, M.A.
Synod Clerk.—Rev. A. HENDERSON, M.A.
Churches and Chapels, 36. Clergy, 39.
Parsonages, 6. Week-day Schools, 15. Daily Services, 5.

Moray and Ross.

Right Rev. ROBERT EDEN, D.D. 1851.

Dean.—Very Rev. J. SMITH, M.A. | *Synod Clerk.*—Rev. W. CHRISTIE, M.A.
Churches and Chapels, 16. Clergy, 16.
Parsonages, 4. Schools, 8. Daily Services, 3.

St. Andrew's, Dunkeld, and Dunblane.

Right Rev. CHAS. WORDSWORTH, D.C.L. 1853.

Dean.—Very Rev. J. TORRY, M.A. | *Synod Clerk.*—Rev. G. G. MILNE, M.A.
Churches and Chapels, 26. Clergy, 29.
Parsonages, 10. Schools, 12. Daily Services, 6.

THE PROGRESS OF THE EPISCOPATE IN THE COLONIES, SHEWN IN A TABULAR FORM.

Western Hemisphere.

1787. **NOVA SCOTIA.**
   1845. FREDERICTON.   1832. NOVA SCOTIA.   NEWFOUNDLAND.

1824. **BARBADOS.**
   1842. GUIANA.   BARBADOS.   1842. ANTIGUA.

1793. **QUEBEC.**
   1850. RUPERT'S LAND.   1850. QUEBEC.   MONTREAL.   1839. TORONTO.   1857. HURON.

1824. **JAMAICA.**
   1856. KINGSTON.   JAMAICA.

1842. **GIBRALTAR.**

1859. ***BRITISH COLUMBIA.**

Eastern Hemisphere.

1814. **CALCUTTA.**
   1835. MADRAS.   1837. CALCUTTA.   1855. BOMBAY.   LABUAN.
   1845. COLOMBO.

1836. **AUSTRALIA.**
   1841. NEW ZEALAND.   1842. TASMANIA.   1847. AUSTRALIA.
   1856. CHRIST CHURCH. NEW ZEALAND.   *WAIAPUA.   1858. NELSON.   1858. WELLINGTON.   1847. MELBOURNE.   1847. SYDNEY. NEWCASTLE.   1847. ADELAIDE.   1856. ADELAIDE. PERTH.

1849. **VICTORIA.**

1850. **SIERRA LEONE.**

1847. **CAPETOWN.**
   1853. GRAHAMSTOWN. CAPETOWN. NATAL.

1854. **MAURITIUS.**

* These Dioceses it is expected will be formed shortly.

Omitting Gibraltar, the tracts over which the Colonial Dioceses extend may be reckoned at upwards of three million square miles, and the population at about 107 millions. There are 495 clergy, and (including the two Bishops-designate) thirty-seven Bishops.

THE COLONIES.

Adelaide.

Right Rev. AUGUSTUS SHORT, D.D. 1847.

Dean—Very Rev. James FARRELL, M.A. 1849.
Archdeacon of South Australia—Ven. W. J. WOODCOCK, 1857.

Population, 81,000.   Square miles, 300,000.   Clergy, 23.

Founded 1847. First Bishop, W. G. BROUGHTON, 1836. Includes, together with Perth, (*q. v.*) Southern Australia. This Diocese, with Melbourne, Newcastle, and Sydney, are divisions of the original Diocese of Australia. Income from Colonial Bishops' Fund, £800.

Antigua.

Right Rev. STEPHEN J. RIGAUD, D.D. 1857.

Archdeacon of Antigua—Ven. George CLARKE, M.A. 1849.
  „   *St. Christopher's*—Ven. H. W. JERMYN, M.A. 1854.

Population, 106,372.   Square miles, 751.   Clergy, 26.

Founded 1842. First Bishop, Dan. G. DAVIS, D.D., 1842. Contains Antigua, Nevis, St. Christopher, Barbada, Montserrat, Anguilla, Virgin Islands, and Dominica. Income from Consolidated Fund, £2,000.

Barbados.

Right Rev. THOMAS PARRY, D.D. 1842.

Archdeacon of Barbados—Ven. Charles LAWSON, M.A. 1842.
  „   *Trinidad*—Ven. George CUMMINS, M.A. 1842.

Population, 308,189.   Square miles, 3,170.   Clergy, 80.

Founded 1824. First Bp., W. H. COLERIDGE, 1824. Diocese contains Barbados, Trinidad, Grenada, Tobago, St. Vincent, St. Lucia. Income from Consolidated Fund, £2,500.

Bombay.

Right Rev. JOHN HARDING, D.D. 1851.

Archdeacon and Commissary—Ven. F. C. P. REYNOLDS, B.A. 1855.

Population, 7,800,000.   Square miles, 65,000.   Clergy, 48.

Founded 1837. First Bishop, T. CARR, 1837. Contains Presidency of Bombay.

Calcutta.

Right Rev. G. E. L. COTTON, D.D. 1858.

Archdeacon—Ven. John Henry PRATT, M.A. 1850.

Population, 72,900,000.   Square miles, 306,012.   Clergy, 150.

Founded 1814. *Bishops*—T. F. MIDDLETON, 1814; REGINALD HEBER, 1823; J. T. JAMES, 1827; J. M. TURNER, 1829; DANIEL WILSON, 1834. Contains Presidency of Bengal. The original Diocese of Calcutta contained also the present Dioceses of Madras and Bombay.

BISHOP'S COLLEGE. *Principal*—Rev. W. KAY, D.D. *Sen. Professor*—Rev. S. SLATER.

Capetown.

Right Rev. ROBERT GRAY, D.D. 1847.

Dean—Very Rev. H. DOUGLAS, M.A. 1856.
Archdeacon of George-Town—Ven. T. E. WELBY, M.A.
  „   *St. Helena*—Ven. R. KEMPTHORNE.

Population, 225,000.   Square miles, 130,046.   Clergy, 38.

Founded 1847. Includes the Cape of Good Hope and Island of St. Helena. The new Diocese of Grahamstown and Natal are divisions of the original Diocese. Income from Colonial Bishoprics' Fund, £800.

Christ Church.

Right Rev. H. J. C. HARPER, D.D. 1856.

Archdeacon—Ven. O. MATHIAS. 1855.

Founded 1856. Formerly under the jurisdiction of the Metropolitan of Australia; now under that of New Zealand, (*q. v.*)

British Columbia.

Rev. GEO. HILLS, M.A. Bishop-designate.

Colombo.

Right Rev. JAMES CHAPMAN, D.D. 1845.
Archdeacon—Ven. J. A. MATHIAS, M.A. 1846.
Population, 1,442,062. Native Clergy, 12. Missionary Clergy, 27.
Square miles, 24,448.
Founded 1845. Consists of the Island of Ceylon. Income from Colonial Funds, £2,000.
ST. THOMAS' COLLEGE, instituted 1851. The College, with an affiliated school, are
in full operation, with more than two hundred Students, and will form the nucleus
of a Theological Training Institution for a native Ministry in Ceylon.

Fredericton.

Right Rev. JOHN MEDLEY, D.D. 1845.
Archdeacon of New Brunswick—Ven. George COSTER, M.A. 1830.
Population, 200,000. Square miles, 26,000. Clergy, 57.
Founded 1845. Includes the Province of New Brunswick. Income from Colonial
Bishoprics' Fund, £1,000.

Gibraltar.

Right Rev. GEORGE TOMLINSON, D.D. 1842.
Archdeacon of Gibraltar—Ven. E. J. BURROW, D.D., F.R.S. 1842.
„ *Malta*—Ven. J. T. H. Le MESURIER, M.A. 1843.
Clergy, 42.
Founded 1842. Includes Gibraltar and the congregations of the Church of England
in the Mediterranean. Income from Colonial Bishoprics' Fund, £1,200.

Grahamstown.

Right Rev. HENRY COTTERILL, D.D. 1856.
Archdeacon of Grahamstown—Ven. N. J. MERRIMAN, M.A. 1847.
„ *Kaffraria*—Ven. J. HARDIE, M.A. 1857.
Population, 340,000. Square miles, 60,000. Clergy, 25.
Founded 1853. First bishop, JOHN ARMSTRONG, 1853. Consists of the Eastern
Provinces, the Sovereignty, and British Kaffraria. Income from Colonial Bishoprics'
Fund, £800.

Guiana.

Right Rev. WILLIAM PIERCY AUSTIN, D.D. 1842.
Archdeacon of Demerara—Ven. H. H. JONES, M.A.
„ *Berbice*—Vacant.
Population, 121,678. Square miles, 134,000. Clergy, 33.
Founded 1842. Includes Demerara, Essequibo, and Berbice. Income from Con-
solidated Fund, £2,000.

Huron.

Right Rev. BENJAMIN CRONYN, D.D. 1857.
Elected by the Synod of the Diocese of Toronto, May, 1857 ; consecrated Oct. 28, 1857.
Clergy, 44.

Jamaica.

Right Rev. AUBREY GEORGE SPENCER, D.D. 1843.
Coadjutor, Rt. Rv. R. COURTENAY, D.D., Bp. of Kingston. 1856.
Archdeacons and Commissaries of Nassau—Ven. J. M. TREW, D.D. 1843.
„ „ *Surrey*—Ven. R. PANTON, D.D. 1847.
„ „ *Middlesex*—Ven. T. STEWART, D.D. 1857.
„ „ *Cornwall*—Ven. J. P. WILLIAMS, D.D. 1847.
Population, 418,847. Square miles, 74,734. Clergy, 108.
Founded 1824. First Bishop, CHRISTOPHER LIPSCOMBE, Cons. 1824. Diocese in-
cludes, besides Jamaica, the Bahamas, British Honduras, and Cayman. Income from
Consolidated Fund, £3,000.
BISHOP'S COLLEGE. *Principal*—Rev. G. J. HANDFORD, M.A.

Labuan. (Borneo.)

Right Rev. F. T. McDougall, D.C.L. 1855.

Population, 6,000,000. Square miles, 260,000. Clergy, 4.

Founded 1855. Contains Labuan and its dependencies. Income from Colonial Bishops' Fund, £500.

Madras.

Right Rev. Thomas Dealtry, D.D. 1849.

Archdeacon—Ven. Vincent Shortland, B.D. 1847.

Population, 13,500,000. Square miles, 144,923. Clergy, 131.

Founded 1835. Bishops, Daniel Corrie, *Cons* 1835; G. T. Spencer, 1837. Consists of Presidency of Madras. The original Diocese included also that of Colombo.

Mauritius.

Right Rev. Vincent W. Ryan, D.D. 1854.

Population, 190,000. Square miles, 1,400. Clergy, 9.

Founded 1854. Contains Mauritius and Seychelles. Income as Senior Chaplain from Colonial Fund, £600; and from the Colonial Bishoprics' Fund, the interest of £6,800.

Melbourne.

Right Rev. Charles Perry, D.D. 1847.

Dean—Very Rev. H. B. Macartnay, LL.D., 1851.

Archdeacon of Geelong—Ven. T. C. B. Stretch, M.A.

——————— *of Melbourne*—Vacant.

——————— *of Portland*—Ven. T. H. Braim, D.D. 1856.

Population, 200,000. Square miles, 80,000. Clergy, 47.

Founded 1847. Consists of the Province of Victoria. Income from Colonial Treasury, £1,000; and from Colonial Bishoprics' Fund, £333 6s. 8d.

Montreal.

Right Rev. Francis Fulford, D.D. 1850.

Dean—Very Rev. J. Bethune, D.D.

Archdeacon—Ven. S. Gilson, M.A. 1857.

Population, 472,405. Square miles, 56,258. Clergy, 56.

Founded 1850. Consists of District of Montreal. Income from Colonial Bishoprics' Fund, £800.

Natal.

Right Rev. John William Colenso, D.D. 1853.

Dean—Very Rev. J. Green, M.A. 1857.

Archdeacon—Ven. C. F. Mackenzie, M.A.

Population, 125,000. Square miles, 18,000. Clergy, 11.

Founded 1853. Consists of the Province of Natal. Income from Colonial Bishoprics' Fund, £800.

Nelson.

Right Rev. Edmund Hobhouse, D.D. 1858.

Archdeacon—Ven. R. B. Paul. 1855.

Founded 1858. Formed, together with Wellington, from the Diocese of New Zealand.

Newcastle.

Right Reverend William Tyrrell, D.D. 1847.

Population, (*see* Sydney). Square miles, 500,000. Clergy, 29.

Founded 1847. Northern Districts of New South Wales. Income from Colonial Treasury, £500; and Colonial Bishoprics' Fund, £333 6s. 8d.

Newfoundland.

Right Rev. EDWARD FEILD, D.D. 1844.

Archd. of Newfoundland and Labrador—Ven. H. M. LOWER, M.A. 1857.

Population, 106,421.   Square miles, 36,022.   Clergy, 50.

Founded 1839. First Bishop, AUBREY G. SPENCER, Cons. 1839. Consists of Newfoundland and the Bermudas. Income by Parliamentary Vote as Archdeacon of Newfoundland and Bermudas, £500; from Colonial Funds, £200; and from the Society for the Propagation of the Gospel, as Bishop, £500.

ST. JOHN'S COLLEGE. *Principal*—

New Zealand.

Rt. Rev. G. AUGUSTUS SELWYN, D.D. (Metropolitan.) 1841.

Archdeacon of Waiapua—Ven. William WILLIAMS, D.C.L. (*Bp.-des.*) 1843.
     „   *Waimate*—Ven. Henry WILLIAMS, M.A. 1845.
     „   *Tauranga*—Ven. Alfred N. BROWN, M.A. 1845.
     „   *Waitemata*—Vacant.
     „   *Kapiti*—Ven. R. B. PAUL, M.A. 1856.
     „   *Akaroa*—Ven. O. MATHIAS, M.A. 1856.

Population, 120,000. Square miles, 95,000. Clergy, with Christ Church, 56.

Founded 1841. Contains New Zealand, Chatham Islands, &c. This Diocese and Tasmania may be considered as divisions of the original Diocese of Australia. Soon after they were formed, the remaining portion was subdivided into Adelaide (*q. v.*), Sydney, Newcastle, and Melbourne. Income from Colonial Bishoprics' Fund, £600.

Nova Scotia.

Right Rev. HIBBERT BINNEY, D.D. 1851.

Archdeacon of Nova Scotia—Ven. Robert WILLIS, D.D. 1825.

Population, 338,465.   Square miles, 22,435.   Clergy, 76.

Founded 1787. *Bishops*—CHARLES INGLIS, cons. 1787; ROBERT STANSER, 1816; JOHN INGLIS, 1825. Includes Prince Edward's Island and Cape Breton. The Dioceses of Fredericton and Newfoundland are also divisions of the original Diocese of Nova Scotia. Income from Interest of Trust Fund by Society for the Propagation of the Gospel, £700.

KING'S COLLEGE, WINDSOR. *Principal*—D. W. PICKETT, M.A.

Perth.

Right Rev. MATHEW BLAGDEN HALE, D.D. 1857.

Dean—Rev. G. P. POWNALL.

Clergy, 9.

Founded 1856. Contains a part of Southern Australia. (*Vide* Adelaide.)

Quebec.

Right Rev. G. JEHOSHAPHAT MOUNTAIN, D.D., D.C.L. 1850.

Population, 417,856.   Square miles, 153,432.   Clergy, 43.

Founded 1793. *Bishops*—JACOB MOUNTAIN, cons. 1793; CHARLES STEWART, 1826. Contains the Districts of Gaspé, Quebec, the three Rivers, and St. Francis. The original Diocese of Quebec contained also the present Dioceses of Rupert's Land, Montreal, and Toronto. Income by Imperial Parliamentary Vote, £1,990.

THE BISHOP'S COLLEGE, LENNOXVILLE. *Chancellor*—Hon. Chief-Justice BOWEN. *Principal*—Jasper H. NICOLLS, M.A.

Rupert's Land.

Right Rev. DAVID ANDERSON, D.D. 1849.

Archdeacon of Assiniboia—Ven. W. COCHRANE. 1853.
     „   *Cumberland*—Ven. J. HUNTER. 1854.

Population, 103,000.   Square miles, 370,000.   Clergy, 16.

Founded 1850. Includes the Territory of the Hudson's Bay Company. Income from Colonial Bishoprics' Fund, £700.

Sierra Leone.

Right Rev. JOHN BOWEN, LL.D. 1857.

Population, 45,000.   Clergy, 14.

Founded 1850. *Late Bishops*—O. E. VIDAL, 1852; J. W. WEEKS, 1855. Comprises the Colonies of the Gambia, Sierra Leone, and other British Settlements on the Western Coast of Africa. Income as Colonial Chaplain, £500; and from Colonial Bishoprics' Fund, £400.

Sydney.

Right Rev. FREDERICK BARKER, LL.D. 1854.

Archdeacon of Cumberland—Vacant.

Population, together with Diocese of Newcastle, 190,000.   Clergy, 63.
Square miles, 100,000.

Founded 1836. First bishop, W. G. BROUGHTON, 1847. Consists of the southern part of New South Wales. Income from General Colonial Revenue, £500; and from Colonial Treasury, £1,000.

Tasmania.

Right Rev. FRANCIS RUSSELL NIXON, D.D. 1842.

Archdeacon of Hobart-Town—Ven. R. R. DAVIES, M.A. 1856.
    ,,   *Launceston*—

Population, 74,464.   Square miles, 24,002.   Clergy, 57.

Founded 1842. Consists of Van Diemen's Land and Norfolk Island. Income from Colonial Funds, £1,000; and also the interest of £5,000 granted by Colonial Bishoprics' Fund.

Toronto.

Rt. Rev. JOHN STRACHAN, D.D., LL.D. 1839.

Archdeacon of Kingston—Ven. G. O'Kill STUART, D.D., LL.D. 1825.
    ,,   *York*—Ven. A. N. BETHUNE, D.D. 1847.

Population	952,004	Townships	370
Square miles	100,000	Clergy	170

Founded 1839. Diocese consists of West Canada. Income from Clergy Revenues in Canada West, £1,250.

TRINITY COLLEGE. *Provost*—G. WHITAKER, M.A.

Victoria.

Right Rev. GEORGE SMITH, D.D. 1849.

Archdeacon of Ningpoo—Vacant.
Clergy, 16.

Founded 1849. Includes Hong Kong, and the Congregations of the English Church in China. Income from Colonial Bishoprics' Fund, £1,000.

Waiapua.

Ven. W. WILLIAMS, D.C.L. *Bishop-designate.*

Wellington.

Right Rev. CHARLES J. ABRAHAM, D.D. 1858.

Archdeacon—Ven. Octavius HADFIELD. 1847.
Founded in 1858, from the Diocese of New Zealand.

MISSIONARY BISHOP AT JERUSALEM.

Right Rev. SAMUEL GOBAT, D.D. 1846.

Clergy, 6.

AMERICA.

THE PROTESTANT EPISCOPAL CHURCH IN THE UNITED STATES OF AMERICA.

The General Convention,

Which meets triennially, is composed of the House of Bishops, consisting of all the diocesan and missionary Bishops in the United States; and of the House of Clerical and Lay Deputies, consisting of four clergymen and four laymen from each diocese.

Secretary of the House of Bishops—Rev. L. P. W. Balch, D.D., Baltimore.

General Institutions.

I. THE GENERAL THEOLOGICAL SEMINARY, NEW YORK.—*Secretary*—Rev. E. N. Mead, Tarrytown.

Students, 39. Alumni, 482. Total Students from commencement, 728.

II. THE DOMESTIC AND FOREIGN MISSIONARY SOCIETY.—*Secretary*—Rev. P. Van Pelt, D.D., Philadelphia.

Home missionary Bishops, 4; missionaries, 126.
Foreign missionary bishops, 2; missionaries, 26; and 28 assistants.
Official Organ—"The Spirit of Missions," published by Dana, New York.

III. THE GENERAL PROTESTANT EPISCOPAL SUNDAY-SCHOOL UNION AND CHURCH BOOK-SOCIETY.—*Secretary*—Rev. A. B. Hart.

The Union publishes books of instruction, and library-books for Sunday-schools and catechetical classes. *Depository*, No. 762, Broadway, New York.

IV. PROTESTANT EPISCOPAL HISTORICAL SOCIETY.—*Secretary*—Rev. B. Franklin, Newcastle, Del.

V. WESTERN CHURCH EXTENSION SOCIETY, embracing Iowa, Minnesota, Wisconsin, Nebraska, and Kansas.—*Corresponding Secs.*—Rev. W. A. Smallwood, D.D., Chicago; Rev. A. N. Littlejohn, New-Haven.

VI. PROTESTANT EPISCOPAL SOCIETY FOR THE PROMOTION OF EVANGELICAL KNOWLEDGE.—*Editor*—Rev. C. W. Andrews, D.D.—*Corresponding Secretary*—Rev. H. Dyer, D.D., New York.

Diocesan Institutions.

Every diocese possesses its own governing body, (as distinct from the General Convention,) entitled, the "Diocesan Convention;" the *Standing Committee* of which consists both of clerical and lay members; in addition to which most have their Board of Missions, and numerous admirable institutions, such as Prayer-book and Tract Committees; Missionary and Benevolent Societies, Relief Funds for Clergy, Widows, Orphans, &c., besides Church Schools and Colleges.

STATISTICAL SUMMARY OF THE EPISCOPAL CHURCH IN AMERICA.

American Dioceses	32	Communicants	122,739
American Bishops (excluding Missionary Bishops)	38	Sunday-School Teachers	11,989
		Sunday Scholars	97,052
Clergy (exclusive of Missionaries)	1,958		

AMERICA.

NAME OF DIOCESE AND BISHOP.	EXTENT.		Clergy.	Communicants.	SUNDAY-SCHOOLS.	
	Square Miles.	Population			Teachers.	Scholars.
ALABAMA, 1844. 43. Rt. Rev. W. H. Cobbs, D.D., Bp. 1844.	50,722	835,192	26	1,240	98	698
CALIFORNIA, 1853. 59. Rt. Rev. W. I. Kip, D.D.	188,982	264,435	10	446	47	238
CAROLINA, NORTH, 1823. 58. Rt. Rev. T. Atkinson, D.D., Bp. 1853.	45,000	868,903	48	2,686	10	1,593
CAROLINA, SOUTH, 1795. 57. Rt. Rev. T. F. Davis, D.D., Bp. 1853.	24,500	668,607	69	5,453	225	2,072
CONNECTICUT, 1784. 19. Rt. Rev. T. C. Brownell, D.D., Bp. 1819 54. Rt. Rev. J. Williams, D.D., As. Bp. 1851.	4,674	370,791	126	10,596	1,044	5,092
DELAWARE, 1841. 38. Rt. Rev. A. Lee, D.D., Bp. 1841.	2,120	91,535	18	895	222	1,784
FLORIDA, 1851. 53. Rt. Rev. F. H. Rutledge, D.D., Bp. 1851.	59,268	110,725	6	385	75	491
GEORGIA, 1841. 37. Rt. Rev. S. Elliott, D.D., Bp. 1841.	58,000	935,690	23	1,580	144	1,405
ILLINOIS, 1851. 55. Rt. Rev. H. J. Whitehouse, D.D. 1851.	55,405	1,300,251	60	2,600	210	1,691
INDIANA, 1849. 50. Rt. Rev. G. Upfold, D.D., Bp. 1849.	33,809	988,393	26	1,118	151	981
IOWA, 1854. 61. Rt. Rev. H. W. Lee, D.D., Bp. 1854.	150,914	509,414	25	671	86	511
KENTUCKY, 1832. 27. Rt. Rev. B. B. Smith, D.D., Bp. 1832.	37,630	1,086,587	29	1,633	269	2,109
LOUISIANA, 1838. 33. Rt. Rev. L. Polk, D.D., Bp. 1838.	46,431	517,763	32	1,551	81	1,520
MAINE, 1847. 49. Rt. Rev. G. Burgess, D.D., Bp. 1847.	30,000	583,169	17	1,063	148	1,072
MARYLAND. 1792. 36. Rt. Rev. W. R. Whittingham, D.D. 1840.	15,959	583,035	144	10,510	773	6,647
MASSACHUSETTS, 1797. 40. Rt. Rev. M. Eastburn, D.D., Bp. 1842.	7,800	1,133,123	78	6,127	400	4,992
MICHIGAN, 1836. 32. Rt. Rev. S. A. M°Coskry, D.D., Bp. 1836.	56,243	509,374	41	1,550	177	1,197
MINNESOTA. *Rt. Rev. J. Kemper, D.D.	166,000	201,000				
MISSISSIPPI, 1850. 51. Rt. Rev. W. M. Green, D.D., Bp. 1850.	47,156	605,948	31	1,049	68	493
MISSOURI, 1844. 44. Rt. Rev. C. S. Hawks, D.D., Bp. 1844.	67,380	682,244	23	981	99	685
NEW HAMPSHIRE, 1844. 42. Rt. Rev. C. Chase, D.D., Bp. 1844.	9,280	317,964	13	626	47	369
NEW JERSEY, 1815. 29. Rt. Rev. G. W. Doane, D.D., Bp. 1832.	8,320	569,499	80	4,012	523	4,366
NEW YORK, 1787. 62. Rt. Rev. H. Potter, D.D., Prov. Bp. 1854.	21,751	1,645,011	310	24,000	2,240	19,356
NEW YORK, WESTERN. 1839. 34. Rt. Rev. W. H. De Lancey, D.D., 1839.	21,463	1,445,011	120	8,901	958	6,129
OHIO, 1819. 28. Rt. Rev. C. P. M°Ilvaine, D.D., Bp. 1832.	39,964	2,215,750	85	5,117	609	4,288
PENNSYLVANIA, 1787. 64. Rt. Rev. S. Bowman, D.D., Bp. 1858.	46,000	2,311,786	173	13,267	1,835	17,630
RHODE ISLAND, 1843. 63. Rt. Rev. T. M. Clark, D.D., Bp. 1854.	1,306	147,554	31	2,607	323	2,387

NAME OF DIOCESE AND BISHOP.	EXTENT.				SUNDAY SCHOOLS.	
	Square Miles.	Population	Clergy.	Communicants.	Teachers.	Scholars.
TENNESSEE, 1834.						
30. Rt. Rev. J. H. OTEY, D.D., Bp. 1834.	45,600	1,002,625	18	914	86	494
TEXAS, 1844.						
46.	367,087	187,403	13	535	36	209
VIRGINIA, 1790.						
22. Rt. Rev. W. MEADE, D.D., Bp. 1829.						
39. Rt. Rev. J. JOHNS, As. Bp. 1842.	61,352	1,421,661	113	6,315	803	4,735
VERMONT, 1832.						
26. Rt. Rev. J. H. HOPKINS, D.D., Bp. 1832.	10,212	314,120	23	1,442	33	603
WISCONSIN, 1835.						
31. Rt. Rev. J. KEMPER, D.D., Bp. 1835.	53,924	552,109	47	1,869	169	1,215

AMERICAN MISSIONS.

ARKANSAS MISSION.
CHINA MISSION, 1844. 45. Rt. Rev. W. J. BOONE, D.D., 1844.
KANSAS MISSION. Rt. Rev. J. KEMPER, D.D.
NEBRASKA MISSION. Rt. Rev. H. W. LEE, D.D.
OREGON & WASHINGTON MSN., 1853. 60. Rt. Rev. T. F. SCOTT, D.D., M.B. 1853.
WESTERN AFRICA MISSION, 1850. 52. Rt. Rev. J. PAYNE, D.D., 1850.
We have not been able to obtain any satisfactory returns relating to the American Missions: the statistics have therefore been omitted.

RETIRED BISHOPS.

CONS.
21. Right Rev. H. U. ONDERDONK, D.D. . . 1827
47. Right Rev. Horatio SOUTHGATE, D.D. . . 1844

LATE BISHOPS OF THE AMERICAN CHURCH.

No.			Cons.	No.			Cons.
1.	S. SEABURY.	*Connecticut.*	1784	15.	J. KEMP.	*Maryland.*	1814
2.	W. WHITE.	*Pennsylvania.*	1787	16.	J. CROES.	*New Jersey.*	1815
3.	S. PROVOST.	*New York.*	1787	17.	N. BOWEN.	*South Carolina.*	1818
4.	J. MADISON.	*Virginia.*	1790	18.	P. CHASE.	*Ohio.*	1819
5.	T. J. CLAGGETT.	*Maryland.*	1792	20.	J. S. RAVENSCROFT.	*N. Carolina.*	1823
6.	R. SMITH.	*South Carolina.*	1795	23.	W. M. STONE.	*Maryland.*	1830
7.	E. BASS.	*Massachusetts.*	1797	24.	B. T. ONDERDONK,	*New York.*	
8.	A. JARVIS.	*Connecticut.*	1797		(Susp.)		1830
9.	B. MOORE.	*New York.*	1801	25.	L. S. IVES.	*North Carolina.*	1831
10.	S. PARKER.	*Massachusetts.*	1804	35.	C. E. GADSDEN.	*South Carolina* .	1840
11.	J. H. HOBART.	*New York.*	1811	41.	J. P. K. HENSHAW.	*Rhode Island.*	1843
12.	A. V. GRISWOLD.	*Eastern Diocese.*	1811	48.	A. POTTER.	*Pensylvania.*	1845
13.	T. DEHON.	*South Carolina.*	1812	56.	J. M. WAINWRIGHT.	*New York Prov.*	1852
14.	R. C. MOORE.	*Virginia.*	1814				

The above list of Bishops of the American Church, together with those now living, and occupying respectively the sees contained in the preceding list, form the whole of the American Episcopacy. Throughout both tables, the number in order is affixed to each Bishop's name,—thus: T. C. Brownell, the nineteenth American Bishop, is the senior Bishop (as to date of consecration) now living. Thos. M. Clark, consecrated in 1854, is the sixty-third American Bishop.

SUMMARY
OF THE ANGLICAN BRANCH OF THE HOLY CATHOLIC CHURCH.

	BISHOPS.	CLERGY.
England (including 2 Archbishops) . . .	28	*circa* 17,000
Scotland	7	,, ,, 200
Ireland	12	,, ,, 2,200
The Colonies (including Waiapua and British Columbia)	38	,, ,, 550
America	40	,, ,, 2,000
Retired Bishops	6	
Total .	131	21,950

UNIVERSITIES, SCHOOLS, &c.

University of Oxford.

	Elected
Chancellor.	
The Rt. Hon. E. G. SMITH STANLEY, EARL OF DERBY, D.C.L.	1852
High Steward.	
The Rt. Hon. WILLIAM COURTENAY, EARL OF DEVON, D.C.L.	1838
Deputy Steward.	
Roundell Palmer, M.A., M.P., Magdalen College	1852
Representatives in Parliament.	
Right Hon. W. E. Gladstone, D.C.L., Christ Church	1847
Sir William Heathcote, Bart., D.C.L., All Souls	1854
Vice-Chancellor.	
Francis Jeune, D.C.L., Master of Pembroke	1858

Pro-Vice-Chancellors.

D. Williams, D.C.L., War. of New C.	R. L. Cotton, D.D., Prov. of Worc·
J. Norris, D.D., Presid. of Corpus.	J. Thompson, D.D., Rector of Linc·

Proctors.

	Elected
Rev. B. Price, M.A., Pembroke College	1858
Rev. C. W. Heaton, B.D., Jesus College ... ..., ...	1858

Pro-Proctors.

Rev. J. M. Holland, M.A., New C.	Rev. J. W. Caldicott, M.A., Jesus C.
Rev. T. H. R. Shand, M.A., B.N.C.	Rev. E. Owen, M.A., Jesus Coll.

Assessor of V.-Chan's. Court, J. R. Kenyon, D.C.L., All Souls' 1840
University Counsel, Sir Richard Bethell, M.P., M.A., Wadham 1846
Registrar of the University, & of the Chancellor's Court, E. W. Rowden, D.C.L., New College - - - 1853—5
Proctors of the Chan.'s Court { H. A. Pottinger, M.A., Worc.; 1857
{ D. Latimer, M.A., Lincoln 1858
Keeper of the Archives, Rev. J. Griffiths, M.A., Wadham Coll. 1857
Bodley's Librarian, Bulkeley Bandinel, D.D., New College - 1813
Sub-Librarians, Rev. S. Reay, B.D., Alban Hall - - 1828
   ,,   Rev. H. O. Coxe, M.A., Corpus - - 1838
Keeper of the Ashmolean Museum, J. Phillips, M.A., Magd. - 1854
Radcliffe's Librarian, H. W. Acland, M.D., All Souls' - 1851
Radcliffe Observer, M. J. Johnson, M.A., Magd. Hall - 1839
Public Orator, Rev. Richard Michell, B.D., Lincoln - 1848
Bampton Lecturer for 1859, George Rawlinson, M.A., Exeter 1858

THE HEBDOMADAL COUNCIL.

HEADS OF HOUSES.	PROFESSORS.	MEMB. OF CONVOC.
The Warden of Wadham.	Rev. E. Cardwell, D.D.	Rev. J. P. Lightfoot, D.D.
The Pres. of St. John's.	Rev. E. B. Pusey, D.D.	Rev. R. Michell, B.D.
The Master of Balliol.	J. D. Macbride, D.C.L.	Rev. J. E. Sewell, M.A.
The Princ. of Brasenose.	Rev. B. Price, M.A.	Rev. O. Gordon, B.D.
The Prov. of Worcester	Rev. W. Jacobson, D.D.	Rev. J. M. Wilson, B.D.
The Dean of Ch. Ch.	Rev. E. Hawkins, D.D.	Rev. H. L. Mansel, B.D.

Besides the official members,—The Chancellor, the Vice-Chancellor, the ex-Vice-Chancellor, and the two Proctors.

Founded.	COLLEGES.	Elected.	M.A. &c.	B.A. S.C.L.	Commoners, &c.	Total on Books.
872. UNIVERSITY. Master . . . . . Rev. Fred. C. Plumptre, D.D. 1836.			150	66	69	285
1262. BALLIOL. Master . . . . Rev. Robert Scott, D.D. 1854.			191	58	99	348
1270. MERTON. Warden . . . . . . R. Bullock-Marsham, Esq., D.C.L. 1826.			101	29	41	171
1314. EXETER. Rector . . . . Rev. John P. Lightfoot, D.D. 1854.			278	79	145	502
1326. ORIEL. Provost . . . . Rev. Edward Hawkins, D.D. 1828.			204	103	77	384
1340. QUEEN'S. Provost . . . . Rev. William Thomson, D.D. 1855.			166	29	56	251
1386. NEW COLLEGE. Warden . . . Rev. D. Williams, D.C.L. 1840.			111	51	26	188
1427. LINCOLN. Rector . . . . Rev. James Thompson, D.D. 1851.			113	44	37	194
1437. ALL SOULS'. Warden . . . . . Rev. F. K. Leighton, M.A. 1858.			91	19	4	114
1456. MAGDALEN. President . . . . Rev. Frederic Bulley, D.D. 1855.			119	70	39	228
1509. BRASENOSE. Principal . . . Rev. E. Hartopp Cradock, D.D. 1853.			279	58	90	427
1516. CORPUS CHRISTI. President . Rev. James Norris, D.D. 1843.			72	43	41	156
1532. CHRIST CHURCH. Dean . . . Very Rev. Henry G. Liddell, D.D. 1855.			459	168	191	818
1554. TRINITY. President . . . . Rev. John Wilson, D.D. 1850.			167	60	79	306
1555. St. JOHN'S. President . . . . . . Rev. Philip Wynter, D.D. 1828.			179	94	71	344
1571. JESUS. Principal . . . . Rev. Chas. Williams, B.D. 1857.			66	48	42	156
1613. WADHAM. Warden . . . . . . Rev. B. P. Symons, D.D. 1831.			167	60	83	310
1624. PEMBROKE. Master . . . . . . Rev. F. Jeune, D.C.L. 1843.			99	58	60	217
1714. WORCESTER. Provost . . . . . Rev. R. L. Cotton, D.D. 1839.			189	90	83	362
1269. St. EDMUND HALL. Principal Rev. John Barrow, D.D. 1854.			43	4	23	70
1325. St. MARY HALL. Principal . . Rev. D. P. Chase, M.A. 1857.			49	10	11	70
1547. St. ALBAN HALL. Principal . . Rev. Edward Cardwell, D.D. 1831.			10	1	10	21
1392. NEW INN HALL. Principal . . Rev. H. Wellesley, D.D. 1847.			20	8	6	34
1602. MAGDALEN HALL. Principal J. D. Macbride, Esq., D.C.L. 1813.			132	32	90	254

N.B.—In the above list, the column M.A. &c., includes D.D., D.C.L., B.D., B.C.L., M.D., and M.A. The Commoners include those whose names are in the Calendar, and who have not taken any Degree.

Founded	PROFESSORS.	Elected
1497	*Divinity (Margaret)*, Rev. Charles Abel Heurtley, D.D., Canon of Ch. Ch.	1853
1535	*Divinity (Regius)*, Rev. W. Jacobson, D.D., Ch. Cb. - - -	1848
1546	*Civil Law (Regius)*, Travers Twiss, D.C.L., University - -	1855
1535	*Medicine (Regius)*, H. W. Acland, M.D., All Souls' - -	1857
1541	*Hebrew (Regius)*, Rev. Edward Bouverie Pusey, D.D., Ch. Ch. -	1828
1546	*Greek (Regius)*, Rev. Benjamin Jowett, M.A., Balliol - -	1855
1618	*Natural Philosophy*, Rev. B. Price, M.A., Pembroke - -	1853
1620	*Astronomy (Savilian)*, W. F. Donkin, M.A., University - -	1842
1619	*Geometry (Savilian)*, Rev. Baden Powell, M.A., Oriel - -	1827
1621	*Moral Philosophy*, Rev. J. M. Wilson, D.D., Corpus - -	1858
1622	*History (Camden)*, Rev. E. Cardwell, D.D., Princ. St. Alban Hall	1826
1626	*Anatomy, (Tomlins')*, Annexed to Regius Professorship of Medicine.	1857
1626	*Music*, Rev. Sir Fred. A. Gore Ouseley, Bart., D.M., Ch. Ch. -	1855
1626	*Music*, Choragus, S. Elvey, D. Mus., Organist, New Coll. -	1848
1636	*Arabic (Laud's)*, Rev. S. Reay, B.D., St. Alban Hall -	1840
1750	*Arabic (Lord Almoner's)*, J. D. Macbride, D.C.L., Princ. Magd. Hall	1813
1708	*Poetry*, Matthew Arnold, M.A., Oriel - - - -	1857
1724	*Modern History (Regius)*, Goldwin Smith, M.A., University -	1858
1758	*Law (Vinerian)*, John R. Kenyon, D.C.L., All Souls' -	1843
1780	*Clinical (Lord Lichfield's)*, H. W. Acland, M.D., All Souls' -	1857
1793	*Botany (Regius)*, C. G. B. Daubeny, M.D., Magdalen - -	1834
1795	*Anglo-Saxon*, J. Bosworth, D.D., Ch. Ch. - - - -	1858
1803	*Anatomy (Aldrich's)*, Annexed to Prælectorship of Anatomy -	1857
——	*Physic (Aldrich's)*, Vacant.	
——	*Chemistry (Aldrich's)*, B. C. Brodie, B.A., Balliol - - -	1855
1825	*Political Economy (Drummond's)*, C. Neate, M.A., Oriel - -	1857
1832	*Sanscrit (Col. Boden's)*, H. H. Wilson, M.A., Exeter - -	1832
1842	*Pastoral Theology (Regius)*, C. Atmore Ogilvie, D.D., Canon of Ch. Ch. -	1842
1842	*Ecclesiastical History (Regius)*, A. P. Stanley, B.D., Ch. Ch. -	1856
1847	*Exegetical (Ireland)*, E. Hawkins, D.D., Provost of Oriel -	1847
1848	*Modern Languages*, Max Müller, Ph. D., University - -	1854
1854	*Latin Literature*, J. Conington, M.A., University - -	1854
1636	**READERS IN**—*Anatomy*, George Rolleston, M.D., Pembroke -	1858
1810	*Experimental Philosophy*, Rev. R. Walker, M.A., Wadham -	1839
1856	*Geology*, J. Phillips, M.A., Magdalen - - - -	1856
	Mineralogy, M. H. Nevil Story-Maskelyne, Wadham - -	1854
1839	*Logic*, Rev. Henry Wall, M.A., Balliol - - - -	1849

SUBJECTS FOR THE PRIZES. 1859.

LATIN VERSE.—India Orientalis.

ENGLISH VERSE (*Newdigate*).—Lucknow. To be in Heroic Couplets.

LATIN ESSAY—Quatenus fabulæ credendum sit de Argonautarum cursu maritimo?

ENGLISH ESSAY.—The Effect produced by the precious metals of America on the Greatness and Prosperity of Spain.

EARL STANHOPE'S PRIZE.—The Causes of the Successes of the Ottoman Turks.

GAISFORD.—1. For Greek prose composition in the style of Herodotus or Plato,— "Pygmæorum Civitas." 2. For Greek Hexameters (original),— "Morte d'Arthur."

ARNOLD PRIZE.—Delphi, considered locally, morally, and politically.

DENYER.—1. The Baptism of Young Children is in anywise to be retained in the Church, as most agreeable with the Constitution of Christ. 2. The Use and Abuse of the Proverb,—"Charity begins at Home."

ELLERTON THEOLOGICAL.—The Lawfulness of Oaths.

QUALIFICATIONS AND DATES.

For those who shall not have exceeded, from date of their Matriculation, 1859—

LATIN VERSE	.	4 years	By Mar. 31.
ENGLISH VERSE	.	4 years	By Mar. 31.
LATIN ESSAY, (shall have exceeded 4, but not)	.	7 years	By Mar. 31.
ENGLISH ESSAY, (shall have exceeded 4, but not)	.	7 years	By Mar. 31.
STANHOPE, (undergraduates,)	. .	16th term	By May 11.
GAISFORD, (undergraduates,)	. .	17th term	By May 7.
ARNOLD, (graduates,)	. .	8 years	By Feb. 1.
DENYER, (at least Deacons entered on their 8th year,)	.	10 years	By Mar. 1.
ELLERTON, at least B.A.'s or B.C.L.'s who have commenced their 16th term 8 weeks previous			To Apr. 27.

But who had not exceeded their 28th term on June 14, 1858.

The Dates at the end of the line are the latest for sending in the Exercises.

University of Cambridge.

Chancellor.   Elected
His Royal Highness The PRINCE-CONSORT, K.G., LL.D., &c. ... 1847

High Steward.
John S. Copley, BARON LYNDHURST, LL.D., Trinity 1840

Vice-Chancellor.
W. H. Bateson, D.D., St. John's   1858

Representatives in Parliament.
Loftus Tottenham Wigram, M.A., Trinity   1852
Right Hon. S. H. Walpole, M.A., Trinity   1856

Commissary.—C. J. Selwyn, M.A., Trinity   1855
Deputy High Steward.—Francis Barlow, M.A., Trinity Hall   ... 1856
Public Orator.—W. G. Clark, M.A., Trinity   1857
Assessor to the Chancellor.—John Tozer, LL.D., Caius   ... 1852
Counsel.—Hon. G. Denman, Trinity. John Baily, Q.C., St. John's.
Librarian.—Rev. Joseph Power, M.A., Clare College 1845
Registrar.—Rev. Joseph Romilly, M.A., Trinity   1832

Council.

W. Whewell, D.D., Trinity
G. E. Corrie, D.D., Jesus
H. Philpott, D.D., St. Catharine's
L. Neville, M.A., Magdalen
Professor Challis, M.A., Trinity
Professor Selwyn, B.D., St. John's
Professor Browne, B.D., Emmanuel
Professor Stokes, M.A., Pembroke

F. Martin, M.A., Trinity
G. E. Paget, M.D., Caius
W. H. Bateson, D.D., St. John's
F. France, M.A., St. John's
H. Latham, M.A., Trinity Hall
W. G. Clark, M.A., Trinity
C. Hardwick, M.A., St. Catharine's
W. M. Campion, M.A., Queen's

Every University Grace must pass the COUNCIL before it can be introduced to the SENATE.

Proctors.—A Long, M.A., King's.   C. K. Robinson, M.A., St. Cath.'s
Pro-Proctors.—G. Williams, B.D., King's.   F. J. Jameson, M.A., St. Cath.
Moderators.—N. M. Ferrers, M.A., Caius.   R. B. Batty, M.A., Eman.

Founded.	COLLEGES.	Mems. of Senate.	Under-grads.	Mems. on Boards.
1257	St. PETER'S COLLEGE. Master H. W. Cookson, D.D. 1848.	163	33	225
1326	CLARE COLLEGE. Master Edward Atkinson, B.D., 1856.	147	42	218
1343	PEMBROKE COLLEGE. Master Gilbert Ainslie, D.D. 1828.	86	29	136
1347	GONVILLE & CAIUS. Master E. Guest, Esq., LL.D., F.R.S. 1852.	256	125	494
1350	TRINITY HALL. Master Thos. C. Geldart, Esq., LL.D. 1852.	81	68	231

CAMBRIDGE.	Mems. of Senate.	Under-grads.	Mems. on Boards.
1351 CORPUS CHRISTI. Master	181	62	284
James Pulling, D.D. 1850.			
1443 KING'S. Provost	101	15	137
Richard Okes, D.D. 1850.			
1449 QUEEN'S. President	163	43	263
George Phillips, D.D. 1858.			
1473 ST. CATHARINE'S COLLEGE. Master .	144	31	216
Henry Philpott, D.D. 1845.			
1496 JESUS. Master	148	39	234
George E. Corrie, D.D. 1849.			
1505 CHRIST'S. Master	202	95	369
James Cartmell, D.D. 1849.			
1511 ST. JOHN'S. Master	904	292	1467
W. H. Bateson, D.D. 1858.			
1519 MAGDALENE. Master	130	51	213
Hon. and Rev. Latimer Neville, M.A. 1854.			
1546 TRINITY. Master	1598	473	2451
William Whewell, D.D. 1841.			
1584 EMMANUEL. Master	215	93	380
George Archdall, D.D. 1835.			
1595 SIDNEY-SUSSEX. Master . . .	75	21	138
Robert Phelps, D.D. 1843.			
1800 DOWNING. Master	41	6	60
Rev. Thomas Worsley, D.D. 1836.			
COMMORANTES IN VILLA	21	0	0
Total . . .	4,656	1,518	7,516

COMPARATIVE VIEW OF MEMBERS ON THE BOARDS.

1748 . . 1,500	1826 . . 4,866	1846 . . 6,487
1816 . . 3,199	1836 . . 5,467	1856 . . 7,453

Founded.	PROFESSORS.		Elected.
1502	*Divinity (Margaret)*, Rev. W. Selwyn, B.D., St. John's	-	1855
1540	*Divinity (Regius)*, James Amiraux Jeremie, D.D., Trinity College	-	1850
—	*Civil Law (Regius)*, John Thomas Abdy, LL.D., Trinity Hall	-	1854
—	*Physic (Regius)*, Henry J. Hayles Bond, M.D., Corpus Christi	-	1851
—	*Hebrew (Regius)*, Thomas Jarrett, M.A., Trinity Coll.	-	1854
1724	*Greek (Regius)*, Rev. W. H. Thompson, M.A., Trinity	-	1853
1632	*Arabic*, Henry Griffin Williams, B.D., Emmanuel	-	1854
—	*Arabic (Lord Almoner's)*, Rev. T. Preston, M.A., Trinity	-	1855
1663	*Mathematics (Lucasian)*, George Gabriel Stokes, M.A., Pembroke	-	1849
1683	*Moral Philosophy*, Rev. J. Grote, B.D., Trinity -	-	1838
1684	*Music*, W. Sterndale Bennett, Mus. D., St. John's	-	1856
1702	*Chemistry*, J. Cumming, M.A., F.R.S., Trinity -	-	1815
1704	*Astronomy (Plumian)* Rev. J. Challis, M.A., F.R.S., Trinity	-	1836
1707	*Anatomy*, William Clark, M.D., F.R.S., Trinity -	-	1817
1724	*Modern History (Regius)*, Rt. Hn. Sir J. Stephen, K.C.B., LL.D., Trin. H.		1849
1724	*Botany*, J. S. Henslow, M.A., F.L.S., St. John's - -	-	1825
1727	*Geology (Woodwardian)*, A. Sedgwick, M.A., F.R.S., Trinity	-	1818
1750	*Astronomy (Lowndes's)*, Vacant.		
1750	*Divinity (Norrisian)*, Rev. Edward Harold Browne, B.D., Emmanuel		1854
1783	*Natural Philosophy (Jacksonian)*, R. Willis, M.A., F.R.S., Caius	-	1837
1800	*Law (Downing)*, Andrew Amos, Esq., M.A., Downing	-	1849
1800	*Medicine (Downing)*, W. W. Fisher, M.D., Downing	-	1841
1808	*Mineralogy*, William Hallows Miller, Esq., M.A., F.R.S., St. John's	-	1832
1828	*Political Economy*, George Pryme, Esq., M.A., Trinity	-	1828
1851	*Archæology (Disney)*, John Howard Marsden, B.D., St. John's	-	1851
1503	*Lady Margaret Preacher*, John Hymers, D.D., F.R.S., St. John's	-	1841
1803	*Christian Advocate*, C. Hardwick, M.A., Catharine Hall	-	1855
1819	*Hulsean Lecturer*, Vacant.		

University of Dublin.

TRINITY COLLEGE, incorporated 1591.
Chancellor—His Grace the Archbishop of Armagh.
Vice-Chancellor—The Right Hon. Francis Blackburne, LL.D.
Visitors—The Chancellor, or in his absence the Vice-Chancellor of the University and the Archbishop of Dublin.
Provost—Rev. Richard Macdonnell, D.D.
Vice-Provost—Rev. Charles Wm. Wall, D.D.
Senior Dean—Rev. Thos. Luby, D.D.
Registrar—Rev. J. H. Todd, D.D.
Catechist—Rev. J. L. Moore, D.D.
Senior Proctor—Rev. Humphrey Lloyd, D.D.
Junior Proctor—Rev. J. W. Stubbs, A.M.
Auditor—Rev. Thos. Luby, D.D.
Junior Dean—Rev. Jas. W. Barlow, A.M.
Senior Lecturer—John Toleken, M.D.
Bursar—A. S. Hart, LL.D.
Librarian—Rev. J. H. Todd, D.D.
There are Thirty Professorships.

University of Durham.

(Incorporated by Royal Charter, 1837.)
Visitor—The Lord Bishop of Durham.
Governors—The Dean and Chapter of Durham.
Warden—Ven. Charles Thorp, D.D., F.R.S.
Sub-Warden—Rev. H. Jenkyns, D.D.
Senate—The Warden, the Professors, the Proctors, and one representative of the Chapter.
Proctors—R. B. Hayward, Esq., M.A., and Rev. J. Waite, M.A.
Pro-Proctors—Rev. Alfred James, M.A., and Rev. R. H. Blakey, M.A.
Registrar—Rev. T. Chevallier, B.D.
Colleges and Halls. Heads.
University College....Ven. Chas. Thorp, D.D., F.R.S., *Master.* R. B. Hayward, Esq., M.A., *Vice-Master.*
Hatfield's Hall..........Rev. John Pedder, M.A., *Principal.*
Bishop Cosin's Hall...Rev. J. J. Hornby, M.A., *Principal.*
There are three Professors, three Readers, and one Lecturer.

Other Universities, &c.

LONDON UNIVERSITY.
Chancellor—The Earl Granville, F.R.S.
Vice-Chancellor—J. G. S. Lefevre, M.A.

GLASGOW UNIVERSITY.
Chancellor—Duke of Montrose.
Vice-Chancellor & Principal—Rev. T. Barclay, D.D.

ST. ANDREW'S.
Chancellor—Duke of Argyll
Rector—Sir R. A. Anstruther, Bt.
ABERDEEN UNIVERSITY.
Chancellor—Earl of Aberdeen.
Rector—John Inglis, LL.D.
Principal—Rev. P. Colin Campbell, D.D.
EDINBURGH UNIVERSITY.
Principal—Rev. John Lee, D.D.

Theological Colleges.

ST. AIDAN'S, BIRKENHEAD.
(Founded 1840, to train Candidates for Orders in the Parochial habits of a Minister of the Gospel, as well as to impart sound Theological Instruction.)
Principal—Rev. J. Baylee, D.D.
Head-Master—Rev. P. Homan, B.A.

ST. BEES'.
(Founded in 1816 by Bp. Law, to supply a good economical Education for Candidates for Holy Orders, and recognised by 3 & 4 Vict. cap. 77.)
Principal—Rev. G. H. Ainger, B.D.

ST. DAVID'S, LAMPETER.
(Incorporated by Royal Charter in 1822, for the Education of Candidates for Holy Orders. A further Royal Charter granted in 1852, to confer the degree

of B.D. on Ordained Members of five years' standing.)
Pr.—Vy. Rev. Llewelyn Lewellin, D.C.L.
Vice-Principal—Rev. R. Williams, D.D.
CHICHESTER.
(Founded by Bishop Otter, 1839.)
Principal—Rev. C. A. Swainson, M.A.
Vice-Principal—Rev. W. H. Davey, B.D.

CUDDESDON THEOLOGICAL COLLEGE.
(Founded 1854.)
Principal—
Vice-Prin.—Rev. H. P. Liddon, M.A.

LICHFIELD.
(Founded 1857.)
Principal—Rev. G. H. Curteis, M.A.

PETERBOROUGH.
Principal—Rev. C. Daymond.

THEOLOGICAL COLLEGES (*continued*).

WELLS THEOLOGICAL COLLEGE.
(Founded 1840.)
Principal—Rev. J. H. Pinder, M.A.
Vice-Principals } Rev. E. Huxtable, M.A.
{ Rev. C. M. Church, M.A.
MISSIONARY COLLEGE OF ST. AUGUSTINE, CANTERBURY.
Founded, as an Abbey, and endowed by King Ethelbert, A.D. 605. Suppressed A.D. 1538. Restored under Royal Charter, as a College for training Missionaries for the Church of England, with a Warden, Sub-Warden, and six Fellows, 1848.)
Warden—Rev. H. Bailey, B.D.
Sub-Warden—Rev. A. P. Moor, M.A.

𝔄 𝔏𝔦𝔰𝔱 𝔬𝔣 ℭ𝔬𝔩𝔩𝔢𝔤𝔢𝔰 𝔞𝔫𝔡 𝔖𝔠𝔥𝔬𝔬𝔩𝔰,
WITH THE NAMES OF THE PRINCIPALS, &c.

METROPOLITAN.

CHARTERHOUSE. *Master*—Ven. Archdeacon Hale. *Master of School*—Rev. R. Elwyn, M.A. *Second Master*—Rev. F. Poynder, M.A.

CHRIST'S HOSPITAL. *Head Master*—Rev. G. A. Jacob, D.D. *Assistant Master*—Rev. I. Thomson, M.A.

CITY OF LONDON SCHOOL. *Head Master*—Rev. G. F. W. Mortimer, D.D.

EAST INDIA COLLEGE. *Principal*—Rev. H. Melvill, B.D. *Dean*—Rev. W. E. Buckley, M.A.

HIGHGATE. *Head Master*—Rev. J. B. Dyne, D.D.

KING'S COLLEGE. *Principal*—Rev. R. W. Jelf, D.D. *Head Master*—Rev. J. R. Major, D.D.

MERCHANT TAYLORS'. *Head Master*—Rev. J. A. Hessey, D.C.L. *Under-Master*—Rev. J. A. L. Airey.

SOUTHWARK, ST. OLAVE'S AND ST. JOHN'S. *Head Master*—Rev. H. Hayman, B.D.

ST. PAUL'S SCHOOL. *High Master*—Rev. H. Kynaston, D.D.

UNIVERSITY COLLEGE. *Chairman of Committee*—J. Taylor, F.R.S.

WESTMINSTER. *Head Master*—Rev. C. B. Scott, M.A. *Under Master*—Rev. T. W. Weare, M.A.

ABINGDON. *Head Master*—W. A. Strange, D.D.

APPLEBY. *Head Master*—Rev. J. Richardson, M.A.

BEDFORD. *Head Master*—Rev. F. Fanshawe, M.A. *Second Master*—Rev. H. Le Mesurier, M.A.

BIRMINGHAM. *Head Master*—Rev. E. H. Gifford, M.A. *Second Master*—Rev. S. Gedge, M.A.

BIRMINGHAM, QUEEN'S COLL. *Warden*—Rev. J. T. Law, (Chancellor). *Principal*—J. K. Booth, M.D.

BRIGHTON COLLEGE. *Principal*—Rev. J. Griffith, M.A.

BROMSGROVE, GRAMMAR-SCHOOL. Rev. J. D. Collis, M.A.

BRUTON. *Head Master*—Rev. J. C. Abrahall, M.A.

BURY ST. EDMUND'S. *Head Master*—Rev. A. H. Wratislaw, M.A. *Second Master*—R. Cayley, B.A.

BURY, LANCASHIRE. *Head Master*—Rev. H. C. Boutflower, M.A.

CANTERBURY, KING'S SCHOOL. *Head Master*—Rev. G. Wallace, M.A.

CARLISLE. *Principal*—Rev. W. A. Beale, M.A.

CHELTENHAM COLLEGE. *Principal*—Rev. W. Dobson, M.A. *Vice-Prin.*—Rev. G. Butler, M.A. *Head Master of School*—Rev. T. A. Southwood, M.A.

CHELTENHAM, GRAMMAR-SCHOOL. *Head Master*—E. R. Humphreys, LL.D.

DULWICH COLLEGE. *Master*—Rev. A. J. Carver, M.A.

DURHAM, GRAMMAR-SCHOOL. *Head Master*—Rev. H. Holden, D.D. *Second Master*—Rev. H. Stokes, M.A.

ELY, GRAMMAR-SCHOOL. *Head Master*—Rev. J. Ingle, M.A.

ETON COLLEGE. *Provost*—Rev. E. C. Hawtrey, D.D. *Vice-Provost*—Rev. T. Carter. *Head Master*—Rev. C. O. Goodford, D.D. *Second Master*—Rev. W. A. Carter, M.A.

GUERNSEY, ELIZABETH COLLEGE. *Head Master*—Rev. A. T. Corfe, M.A.

HALSTEAD GRAMMAR-SCHOOL, ESSEX. *Head Master*—Rev. R. G. Watson.

HARROW. *Head Master*—Rev. C. J. Vaughan, D.D. *Lower Master*—Rev. W. Oxenham, M.A.

HOUGHTON-LE-SPRING. *Head Master*—Rev. G. Moultrie.

HURSTPIERPOINT. *Head Master*—Rev. E. C. Lowe, M.A. *Second Master*—Rev. C. H. Lomax.

IPSWICH. *Head Master*—Rev. H. A. Holden, M.A. *Second Master*—Rev. F. W. Greenfield, M.A.

ISLE OF MAN, K. W. COLLEGE. *Principal*—Rev. R. Dixon, D.D. *Vice-Principal* —Rev. T. E. Brown, M.A.

LANCASTER, GRAMMAR-SCHOOL. *Head Master*—Rev. T. F. Lee.

LEAMINGTON COLLEGE. *Principal*—Rev. E. St. John Parry, M.A.

LEEDS. *Head Master*—Rev. A. Barry, M.A. *Second Masters*—Rev. C. Moberly, M.A.; Rev. J. B. Winter.

LEICESTER COLLEGIATE SCHOOL. *Head Master*—Rev. A. Hill, M.A.

LIVERPOOL COLLEGIATE INSTITUTION. *Principal*—Rev. J. S. Howson, M.A.

,, ROYAL INSTITUTION SCHOOL. *Head-Master*—Rev. D. W. Turner, M.A.

LOUTH. *Head Master*—Rev. G. S. Hodgkinson.

LYNN REGIS. *Head Master*—Rev. Thomas White.

MACCLESFIELD. *Head Master*—Rev. T. B. Cornish, M.A.

MANCHESTER. *High Master*—Rev. N. Germon, M.A. *Second Master*—R. Thompson, M.A.

MARLBOROUGH COLLEGE. *Head Master*—Rev. G. G. Bradley.

MARLBOROUGH, GRAMMAR-SCHOOL. *Head Master*—Rev. F. H. Bond, M.A.

OTTERY ST. MARY. *Head Master*—Rev. S. W. Cornish, D.D.

OXFORD, MAGDALEN COLLEGE SCHOOL. *Head Master*—Rev. J. E. Millard, B.D.

RADLEY, ST. PETER'S COLLEGE. *Warden*—Rev. W. Sewell, D.D.

READING. *Head Master*—Rev. R. Appleton, M.A. *Second Master*—Rev. J. H. Appleton, B.A.

REPTON. *Head Master*—Rev. S. A. Pears, D.D. : *Second Master*—Rev. G. M. Messiter, M.A.

RICHMOND, YORKSHIRE. *Head Master*—Rev. James Tate, M.A.

RIPON. *Head Master*—Rev. J. Macmichael, B.D.

ROCHESTER, GRAMMAR-SCHOOL. *Head Master*—Rev. R. Whiston, M.A.'

RUGBY. *Head-Master*—Rev. F. Temple, D.D. *Assistant Masters*—Rev. C. A. Anstey, M.A.; Rev. J. H. Buckoll, M.A.; Rev. C. T. Arnold, M.A.; Rev. T. S. Evans, M.A.

RUTHVEN, GRAMMAR-SCHOOL. *Head Master*—Rev. E. L. Barnwell, M.A.

SEDBERG. *Head Master*—Rev. L. H. Evans, M.A. [James, M.A.

SHERBORNE. *Head Master*—Rev. H. D. Harper, M.A. *Under Master*—Rev. T.

SHOREHAM, ST. NICOLAS COLLEGE. *Provost*—Rev. N. Woodard, B.A.

,, GRAM.-SCHOOL. *Head Master*—Rev. J. Branthwaite, M.A.

SHREWSBURY. *Head Master*—Rev. B. H. Kennedy, D.D. *Second Master*—Rev. William Burbury, M.A.

ST. BEES' GRAMMAR-SCHOOL. *Head Master*—Rev. G. H. Heslop, M.A.

THAME, GRAMMAR-SCHOOL. *Head Master*—Rev. T. B. Fooks, D.C.L.

TONBRIDGE. *Head Master*—Rev. J. Ind Welldon, D.C.L.

WIMBORNE. *Head Master*—Rev. W. Fletcher, D.D.

WINCHESTER. *Warden*—Rev. R. S. Barter, B.C.L. *Head-Master*—Rev. G. Moberley, D.C.L. *Second Master*—Rev. F. Wickham, M.A.

IRELAND.

BELFAST, QUEEN'S COLL. *President*—Rev. P. S. Henry, D.D.

CORK, QUEEN'S COLLEGE. *President*—Sir Robert Kane.

GALWAY, QUEEN'S COLLEGE. *President*—Edward Berwick, Esq., B.A. *Vice-President*—Rev. J. D. Kelly, M.A.

WHITCHURCH, ST. COLUMBA'S COLLEGE. *Warden*—

SCOTLAND.

EDINBURGH ACADEMY. *Master*—Rev. J. S. Hodson, D.D.

EDINBURGH, HIGH SCHOOL. *Rector*—Leonard Schmidtz, LL.D.

GLENALMOND, TRINITY COLLEGE. *Warden*—Rev. John Hannah, DD. *Sub-Warden* —Rev. R. H. Witherby. *Tutor*—Rev. W. Bright.

PERTH, ST. NINIAN'S. *Provost*—Very Rev. E. B. Knottesford Fortescue, M.A.

Committee of Council on Education.

(Founded in 1839. Privy Council-office, Downing-street.)

Lord President of the Council, Lord Keeper of the Privy Seal, the Earl of Derby, Rt. Hon. Lord Stanley, Rt. Hon. S. H. Walpole, Rt. Hon. Sir J. S. Pakington, the Chancellor of the Exchequer, Rt. Hon. J. W. Henley, Rt. Hon. T. H. Sotheron-Estcourt, Rt. Hon. C. B. Adderley, *Vice-President*.

SOCIETIES AND INSTITUTIONS.

𝔈𝔡𝔲𝔠𝔞𝔱𝔦𝔬𝔫𝔞𝔩.

THE SOCIETY FOR PROMOTING CHRISTIAN KNOWLEDGE. Founded 1698. *Secs.*—Rev. Thomas Boyles Murray, M.A.; Rev. John Evans, M.A.; Rev. John David Glennie, M.A. *Soc. house*, 67, Lincoln's-inn-fields. *Depositories*, 77, Great Queen-street; 4, South side of the Royal Exchange, Cornhill; 16, Hanover-street, Hanover-square.

THE NATIONAL SOCIETY FOR PROMOTING THE EDUCATION OF THE POOR in the Principles of the Established Church throughout England and Wales. Instituted 1811, incorporated 1817. *Sec.*—Rev. John G. Lonsdale. *Depositing Sec.*, Rev. A. Wilson. *Travelling Sec.*—Frederick S. Warren, Esq. *Organising Secs.*, Diocese of London—Rev. R. Chaffer; Carlisle, Rev. J. Brunskill, Rev. R. K. Cornish; Manchester, Rev. P. Marshall; St. Asaph, Rev. H. P. Ffoulkes. *Travelling Agent*—Mr. Richard H. Bower.

THE WELSH EDUCATION COMMITTEE OF THE NATIONAL SOCIETY. Established 1846. The Treasurer, Secretary, and officers for conducting the business of the Committee are the same as those who act for the National Society.

DIOCESAN SOCIETIES AND BOARDS OF EDUCATION. These Societies or Boards are in direct connection with the National Society, and under the presidency of the Bishop of the Diocese.

HOME AND COLONIAL SCHOOL SOCIETY. For the Education of Teachers, and for the Improvement and Extension of the Infant-School System, and of Education in general, on Christian Principles, at Home and abroad. Gray's-inn-road, near King's-cross. Instituted 1836. *Hon. Sec.*—John Stuckey, Esq. *Assistant Sec.*—Charles Reynolds, Esq.

CHURCH OF ENGLAND EDUCATION SOCIETY. 11, Adam-street, Adelphi, London. Instituted May 25, 1853. *Hon. Secs.*—Rev. G. E. Tate; W. Taylor, Esq. *Clerical Sec.*—Rev. R. Gunnery.

BETTON'S CHARITY. Bequeathed 1723. £5,000 appointed annually to Church of England Schools.

BEVAN CHARITY. Bequeathed 1730 and 1779. £900 to Newport School, Pembrokeshire.

𝔐𝔦𝔰𝔰𝔦𝔬𝔫𝔞𝔯𝔶.

SOCIETY FOR THE PROPAGATION OF THE GOSPEL IN FOREIGN PARTS. 79, Pall-Mall, s. w. Incorporated by Royal Charter, 1701. *Sec.*—Rev. E. Hawkins.

COLONIAL BISHOPRICS' FUND. 79, Pall-Mall, s. w. *Hon. Sec.*—Rev. Ernest Hawkins. *Treasurer*—J. G. Hubbard, Esq.

SOCIETY FOR PROMOTING THE EMPLOYMENT OF ADDITIONAL CURATES IN POPULOUS PLACES. 7, Whitehall. *Sec.*—W. R. Cosens, M.A. *Income.*—£20,000.

CHURCH BUILDING SOCIETY. 7, Whitehall. *Sec.* Rev. G. Ainslie, M.A.

LONDON DIOCESAN CHURCH BUILDING SOCIETY, AND METROPOLIS CHURCHES FUND. 79, Pall-Mall. *Hon. Sec.*—Rev. T. F. Stooks. *Sec.*—G. C. Silk.

SCOTTISH EPISCOPAL CHURCH SOCIETY. *Sec.*—Rev. F. Garden.

CHURCH MISSIONARY SOCIETY. 14, Salisbury-square. *Secs.*—Revs. H. Venn and J. Chapman.

COLONIAL CHURCH AND SCHOOL SOCIETY. 9, Serjeant's Inn, Fleet-street. *Secs.*—Rev. Mesac Thomas and H. W. Green, Esq.

CHURCH PASTORAL AID SOCIETY. Temple Chambers, Falcon-court. *Sec.*—Rev. E. J. Speck. *Lay Sec.*—R. Laughton, Esq.

FUND FOR PROMOTING FEMALE EDUCATION. 4, St. Martin's-place. *Hon. Sec.*—W. T. Haly.

CHURCH OF ENGLAND SCRIPTURE READERS' ASSOCIATION. 9, Spring-gardens. *Cler. Sec.*—Rev. J. M. Roberton. *Lay Sec.*—J. Roddain Tate, Esq.

CHURCH OF ENGLAND YOUNG MEN'S SOCIETY FOR MISSIONS. 16, Salisbury-square. *Sec.*—J. Catchpole.

LONDON MISSIONARY SOCIETY. *Treasurer*—Sir C. Eardley, Bart.

LONDON SOCIETY FOR PROMOTING CHRISTIANITY AMONG THE JEWS. 16, Lincoln's-Inn-Fields. *Secs.*—Rev. C. J. Goodheart, and Capt. H. L. Layard.

Benebolent.

CHURCH PENITENTIARY ASSOCIATION. 35, Lincoln's-Inn-Fields. *Hon. Secs.*—Rev. T. Poynder and B. Lancaster, Esq.

HOUSE OF CHARITY FOR DISTRESSED PERSONS. 9, Rose-street, Soho. *Warden*—Rev. J. C. Chambers. *Hon. Secs.*—W. C. Cocks and C. Foster, Esqs. *Income*—£1,123. *Inmates*—Irregular; about 300 per annum.

FRIEND OF THE CLERGY, FOR ALLOWING PERMANENT PENSIONS, &c. 4, St. Martin's-place. *Sec.*—H. J. M. Bramall, Esq. *Subscription.*—£1 1s.

CLERGY ORPHAN INCORPORATED SOCIETY. 67, Lincoln's-Inn-Fields. *Hon. Sec.*—Rev. J. D. Glennie. *Children*—137.

CLERGY PROVIDENT SOCIETY. 5, Mitre-court, Fleet-street. *Secs.*—Rev. J. B. Sweet and C. B. Hallward, Esq.

CORPORATION OF THE SONS OF THE CLERGY. 2, Bloomsbury-place. *Reg.*—C. J. Baker.

HOME FOR PENITENT FEMALES. 57, White-Lion-street. *Matron.*—Mrs. Winstanley.

NURSING SISTERS' INSTITUTION. 4, Devonshire-square. *Hon. Sec.*—Miss E. Wilson.

ANGLO-AMERICAN CHURCH EMIGRANTS AID SOCIETY. 79, Pall-Mall. *Sec.*—Rev. H. Caswall.

Miscellaneous.

RELIGIOUS TRACT SOCIETY. 56, Paternoster-row. *Clerical Sec.*—Rev. A. Nicholson. *Lay Sec.*—George H. Davis, Esq.

PRAYER-BOOK AND HOMILY SOCIETY. 18, Salisbury-square. *Sec.*—Rev. C. Smalley; *Assisting Sec.*—Rev. T. Seaward.

BRITISH AND FOREIGN BIBLE SOCIETY. 10, Earl-street, Blackfriars. *Secs.*—Rev. J. Mee and S. B. Bergne.

CONVOCATION, SOCIETY FOR THE REVIVAL OF. 39, Essex-street, Strand. *Sec.*—G. J. Ottaway, Esq. *Subscription.*—10s.

TITHE REDEMPTION TRUST. 1, Adam-street, Adelphi. *Sec.*—Wm. T. Young, Esq.

CHORAL FUND SOCIETY. 13, North-street, Westminster. *Sec.*—W. W. Grice.

CHURCH OF ENGLAND LITURGICAL REVISION SOCIETY. 25, Bedford-row. *Sec.*—C. Bird, Esq.

EVANGELICAL ALLIANCE. 7, Adam-street, Adelphi. *Sec.*—J. P. Dobson.

Church Unions.

*LONDON UNION ON CHURCH MATTERS. *Sec.*—Sydney G. R. Strong, Esq. 5, Mitre-court, Temple.

*METROPOLITAN CHURCH UNION. *Sec.*—G. J. Ottaway, Esq. 39, Essex-st., Strand.

BIRMINGHAM. *Sec.*—Rev. Charles Gooch. 101, New-street, Birmingham.

*BRISTOL. *Sec.*—Rev. J. J. Coles. 21, High-street, Bristol.

COVENTRY. *Sec.*—R. H. Minster, Esq. Trinity Pass, Coventry.

EXETER. *Sec.*—T. T. Daunt, Esq. 11, Windsor-place, Plymouth.

*GLOUCESTER. *Sec.*—Rev. J. J. Barlow. Gloucester.

LINCOLNSHIRE AND NOTTS. *Secs.*—Rev. W. B. Caparn, West Torrington.

CHE-TER. *Sec.*—Rev. Cecil Wray. St. Martin's, Liverpool.

*MANCHESTER CHURCH SOCIETY. *Sec.*—Daniel Herford, Esq.; *Assistant Sec.*—J. T. Simpson, Esq. 14, Ridgefield, Manchester.

NORTHAMPTON. *Sec.*—

NORWICH. *Sec.*—W. Foster, Esq. Orford-hill, Norwich.

SOUTH CHURCH UNION. *Sec.*—F. Gill, Esq. Lewes.

WARWICK AND LEAMINGTON. *Sec.*—

YORKSHIRE. *Sec.*—Rev. W. Pound. Malton, Yorkshire.

Ecclesiastical Courts.

COURT OF ARCHES. Hours, 10 to 4. *Official Principal*—Right Hon. Sir John Dodson, Knt., D.C.L. *Registrar*—Wm. Townsend, Esq.

VICAR-GENERAL'S OFFICE. Bell-yard, Doctors' Commons. *Vicar-General of the Province of Canterbury*—Right Worshipful Travers Twiss, D.C.L. *Dean of Peculiars*—The Rt. Hon. Stephen Lushington. *Registrar*—F. H. Dyke, Esq.

COURT OF FACULTIES. Knightrider-street. Hours, 10 to 4. *Master*—The Rt. Hon. Stephen Lushington. *Registrar*—The Hon. J. H. T. Manners Sutton.

CONSISTORY COURT OF THE BISHOP OF LONDON. Godliman-street. Hours, 10 to 4. *Judge*—Rt. Worshipful Travers Twiss, D.C.L. *Registrars*—John Shepherd, Esq., and John Benj. Lee, Esq. *Record Keeper*—John Collis.

Public Ecclesiastical Offices, &c.

CHARITY COMMISSIONERS for England and Wales. 8, York-st., St. James's-sq.
Commissioners—Right Hon. C. B. Adderley, M.P.; P. Erle, Q.C.; J. Hill, and J. Campbell, Q.C. Secretary—Henry Morgan Vane.

ECCLESIASTICAL COMMISSIONERS for England. 11, Whitehall-pl. Hours, 10 to 4.
Commissioners—The Archbishops and Bishops of England and Wales, the Lord Chancellor, First Lord of the Treasury, President of the Council, Home Secretary, Chancellor of the Exchequer, the Lord Chief Justice of England, Master of the Rolls, Lord Chief Justice of the Common Pleas, the Lord Chief Baron of the Exchequer, the Judge of the Admiralty Court, Deans of Canterbury, St. Paul's, and Westminster, Earls of Chichester and Harrowby, Viscount Eversley, the Rt. Hons. Sir James R. G. Graham, Bart., M.P., Edward Cardwell, M.P., Sir J. G. Shaw Lefevre, K.C.B., William Deedes, Esq., M.P.

Church Estate Commissioners—Earl of Chichester, Viscount Eversley, and William Deedes, Esq., M.P. Secretary—J. J. Chalk, Esq.

GENERAL REGISTER OFFICE. Somerset-house. Registrar-General—George Graham, Esq.; Chief Clerk—Horace Mann, Esq.

BURIAL ACTS OFFICE. 4, Old Palace-yard, Westminster. Hours 10 to 4.
Medical Inspectors—R. D. Grainger, Esq., P. H. Holland, Esq. Clerk—T. Baker, Esq.

WAR CHAPLAINS' DEPARTMENT. Office—War-Office, Pall-Mall. Chaplain-General to the Forces—Rev. G. R. Gleig, M.A.

QUEEN ANNE'S BOUNTY, FIRST-FRUITS AND TENTHS' OFFICES. Next to 3, Great Dean's-yard, Westminster. Secretary's Hours, 10 to 4; Treasurers, 10 to 2.
Governors—Her Majesty's Privy Council, the Archbishops and Bishops of England, the Deans of Cathedral Churches, and the Learned Judges. Secretary and Treasurer—Christopher Hodgson, Esq.
The First Fruits are payable by every new Incumbent within three months after his induction. The yearly tenths become due on the 25th of December, and are to be paid early in the following year. Fees on Payment of First Fruits :— Under £40 in the King's Books, the fees are £1 16s. 6d. ; above £40, the fees are £2 8s.

COPYHOLD INCLOSURE AND COMMISSION OFFICE. 3, St. James's-square.
Commissioners—Wm. Blamire, Esq., G. Darby, Esq.

Ancient Collegiate Institutions, &c.
COLLEGIATE CHAPTERS.

WESTMINSTER. Dean—The Very Rev. Richard Chenevix Trench, D.D., Dean of the Order of the Bath.
WINDSOR. Dean—The Hon. and Very Rev. Gerald Valerian Wellesley, M.A., Registrar of the Order of the Garter.
BRECON. Dean and Treasurer—The Lord Bishop of St. David's.
MIDDLEHAM. (Founded in 1478 by Richard Duke of Gloucester.) Visitor—The Queen. Dean—Very Rev. H. Birch, M.A.
ST. KATHARINE'S Hospital, Regent's Park. (Founded by Queen Eleanor, Widow of Hen. III., A.D. 1273.) Visitor—The Queen. Master—The Hon. William Ashley.
SOUTHWELL. Canon Residentiary and Vicar-General—Archdeacon Wilkins, D.D. Rector—John Murray Wilkins, M.A.
HEYTESBURY. Canons—E. B. Elliott, M.A., John Knight, M.A., W. H. Pearson, M.A.

DEANS OF PECULIARS.

Battle. The Very Rev. J. Littler, M.A.
Bocking. The Very Rev. Henry Carrington, M.A.; The Very Rev. Henry Barry Knox, M.A.
Guernsey. The Very Rev. W. Guille, M.A.

Jersey. The Very Rev. William Corbet Le Breton, M.A.
St. Burian. The Hon. and Very Rev. F. H. R. Stanhope, M.A.

The Royal Family.

THE QUEEN. (ALEXANDRINA) VICTORIA, Queen of the United Kingdom of Great Britain and Ireland; only Child of EDWARD DUKE OF KENT; born May 24, 1819.

Succeeded to the Throne on the Decease of her Uncle, KING WILLIAM IV., June 20, 1837.

Proclaimed June 21, 1837; Crowned June 28, 1838.

Married HIS ROYAL HIGHNESS ALBERT, Prince of Saxe Cobourg and Gotha, Feb. 10, 1840.

Issue.

Victoria Adelaide Mary Louisa, *Princess Royal*, born Nov. 21, 1840.
Albert Edward, *Prince of Wales, and Earl of Dublin*, K.G., *b.* Nov. 9, 1841.
Alice Maud Mary, *born* April 15, 1843.
Alfred Ernest Albert, *born* Aug. 6, 1844.
Helen Augusta, *born* May 25, 1846.

Louisa Caroline Alberta, *b.* March 18, 1848.
Arthur William Patrick Albert, *born* May 1, 1850.
Leopold George Duncan Albert, *born* April 7, 1853.
Beatrice Mary Victoria Feodore, *born* April 14, 1857.

GEORGE FREDERICK, King of Hanover, K.G., K.P., G.C.B., G.C.H., *born* May 27, 1819.
Duke of Cambridge, K.G., G.C.H., G.C.M.G., *born* March 26, 1819.

Duchess of Kent, *born* Aug. 17, 1786.
Grand Duchess of Mecklenburg Strelitz, *born* July 19, 1822.
Princess Mary of Cambridge, *born* Nov. 27, 1833.

HER MAJESTY'S CHIEF OFFICERS OF STATE.

ENGLAND.

THE CABINET.

First Lord of the Treasury, Earl of Derby
Lord High Chancellor, Lord Chelmsford
Chancellor of the Exchequer, Rt. Hon. Benj. Disraeli
Lord President of the Council, Marquis of Salisbury
Postmaster-General, Lord Colchester
Lord Privy Seal, Earl of Hardwicke
Secretary of State. Home Department, Right Hon. S. H. Walpole
Secretary of State, Foreign Affairs, Earl of Malmesbury
Ditto, Colonies, Sir E. B. Lytton, Bart.
Ditto, War Department, Rt. Hon. J. Peel
First Lord of the Admiralty, Rt. Hon. Sir J. S. Pakington, Bart.
Pres. of the Board of Control, Lord Stanley
Pres. of the Board of Trade, Rt. Hon. J. W. Henley
Chancellor of the Duchy of Lancaster, Duke of Montrose

HER MAJESTY'S HOUSEHOLD.

Lord Steward, Marquis of Exeter
Lord Chamberlain, Earl De La Warr
Master of the Horse, Duke of Beaufort

PUBLIC OFFICERS, &c.

Lord Great Chamberlain, Lord Willoughby d'Eresby
Earl Marshal, Duke of Norfolk
Vice-Pres. of Board of Trade, and Paymaster-Gen., Earl of Donoughmore
General Commanding-in-Chief, H. R. H. Duke of Cambridge
Master of the Mint, Thomas Graham, D.C.L.
President of the Poor-Law Board, Rt. Hon. T. H. S. S. Estcourt

President of the Board of Health, Rt. Hon. C. B. Adderley
Chief Commissioner of Works and Public Buildings, Rt. Hon. Lord J. J. R. Manners

LAW OFFICERS.

Lords Justices of Chancery, Sir J. L. K. Bruce, Sir G. J. Turner
Vice-Chancellors, Sir R. T. Kindersley, Sir John Stuart, Sir W. Page Wood
Master of the Rolls, Rt. Hon. Sir John Romilly
Attorney-Gen., Sir Fitz Roy Kelly
Solicitor-Gen., Sir H. M'C. Cairns
Judge-Adv.-Gen., J. W. Mowbray, Esq.

IRELAND.

Lord-Lieut., Earl of Eglintoun
Lord High Chanc., Rt. Hon. J. Napier
Master of the Rolls, Rt. Hon. T. B. C. Smith
Lord Almoner, Abp. of Armagh
Chief Sec. and Keeper of Privy Seal, Lord Naas
Attorney-Gen., Rt. Hon. J. Whiteside.
Solicitor-Gen., Edm. Hayes, Esq. LL.D.
Comm. of the Forces, Gen. Lord Seaton

SCOTLAND.

Keeper of the Great Seal, Earl of Selkirk
Keeper of the Privy Seal, Lord Panmure
High Commiss. to General Assembly of the Church of Scotland, Earl of Mansfield
Lord Pres. and Lord Justice-General, Rt. Hon. Duncan McNeill
Lord Clerk-Registrar, Marq. of Dalhousie, K. T.
Lord Justice Clerk, Rt. Hon. J. Inglis
Lord Advocate, Rt. Hon. C. Baillie.
Solicitor-General, David Mure, Esq.
Commander of the Forces, Maj.-Gen. Visc. Melville, K.C.B.

House of Peers.

SUMMARY OF THE HOUSE OF PEERS.

Peers of the Blood Royal	3	Bishops(24), one being a Temporal Peer	23
Archbishops	2	Barons	198
Dukes	20	Scotch Representative Peers	16
Marquesses	21	Irish Representative Peers, 28, one of	
Earls	112	whom is also a Peer of Great Britain	27
Viscounts	23	Irish Spiritual Peers	4
	181		**268**

Total *449

* Of whom 14 are Minors, making the actual number of the House of Peers 435.

ABERCORN, M. *Chesterfield-house, South Audley-street,* w.
Abercromby, L. (a minor, born 1838)
Aberdeen, E. *7 Argyll-street,* w.
Abergavenny, E. *58 Portland-place,* w.
Abingdon, E. *18 Grosvenor-street,* w.
Abinger, L. *10 Park-pl. St. James's,* w.
Ailesbury, M. *78 Pall-Mall,* s.w.
Ailsa, M. *Thomas's-hot. Berkeley-sq.* w.
Airlie, E. *27 Berkeley-square,* w.
Albemarle, E. *11 Grosvenor-square,* w.
Amherst, E. *43 Grosvenor-street,* w.
Anglesey, M. *6 Clifford-street,* w.
Argyll, D. *Campden-hill, Kensington,* w.
ARMAGH, Abp. *30 Chas.-st. St. Jas's.* w.
Arundell, L. *40 Connaught-terrace,* w.
Ashburnham, E. *30 Dover-street,* w.
Ashburton, L. *82 Piccadilly,* w.
Athol, D. *St. George's-hot. Albem.-st.* w.
AUCKLAND, L. (Bishop of Bath & Wells), *2 Grosvenor-cres. Belgrave-sq.* s. w.
Audley, L. *4 Campden-hill-rd. Kensington,* w.
Aveland, L. *12 Belgrave-square,* s.w.
Aylesford, E. *Carlton-club,* s.w.
Bagot, L. *Dover-house, Whitehall,* s.w.
BANGOR, Bp. *Maurigy's-hotel,* s.w.
Bangor, V. *Carlton-club,* s.w.
Bantry, E. *Thomas's-hotel, Berk.-sq.* w.
Bateman, L. *37 Brook-street,* w.
Bath, M. *44 Berkeley-square,* w.
Bathurst, E. *4 Wilton-crescent,* s.w.
Bayning, L.
Beauchamp, E. *19 Grosvenor-place,* s.w.
Beaufort, D. *10 St. James's-square,* s.w.
Beaumont, L. (a minor, born 1848)
Bedford, D. *6 Belgrave-square,* s.w.
Belhaven & Stenton, L. *30 Albem.-st.* w.
Belmore E. *56 Eaton place,* s.w.
Belper, L. *88 Euston-square,* w.
Berkeley, E.
Berners, L. *16 Grafton-street,* w.
Berwick, L.
Bessborough, E. *40 Chas.-st. Berk.-sq.* w.
Beverley, E. *8 Portman-square,* w.
Blantyre, L. *Stafford-hou. St. Jas's.* s.w.
Blayney, L. *Carlton-club,* s.w.
Bolingbroke, V. *1 Chandos-street,* w.
Bolton, L. *York-hotel, Albem.-st.* s.w.

Boston, L. *4 Belgrave-square,* s.w.
Bradford, E. *43 Belgrave-square,* s.w.
Braybrooke, L. *10 New Burling.-st.* w.
Breadalbane, M. *21 Park-lane,* w.
Bristol, M. *6 St. James's-square,* s.w.
Brougham & Vaux, L. *4 Grafton-st.* w.
Broughton, L. *42 Berkeley-square,* w.
Brownlow, E. (a minor, born 1842)
Buccleuch, D. *Mont.-hou. Whitehall,* s.w.
Buckingham, D. *Carlton-club,* s.w.
Buckinghamshire, E. *6 Eaton-place,* s.
Bute, M. (a minor, born 1847)
Byron, L. *48 Eaton-place,* s.w.
Cadogan, E. *138 Piccadilly,* w.
Caithness, E. *17 Hill-street,* w.
Calthorpe, L. *33 Grosvenor-square,* w.
CAMBRIDGE, D. *St. James's-palace,* s.w.
Camden, M. *5 Carlton-house-ter.* s.w.
Camoys, L. *11 Old Bond-street,* w.
Campbell, L. *Stratheden-house, Knightsbridge,* s.w.
Camperdown, E. *1 Wilton-terrace,* s.w.
Canning, V. *(Abroad)*
CANTERBURY, Abp. *Lambeth-palace,* s.
Canterbury, V. *4 Bolton-row,* w.
Cardigan, E. *36 Portman-square,* w.
Carew, L. *28 Belgrave-square,* s.w.
CARLISLE, Bp. *64 Russell-square,* w.c.
Carlisle, E. *12 Grosvenor-place,* s.w.
Carnarvon, E. *3 Park-st. Westminst.* s.w.
Carrington, L. *8 Whitehall,* s.w.
Carysfort, E. *28 Lowndes-street,* s.w.
CASHEL, Bp. *105 Jermyn-street,* s.w.
Castlemaine, L. *35 Pall-Mall,* s.w.
Cathcart, E. *United-Service-club,* s.w.
Cawdor, E. *74 South-Audley-street,* w.
Charlemont, E.
Chelmsford, L. *7 Eaton-square,* s.w.
CHESTER, Bp. *Euston-hotel,* n.w.
Chesterfield, E. *33 Dover-street,* w.
CHICHESTER, Bp. *43 Queen Anne-st.* w.
Chichester, E. *22 Grosvenor-place,* s.w.
Cholmondeley, M. *12 Carlton-h.-ter.* s.w.
Churchill, L. *33 Albemarle-street* w.
Clancarty, E. *National-club,* s.w.
Clanricarde, M. *2 Carlton-house-ter.* s.w.
Clanwilliam, E. *32 Belgrave-square,* s.w.
Clare, E. *39 South-street,* w.
Clarendon, E. *1 Grosv.-cres.Belg.-sq,* s.w.

HOUSE OF PEERS.

Clarina, L.   *Carlton-club*, s.w.
Cleveland, D. 17 *St. James's square*, s.w.
Clifden, V. *Dover-house, Whitehall*, s.w.
Clifford, L.
Clinton, L.   *Travellers'-club*, s.w.
Clonbrock, L. 11 *Clarges-street*, w.
Cloncurry, L.   *White's-club*, s.w.
Colchester, L. 34 *Berkeley-square*, w.
Colville of Culross, L. 42 *Eaton-pl.* s.w.
Combermere, V. 48 *Belgrave-sq.* s.w.
Congleton, L. 22 *Cumberland-street.* w.
Conyngham, M. 5 *Hamilton-place*, w.
Cork and Orrery, E. 1 *Grafton-street*, w.
Cottenham, E.   15 *Park-lane*, w.
Courtown, E. 92 *Eaton-place*, s.w.
Coventry, E. (a minor, born 1838)
Cowley, E.   (*Abroad*)
Cowper, E.   17 *Curzon-street*, w.
Cranworth, L. 40 *Upper Brook-st.* w.
Craven, E. 16 *Charles-st. Berk.-sq.* w.
Crawford & Balcarres, E. 21 *Berk.-sq.* w.
Cremorne, L. 3 *Great Stanhope-st.* w.
Crewe, L.   28 *Hill-street*, w.
Crofton, L.   *Carlton-club*, s.w.
CUMBERLAND, D.   (*King of Hanover*)
Dacre, L. 45 *Upper Grosvenor-st.* w.
Dalhousie, M.   *Carlton-club*, s.w.
Darnley, E.   *Claridge's-hotel*, w.
Dartmouth, E. 40 *Grosvenor-square*, w.
De Freyne, L. 54 *Parliament-st.* s.w.
De Grey, E. 4 *St. James's-square*, s.w.
Delamere, L. 12 *Hereford-street*, w.
De La Warr, E. 17 *Up. Grosvenor-st.* w.
De L'Isle & Dudley, L.
De Mauley, L. 49 *Grosvenor-street*, w.
Denbigh, E. 49 *Eaton-square*, s.w.
Denman, L.
Derby, E. 23 *St. James's-square*, s.w.
DERRY, Bp.
De Ros, L.   36 *Curzon-street*, w.
Desart, E.   28 *Bruton-street*, w.
De Saumarez, L. *University-club*, s.w.
De Tabley, L. 1 *Upper Brook-street*, w.
De Vesci, V. 4 *Carlton-ho.-terrace*, s.w.
Devon, E. 18 *Grosvenor-street*, s.w.
Devonshire, D. 10 *Belgrave-square*, s.w.
Digby, L. 31 *Old Burlingto -street*, w.
Donegal, M. 22 *Grosvenor-square*, w.
Doneraile, V.   *Claridge's-hotel*, w.
Donoughmore, E. 29 *Dover-street*, w.
Dorchester, L.
Dormer, L.   *Brookes's-club*, s.w.
Downes, L. 19 *Grafton-street*, w.
Downshire, M. 24 *Belgrave-square*, s.w.
Drogheda, M.   *Carlton-club*, s.w.
DUBLIN, Abp.
Ducie, E.   30 *Prince's-gate*, w.
Dufferin, L. *Travellers'-club*, s.w.
Dunfermline, L.   (*Abroad*)
Dungannon, V. 3 *Grafton-street*, w.
Dunmore, E. (a minor, born 1841)
Dunsandle, L.   *Carlton-club*, s.w.
DURHAM, Bp. 27 *Parliament-st.* s.w.
Durham, E. 122 *Park-st. Grosv.-sq.* w.
Dynevor, L. 7 *Prince's-gar. Hyde-pk.*s.w.
Ebury, L. 107 *Park-st. Grosv.-sq.* s.w.
Effingham, E. 57 *Eaton-place*, s.w.
Eglintoun, E.

Egmont, E. 26 *St. James's-place*, s.w.
Eldon, E. (a minor, born 1845)
Elgin, E.   (*Abroad*)
Ellenborough, E. 115 *Eaton-square*, s.w.
Ellesmere, E. *Cleveland-sq. St. Jas's.*s.w.
Elphinstone, L.   (*Abroad*)
ELY, Bp.   37 *Dover-street*, w.
Ely, M. (a minor, born 1849)
Enfield, V. 5 *St. James's-square*, s.w.
Enniskillen, E. 97 *Mount-street*, w.
Erne, E. 95 *Eaton-square*, s.w.
Errol, E.   *Reform-club*, s.w.
Erskine, L. *Bacon's-hot. Hyde-pk.-sq.* w.
Essex, E. 21 *Chesham-street*, s.w.
Eversley, V. 69 *Eaton-place*, s.w.
EXETER, Bp.   *Clarendon-hotel*, w.
Exeter, M. 36 *Grosvenor-square*, w.
Exmouth, V. 29 *Montague-square*, w.
Falkland, V. 32 *Albemarle-street*, w.
Falmouth, V. 2 *St. James's-square*, s.w.
Farnham, L.   44 *Brook-street*, w.
Ferrers, E. 39 *Clarges-street*, w.
Feversham, L. 25 *Belgrave-square*, s.w.
Fife, E.   22 *Bruton-street*, w.
Fingall, E. 12A *George-st. Han.-sq.* w.
Fitzwilliam, E. 4 *Grosvenor-square*, w.
Foley, L. 26 *Grosvenor-square*, w.
Forester, L. 6 *Audley-square*, w.
Fortescue, E. 17 *Grosvenor-square*, w.
Gage, V.   4 *Whitehall-yard*, s.w.
Gainsborough, E. 11 *Chandos-street*, w.
Galloway, E. 116 *Eaton-square*, w.
Gardner, L. 46 *Dover-street*, w.
Gifford, L.   49 *Pall-Mall*, s.w.
Glasgow, E.   *Grillion's-hotel*, w.
Glenelg, L.   *H 4 Albany*, w.
GLOUCESTER & BRISTOL, Bp. 4 *Charles-street, St. James's*, s.w.
Godolphin, L.
Gosford, E. 59 *Lower Grosvenor-st.* w.
Gough, V. 25 *Hyde-park-gardens*, w.
Grafton, D. 47 *Clarges-street*, w.
Granard, E. 13 *Eaton-square*, s.w.
Grantley, L. 10 *Wilton-place*, s.w.
Granville, E. 16 *Bruton-street*, w.
Gray, L.   *Carlton-club*, s.w.
Grey, E. 13 *Carlton-house-terrace*, s.w.
Guilford, E. 48 *Grosvenor-street*, w.
Haddington, E. 43 *Berkeley-square*, w.
Hamilton, D. 22 *Arlington-street*, s.w.
Harborough, E.
Hardinge, V. 20 *Hanover-square*, w.
Hardwicke, E. 37 *Portman-square*, w.
Harewood, E. *Harewood-pl. Han.-sq.* w.
Harrington, E. 13 *Kensing.-pal.-gar.* w.
Harris, L.   (*Abroad*)
Harrowby, E. 39 *Grosvenor-square*, w.
Hastings, L. 45 *York-ter. Reg.-pk.* N.W.
Hastings, M. (a minor, born 1842)
Hatherton, L.
Hawke, L.
Headfort, M.   *Brookes's-club*, s.w.
HEREFORD, Bp. 107 *Eaton-place*, s.w.
Hereford, V. (a minor, born 1843)
Hertford, M. 13 *Berkeley-square*, w.
Heytesbury, L. *Burlington-hotel*, w.
Hill, V. *Thomas's-hotel, Berkeley-sq.* w.
Holland, L. *Holland-ho. Kensington*, w

Home, E. *Montague-ho. Whitehall,* s.w.
Hood, V. (a minor, born 1838)
Hopetoun, E. *Long's-hotel, Bond-st.* w.
Howard de Walden, L.   (*Abroad*)
Howden, L.
Howe, E.   8 *South Audley-street,* w.
Huntingdon, E.   *Union-club,* s.w.
Huntly, M.   10 *Suffolk-street,* s.w.
Ilchester, E.   31 *Old Burlington-st.* w.
Jersey, E.   38 *Berkeley-square,* w.
Keane, L.   *United Service-club* s.w.
Kenmare, E.   54 *Eaton-place,* s.w.
Kenyon, L.   9 *Portman-square,* w.
Kilmaine, L.   47 *Dover-street,* w.
Kingston, E.   35 *Park-st. Grosv.-sq.* w.
Kinnaird, L.   33 *Grosvenor-street,* w.
Kinnoul, E.   24 *Portman-square,* w.
Kintore, E.
Lanesborough, E. 8 *Gt. Stanhope-st.* w.
Lansdowne, M. 54 *Berkeley-square,* w.
Lauderdale, E.   *Maurigy's-hotel,* s.w.
Leeds, D.   *Clarendon-hotel,* w.
Leicester, E.
Leigh, L.   30 *Portman-square,* w.
Leinster, D. 6 *Carlton-house-ter.* s.w.
Leitrim, E. *Jun. United-Ser.-club,* s.w.
Leven & Melville, E.
Lichfield, E.   34 *Albemarle-street,* w.
LICHFIELD, Bp. 4 *Ches.-pl. Reg.-pk.* N.W.
Lifford, V.   *Carlton-club,* s.w.
Lilford, L.   10 *Grosvenor-place,* s.w.
Limerick, E.   79 *Chester-square,* s.w.
LINCOLN, Bp.
Lindsey, E.
Lismore, V.   41 *Wilton-crescent,* s.w.
LLANDAFF, Bp.   6 *Chandos-street,* w.
Londesborough, L. 8 *Carlt.-ho.-ter.* s.w.
LONDON, Bp.   22 *St. James's-sq.* s.w.
Londonderry, M.   37 *Grosvenor-sq.* w.
Longford, E.   24 *Bruton-street,* w.
Lonsdale, E. 14 *Carlton-house-ter.* s.w.
Lothian, M.   59 *Eaton-square,* s.w.
Lovat, L.   *Reform-club,* s.w.
Lovelace, E.
Lucan, E.   20 *Hanover-square,* w.
Lurgan, L. *Claridge's-ho. Brook-st.* w.
Lyndhurst, L. 25 *George-st. Han.-sq.* w.
Lyons, L.
Lyttelton, L. 24 *St. James's-square,* s.w.
Macaulay, L. *Holly-lodge, Kensington,* w.
Macclesfield, E.   9 *Conduit-street,* w.
Malmesbury, E. 8 *Whitehall-gard.* s.w.
Manchester, D. 1 *Great Stanhope-st.* w.
MANCHESTER, Bp.   *Cox's-hotel,* s.w.
Manners, L. 56 *Upper Brook-street,* w.
Mansfield, E. *Caen-wood, Highgate,* N.W.
Manvers, E.   13 *Portman-square,* w.
Marlborough, D.   36 *Brook-street,* w.
Massereene, V.   *Athenæum,* s.w.
Maynard, V. 38 *Grosvenor-square,* w.
Mayo, E.   52 *Eaton-square,* w.
Meath, E.   52 *Grosvenor-street,* w.
Melville, V. 7 *Portugal-st. Grosv.-sq.* w.
Methuen, L.   4 *Connaught-place,* w.
Middleton, L. 33 *Albemarle-street,* s.w.
Midleton, V.   65 *Eaton-place,* s.w.
Minto, E.   48 *Eaton-square,* s.w.
Monson, L. 1 *Lincoln's-inn-fields,* w.c.

Monteagle, L. 7 *Park-st. Westmins.* s.w.
Montrose, D.   45 *Belgrave-square,* s.w.
Moray, E.
Morley, E. *Kent-house, Knightsbr.* s.w.
Mornington, E.   *Clarendon-hotel,* w.
Mostyn, L. 9 *Lower Seymour-street,* w.
Mountcashell, E.   *National-club,* s.w.
Mount-Edgcumbe, E.
Munster, E.   35 *Rutland-gate,* s.w.
Nelson, E. 3 *Seamore-pl. Curzon-st.* w.
Newcastle, D.   17 *Portman-square,* w.
Norfolk, D. 21 *St. James's-square,* s.w.
Normanby, M.   (*Abroad*)
Northampton, M.   145 *Piccadilly,* w.
Northumberland, D. *Charing-cross,* s.w.
Northwick, L. 2 *St. James's-place,* s.w.
Onslow, E.
Orford, E.   7 *Halkin-street west,* s.w.
Orkney, E.   3 *Ennismore-place,* s.w.
Ormonde, M. (a minor, born 1844)
Overstone, L. 2 *Carlton-gardens,* s.w.
OXFORD, Bp.   26 *Pall Mall,* s.w.
Panmure, L. 37 *Chesham-place,* s.w.
Pembroke, E.
PETERBOROUGH, Bp. 16 *Suffolk-st.* s.w.
Petre, L.   16 *Montagu-square,* w.
PLUNKET, L. (Bp.Tuam) *National-cl.* s.w.
Poltimore, L. 25 *Grosvenor-square,* w.
Polwarth, L.   *Carlton-club,* s.w.
Pomfret, E. 62A *Grosvenor-street,* w.
Ponsonby, L.
Portarlington, E. *Claridge's-hotel,* w.
Portland, D. 19 *Cavendish-square,* w.
Portman, L. 5 *Prin.'s-ga. Hyde-pk.* s.w.
Portsmouth, E. 57 *St. James's-st.* s.w.
Poulett, E.
Powis, E.   45 *Berkeley-square,* w.
Radnor, E.
Raglan, L.   58 *Rutland-gate,* s.w.
Ranfurly, E. (a minor, born 1849)
Ravensworth, L. *Percy's-cr.Fulham,* s.w.
Rayleigh, L.   *University-club,* s.w.
Redesdale, L. 6 *Park-pl. St. Jas.'s,* s.w.
Ribblesdale, L.
Richmond, D.   51 *Portland-place,* w.
RIPON, Bp. 4 *Gloucester-square,* w.
Ripon, E.   1 *Carlton-gardens,* s.w.
Rivers, L.   *Travellers'-club,* s.w.
ROCHESTER, Bp. 77 *Chester-square,* s.w.
Roden, E.   124 *Pall Mall,* s.w.
Rodney, L.
Romney, E.   37 *Davies-street,* w.
Rosebery, E.   139 *Piccadilly,* w.
Rosse, E.   25 *Cambridge-square,* w.
Rosslyn, E.   *White's-club,* s.w.
Rossmore, L.   *Brookes's-club,* s.w.
Roxburghe, D.   *Clarendon-hotel,* w.
Rutland, D.   22 *Prince's-gate,* s.w.
St. Alban's, D. (a minor, born 1840)
St. Asaph, Bp. 43 *Great Ormond-st.* w.c.
St. David's, Bp. 1 *Regent-street,* s.w.
St. Germans, E.   36 *Dover-street,* w.
St. John, L.
St. Leonards, L.
St. Vincent, V.   *Clarendon-hotel,* w.
Salisbury, M. 20 *Arlington-street,* s.w.
SALISBURY, Bp.   44 *Curzon-street,* w.
Sandwich, E.   26 *Curzon-street,* w.

HOUSE OF PEERS.

Sandys, L.	14 *Curzon-street*, w.	Tankerville, E.	23 *Hertford-street*, w.
Saye & Sele, L.		Templemore, L.	32 *Bruton-street*, w.
Scarborough, E.		Tenterden, L.	12 *Wilton-street*, s.w.
Scarsdale, L.		Teynham, L. 18 *Petersb.-pl. Baysw.* w.	
Seafield, E. *Claridge's-hot. Brook-st.* w.		Thurlow, L.	
Seaton, L. *United Service-club*, s.w.		Torrington, V. 4 *Warwick-sq. Pim.* s.w.	
Sefton, E. 53 *Grosvenor-place*, s.w.		Townshend, M. 6 *Stratford-place*, w.	
Selkirk, E. *Carlton-club*, s.w.		Truro, L. 29 *Dover-street*, w.	
Shaftesbury, E. 24 *Grosvenor-sq.* w.		Tweeddale, M. 16 *Chesham-place*, s.w.	
Shannon, E.		Vane, E. 14 *Chapel-st. Grosv.-sq.* w.	
Sheffield, E. 20 *Portland-place*, w.		Vaux of Harrowden, L. *Brookes'-cl.* s.w.	
Shelburne, E. *Lansd.-hou. Berk.-sq.* w.		Vernon, L.	
Sherborne, L.		Verulam, E. 6 *Gt. Stanhope-street*, w.	
Shrewsbury, E. 4 *Lowndes-street*, s.w.		Vivian, L. *Brookes's-club*, s.w.	
Sidmouth, V. *Batt's-hotel, Dover-st.* w.		Waldegrave, E. 4 *Harley-street*, w.	
Sinclair, L. *United Service-club*, s.w.		WALES, H. R. H. Prince	
Skelmersdale, L.		Walsingham, L. 23 *Arlington-st.* s.w.	
Sligo, M. 2 *Mansfield-street*, w.		Ward, L. *Dudley-house, Park-lane*, w.	
Somers, E. 45 *Grosvenor-place*, s.w.		Warwick, E. 1 *Stable-yd. St. Jas.'s*, s.w.	
Somerset, D.		Waterford, M. 44 *Brook-street*, w.	
Sondes, L. 32 *Grosvenor-square*, w.		Wellington, D. *Apsley-house, Piccad.* w.	
Southampton, L. 58 *Grosvenor-st.* w.		Wemyss, E.	
Spencer, E. 27 *St. James's-place*, s.w.		Wenlock, L. 29 *Berkeley-square*, w.	
Stafford, L. 24 *Mount-street*, w.		Wensleydale, L. 56 *Pk.-st. Grosv.-sq.* w.	
Stair, E.		Westmeath, M. *Devonsh.-terr.Baysw.*w.	
Stamford, E. 33 *Hill-street*, w.		Westminster, M. 33 *Up. Grosv.-st.* w.	
Stanhope, E. 3 *Grosv.-pl.-houses*, s.w.		Westmoreland, E. 16 *Cavendish.-s1.* w.	
Stanley of Alderley, L. 40 *Dover-st.* w.		Wharncliffe, L. 15 *Curzon-street*, w.	
Stourton, L.		Wicklow, E. 2 *Cavendish-square*, w.	
Stradbroke, E. 52 *Jermyn-street*, s.w.		Willoughby de Broke, L. 50 *Grosv.-st.*w.	
Strafford, E. 44 *Grosvenor-street*, w.		Willoughby d'Eresby, L. 142 *Piccad.* w.	
Strangford, V. *(Abroad)*		Wilton, E. 7 *Grosvenor-sq.* w.	
Stratford de Redcliffe, V. 29a *Grosv.-sq.*w.		WINCHESTER, Bp. 19 *St. James's.* s.w.	
Strathallan, V. 44 *Chas.-st., Berk.-sq.* w.		Winchester, M. 2 *Clarges-street*, w.	
Strathmore,E. 9 *St.Geo.-rd.Pimlico,*s.w.		Winchilsea, E. *Carlton-club*, s.w.	
Stuart de Decies, L. 43 *Albemarle-st.* w.		Wodehouse, L. *(Abroad)*	
Sudeley, L. 35 *Dover-street*, w.		WORCESTER, Bp. 24 *Grosvenor-pl.* s.w.	
Suffield, L. 11 *Berkeley-square*, w.		Wrottesley, L. 1 *Albemarle-street*, w.	
Suffolk, E.		Wynford, L. 7 *Park-pl. St. Jas's.* s.w.	
Sutherland, D. *Stafford-h. St.Jas.'s*, s.w.		Yarborough, E. 17 *Arlington-st.* s.w.	
Sydney, V. 3 *Cleveland-square*, s.w.		YORK, Abp. 41 *Belgrave-square*, s.w.	
Talbot de Malahide, L. *Athenæum*, s.w.		Zetland, E. 19 *Arlington-street*, s.w.	

Rotation of Irish Representative Bishops in Parliament—By Act 3 and 4 William IV. c. 37,the Archbishops of ARMAGH and Dublin sit in the House of Lords alternately from Session to Session : and the Rotation of the Bishops' Sees is now as follows :—MEATH, Cashel, Tuam, Derry, Limerick, Down, Ossory, CORK, KILLALOE, KILMORE.

PEERESSES in their Own Right.

Title.	DUCHESS.	Family Name.	
Inverness	Underwood ...	...	1840.

Title.	Family Name.	BARONESSES.	Title.	Family Name.	
Le De Spencer	Stapleton	1264	Windsor	Windsor Clive	1531
De Clifford	Russell	1299	North	North	1554
De la Zouche	Curzon	1308	Ruthven	Ruthven	1651
Grey de Ruthyn ...	Yelverton	1324	Nairn and Keith ...	Elphinstone	1681
Sempill	Sempill	1489	Wenman	Wykenham	1834
Braye	Otway Cave ...	1529	Stratheden	Campbell ...	1836
Wentworth	Noel Byron ...	1529			

OFFICERS OF THE HOUSE OF PEERS.

Clerk of the Parliaments, J. G. Shaw Lefevre, Esq., K.C.B.
Deputy-Clerk of the Parliaments, (Clerk-Assistant), William Rose, Esq.
Reading-Clerk, and Clerk of the Private Committees, L. Edmunds, Esq.
Counsel to Chairman of Committees, R. J. Palk, Esq.
Chief Clerk. H. Stone Smith, Esq.
Principal Clerk for Bills, W. E. Walmisley, Esq.
Librarian, J. F. Leary, Esq., F.S.A.

House of Commons.

SUMMARY OF THE HOUSE OF COMMONS.

ENGLAND.	MEMBS.	SCOTLAND.	MEMBS.
40 Counties	143	33 Counties	30
Isle of Wight	1	7 Cities and Towns	9
185 Cities, Boroughs, &c., with 2 contributory Boroughs	319	14 Districts of Burghs	14
2 Universities	4	**IRELAND.**	
WALES.—12 Counties	15	32 Counties	64
14 Boroughs, with 45 contributory Boroughs	14	33 Cities and Boroughs	39
		1 University	2
	496		158
Total	.	.	654

Adair, Hugh Edward — *Ipswich*
*Adams, William Henry — *Boston*
Adderley, Charles Bowyer — *Staffordsh. N.*
*Adeane, Henry John — *Cambridgeshire*
Agnew, Sir Andrew, Bt. — *Wigtonshire*
*Akroyd, Edward — *Huddersfield*
Alcock, Thomas — *Surrey, E.*
Alexander, John — *Carlow*
Anderson, Sir James — *Stirling, &c.*
*Annesley, Capt. Hon. Hugh — *Cavan*
Antrobus, Edmund — *Wilton*
Arbuthnott, Gen. Hon. H. — *Kincardinesh.*
Archdall, Capt. Mervyn E — *Fermanagh Co.*
*Ashley, Lord — *Kingston-on-Hull*
Atherton, William, Q.C. — *Durham*
*Ayrton, Acton Smee — *Tower Hamlets*
Bagshaw, John — *Harwich*
Bagshaw, Robert John — *Harwich*
Bagwell, John — *Clonmel*
Bailey, Crawshay — *Monmouth, &c.*
Bailey, Sir Joseph, Bart. — *Brecknockshire*
Baillie, Henry James — *Inverness-shire*
Baines, Rt. Hon. Matt. Talbot, Q.C. — *Leeds*
Ball, Edward — *Cambridgeshire*
Baring, Alex. Hugh — *Thetford*
Baring, Rt. Hn. Sir F. T., Bt. — *Portsmouth*
Baring, Henry Bingham — *Marlborough*
Baring, Thomas — *Huntingdon*
*Baring, Thomas George — *Penryn, &c.*
*Barnard, Thomas — *Bedford*
Barrow, Wm. Hodgson — *Nottinghamsh. S.*
Bass, Michael Thomas — *Derby*
*Bathurst, Allen Alexander — *Cirencester*
Baxter, William Edward — *Montrose, &c.*
*Beach, Wm. Wither Bramston — *Hants. N.*
*Beale, Samuel — *Derby*
Beamish, Francis Bernard — *Cork City*
Beaumont, Wentw. Blackett — *Northumb. S.*
Bective, Earl of — *Westmoreland*
*Beecroft, George Skirrow — *Leeds*
Bennet, Capt. Philip — *Suffolk, W.*
Bentinck, Geo. W. Pierrepont — *Norfolk, W.*
Beresford, Rt. Hon. William — *Essex, N.*
Berkeley, Hon. F. H. Fitzhard. — *Bristol*
Berkeley, Capt. F. W. Fitzh. — *Cheltenham*
*Bernard, Thos. Tyringham — *Aylesbury*
Bernard, Capt. Hon. Wm. S. — *Bandon*
Bethell, Sir Richard, Q.C. — *Aylesbury*
Biddulph, Col. R. Middleton — *Denbighsh.*
Biggs, John — *Leicester*
Black, Adam — *Edinburgh*
Blackburn, Peter — *Stirlingshire*
*Blake, John Aloysius — *Waterford City*
Bland, Loftus Henry — *King's Co.*
Boldero, Lt.-Col. Henry Geo. — *Chippenham*

Bonham-Carter, John — *Winchester*
Booth, Geo. Sclater — *Hants, N.*
Booth, Sir Robert Gore, Bt. — *Sligo Co.*
*Botfield, Beriah, F.R.S. — *Ludlow*
Bouverie, Rt. Hon. Ed. P. — *Kilmarnock, &c.*
*Bouverie, Hon. Philip Pleydell — *Berksh.*
*Bovill, William, Q.C. — *Guildford*
Bowyer, George — *Dundalk*
*Boyd, John — *Coleraine*
Brady, John — *Leitrim*
Bramston, Thomas William — *Essex, S.*
Brand, Hon. Hen. B. William — *Lewes*
*Bridges, Sir Brook Wm., Bt. — *Kent, E.*
Bright, John — *Birmingham*
*Briscoe, John Ivatt — *Surrey, W.*
*Brocklehurst, John — *Macclesfield*
*Brown, James — *Malton*
Brown, William — *Lancashire, S.*
Brown, Lord John Thos. — *Mayo Co.*
Bruce, Maj. C. L. Cum. — *Elgin & Nairnsh.*
Bruce, Rt. Hn. Ld. Ernest A. C.B. — *Marlboro'*
Bruce, Henry Austin — *Merthyr Tydvil*
*Bruen, Henry — *Carlow Co.*
Buchanan, Walter — *Glasgow*
Buckley, Maj.-Gen. Edw. Pery — *Salisbury*
Bulkeley, Sir Richard Bulkeley Williams, Bart. } — *Anglesey*
*Buller, James Wentworth — *Devon, N.*
Bunbury, Capt. W. B. McC. — *Carlow Co.*
n Burghley, Lord — *Northamptonsh., N.*
Burke, Sir Thomas John, Bt. — *Galway Co.*
Burrell, Sir C. Merrik, Bt. — *New Shoreham*
*Bury, Viscount — *Norwich*
*Butler, Chas. Salisbury — *Tower Hamlets*
Butt, Isaac, LL.D. — *Youghal*
*Buxton, Charles — *Newport, I. of W.*
n Byng, Hon. Geo. Hen. Chas. — *Middlesex*
*Caird, James — *Dartmouth, &c.*
Cairns, Sir Hugh M'Calmont — *Belfast*
*Calcraft, John Hales — *Wareham*
*Calcutt, Francis Macnamara — *Clare Co.*
*Campbell, R. James Roy — *Weymouth, &c.*
*Carden, Sir Robt. Walter — *Gloucester*
Cardwell, Rt. Hon. Edward — *Oxford*
Carnac, Sir John Rivett, Bt. — *Lymington*
*Cartwright, Col. Henry — *Northamp. N.*
Castlerosse, Rt. Hon. Viscount — *Kerry*
*Cavendish, Hon. W. G. — *Bucks.*
Cavendish, Hon. Geo. H. — *Derbyshire, N.*
Cayley, E. Stillingfleet — *York, N. Riding*
Cecil, Lord Robt. T. Gascoigne — *Stamford*
*Charlesworth, John C. D. — *Wakefield*
Cheetham, John — *Lancashire, S.*
Child, Smith — *Staffordshire, N.*
*Cholmeley, Sir J. M. J., Bt. — *Lincolnsh. N.*

Christy, Samuel *Newcastle-under-Lyme*
*Churchill, Ld. Alfred Spencer *Woodstock*
*Clark, Hon. W. C. W. *Norfolk, E.*
Clark, James Johnston *Londonderry*
Clay, James *Kingston-on-Hull*
*Clifford, Charles Cavendish *I. of Wight*
Clifford, Lt.-Col. Hen. Morgan *Hereford*
Clinton, Lord R. R. P. *Nottinghamsh. N.*
Clive, George *Hereford*
Clive, Hon. Robt. Windsor *Shropshire, S.*
*Close, Maxwell Charles *Armagh Co.*
Cobbett, John Morgan *Oldham*
Cobbold, John Chevallier *Ipswich*
Codrington, Sir C. W., Bt. *Gloucestersh. E.*
Codrington, Lt.-Gen. Sir Wm. J., K.C.B. } *Greenwich*
Cogan, William Henry Ford *Kildare Co.*
*Coke, Lt.-Col. Hon. W.C.W. *Norfolk, E.*
Cole, Lt.-Col. Hon. H. A. *Fermanagh Co.*
*Colebrooke, Sir Thos. E., Bt. *Lanarksh.*
Collier, Robert Porrett, Q.C. *Plymouth*
*Collins, Thomas, Jun. *Knaresborough*
Colvile, Charles Robert *Derbyshire, S.*
Coningham, William *Brighton*
Conolly, Thomas *Donegal Co.*
*Conyngham, Lord Francis N. *Clare Co.*
*Cooper, Edward Joshua *Sligo Co.*
Coote, Sir Chas. Henry, Bt. *Queen's Co.*
*Copeland, Ald. Wm. T. *Stoke-on-Trent*
Corbally, Matthew Elias *Meath*
Corry, Rt. Hon. H. T. Lowry *Tyrone Co.*
*Cotterell, Sir H. Geers, Bt. *Herefordsh.*
Cowan, Charles *Edinburgh*
Cowper, Rt. Hon. W. Francis *Hertford*
*Cox, William *Finsbury*
Craufurd, Edw. Henry John *Ayr, &c.*
*Crawford, Robt. Wygram *London*
Crook, Joseph *Bolton*
*Cross, Richard Assheton *Preston*
Crossley, Frank *Halifax*
Cubitt, Alderman William *Andover*
*Curzon, Viscount *Leicester, S.*
*Dalglish, Robert *Glasgow*
Dalkeith, Earl of *Edinburgh Co.*
*Damer, Capt. L. S. W. D. *Portarlington*
Dashwood, Sir Geo. Hen., Bt. *Wycombe*
*Davey, Richard *Cornwall, W.*
Davie, Sir H. R. Ferg., Bt. *Haddington*
Davison, Richard *Belfast*
Deasy, Rickard, Q.C. *Cork Co.*
Deedes, William *Kent, E.*
Denison, Edm. Beckett *York, W. Riding*
n Denison, Rt. Hon. J. Evelyn (*Speaker*) } *Nottinghamsh. N.*
*Denison, Hon. W. H. Forester *Beverley*
Dent, John Dent *Scarbro'*
De Vere, Stephen Edward *Limerick Co.*
Devereux, John Thomas *Wexford*
Dillwyn, Lewis Llewellyn *Swansea*
Disraeli, Rt. Hon. Benjamin *Bucks.*
Divett, Edward *Exeter*
*Dobbs, William Cary *Carrickfergus*
Dod, John Whitehall *Shropshire, N.*
*Dodson, John George *Sussex, E.*
Drummond, Henry, F.R.S. *Surrey, W.*
*Du Cane, Charles *Essex, N.*
*Duff, Maj. L. G. *Banffshire*
Duff, Mountstuart E. Grant *Elgin, &c.*

Duke, Sir James, Bt. *London*
*Dunbar, Sir William, Bt. *Wigton, &c.*
Duncan, Viscount *Forfarshire*
Duncombe, Adm. Hon. Ar. *York, E. Riding*
Duncombe, Col. Hon. Oct. *York, N. Riding*
Duncombe, Thomas Slingsby *Finsbury*
Dundas, Frederick *Orkney & Shetland*
Dundas, George *Linlithgow*
*Dunkellin, Lord *Galway*
Dunlop, Alexander Murray *Greenock*
Dunne, Michael *Queen's Co.*
Du Pré, Caledon George *Bucks.*
*Dutton, Hon. Ralph Heneage *Hants. S.*
East, Sir J. Buller, Bt. D.C.L. *Winchester*
Ebrington, Viscount *Marylebone*
Edwards, Major Henry *Beverley*
Egerton, Edw. Christopher *Macclesfield*
Egerton, Sir P. de Mal. G. Bt. *Cheshire, S.*
*Egerton, Wilbraham *Cheshire, N.*
Elcho, Lord *Haddingtonshire*
Ellice, Rt. Hon. Edward *Coventry*
Ellice, Edward, Jun. *St. Andrew's, &c.*
Elliot, Hon. John Edmund *Roxburgsh.*
*Ellis, Capt. Hon. L.G.F. Agar *Kilkenny Co.*
Elmley, Viscount *Worcestershire, W.*
*Elphinstone, Sir J. D.H., Bt. *Portsmouth*
*Elton, Sir Arthur Hallam, Bart. *Bate*
Emlyn, Viscount *Pembrokeshire*
*Ennis, John *Athlone*
Esmonde, John *Waterford Co.*
Estcourt, T. H. S. Sotheron *Wiltshire, N.*
Euston, Earl of *Thetford*
Evans, Lt.-Gen. Sir De Lacy, G.C.B. } *Westminster*
*Evans, Thomas William *Derbyshire, S.*
Ewart, Joseph Christopher *Liverpool*
Ewart, William *Dumfries, &c.*
Ewing, Humphrey E. C. *Paisley*
Fagan, William Trant *Cork*
Farnham, Edward Basil *Leicestersh. N.*
*Farquhar, Sir Walter M. T., Bt. *Hertford*
Fellowes, Edward *Huntingdonshire*
Fenwick, Henry *Sunderland*
Fergus, John *Fifeshire*
Ferguson, Sir Robt. A., Bt. *Londonderry*
Ferguson, Lt.-Col. Robert *Kirkaldy, &c.*
*Finlay, Alex. Struthers *Argyllshire*
FitzGerald, Rt. Hon. J. D. *Ennis*
FitzGerald, W. R. Seymour V. *Horsham*
FitzRoy, Rt. Hon. Henry *Lewes*
Fitzwilliam, Hon. C. Wm. W. *Malton*
Fitzwilliam, Hon. G. Went. *Peterborough*
*Foley, Hen. J. Went. H. *Staffordsh. S.*
Foley, J. Hodgetts Hod. *Worcestersh. E.*
*Foljambe, Francis J. Savile *E. Retford*
*Forde, Lt.-Col. William B. *Downshire*
Forester, Col. Rt. Hn. G.C.W. *Wenlock*
Forster, Charles *Walsall*
Forster, Sir George M., Bt. *Monaghan*
Fortescue, Chichester Sam. *Louth*
*Fortescue, Hon. Dudley F. *Andover*
*Foster, Wm. Orme *Staffordshire, S.*
Fox, Wm. Johnson *Oldham*
Franklyn, George Woodroffe *Poole*
*Fraser, Sir Wm. Augustus *Barnstaple*
Freestun, Col. Wm. Lockyer *Weymouth*
French, Col. Fitzstephen *Roscommon*
Gallwey, Sir Wm. Payne, Bt. *Thirsk*

HOUSE OF COMMONS.

Galway, Viscount   *East Retford, &c.*
*Gard, Richard Sommers   *Exeter*
*Garnett, Wm. James   *Lancaster*
Gaskell, James Milnes   *Wenlock*
*Gibson, Rt. Hn. T. M. *Ashton-un.-Lyne*
Gifford, Earl of   *Totnes*
*Gilpin, Charles   *Northampton*
Gilpin, Col. Rich. Thos.   *Bedfordshire*
Gladstone, Rt. Hon. W. Ewart *Oxford U.*
Glyn, George Carr   *Kendal*
*Glyn, George Grenfell   *Shaftesbury*
Goddard, Ambrose Lethbridge *Cricklade*
×Goderich, Viscount   *York, W. Riding*
*Gore, W. R. Ormsby   *Leitrim*
Grace, Oliver Dowel John *Roscommon*
Graham, Rt. Hon. Sir J.R.G.,Bt. *Carlisle*
*Gray, Capt. William   *Bolton*
Greaves, Edward   *Warwick*
Greenall, Gilbert   *Warrington*
Greene, Capt. John   *Kilkenny Co.*
*Greenwood, John   *Ripon*
*Greer, Sam. McCurdy *Londonderry Co.*
*Gregory, William Henry *Galway Co.*
Gregson, Samuel   *Lancaster*
*Grenfell, Chas. Pascoe   *Preston*
Grenfell, Charles William   *Windsor*
Greville, Col. Fulke Southwell *Longford*
Grey, Rt. Hon. Sir Geo.Bt.G.C.B. *Morpeth*
Grey, Ralph William   *Liskeard*
*Griffith, Christopher Darby *Devizes*
Grogan, Edward   *Dublin*
Grosvenor, Earl   *Chester*
*Gurdon, Brampton   *Norfolk, W.*
Gurney, John Henry   *King's Lynn*
*Gurney, Samuel   *Penryn, &c.*
*Hackblock, William   *Reigate*
Haddo, Lord   *Aberdeenshire*
Hadfield, George   *Sheffield*
Hall, Rt. Hon. Sir Benj., Bt. *Marylebone*
Hall, Major-Gen. John   *Buckingham*
Hamilton, Rt. Hn. Lord Claud *Tyrone Co.*
Hamilton, George Alexander *Dublin U.*
Hamilton, James Hans   *Dublin Co.*
Hamilton, J. G. C.   *Falkirk, &c.*
*Hanbury, Hon. Capt. C.S.B. *Leominster*
*Hanbury, Robert   *Middlesex*
*Handley, John   *Newark*
Hankey, Thomson   *Peterborough*
Hanmer, Sir John, Bt.   *Flint, &c.*
Harcourt, Geo. Granville V. *Oxfordshire*
*Hardcastle, Joseph Alfred *Bury St.Edm.*
Hardy, Gathorne   *Leominster*
*Harris, John Dove   *Leicester*
*Hartington, Marquess of, *Lancashire*
*Hassard, Mich. Dobbyn *Waterford City*
*Hatchell, John   *Wexford Co.*
*Hay, Cpt. Lord John,R.N.,C.B. *Wick,&c.*
Hayes, Sir Edm. Sam., Bt. *Donegal Co.*
Hayter, Rt. Hon. Sir W. G., Q.C. *Wells*
Headlam,Thos.E.,Q.C. *Newcast.-on-Tyne*
Heard, John Isaac   *Kinsale*
Heathcoat, John   *Tiverton*
Heathcote, Hon. Gilbert Hen. *Rutland*
Heathcote, Sir Wm., Bt. D.C.L. *OxfordU.*
Henchy, David O'Connor *Kildare Co.*
Heneage, George Fieschi   *Lincoln*
Henley, Rt. Hon. Jos. Warner *Oxfordsh.*
Henniker, Lord   *Suffolk, E.*

Herbert, Rt. Hon. Hen.Arthur *KerryCo.*
Herbert, Col. Hon. Percy E., C.B. *Ludlow*
Herbert, Rt. Hon. Sidney *Wiltshire, S.*
*Hill, Hon. Rowland Clegg *Shropshire,N.*
Hill, Lord Arthur Edwin *Downshire*
*Hodgson, Kirkman Daniel *Bridport*
*Hodgson, Wm. Nicholson   *Carlisle*
Holford, Robert Stayner *Gloucestersh.E.*
Holland, Edward   *Evesham*
*Hope,Alex.Jas. B. Beresford *Maidstone*
*Hopwood, John Turner   *Clitheroe*
*Hornby, William Henry   *Blackburn*
Horsfall, Thomas Berry   *Liverpool*
Horsman, Rt. Hon. Edward   *Stroud*
Hotham, Lord   *York, E. Riding*
Howard, Hon. C. W. G. *Cumberland, E.*
Howard, Lord Edward Geo. F. *Arundel*
Hudson, George   *Sunderland*
*Hugessen, E. H. Knatchbull *Sandwich*
Hughes, Wm. Bulkeley *Carnarvon, &c.*
Hume, Wm. W. Fitzwilliam *Wicklow*
*Hunt, George Ward *Northamp. N.*
Hutt, William   *Gateshead*
*Ingestre, Viscount   *Stafford*
Ingham, Robert, Q.C. *South Shields*
*Inglis, Rt. Hon. John   *Stamford*
Ingram, Herbert   *Boston*
Jackson, William *Newcastle-un.-Lyme*
Jermyn, Rt. Hon. Earl *Bury St. Edm.*
*Jervoise, Sir Jervoise C., Bt. *Hants. S.*
*Johnstone, Hon. H. Butler *Canterbury*
Johnstone, John Jas. Hope *Dumfriessh.*
Johnstone, Sir J. V. B., Bt. *Scarborough*
Jolliffe, Capt. Hedworth Hylton *Wells*
Jolliffe, Sir W. G. Hylton, Bt. *Petersfield*
Jones, David   *Carmarthenshire*
Keating, Sir Henry Singer, Q.C. *Reading*
*Kekewich, S. T.   *Devon, S.*
Kelly, Sir FitzRoy, Q.C.   *Suffolk, E.*
Kendall, Nicholas   *Cornwall, E.*
Ker, Richard   *Downpatrick*
Kerrison, Sir Edw. Clarence, Bt. *Eye*
Kershaw, James   *Stockport*
*King, Edward Bolton *Warwickshire, S.*
King, Hon. Peter John Locke *Surrey, E.*
King, Jas. King   *Herefordshire*
*Kinglake, Alex. William *Bridgwater*
*Kinglake, Serj. John Alex. *Rochester*
Kingscote,Lt-Col.R.N.F. *Gloucestersh. W*
Kinnaird, Hon. Ar. Fitzgerald *Perth*
Kirk, William   *Newry*
Knatchbull, Lt.-Col. W. F. *Somerset, E.*
Knight, Fred. Winn *Worcestershire, W.*
Knightley, Rainald *Northamptonsh. S.*
Knox, Lt.-Col. Brownlow W. *Marlow*
Knox, Maj. Hon. W. Stuart *Dungannon*
Labouchere, Rt. Hon. Henry *Taunton*
Langston, James Haughton   *Oxford*
Langton, Wm. Henry Gore   *Bristol*
Langton, Wm. H. P. G. *Somersetsh. W.*
Laslett, William   *Worcester City*
*Laurie, John   *Barnstaple*
*Lefroy, Anthony   *Dublin Univ.*
Legh, George Cornwall   *Cheshire, N.*
Lennox, Lord Alex. F. C. G. *Shoreham*
Lennox, Lord H. Geo. C. G. *Chichester*
Leslie, Charles Powell *Monaghan Co.*
*Levinge, Sir R. G. A., Bt. *Westmeath*

HOUSE OF COMMONS.

Lewis, Rt. Hn. Sir G. C., Bt.	*Radnor, &c.*
Liddell, Hon. Hen. Geo.	*Northumb. S.*
*Lincoln, Earl of	*Newark*
Lindsay, William Schaw	*Tynemouth*
Lisburne, Earl of	*Cardigan*
*Locke, John	*Southwark*
Locke, Joseph	*Honiton*
Lockhart, Allan Eliott	*Selkirkshire*
Long, Walter	*Wiltshire, N.*
*Lopes, Sir Massey, Bt.	*Westbury*
Lovaine, Lord	*Northumb. N.*
Lowe, Rt. Hon. Robert	*Kidderminster*
Lowther, Col. Hon. H. C.	*Westmoreland*
Lowther, Capt. Henry	*Cumberland, W.*
Luce, Thomas	*Malmesbury*
*Lyall, George	*Whitehaven*
*Lygon, Hon. Frederick	*Tewkesbury*
Lytton, Sir E. G. E. L. Bulwer, Bt.	*Herts.*
Macartney, George	*Antrim*
*Macaulay, Kenneth	*Cambridge*
MacEvoy, Edward	*Meath*
*Mackie, James	*Kirkcudbright*
Mackinnon, William Alex.	*Rye*
*Mackinnon, W. Alex., Jun.	*Lymington*
Magan, Capt. William Henry	*Westmeath*
*Maguire, John Francis	*Dungarvon*
*Mainwaring, Townshend	*Denbigh, &c.*
Malins, Richard, q.c.	*Wallingford*
*Mangles, Capt. Chas. E.	*Newport, I. W.*
Manners, Rt. Hn. Ld. J. J. R.	*Leicester, N.*
March, Earl of	*Sussex, W.*
Marjoribanks, Dudley Coutts	*Berwick*
*Marsh, Matthew Henry	*Salisbury*
Marshall, William	*Cumberland, E.*
Martin, Charles Wykeham	*Kent, W.*
Martin, John	*Tewkesbury*
Martin, Philip Wykeham	*Rochester*
nMassey, Wm. Nathaniel	*Salford*
Matheson, Alexander	*Inverness, &c.*
Matheson, Sir J., Bt.	*Ross & Cromarty*
Maxwell, Lt.-Col. Hon. J. P.	*Cavan Co.*
McCann, James	*Drogheda*
*McCarthy, Alexander	*Cork Co.*
*McClintock, John	*Louth Co.*
McMahon, Patrick	*Wexford Co.*
*Melgund, Viscount	*Clackmannan, &c.*
Mellor, John, q.c.	*Great Yarmouth*
Meux, Sir Henry, Bt.	*Hertfordshire*
Miles, William	*Somersetshire, E.*
*Miller, Stearne Ball	*Armagh*
*Miller, Taverner John	*Colchester*
*Mills, Arthur	*Taunton*
Mills, Thomas	*Totnes*
Milnes, Richard Monckton	*Pontefract*
Mitchell, Thomas Alexander	*Bridport*
Moffatt, George	*Ashburton*
Moncreiff, Rt. Hon. James	*Leith, &c.*
Monsell, Rt. Hon. William	*Limerick Co.*
*Monson, Wm. John	*Reigate*
Montgomery, Sir G. G., Bt.	*Peebles-shire*
Moody, Charles Aaron	*Somerset, W.*
Moore, John Bramley	*Maldon*
Morgan, Ch. Oct. Swinn.	*Monmouthsh.*
Morris, David	*Carmarthen*
M.styn, Hon. Thos. E. M. L.	*Flintshire*
Moworay, John Robert	*Durham*
Mullings, Joseph Randolph	*Cirencester*
nNaas, Rt. Hon. Lord	*Cockermouth*
Napier, Adm. Sir C. K.C.B.	*Southwark*
Neeld, John	*Cricklade, &c.*
Newark, Viscount	*Nottingham, S.*
Newdegate, C. Newdigate	*Warwicksh. N.*
Newport, Viscount	*Shropshire, S.*
*Nicoll, Donald	*Frome*
Nisbet, Robert Parry	*Chippenham*
Noel, Hon. Gerard James	*Rutland*
Norreys, Sir Den. Jephson, Bt.	*Mallow*
*Norris, John Thomas	*Abingdon*
North, Frederick	*Hastings*
North, Lt.-Col. John Sidney	*Oxfordshire*
*Northcote, Sir Staf. H., Bt.	*Stamford*
O'Brien, Patrick	*King's Co.*
O'Brien, Sir Timothy, Bt.	*Cashel*
O'Connell, Capt. Daniel	*Tralee*
O'Donoghoe, D.	*Tipperary*
*Ogilvy, Sir John, Bt.	*Dundee*
*Onslow, Guildford	*Guildford*
nOsborne, Ralph Bernal	*Dover*
Ossulston, Lord	*Northumb. N.*
Owen, Sir John, Bt.	*Pembroke*
Packe, Charles William	*Leicestersh. S.*
Paget, Lord Alfred Henry	*Lichfield*
Paget, Charles	*Nottingham*
*Paget, Lord Clarence Edw.	*Sandwich*
Pakenham, Lt.-Col. Thos. H.	*Antrim*
Pakington, Rt.Hn.Sir J. S., Bt.	*Droitwich*
Palk, Lawrence	*Devon, S.*
Palmer, Robert	*Berkshire*
*Palmer, Roger Wm. Henry	*Mayo Co.*
Palmerston, Rt.Hn.Visc. K.G. &c.	*Tiverton*
Patten, Col. John Wilson	*Lancash. N.*
*Paull, Henry	*St. Ives*
Paxton, Sir Joseph	*Coventry*
*Pease, Henry	*Durham Co. S.*
Pechell, Sir G. R. Brooke, Bt.	*Brighton*
Peel, Major-Gen. Jonathan	*Huntingdon*
Peel, Sir Robert, Bt.	*Tamworth*
Pennant, Col. Hon. E. G. D.	*Carnarvonsh.*
Percy, Hon. Joceline Wm.	*Launceston*
Perry, Sir Thos. Erskine	*Devonport*
Pevensey, Viscount	*Sussex, E.*
Philipps, John Henry	*Haverfordwest*
*Philips, Robert Needham	*Bury, Lanc.*
Pigott, Francis	*Reading*
Pilkington, James	*Blackburn*
Pinney, Col. William	*Lyme Regis*
nPortman, Hon. Wm. H. B.	*Dorsetshire*
*Powell, Francis Sharp	*Wigan*
Power, Nicholas Mahon	*Waterford Co.*
Price, William Philip	*Gloucester*
Pritchard, John	*Bridgnorth*
*Proby, Hon. Granv. Leveson	*Wicklow*
*Pryse, Capt. Edw. Lewis	*Cardigan, &c.*
Pugh, David	*Montgomery*
*Pugh, David	*Carmarthenshire*
*Puller, Christopher Wm. G.	*Herts.*
*Ramsay, Sir Alexander, Bt.	*Rochdale*
nRamsden, Sir John Wm., Bt.	*Hythe*
Raynham, Viscount	*Tamworth*
Rebow, John Gurdon	*Colchester*
Repton, Geo. William John	*Warwick*
Ricardo, John Lewis	*Stoke-on-Trent*
Ricardo, Osman	*Worcester*
Rich, Henry	*Richmond*
*Richardson, Jonathan	*Lisburn*
Ridley, George	*Newcastle-on-Tyne*
Robartes, Thos. Jas. Agar	*Cornwall, E.*
Robertson, Patrick Francis	*Hastings*

HOUSE OF COMMONS.

Roebuck, John Arthur — *Sheffield*
*Rolt, John — *Gloucestershire, W.*
Rothschild. Baron Lionel N. de — *London*
*Roupell, William — *Lambeth*
Rushout, Lt.-Col. Hon. G. — *Worcester, E.*
Russell, A. J. E. — *Tavistock*
Russell, Fras. Chas. — *Hastings Bedfordsh.*
Russell, Francis William — *Limerick*
Russell, Rt. Hon. Lord John — *London*
*Russell, Sir William, Bt. — *Dover*
Rust, James — *Huntingdonshire*
*St. Aubyn, John — *Cornwall*
*Salisbury, Enoch Gibbon — *Chester*
Sandon, Viscount — *Lichfield*
*Schneider, Henry William — *Norwich*
Scholefield, William — *Birmingham*
*Scott, Major Edward — *Maidstone*
Scott, Hon. Francis — *Berwickshire*
Scrope, George Poulett — *Stroud*
Seymer, Henry Ker — *Dorsetshire*
Seymour, Henry Danby — *Poole*
Shafto, Robt. Duncombe — *Durham Co. N.*
Shelley, Sir John Vill., Bt. — *Westminster*
*Sheridan, Henry Brinsley — *Dudley*
Sheridan, Richard Brinsley — *Dorchester*
Shirley, Evelyn Philip — *Warwickshire, S.*
Sibthorp, Major Gervaise T. W. — *Lincoln*
*Slaney, Robert Aglionby — *Shrewsbury*
*Smith, Augustus — *Truro*
Smith, John Abel — *Chichester*
Smith, John Benjamin — *Stockport*
*Smith, Maj.-Gen. Sir J. M. F. — *Chatham*
Smith, Martin Tucker — *Wycombe*
Smith, Rt. Hn. R. Vernon — *Northampton*
Smollett, Alexander — *Dumbartonshire*
Smyth, Col. John George — *York*
Somerset, Col. Edw. A. — *Monmouthshire*
Somerville, Rt.Hon.Sir W.M.Bt. — *Canterb.*
Spaight, James — *Limerick*
Spooner, Richard — *Warwickshire, N.*
Stafford, Marquis of — *Sutherlandshire*
Stanhope, James Banks — *Lincolnsh. N.*
Stanley, Lord — *Lynn Regis*
nStanley, Hon. Wm. Owen — *Beaumaris*
*Stapleton, John — *Berwick*
Steel, John — *Cockermouth*
Stephenson, Robert, F.R.S. — *Whitby*
*Steuart, Andrew — *Cambridge*
Stewart, Sir M. R. Shaw, Bt. — *Renfrewsh.*
Stirling, William — *Perthshire*
*Stuart, Lord Pat. Jas. H. C. — *Ayrshire*
*Stuart, Lt.-Col. Jas. F. D. C. — *Cardiff*
Sturt, Capt. Chas. Napier — *Dorchester*
Sturt, Henry Gerard — *Dorsetshire*
Sullivan, Michael — *Kilkenny*
*Sykes, Col. William Henry — *Aberdeen*
Talbot, Christ. Rice Mans. — *Glamorgansh.*
Tancred, Henry William — *Banbury*
Taylor, Simon Watson — *Devizes*
Taylor, Lt.-Col. Thom. Edw. — *Dublin Co.*
Tempest, Ld. F. A. C. V. — *Durham Co. N.*
*Thompson, Maj.-Gen. T. P. — *Bradford*
Thornely, Thomas — *Wolverhampton*
Thornhill, William Pole — *Derbyshire, N.*
Tite, William — *Bath*
*Tollemache, Hon. Fred. Jas. — *Grantham*
Tollemache, John — *Cheshire, S.*
Tomline, George — *Shrewsbury*
Tottenham, Charles — *New Ross*
*Townsend, John — *Greenwich*

Traill, George — *Caithness*
*Trefusis, Hon. Chas. H. R. — *Devon, N.*
*Trelawny, Sir John S., Bt. — *Tavistock*
Trollope, Rt. Hn. Sir J.,Bt. — *Lincolnsh. S.*
*Trueman, Charles — *Helston*
*Turner, James Aspinall — *Manchester*
Tynte, Col. Chas. J. K. F.R.S. — *Bridgwater*
Vance, John — *Dublin*
Vane, Lord Harry George — *Durham, S.*
Vansittart, George Henry — *Berks.*
*Vansittart, William — *Windsor*
Verner, Sir William, Bt. — *Armagh Co.*
*Verney, Sir Harry, Bt. — *Buckingham*
Villiers, Rt. Hon. C. P. — *Wolverhampton*
*Vivian, Capt. Hon. John C.W. — *Bodmin*
nVivian, Henry Hussey — *Glamorganshire*
Waddington, Harry Spencer — *Suffolk, W.*
Walcott, Rr.-Adm. J. E. — *Christchurch*
*Waldron, Lawrence — *Tipperary*
Walpole, Rt.Hon. Spenc. H. — *Camb.Univ.*
Walsh, Sir John Benn, Bt. — *Radnorshire*
Walter, John — *Nottingham*
*Warre, John Ashley — *Ripon*
Warren, Samuel — *Midhurst*
Watkins, Col. Lloyd V. — *Brecknock*
Weguelin, Thos. Matthias — *Southampton*
*Welby, Wm. Earle — *Grantham*
*Western, Thomas Sutton — *Maldon*
*Westhead, J. Procter Brown — *York*
nWhatman, James — *Kent, W.*
Whitbread, Samuel — *Bedford*
*White, Col. Henry — *Longford*
*White, James — *Plymouth*
Whiteside, Rt. Hon. James — *Enniskillen*
Whitmore, Henry — *Bridgnorth*
Wickham, Henry Wickham — *Bradford*
Wigram, Loftus Tottenham — *Cambr. Univ.*
Wilcox, Brodie McGhie — *Southampton*
Williams, Lt.-Col. T. Peers — *Marlow*
Williams, Maj.-Gen. Sir W. F.,Bt. — *Calne*
Williams, William — *Lambeth*
Willoughby, Sir Henry P. Bt. — *Evesham*
*Willson, Anthony — *Lincolnshire, S.*
*Willyams, Edw. W. Brydges — *Truro*
nWilson, James — *Devonport*
*Windham, M.Gen.C.Ashe,CB. — *NorfolkE.*
*Wingfield, Richard Baker — *Essex, S.*
Winnington, Sir Thos. Edw. Bt. — *Bewdley*
Wise, John Ayshford — *Stafford*
Wood, Rt. Hon. Sir Chas. Bt. — *Halifax*
*Wood, William — *Pontefract*
Woodd, Basil Thomas — *Knaresborough*
*Woods, Henry — *Wigan*
*Worsley, Lord — *Great Grimsby*
*Wortley, Major A. H. P. S. — *Honiton*
Wortley, Rt. Hon. J. A. Stuart — *Buteshire*
Wrightson, William Battie — *Northallerton*
*Wyld, James — *Bodmin*
nWyndham, Gen.Henry — *Cumberland, W.*
Wyndham, Capt. Henry — *Sussex, W.*
Wyndham, William — *Wilts. S.*
Wynn, Lt.-Col. H.W.W. — *Montgomerysh.*
Wynn, Sir W. Williams, Bt. — *Denbighsh.*
Wynne, Rt. Hon. John Arthur — *Sligo*
Wynne, W. Watkin E. — *Merionethshire*
Wyvill, Marmaduke — *Richmond*
Yorke, Hon. Eliot Thomas — *Cambridgsh.*
Young, A. W. — *Great Yarmouth*
Galway, Manchester, and Hereford-shire—Vacant.

PUBLIC INCOME OF THE UNITED KINGDOM,
from March 31, 1857, *to March* 31, 1858.

Net Income after deducting Expenses of Collection, &c.   **Gross Income.**

	Net Income	Gross Income
Customs	£21,985,231	£23,109,105
Excise	16,973,508	17,825,000
Stamps	7,241,902	7,415,719
Land Taxes, &c.	2,981,354	3,152,033
Property Tax, &c.	11,260,341	11,586,115
Post-Office	1,206,647	2,920,000
Crown Lands	276,654	276,654
Office Fees and Hereditary Revenue	172,026	172,026
Miscellaneous (e.g. East India Company, Old Stores, &c.)	1,424,861	1,424,861
Total	63,522,524	67,881,513
Excess of Expenditure over Income		2,497,346
		£70,378,859

PUBLIC EXPENDITURE OF THE UNITED KINGDOM,
from March 31, 1857, *to March* 31, 1858.

DEBT—Interest and Management of Public Debt	(Ac. No. 29)	23,573,973
Terminable Annuities and Unclaimed Dividends	(„ „)	4,068,487
Interest of Exchequer Bonds and Bills	(„ 30)	984,643
CONSOLIDATED FUND—Civil List	(„ 31)	401,258
Annuities and Pensions	(„ 32)	334,997
Salaries and Allowances	(„ 33)	157,549
Diplomatic Salaries and Pensions	(„ 34)	158,934
Courts of Justice	(„ 35)	563,225
Miscellaneous Charges	(„ 36)	178,030
Compensation to Denmark for Sound Dues	(„ „)	1,125,206
SUPPLY SERVICE—Army, including Ordnance	(„ 57)	12,915,157
Navy	(„ „)	10,590,000
Persian and Chinese Expeditions	(„ „)	1,490,693
Civil Services	(„ „)	7,227,719
Exchequer Bonds Redeemed and Sinking Fund	(„ „)	2,250,000
Total		66,019,871
Expenses in the REVENUE Departments		4,358,988
Grand Total		**£70,378,859**

TRADE OF THE UNITED KINGDOM.
An Account of Value of Imports and Exports of the United Kingdom during 1855, 1856, *and* 1857.

	1855.	1856.	1857.
IMPORTS, calculated at official rates of valuation	£117,284,881	131,937,763	136,215,849
EXPORTS, Produce and Manufactures of U. K., at official rates	226,920,262	258,505,653	255,396,713
—— Foreign and Colonial Merchandize, at official rates	31,494,391	33,423,724	30,797,818
Total Exports	258,414,653	291,929,377	286,194,531

NAVIGATION OF THE UNITED KINGDOM.

	Vessels Built in 1857.		Total Vessels registered, Dec. 31, 1557.		
	Vessels.	Tons.	Vessels.	Tons.	Men.
England	1,014	192,761	20,485	3,594,687	167,805
Scotland	225	51,533	3,508	639,557	32,135
Ireland and the Isles	85	11,243	3,104	324,496	19,943
British Plantations	721	167,940	9,917	960,414	64,252
Total	2,045	423,477	37,014	5,519,154	284,135

SOME OF THE ITEMS OF THE PUBLIC INCOME.

CUSTOMS.—Books *Net Produce* £5,314	EXCISE.—Hops . *Net Produce* 477,035
Butter 103,004	Hackney Carriages . . 80,130
Cheese 48,315	Licences . . . 1,424,663
Cocoa, &c. . . . 12,326	Malt 5,326,023
Coffee 481,409	Paper 1,119,433
Corn, Meal, and Flour 486,026	Railways . . . 348,611
Currants . . . 229,165	Spirits . . . 8,963,874
Eggs 21,377	STAMPS.—Deeds . . . 1,331,788
Figs 31,063	Probates of Wills . 1,187,228
Flowers, Artificial . 19,349	Bills of Exchange . 523,616
Gloves of Leather . 49,652	Receipts and Drafts . 281,115
Hops 44,440	Marine Insurances . 319,508
Iron and Steel, Wrought . 1,317	Licenses and Certificates . 217,599
Oranges and Lemons . 31,881	Newspapers and Supplements 153,420
Paper of all Sorts . 11,250	Legacies and Successions . 1,845,205
Pepper 96,318	Fire Insurances . . 1,356,069
Raisins . . . 96,177	Cards and Dice . . 13,634
Rice 28,705	Divorce Causes . . 196
Silk Manufactures . 231,490	TAXES.—Land . . . 1,142,173
Rum 1,381,693	Inhabited Houses . 754,044
Brandy . . . 882,137	Servants . . . 192,760
Geneva and other Sorts . 35,933	Carriages . . . 300,597
Sugar, Unrefined . 5,119,079	Horses . . . 351,006
Tea . . . 5,459,699	Dogs 197,604
Tobacco and Snuff . 5,272,471	Hair-Powder . . 1,265
Wine 1,733,729	Armorial Bearings . 53,494
Wood and Timber . 580,571	Game-Duty . . . 129,943

SOME OF THE ITEMS OF THE PUBLIC EXPENDITURE.

CONSOLIDATED FUND.

ANNUITIES AND PENSIONS, (Ac. 32.)	Parliament Salaries . . 84,680
To the Royal Family . £140,887	Poor-Law Commission . 216,293
For Civil and Military Services 194,110	Mint, including Coinage . 38,829
SALARIES AND ALLOWANCES, (Ac. 33.)	Printing and Stationery . 406,275
House of Commons . . £5,662	Postage of Public Departments 103,410
Exchequer and Audit-Office . 8,300	Prosecutions formerly paid by
Lunacy Commission . 12,527	County Rates . . 195,000
Scotch Clergy . . . 17,040	County Police . . 120,000
West India Clergy . . 20,300	Metropolitan Police . 103,306
Lord-Lieutenant of Ireland . 20,000	Irish Constabulary . 643,155
Maynooth College . . 26,360	Prison Establishments . 417,822
Queen's Colleges, Ireland . 21,000	Maintenance in County Gaols 182,704
DIPLOMATIC SERVICE, (Ac. 34.)	Transportation . . 28,000
Ambassadors, Envoys, &c. . 139,404	Colonial Convict Establishments 293,605
Pensions . . . 19,520	Education, Great Britain . 597,446
COURTS OF JUSTICE, (Ac. 35.)	Ditto, Ireland . . . 217,641
Court of Chancery . . 39,850	Ditto, Science and Art . 79,530
Queen's Bench . . . 31,602	British Museum . . 111,987
Common Pleas . . 27,000	National Gallery . . 28,639
Exchequer . . . 27,000	Clergy, North America . 7,397
Metropolitan Police Courts . 27,900	Consuls abroad . . 192,587
Miscellaneous Salaries . 7,425	Superannuations, &c. . 162,037
Compensations in above Deps. 36,299	Dissenting Ministers, Ireland . 39,309
Judges of County Courts . 78,598	Ecclesiastical Commission . 4,461
Miscellaneous Compensations 289,663	Charity Commission . 18,022
Ireland . . . 138,157	Metropolitan Churches Fund . 10,000
Ditto, Compensations . 15,722	REVENUE DEPARTMENTS.
MISCELLANEOUS SERVICES.	CUSTOMS—Expenses of Collecting 843,757
Interest on Loans . . 130,783	INLAND REVENUE, ditto . 1,339,249
Greenwich Hospital . 20,000	POST OFFICE—Chief Offices . 464,134
Secret Service . . . 10,000	Provincial Offices . . 509,301
Compensation to D. of Cornwall 16,217	Foreign and Colonial . 19,872
SUPPLY SERVICE.	Conveyance of Mails . 727,066
ARMY—Land Forces, &c. . 9,223,535	Surveyors, Buildings, &c. . 28,480
Works, Stores, &c. . 3,690,622	Postage Labels . . 27,187
CIVIL SERVICES, (Ac. 57)—Mar-	Total Cost of Post-Office . 1,776,041
riage portion, Princess Royal . 40,000	SUPERANNUATIONS—Revenue . 454,198
Royal Palaces . . . 69,575	Ditto, Post-Office . . 36,400
Royal Parks . . . 111,114	WOODS AND FORESTS—
New Houses of Parliament . 131,883	Salaries, &c. . . . 21,717
Harbours of Refuge . 259,000	Local Officers, &c. . . 16,024
	Pensions, &c., charged . 132,618

STATISTICS OF GREAT BRITAIN.

FROM THE CENSUS OF MARCH 31, 1851.

	POPULATION.			HOUSES.		
	Males.	Females.	Persons.	Inhabit-ed.	Unin-habited.	Build-ing.
England and Wales - -	8,781,255	9,146,384	17,927,609	3,278,039	153,494	26,571
Scotland - -	1,375,479	1,513,263	2,888,742	370,308	12,146	2,420
Islands in British Seas -	66,854	76,272	143,126	21,845	1,095	203
Total of Great Britain - -	10,223,558	10,735,919	20,959,477	3,670,192	166,735	29,194

INCREASE OF POPULATION.

	POPULATION.			HOUSES.		
	Males	Females.	Persons.	Inhabited.	Unin-habited.	Build-ing.
1801	5,030,226	5,548,730	10,578,956	1,882,476	67,320	,,
1811	5,737,261	6,312,859	12,050,120	2,113,897	62,664	18,626
1821	6,874,675	7,306,590	14,181,265	2,443,393	82,791	21,777
1831	7,934,201	8,430,692	16,364,893	2,866,595	133,331	27,553
1841	9,077,004	9,581,368	18,658,372	3,465,987	198,141	30,810
1851	10,223,558	10,735,919	20,959,477	3,670,192	166,735	29,194

AGES OF THE PEOPLE IN GREAT BRITAIN.

	Males.	Females.		Males.	Females.
Under 5	1,374,444	1,362,515	Above 55	293,416	318,237
Above 5	1,230,590	1,218,109	60	262,461	301,114
10	1,134,290	1,111,594	65	174,935	206,636
15	1,025,419	1,045,317	70	133,187	160,664
20	930,048	1,030,456	75	75,474	95,479
25	808,705	903,733	80	37,648	51,356
30	710,890	768,711	85	12,390	18,203
35	612,374	649,642	90	2,823	4,964
40	548,694	581,437	95	584	1,130
45	452,542	475,268	100	111	208
50	402,533	431,146			

Total, all ages—Males, 10,223,558 ; Females, 10,735,919.

THE CONJUGAL CONDITION OF THE PEOPLE.

Bachelors.	Husbands.	Widowers.	Spinsters.	Wives.	Widows.
1,689,116	3,386,811	382,858	1,767,194	3,435,917	795,273

N.B.—In this return those only aged 20 years and upwards are included.

STAMPS, LEASES, AGREEMENTS, &c.

BILLS AND PROMISSORY NOTES.

Inland Bill of Exchange, Draft, or Order for Payment to the Bearer, or to Order, at any time otherwise than on demand, of any sum of money

Exceeding	Not exceeding	£	s.	d.
	£5	0	0	1
£5	10	0	0	2
10	25	0	0	3
25	50	0	0	6
50	75	0	0	9
75	100	0	1	0
100	200	0	2	0
200	300	0	3	0
300	400	0	4	0
400	500	0	5	0
500	750	0	7	6
750	1,000	0	10	0
1,000	1,500	0	15	0
1,500	2,000	1	0	0
2,000	3,000	1	10	0
3,000	4,000	2	0	0
4,000 and upwards		2	5	0

Promissory Notes at the same rates as Inland Bills.

RECEIPTS.

	s.	d.
For sums of £2 and upwards	0	1
Draft, or Order, for the payment of any sum of money to the Bearer, or to Order, on demand	0	1
Letters of Credit	0	1

Receipts or acknowledgments for bills, monies, or securities, sent through the post, require to be stamped exactly the same as if passed by hand.

By the New Act, unstamped cheques are not allowed to circulate beyond 15 miles from the Bank; and any person sending or remitting such a cheque beyond that distance, or receiving such cheques in payment, will be liable to a fine of £50.

CROSSED CHEQUES.—A Draft crossed with a banker's name is to be payable *only* to or through some banker.

LEASES.

Lease or tack of any lands, tenements, hereditaments, or heritable subjects at a yearly rent, without any sum of money by way of fine, premium, or grassum paid for the same. Yearly rent—

Exceeding	Not exceeding	s.	d.
	£5	0	3
£5	10	0	6
10	15	0	9
15	20	1	0
20	25	1	3
25	50	1	10
50	75	2	5
75	100	3	0

And where the same shall exceed £100, then for every £50, or any fractional part of £50, 5s.

Over 100 years the rate is double.

CONVEYANCES.

Where the purchase or consideration money therein or thereupon expressed shall not exceed £25 ... 0 2 6

Exceeding	Not exceeding	£	s.	d.
£25	£50	0	5	0
50	75	0	7	6
75	100	0	10	0
100	125	0	12	6
125	150	0	15	0
150	175	0	17	6
175	200	1	0	0
200	225	1	2	6
225	250	1	5	0
250	275	1	7	6
275	300	1	10	0
300	350	1	15	0
350	400	2	0	0
400	450	2	5	0
450	500	2	10	0
500	550	2	15	0
550	600	3	0	0

And where the purchase or consideration money shall exceed £600, then for every £100, and also for any fractional part of £100, 10s.

AGREEMENTS.

Where the subject-matter thereof shall be of the value of £20 or upwards, and less than 2,160 words, 2s. 6d.; if 2,160 words or upwards, then for every entire 1,080 words over and above the first 1,080, a further progressive duty of 2s. 6d.

BONDS AND MORTGAGES.

Exceeding	Not exceeding	s.	d.
	£50	1	3
£50	100	2	6
100	150	3	9
150	200	5	0
200	250	6	3
250	300	7	6

And where the same shall exceed £300, then for every £100, and also for any fractional part of £100, 2s. 6d.

And where any such bond or mortgage shall contain 2,160 words or upwards, then for every entire quantity of 1,080 words contained therein, over and above the first 1,080 words, there shall be charged the further progressive duty following; viz., where such bond or mortgage shall be chargeable with any *ad valorem* stamp-duty, not exceeding 10s., a further progressive duty equal to the amount of such *ad valorem* duty or duties; and in every other case, a further progressive duty of 10s.

A Table of the Kings and Queens of England since the Norman Invasion,

With the exact date of the Commencement of each Reign.

The legal maxim, that "the king never dies," in virtue of which the accession of each monarch is ascribed to the same day as the demise of his predecessor, was unknown in the earlier periods of our history. From William I. to Henry III. inclusive, the reign of each king was considered only to commence at his coronation, the doctrine of hereditary right not being fully accepted, and the interregnum thus occasioned extended from three days in the case of Henry I., to nearly two months in those of Henry II. and Richard I. From Edward II. to Henry VIII. the accession is ascribed to the day following the death or deposition of the preceding king, (Edward I., Edward III., Edward V., and Richard III., are exceptional cases); but from Edward VI. to the present day the above-cited maxim has prevailed.

	Title.		Duration. Years.
THE HOUSE OF NORMANDY.			
WILLIAM I.	Obtained the Crown by Conquest. His reign dates from his coronation, Dec. 25.	. 1066	
	Died Sept. 9.	. 1087	21
WILLIAM II.	Fourth son of William I., crowned Sept. 26.	. 1087	
	Died Aug. 2.	. 1100	13
HENRY I.	Youngest son of William I., crowned Aug. 5.	. 1100	
	Died Dec. 1.	. 1135	35
THE HOUSE OF BLOIS.			
STEPHEN	Third son of Stephen, Count of Blois, by Adela, fifth daughter of William I. Crowned (St. Stephen's Day) Dec. 26.	. 1135	
	Died Oct. 25.	. 1154	19
THE HOUSE OF PLANTAGENET.			
HENRY II.	Son of Geoffrey Plantagenet, earl of Anjou, by Matilda, only daughter of Henry I. Crowned Sunday, Dec. 19.	. 1154	
	Died July 6.	. 1189	35
RICHARD I.	Eldest surviving son of Henry II. Crowned Sunday, Sept. 3.	. 1189	
	Died	. 1199	10
JOHN	Fifth and youngest son of Henry II. Crowned (Ascension-day) May 27.	. 1199	
	Died Oct. 19.	. 1216	18
HENRY III.	Eldest son of John, crowned Oct. 28.	. 1216	
	Died Nov. 16.	. 1272	57
EDWARD I.	Eldest son of Henry III. Proclaimed Nov. 20, 1272, crowned Aug. 2, 1274.	. 1272	
	Died July 7.	. 1307	35
EDWARD II.	Eldest surviving son of Edward I. Succeeded Saturday, July 8.	. 1307	
	Deposed Jan. 20.	. 1327	20
EDWARD III.	Eldest son of Edward II. Succeeded Jan. 25.	. 1327	
	Died June 21.	. 1377	51
RICHARD II.	Son of the Black Prince, eldest son of Edward III., began to reign June 22.	. 1377	
	Deposed Sept. 29.	. 1399	23
THE HOUSE OF LANCASTER.			
HENRY IV.	Son of John of Gaunt, fourth son of Edw. III., began to reign Sept. 30.	. 1399	
	Died March 20.	. 1413	14
HENRY V.	Eld. son of Henry IV., began to reign March 21.	. 1413	
	Died Aug. 31.	. 1422	10
HENRY VI.	Only son of Henry V., began to reign Sept. 1.	. 1422	
	Deposed March 4, 1461; restored Oct. 9, 1470; deposed April, 1471.		39

THE HOUSE OF YORK.

			Dura-tion. Years
EDWARD IV.	His grandfather, Richard, was son of Edmund, fifth son of Edw. III.; and his grandmother, Anne, was great-granddaughter of Lionel, third son of Edw. III. Began to reign March 4.	1461	
	Died April 9.	1483	23
EDWARD V.	Eldest son of Edw. IV., began to reign April 9. . .	1483	
	Date of death unknown.		0
RICHARD III.	Younger br. of Edw. IV., beg. to reign June 26. .	1483	
	Died August 22.	1485	3

THE HOUSE OF TUDOR.

HENRY VII.	His father was Edmund, eldest son of Owen Tudor and Queen Catharine, widow of Hen. V.; and his mother was Margaret Beaufort, great-granddaughter of John of Gaunt.		
	Succeeded Aug. 22.	1485	
	Died April 21.	1509	24
HENRY VIII.	Only surviving son of Henry VII.		
	Began to reign April 22.	1509	
	Died Jan. 28.	1547	38
EDWARD VI.	Son of Henry VIII. by Jane Seymour.		
	Began to reign Jan. 28.	1547	
	Died July 6.	1553	7
[LADY JANE GREY	Documents are in existence bearing her seal as Queen, dated as early as July 9, and as late as July 18. .	1553]	
MARY	Daughter of Henry VIII. by Catherine of Arragon.		
	Reign reckoned from July 6, (death of Edw. VI.) .	1553	
	Died Nov. 17.	1558	6
ELIZABETH	Daughter of Henry VIII. by Anne Boleyn . .		
	Began to reign Nov. 17.	1558	
	Died March 24.	1603	45

THE HOUSE OF STUART.

JAMES I.	Son of Mary Queen of Scots, granddaughter of James IV. and Margaret, eldest daughter of Henry VII.		
	Began to reign March 24.	1603	
	Died March 27.	1625	23
CHARLES I.	Only surviving son of James I.		
	Began to reign March 27.	1625	
	Died Jan. 30.	1649	24
INTERREGNUM.	Commonwealth commenced Jan. 30. . . .	1649	
CHARLES II.	Eldest son of Charles I., king de jure, Jan. 30, 1649, de facto, May 29.	1660	
	Died Feb. 6.	1685	37
JAMES II.	Only surviving son of Charles I.		
	Began to reign Feb. 6.	1685	
	Abdicated Dec. 11.	1688	4
WILL. III.	Son of William of Nassau, by Mary, daughter of Charles I.	1689	14
MARY	Eldest daughter of James II.	1689	6
	Began to reign Feb. 13.		
	Mary died Dec. 27, 1694; William died March 8. .	1702	
ANNE	Daughter of James II., began to reign Mar. 8. .	1702	
	Died Aug. 1.	1714	13

THE HOUSE OF HANOVER.

GEORGE I.	Eldest son of the Elector of Hanover, by Sophia, daughter of Fred. V., King of Bohemia, and Elizabeth, daughter of James I.		
	Began to reign Aug. 1.	1714	
	Died June 11.	1727	13
GEORGE II.	Only son of George I., began to reign June 11. .	1727	
	Died Oct. 25.	1760	34
GEORGE III.	Grandson of George II., began to reign Oct. 25. .	1760	
	Died Jan. 29.	1820	60
GEORGE IV.	Eldest son of George III., began to reign Jan. 29. .	1820	
	Died June 26.	1830	11
WILLIAM IV.	Third son of George III., began to reign June 26. .	1830	
	Died June 20.	1837	7
VICTORIA	Daughter of Edward, Duke of Kent, fourth son of George III.		
	Began to reign June 20.	1837	

WHOM GOD PRESERVE.

POSTAL REGULATIONS.

THE UNITED KINGDOM.

[A] LETTERS—From any part of the United Kingdom to another are charged— Not exceeding half-an-ounce, 1d.; not exceeding an ounce, 2d.; and 2d. for every additional ounce, or part of an ounce. *The Postage* must be prepaid by affixing Stamps. *Unpaid letters* to be charged Double Postage on delivery; or if insufficiently paid, double the amount of such insufficiency.

[B] NEWSPAPERS.—A *Stamped* Newspaper will pass free through the post, provided (a) that the paper be so folded as to leave the stamp exposed to view, and distinctly visible on the outside. (b), That the Paper must be posted within fifteen days of the date of publication, or the stamp is of no avail. Newspapers *Unstamped* or with writing thereon will be subject to the same laws as the Book Postage.

[C] BOOKS, Manuscripts, Proofs, Pamphlets, &c., are charged—For a packet not exceeding 4 oz., 1d.; 8 oz., 2d.; 16 oz., 4d.; 1¼ lb., 6d.; and so on, 2d. being charged for every additional half-pound.

The Postage must be prepaid in Stamps. *Every packet* must be sent either without a cover or in a cover open at the ends or sides, so as to admit of the contents being removed for examination. *The packet* must not contain anything sealed or closed against inspection, or *any communication of the nature of a letter.*

POSTAL TABLE BETWEEN ENGLAND AND THE CONTINENT.

DESTINATION.		LETTERS. Not ex. ½ oz. (s. d.)	Not ex. ½ oz. (s. d.)	Reg. News. under 4 oz. (s. d.)
Austria	v. B.	0 8	0 8	*0 1
	v. F.	0 8	1 4	*0 1
Baden & Bavaria	v. F.	0 6	1 0	*0 1
	v. B.	0 8	0 8	*0 1
Belgium, (if prepaid)		0 4	0 4	*0 1
"	v. F.	0 6	0 6	*0 1
Bremen and Holland	v. B.	0 8	0 8	*0 1
	v. F.	0 6	1 0	*0 1
Brunswick	v. B.	0 8	0 8	*0 1
	v. F.	0 8	1 4	*0 1
Cadiz and Vigo	v. S.	*2 2	*2 2	*0 1
	v. F.	*0 8	*0 11	*0 1
Coburg (Saxe)	v. B.	0 8	0 8	*0 1
	v. F.	0 6	1 0	*0 1
Denmark	v. B.	0 11	0 11	*0 1
	v. F.	0 9	1 6	*0 1
France & Algeria if prep.		0 4	0 8	*0 1
Frankfort	v. B.	0 8	0 8	*0 1
	v. F.	0 6	1 0	*0 1
Greece	v. B.	1 3	1 3	...
	v. F.	0 11	1 10	*0 1
Hanover	v. B.	0 8	0 8	*0 1
	v. F.	0 8	1 4	*0 1
Hesse	v. B.	0 8	0 8	*0 1
	v. F.	0 6	1 0	*0 1
Ionian Islands	v. B.	1 0	1 0	...
	v. F.	*1 2	*2 4	*0 1
Lubeck	v. B.	0 8	0 8	*0 1
	v. F.	0 6	1 0	*0 1
Lucca	v. F.	0 7	1 4	*0 1
Luxemburg (Duchy of)	v. F.	0 6	1 0	*0 1
	v. B.	*0 6	*0 6	*0 1
Malta	v. M.	*0 9	1 0	*0 3
"	v. S.	*0 6	0 6	*0 1
" by F. Packet	v. M.	*0 9	1 0	*0 1

DESTINATION.		LETTERS. Not ex. ½ oz. (s. d.)	Not ex. ½ oz. (s. d.)	Reg. News. under 4 oz. (s. d.)
Norway	v. B.	1 5	1 5	*0 1
	v. F.	1 2	2 4	*0 1
Oldenburg	v. B.	0 8	0 8	*0 1
	v. F.	0 8	1 4	*0 1
Papal States	v. F.	0 11	1 10	*0 1
" and Naples	v. M.	0 11	1 10	*0 1
Poland	v. B.	1 0	1 0	*0 1
	v. F.	1 2	2 4	*0 1
Portugal		*1 9	*1 9	*0 1
"	v. B.	*0 8	*0 11	*0 1
Prussia	v. B.	0 8	0 8	*0 1
" Rhenish	v. F.	0 6	1 0	*0 1
" Other parts	v. F.	0 8	1 4	*0 1
Russia	v. B.	1 0	1 0	*0 1
	v. F.	1 2	2 4	*0 1
Sardinia (if prep.) otherwise, a fine of 6d. on delivery	v. F.	0 6	1 0	*0 1
	v. B.	1 0	1 0	*0 3
Saxony	v. B.	0 8	0 8	*0 1
	v. F.	0 8	1 4	*0 1
Sicilies (Two)	v. F.	0 11	1 10	*0 1
	v. B.	*0 8	*0 8	*0 3
Spain	v. S.	*2 2	*2 2	*0 1
Sweden	v. B.	1 2	1 2	*0 1
	v. F.	1 2	2 4	*0 1
Switzerland	v. F.	0 6	1 0	*0 1
	v. B.	1 0	1 0	*0 1
Turkey	v. B.	*0 8	0 8	*0 2
	v. F.	1 3	2 6	*0 1
Tuscany	v. F.	0 7	1 2	*0 1
	v. B.	0 11	0 11	*0 3
Venetian Lombardy	v. F.	0 8	1 4	*0 1
	v. B.	0 10	0 10	*0 1
Wurtemburg	v. F.	*0 6	*1 0	*0 1
	v. B.	0 8	0 8	*0 1

v. B. expresses *via* Belgium; *v. F.*, *via* France; *v. M.*, *via* Marseilles; and *v. S.*, *via* Southampton.   *Prepayment compulsory.

LONDON BANKERS.

Bank of Australasia, 8, Austin Friars
Bank of British North America, 7, St. Helen's-place
Bank of England, Threadneedle-st. ; 1, Old Burlington-street
Bank of London, 52, Threadneedle-st. ; 450, West Strand
Barclay, and Co., 54, Lombard-street
Barnett, Hoares, & Co., 62, Lombard-St.
Biggerstaff, W. & J. 8, West Smithfield ; 6, Cattle-market, Islington
Bosanquet, Franks, Whatman, and Co., 73, Lombard-St.
British Colonial, 80, Coleman-street
Brown, Janson, & Co., 32, Abchurch-lane
Brown, John, & Co., 25, Abchurch-lane
Call, Sir W. B., Bt., Marten, and Co., 25, Old Bond-street
Challis and Son, 37, West Smithfield
Chartered Bank of Asia, 32, Great Winchester-street
Chartered Bank of India, Australia, and China, Gresham-hse, Threadneedle-st.
Child & Co., 1 Fleet-street, Temple-bar
City Bank, Threadneedle-street
Cocks & Biddulph, 43, Charing-cross
Colonial Bank, 13, Bishopsg.-st. Within
Commercial Bank of London, 6 Lothbury, 6, Henrietta-st., Covent Garden
Coutts and Co., 59, Strand
Cunliffe, Roger, Son, & Co., Bucklersbury
Cunliffes, Brooks, & Co., 24, Lombard-St.
Currie and Co., 29, Cornhill
Davies, Robert, & Co., 187, Shoreditch
Dimsdale, Drewett, Fowler, & Barnard, 50, Cornhill
Dixon & Brooks, 25, Chancery-lane
Drummond Messrs., 49, Charing-cross
English, Scottish, & Australian chartered Bank, 61A, Moorgate-street
Exchange Bank, A. Bauer, and Co., 113, Leadenhall-street
Feltham, John, & Co., 42, Lombard-st.
Fuller and Co., 66, Moorgate-street
Glyn, Sir R. P., Mills, & Co., 67, Lombard-st.
Goslings and Sharpe, 19, Fleet-street
Hallett, and Co., 14, Great George-street
Hanburys & Lloyd, 60, Lombard-street
Hankey Messrs., 7, Fenchurch-street
Herries, Farquhar, and Co., 16, St. James's-street
Heywood & Co., 4, Lombard-street
Hill and Sons, 17, West Smithfield
Hoare, Messrs., 37, Fleet-street
Hopkinson and Co., 3, Regent-street
Ionian Bank, 6, Great Winchester-street
Johnston, H. & J., & Co., 28, Cannon-st.
Jones, Loyd, and Co., 43, Lothbury
Janvrin, De Lisle, & Co., 14, Austin Friars
Kemp, Clay, & Co., Lombard-street ; 7, Nicolas-lane
Lacy and Son, 60, West Smithfield ; 11, Bank-buildings
London Chartered Bank of Australia, 17, Cannon-street
London and County Joint Stock Banking Company, 21, Lombard-street ; Albert Gate, Knightsbridge ; 22½, Connaught-terrace, Edgware-road ; 441, Oxford-st. ; 201, High-street, Borough

London and Eastern Banking Corporation, 27, Cannon-st. ; 136, Westbourne-terrace ; 20, Pall-Mall ; 44, Mark-lane
London Joint Stock Bank, 5, Prince's-st., Bank ; 69, Pall Mall
London and Westminster Bank, 41, Lothbury ; 1, St. James's-sq. ; 214, High Holborn ; 3, Wellington-st., Borough ; 87, High-st., Whitechapel ; 4, Stratford-pl., Oxford-st. ; Temple-bar
Lubbock, Sir J. W., Bt., and Co., 11, Mansion-house-street
Martin and Co., 68, Lombard-street
Masterman, Peters, & Co., Nicholas-lane
McGregor, R. G., & Co., 10, Old Jewry
Melbourne, Sydney, and Adelaide Chartered Bank, 9, Moorgate-street
Mercantile Bank of India, 50, Broad-st City
National Bank of Ireland, Old Broad-st.
National Provincial Bank of England, 112, Bishopgate-street-Within
National Security Bk., 29, Gt. St. Helen's
North Western Bank of India, Gresham House, Old Broad-street
Olding & Co., 29, St. Clement's-lane
Ommanney, Son, & Co., 40, Charing-cross
Oriental Bank Corporation, 7, Walbrook
Ottoman Bank, 26, Old Broad-street
Praed, Fane, Praed, and Co., 189, Fleet-street
Prescott & Co., 62, Threadneedle-street
Price, Sir C., Bt., & Co., 3, King Wm.-st.
Provincial Bank of Ireland, 42, Old Broad-street
Puget, Bainbridge, & Co., 12, St. Paul's churchyard
Ransom and Co., 1, Pall-Mall East
Robarts, Curtis, & Co., 15, Lombard-st.
Samuel & Montague, 22, Cornhill
Sapte, Muspratt, Banbury, and Co., 77, Lombard-street
Scott, Sir S., Bt., & Co., 1, Cavendish-sq.
Seale, Lowe, & Co., 15½, Leicester-place
Shank, J., 4, Cattle-market, Islington
Smith, Payne, & Smith, 1, Lombard-st.
South Australian Company, 54, Old Broad-street
Spielmann and Co., 79, Lombard-street
Spooner, Attwoods, and Co., 27, Gracechurch-street
Stevenson, Salt, & Sons, 20, Lombard-st.
Stride, J. and W. S., 41, West Smithfield ; 8, Cattle-market, Islington
Twining, Messrs., 215, Strand

Union Bk. of Australia, 38, Old Broad-st
Union Bank of London, 2, Princes-st., Bank ; Argyll-pl. ; 4, Pall-Mall East ; 13, Fleet-street
Unity Joint Stock Mutual Association, 10, Cannon-st. ; 1, New Coventry-st.
Ward, T. G., 15, West Smithfield ; 4, Bank-buildings, Caledonian-road, Islington
Western Bank of London, 21, Hanover-square
White & Co., 11, Haymarket
Williams, Deacon, Labouchere, and Co., 20, Birchin-lane
Willis, Percival, & Co., 76, Lombard-st.

PART II.

The Diocese of Oxford.

NOTICE.

In the following pages, the information relating to the various Societies in the Diocese has been given, as far as was found practicable, to the present time, or in accordance with their last report. Assistance from the different Secretaries was freely and kindly offered to us, but a difficulty arose in stating precisely the kind of information required, or the space that could be devoted to each Society. This difficulty will not occur in future issues, and next year we hope to avail ourselves more largely of the proffered assistance. The same remark applies to the Schools, &c.

With regard to the "Record," we need scarcely point out how much depends upon the co-operation of our subscribers, and we believe there are few who will not be ready to afford us information of such events which take place from time to time in their parishes, as will interest those of other parishes, or be deemed of sufficient importance to be chronicled in this department. As the number of entries will, without doubt, be considerably increased, we would not only recommend, but request, *conciseness* in narrating what takes place. Short Biographical Notices of Clergymen deceased during the year is a feature that should also find a place in the Record.

As to the list of Parishes, Clergy, Church Accommodation, &c., we can only say that we have employed all means within our power to ensure both completeness and accuracy. Of course there must be errors in so long and so varying a list, compiled for the first time, but we look to our friends to point them out before the next year's issue.

The Miscellaneous information at the end of the Calendar, we also feel, is capable of additions and improvements, which we hope a cordial and extensive patronage will enable us, as years roll on, to effect.

Next year the issue will take place earlier in December. Corrections, information, and suggestions will be received up to the 25th of November, 1859,

Addressed to   THE EDITOR OF THE DIOCESAN CALENDAR,

Care of MESSRS. PARKER,

BROAD-STREET, OXFORD.

THE DIOCESE OF OXFORD.

DORCHESTER was an episcopal see instituted under Birinus, and after it had existed 460 years, Remigius, (under William the Conqueror,) removed it to Lincoln about the year 1086.

Henry VIII., upon the dissolution of the monasteries, added six sees, and amongst them that of Oxford, which he took out of Lincoln, and by patent, 34 Henry VIII., Jan. 6, (1542,) the King largely endowed the bishoprick. It was then seated at Osney; but in 1546, on the removal of it to the priory of St. Frideswide, several manors and demesnes, and the palace of Gloucester-hall, Oxford, were taken from it. At the same time other manors and impropriations were added to the see; and Edward VI., by patent in 1547, granted additional rectories and advowsons to the bishoprick.

But Queen Elizabeth kept the bishoprick vacant forty-one years out of her forty-four years' reign, and in that interval stripped it of its endowments, and in lieu thereof bestowed on the see the following livings :—

Stanton Harcourt, Rectory; Culham, Vicarage; Cuddesdon; Banbury, Prebend and Rectory; Cropredy, Prebend; Burford, Rectory, *cum* Fulbrook Chapelry; Ambrosden.

The see then being reduced, and no palace appropriated for the bishops, King Charles the First was pleased to grant to Bishop Bancroft and his successors a pension of £100 per annum out of his forests of Shotover and Stow-wood, with licence to unite the vicarage of Cuddesdon to the rectory; and this Bishop built a palace at Cuddesdon, which was burned down in the Rebellion, and continued a ruin till Bishop Fell, after the Restoration, rebuilt it. The above endowments were under the Ecclesiastical Commission commuted for the fixed sum of £5,000 per annum.

Bishops of Oxford.

	Admitted to the See.
1. ROBERT KING, first and only Bishop of Osney, and afterwards first Bishop of Oxford	1542
Thomas Goldwell, nominated to the see by Queen Mary, whose death took place previous to his institution	1558
2. Hugh Curwen, Archbishop of Dublin, and Lord Chancellor of Ireland, translated to Oxford	1567
See vacant twenty-one years.	
3. John Underhill, Rector of Lincoln College	1589
See again vacant eleven years.	
4. John Bridges, Dean of Salisbury	1604
5. John Howson, Student of Christ Church	1619
6. Richard Corbett, Dean of Christ Church	1628
7. John Bancroft, Master of University College. He largely endowed the see, and built an episcopal residence at Cuddesdon	1632
8. Robert Skinner, Bishop of Bristol, (deprived during the Commonwealth, but restored 1660,)	1641
9. William Paul, Dean of Lichfield	1663
10. Walter Blandford, Warden of Wadham College	1665

	Admitted to the See.
11. Nathaniel Crew, Rector of Lincoln, and Dean of Chichester .	1671
12. Henry Compton	1674
13. John Fell, Dean of Christ Church . . .	1675
14. Samuel Parker, Archdeacon of Canterbury . .	1686
15. Timothy Hall	1688
16. John Hough, President of Magdalen . . .	1690
17. William Talbot, Dean of Worcester . . .	1699
18. John Potter, Regius Professor of Divinity at Oxford .	1715
19. Thomas Secker, Bishop of Bristol . . .	1737
20. John Hume, Bishop of Bristol . . .	1758
21. Robert Louth, Bishop of St. David's . . .	1766
22. John Butler	1777
23. Edward Smallwell, Bishop of St. David's . .	1788
24. John Randolph, Regius Professor of Greek, Editor of the *Enchiridion Theologicum*	1799
25. Charles Moss ; bequeathed £3,000 to endow Wheatley School	1807
26. William Jackson, Regius Professor of Greek . .	1812
27. Hon. Edward Legge, Dean of Windsor, and Warden of All Souls'	1815
28. Charles Lloyd, Regius Professor of Divinity . .	1827
29. Richard Bagot, Dean of Canterbury . . .	1829

30. 𝕿𝖍𝖊 𝖕𝖗𝖊𝖘𝖊𝖓𝖙 𝕷𝖔𝖗𝖉 𝕭𝖎𝖘𝖍𝖔𝖕 𝖔𝖋 𝖙𝖍𝖊 𝕯𝖎𝖔𝖈𝖊𝖘𝖊 *,

The Right Reverend SAMUEL WILBERFORCE, D.D.,
Who was consecrated on the thirtieth day of November, 1845, upon the translation of the Hon. and Right Rev. Richard Bagot, D.D., to the bishoprick of Bath and Wells.

Residence—Cuddesdon Palace, near Wheatley, Oxon.

Archdeacons.

Ven. Chas. Carr Clerke, D.D., *Oxford*	1830
—— Edward Bickersteth, M.A., *Buckingham*.	1853
—— James Randall, M.A., *Berks*	1855

Chancellor of the Diocese.

Worshipful Robert Joseph Phillimore, D.C.L., Q.C., M.P. 1855

Proctors for the Diocese.

Richard W. Jelf, D.D.   Francis Knyvett Leighton, D.D.
Charles Lloyd, M.A.

The *Surrogates* will be found in the List of the Clergy, each being marked with **S**.   In the Index an asterisk is attached.

Chaplains.

The Dean of Westminster.	E. M. Goulburn, D.D.
Archdeacon Clerke, D.D.	Charles Lloyd, M.A.
Archdeacon Randall, M.A.	T. V. Fosbery, M.A.

Registrars—The Rev. Messrs. Bagot.   *Dep.*—J. M. Davenport, Esq., xford.

Sec. to Bishop—John M. Davenport, Esq., Oxford.

* Formerly of Oriel College, Oxford, M.A. 1829, B.D. and D.D. 1847. In 1830 he was appointed Rector of Brightstone, Isle of Wight; in 1839, Archdeacon of Surrey, Rector of Alverstoke, and Chaplain to Prince Albert; in 1840, Canon of Winchester ; in 1844, Sub-Almoner to the Queen; in 1845, Dean of Westminster. On the 30th November, 1845, he was consecrated Lord Bishop of Oxford, to which was attached the Office of Chancellor of the Order of the Garter. In November, 1847, he was appointed Lord High Almoner to the Queen.

The Cathedral, Christ Church.

Dean of Christ Church—Very Rev. HENRY GEO. LIDDELL, D.D., 1855.

Canons.

F. Barnes, D.D.	1810	W. Jacobson, D.D.ᵈ	1848
Edward B. Pusey, D.D. ᵇ ...	1828	C. A. Ogilvie, D.D.ᵉ	1849
Richard W. Jelf, D.D.	1830	C. A. Heurtley, D.D.ᶠ	1853
Archd. Clerke, D.D., *Sub-D.*ᶜ	1845	A. P. Stanley, D.D.ᵍ	1858

Chaplains.

A. Hackman, M.A., *Precentor.*	Thomas Evans, M.A.
George Fereman, M.A.	Arthur James Williams, M.A.
John Baker, M.A.	William Morrison, M.A.
William Price, M.A.	William Sanders, M.A.

Master of the Cathedral School—Rev. John Baker, M.A.
Chapter Clerk—C. W. Lawrence, Esq., M.A.
Organist—C. W. Corfe, Mus. Doc.
8 Singing Men, 12 Choristers.

The Chapter, Windsor.

Dean—Hon. and Very Rev. GERALD WELLESLEY, M.A., 1854, Registrar of the Order of the Garter.

Canons.

Hon. H. C. Cust, M.A.	1813	Hon. E. G. Moore, M.A.......	1834
Charles Proby, M.A.	1814	Lord Wrioth. Russell, M.A.	1840
William Canning, M.A.	1828	Fred. Anson, jun., M.A.	1845

They all have residences. Proceeds of six suspended Canonries paid over to the Ecclesiastical Commissioners.

Minor Canons.

B. Pope, M.A.	1817	John Gore, B.A.	1829
Christopher Packe, M.A.....	1821	Seymour Neville, M.A.	1847
H. Butterfield, M.A.	1828		

Divinity Lecturer—George Frewer, M.A.
Chapter Clerk—T. Batcheldor, Esq. | *Organist*—G. J. Elvey, Mus. D.
12 Lay Clerks.—10 Choristers.

Cuddesdon Theological College.

Visitor—The Lord Bishop of Oxford.
Principal—
Vice-Principal—The Rev. Henry P. Liddon, M.A., (Student of Ch. Ch.)
Chaplain and Precentor—The Rev. Edw. King, M.A., (Oriel College.)

The College was founded by the present Bishop. The building was erected by subscriptions raised within the diocese and elsewhere, and opened on Thursday in Trinity-week, 1854, and has been, ever since its foundation, self-supporting.

The College is under the immediate direction of the Lord Bishop of Oxford, and is intended as a place of residence for religious preparation and theological study between graduating at the University and taking Holy Orders.

ᵇ Annexed to Reg. Prof. of Hebrew. ᶜ Ann. to Archdeaconry of Oxford, and charged with the payment of £300 per annum to the Archdeacon of Buckingham. ᵈ Ann. to Reg. Prof. of Divinity. ᵉ Ann. to Reg. Prof. of Past. Theol. ᶠ Ann. to Marg. Prof. of Divinity. ᵍ Ann. to Reg. Prof. of Ecclesiastical History.

The College is open to all who have passed the final examination at Oxford, Cambridge, Durham, Trinity College, Dublin, and King's College, London, and Students admitted to the college are not in any way pledged to take cures within the diocese of Oxford.

The Lord Bishop of Oxford, and others of the bishops, will accept the full year's residence at Cuddesdon in lieu of the Cambridge Voluntary, or the Theological Lectures at Oxford.

Those who, being already in Deacon's Orders, are desirous of retirement and study before becoming candidates for the Priesthood, may be admitted for short periods, so long as there is room in the College.

The ordinary period of residence extends over one year, and the lectures are so arranged as to be completed in that period.

The course of lectures comprehends the study of the Holy Scriptures, the Articles and Liturgy of the Church of England, the standard theological writers of the English Church, especially Pearson and Hooker, some portions of the Catholic Fathers, Church History, and, when desired, the elements of Hebrew. Attention is also given to the composition of sermons.

Facilities are given for acquiring some knowledge of parochial work in the parish of Cuddesdon and its neighbourhood, under the direction of the parochial clergy, and Church music is taught by one of the resident officers of the College.

The foundation of religious habits being one principal object of such an institution, direction and assistance is given in acquiring such habits. The students attend daily prayers every morning in the parish church, and every evening in the College chapel. Opportunities are afforded for frequent Communion, and books of private devotion are recommended for the students' use. The living is collegiate; all meals are taken in common, and all live under one roof, as in colleges at the University.

Any further particulars may be ascertained by reference to

The Rev. The PRINCIPAL, Cuddesdon College, Wheatley.

The Diocesan Training College, Culham.

Established 1839. Removed to Culham 1853.

President—The Lord Bishop of Oxford.

Committee of Management—Elected by the Diocesan Board.

Hon. Secretary to the Committee—Rev. J. Slatter.

Principal—Rev. A. R. Ashwell, M.A.

Vice-Principal—Rev. F. G. Fleay, M.A.

Tutor—Rev. W. J. Pickard.   *Normal Master*—Mr. G. Pain.

The Rev. the Principal is the *Corresponding Secretary.*

Situation, &c.—At Culham, Abingdon, half-a-mile from the Culham Station on the Oxford Branch of the Great Western Railway.

Accommodation.—The buildings, opened Jan. 29, 1853, comprise, in addition to a residence for the Principal, accommodation for a hundred students. There is a chapel and a practising-school attached.

Inspection.—The College annually inspected by H.M.'s Inspectors.

Period of Training.—From one to three years, according to the age, character, and attainments of students. Masters already appointed to schools will be admitted for short periods.

Age of Admission.—At least fifteen years.

Terms.—20*l.* a-year, and 2*l.* for washing, payable quarterly, in advance. Students will also find it desirable to purchase books to the amount of £2 or £2 10*s.* per annum.

Queen's Scholars.—Holders of Queen's Scholarships, of whichever class, are admitted free of further charge.

Exhibitions.—The endowed Exhibitions are—The Lord Bishop's, 10*l.*, for the diocese; H.R.H. Prince Albert's, 15*l.*, Windsor Deanery; Sympson's, by Merton College, 40*l.*, parishes connected with the College; Mr. Eyres, 15*l.*, Newbury Deanery; Mr. Bowles', 10*l.*, Wantage Deanery; ditto, 10*l.*, Abingdon; Mr. Pusey's, 10*l.*, Faringdon; Windsor and Eton Church Union, 15*l.*, Windsor and Eton; the Board, two of 10*l.* each, the diocese. Those which are founded for the benefit of deaneries are appointed to by the Inspectors. The regulations for them are dependent on the Lord Bishop.

The following is a statement of the results of the first five years' work of Culham College: i.e. to January 1858 :—

Schoolmasters sent out bearing Government certificates of merit	75
Ditto, *not* certificated	19
Ditto, in colonial service	4
Left from ill-health 3, As incompetent 3, Expelled 4 .	10
Total	108
Number in residence, Nov., 1858 . . .	65

N.B. The chapel services are at 7.30 a.m., and 8.45 p.m., daily. On Sundays and Festivals the hours of service are 7.30 a.m., 11 a.m., and 8.45 p.m.

DIOCESAN SOCIETIES.
THE OXFORD DIOCESAN SPIRITUAL HELP SOCIETY.

THIS Society was inaugurated at a meeting held in the Sheldonian Theatre, Oxford, on June 2nd, 1857. The main object is to afford to the most necessitous of the diocesan clergy, permanent or temporary pecuniary aid in the maintenance of a curate.

"The Society consists, under the presidency of the Bishop of the diocese, of all annual subscribers of £1 and upwards, (all annual subscriptions to be considered due on the first day of January, and payable in advance ;) and all clergy of the diocese, being subscribers to any amount, are members. All donors of £50 and upwards are life-members.

"The Committee are empowered (at the annual meeting in February) to make annual grants (*a*) towards the maintenance of curates in those parishes and districts which shall appear to be most in need of such assistance.

(*b*) "At any quarterly meeting, to make grants, in cases of emergency, for the supply of a curate for a term not exceeding three months.

(*c*) "To make grants for the remuneration of preachers who, under the sanction of the Bishop, may assist parochial clergymen who desire their aid for special purposes on special occasions.

"All applications must be made according to a printed form, to be supplied by the *Secretary*, Rev. H. Swabey, 33, Spring-gardens, London."

Treasurer—Rev. C. F. Plumptre, Master of University College, Oxford.

Subscriptions and donations may be paid to the Treasurer, or the Rural Deans of the Diocese, or at the Old Bank.

Statement of accounts up to Nov. 1, 1858 :—

Receipts.	£ s. d.		£ s. d.
From Parochial Collections, Donations, Subscriptions, and interest of money invested	2,739 5 5	Invested in Consols . . Paid in grants, &c. . . Expenses of printing, stationery, &c. . . .	2,219 10 6 / 37 3 6 / 5 14 2
Balance in Treasurer's hands	476 17 3		2,262 8 2

Annual grants to the amount of £360 become due in Feb., 1859 ; besides which, quarterly grants have been made in cases of emergency at the rate of £300 per annum ; these will, in all probability, be confirmed as annual grants at the next February quarterly meeting; so that at that time (independently of new grants, which will then be applied for) the Society will be answerable for £660 a-year. To enable the Society to continue these grants, and to extend its usefulness, an increase of *annual subscriptions* is much needed.

THE DIOCESAN SOCIETY FOR THE INCREASE OF CHURCH ACCOMMODATION, AND OF THE NUMBER OF PARSONAGE-HOUSES. ESTABLISHED FEB. 8, 1847.

ELECTED MEMBERS OF THE COMMITTEE.

Oxon.—His Grace the Duke of Marlborough, J. H. Langston, Esq. M.P., H. Norris, Esq., H. Barnett, Esq., Dr. Guest, W. Ward, Esq., Rev. J. H. Ashhurst, Rev. Joseph Dodd, Rev. John Slatter.

Berks. — The Lord Viscount Barrington, Charles Eyre, Esq., J. S. Bowles, Esq., Charles Sawyer, Esq., J. K. Hedges, Esq., W. Mount, Esq., Rev. H. H. Swinny, Rev. Walter Levett, Rev. J. C. Clutterbuck.

Bucks.—The Marquis of Chandos, T. Raymond Baker, Esq., J. G. Hubbard, Esq., Philip Wroughton, Esq., Frederick Morrell, Esq., P. D. P. Duncombe, Esq., Rev. C. D. Goldie, Rev. A. P. Cust, Rev. H. Drummond.

Auditors—Ven. Archdeacon Clerke, and

Treasurers—Messrs. Parsons and Co., Old Bank, Oxford.

Honorary Secretary—Rev. R. Gordon, Elsfield, near Oxford, from whom *Forms of Application* for aid may be obtained.

Diocesan Architect—George Edmund Street, Esq., 33, Montague-place, Bedford-square, London, W.C.

The following table exhibits the transactions from Oct. 1, 1857, to Oct. 1, 1858 :—

		Sittings.			
	Free.	Approp.	Total.	Grants.	Expended.
New churches, 5	1,067	30	1,097	£590	£9,800
Restored chs. . 8	540	..	540	640	6,335
Parsonages . 4	....	..	....	290	3,840
17	1,607	30	1,637	£1,520	£19,975

OXFORD DIOCESAN BOARD OF EDUCATION.

Quarterly Meetings held at the Diocesan Registry, New Road.

Secretary—Rev. T. Menzies, Brasenose College, Oxford.

Educational Societies or Boards, in direct connection with the National Society, and under the presidency of the Bishop of the diocese, have now been established throughout the kingdom. Some of them date their foundation from 1811, when the National Society was first established; but they were generally, on the suggestion of the Society, remodelled in 1839. The Boards have separate funds from the parent Society, and have in connection with them Rural Deanery or local Boards, about three hundred in number, with separate Secretaries to act for each district.

The Oxford Diocesan Board supports in part an institution for training masters at Culham, already mentioned, p. 74, which is to serve also for the diocese of Gloucester and Bristol, and the latter trains school-mistresses for the diocese of Oxford. It votes grants in aid of local efforts to build and establish schools, carries on a system of diocesan inspection, and distributes prizes. It also assists in establishing middle and commercial schools.

"Two funds have been formed in connexion with the National Society. The one to be expended in small grants for the purchase of books and school apparatus; the other in grants to aid school managers in rural districts to engage the services of registered or certificated teachers, in order to secure capitation and other allowances from the Committee of Council on Education."

DIOCESAN INSPECTORS.

The National Society, on the appointment of Inspectors by her Majesty, ceased to employ salaried officers for the inspection of schools; but, on behalf of the Church, the work of inspection has been extensively carried on, through the instrumentality of the Bishop of the diocese, and the Diocesan Boards, by the appointment of clergymen and laymen to act for the most part as gratuitous Inspectors.

ARCHDEACONRY OF OXON.
Rural Deanery.
ASTON—
BICESTER—Rev. H. Gough.
CHIPPING NORTON—Rev. J. M. Talmage.
CUDDESDON—Rev. J. Slatter.
DEDDINGTON—Rev. J. Murray.
　　　　　Rev. A. W. Noel.
HENLEY—Rev. T. B. Morrell.
　　　　Rev. W. H. Ridley.
ISLIP—Rev. H. Gough.
NETTLEBED—Rev. G. K. Morrell.
OXFORD—Rev. J. Riddell.
WITNEY—Rev. G. C. Rolfe.
　　　　Rev. T. W. Goodlake.
WOODSTOCK—Rev. C. W. M. Bartholomew.

ARCHDEACONRY OF BERKS.
ABINGDON—Rev. J. C. Clutterbuck.
　　　　　Rev. Jos. Moore.
　　　　　Rev. W. Jephson.

MAIDENHEAD—Rev. G. H. Hodson.
NEWBURY—
READING—Rev. S. Sturges.
　　　　Rev. A. A. Cameron.
WALLINGFORD—Rev. J. L. Hoskyns.
WANTAGE—Rev. W. J. Butler.

ARCHDEACONRY OF BUCKINGHAM.

AMERSHAM—Rev. T. Evetts.
BUCKINGHAM—Rev. J. Cockerton.
　　　　　Rev. C. Coker.
BURNHAM—Rev. C. D. Goldie, *Colnbrook.*
MURSLEY—1st Portion.
MURSLEY—2nd Portion.
NEWPORT PAGNEL—Rev. J. Tarver.
　　　　　Rev. H. Burney.
WADDESDON—Rev. J. Statter.
WENDOVER—Rev. W. Rawson.
WYCOMBE—Rev. F. Ashpitel.

DIOCESAN SCHOOLMASTERS' ASSOCIATIONS.
THE WINDSOR AND ETON ASSOCIATION.

President—The Lord Bishop of Oxford.
Vice-Presidents—The Vicars of Burnham and Windsor.

Joint Secretaries — Rev. C. D. Goldie, and Mr. R. Blythe, St. Mark's School, Windsor.

This Association, for the improvement of masters of Church schools, and intended to furnish the opportunity of religious fellowship and social intercourse between the clergy and schoolmasters, consists of forty-two members—twenty-five clergymen and seventeen masters. The meetings of the Association, which are bi-monthly, generally take place at the Windsor Infant-School.

HENLEY-ON-THAMES DEANERY ASSOCIATION.

Patron—The Bishop of Oxford.
President—The Rural Dean.

Treasurers and Secretaries—Rev. T. B. Morrell, Rector of Henley, and Mr. E. J. Rawlins.

This Association at present consists of thirteen clergymen and six schoolmasters.

THE VALE OF AYLESBURY ASSOCIATION.

President — The Ven. Archd. Bickersteth.

Hon. Secretary—Rev. J. Wood, Aylesbury.

During the last year various interesting and instructive papers have been read at the bi-monthly meetings of this Association. The subjects have been as follows :—
On "Church Music ;" by the Rev. A. P. Cust.
On the "Formation and Improvement of Church Choirs;" by Mr. Worall.
On the "Management of Boys in School;" by the Rev. Thos. Gwynn.
On the "Reports of her Majesty's Inspectors" for 1857 ; by the Rev. P. T. Ouvry.
On the "Course of Instruction in National Schools ;" by Mr. G. Mills.
The "Resolution" recorded in the last Report respecting a "Choral Class," has led to the establishment of a "Church Choral Society" for the Vale of Aylesbury, an account of which will be given elsewhere.

An Association of the Society for the Propagation of the Gospel has been formed.

Treasurer—Z. D. Hunt, Esq.   *Secretary*—The Ven. Archd. Bickersteth. Amount remitted for the year ending 1857, £69 12s. 1d.

BANBURY DEANERY ASSOCIATION.

Secretary—Rev. H. D. Harrington, Vicarage, South Newington.

WINDSOR AND ETON CHURCH UNION.

To promote the interest of the National Society for the Education of the Poor, the Society for Promoting Christian Knowledge, the Society for Building, &c. Churches, the Additional Curates Society, and of local objects in conformity with the above Societies.

Established Nov. 5, 1838.

Patron—Her Majesty the Queen.
President—The Lord Bishop of Oxford.
Treasurer—Rev. Henry J. Ellison.
General Secretary—Rev. W. Crawford Bromehead.

CHARITY FOR THE RELIEF OF WIDOWS AND ORPHANS OF CLERGY IN THE ARCHDEACONRY OF OXFORD.

THE widows and orphans to be relieved, are those of such clergymen as, at the time of their death, were possessed of some ecclesiastical preferment or curacy within the county of Oxford.

Subscriptions received by the Treasurer for the year 1856.

	£	s.	d.		£	s.	d
Oxford	39	17	0	Woodstock	24	3	0
Cuddesdon	14	14	0	Chipping Norton	13	13	0
Bicester	27	4	6	Henley	27	6	0
Aston	16	5	6	Deddington	22	8	0
Witney	20	6	6				
				Total	205	17	6
				Dividends, from Legacies, &c.	164	18	9

Treasurer—The Venerable Archdeacon Clerke.
Stewards—Cuddesdon, Rev. H. A. Tyndale ; Bicester, Rev. W. Brown ; Aston, Rev. C. R. Conybeare ; Witney, Rev. H. Gregory ; Woodstock, Rev. W. B. Lee ; Chipping Norton, Rev. T. Harris ; Henley, Rev. R. Powys ; Deddington, Rev. H. D. Harrington.

CHARITY FOR THE RELIEF OF WIDOWS AND ORPHANS OF CLERGY IN THE ARCHDEACONRY OF BERKS,

Who have been possessed of some benefice or curacy in the county, and in some cases of distressed clergymen themselves; also (failing such cases) to provide exhibitions of not more than £20 per ann. towards the education of children of the poorer clergy in the county of Berks.

Treasurer—Rev. J. Leigh Hoskyns, Aston Tirrold.

Stewards—*Abingdon.* Rev. J. Moore, Rev. H. R. Dupré. *Reading.* Rev. F. J. Eyre, T. V. Fosbery. *Newbury.* Rev. T. A. Houblon. *Wokingham.* Rev. T. Morres. *Wallingford.* Rev. J. Langley.

BISHOP BURGESS'S FUND FOR THE RELIEF OF DISTRESSED CLERGYMEN.

Treasurer and Sec.—Rev. J. Leigh Hoskyns, Aston Tirrold.

BOOK-HAWKING ASSOCIATION.

At a meeting of Rural Deans, held at Oxford in February, 1855, the whole diocese was divided into five districts, each to be distinct and independent as to funds and management; each, however, to adhere to the same general rules. The sales began in some of the districts during the summer and autumn of 1855. The following is a rough abstract of the sales effected up to the present time:—

	1855–56.	1856–57.	1857–58.
In North Bucks. division . . .	£128	£160	No return.
In South Bucks. and East Berks. .	137	150	
In West Berks.	,,	140	
In South Oxfordshire . . .	,,	88	
In North Oxfordshire . . .	90	90	

THE OXFORD ARCHITECTURAL SOCIETY.

Established for the purpose of promoting the study of Gothic Architecture, and to furnish suggestions, so far as may be within its province, for improving the character of ecclesiastical edifices hereafter to be erected.

Society's Museum—Music-room, Holywell-street.

Members—About 700.

Hon. Secs.—W. H. Lowder, St. Edmund Hall, and R. P. Lightfoot, Balliol College.

Curator—Mr. W. A. Dicks, at the Museum.

THE ARCHITECTURAL AND ARCHÆOLOGICAL SOCIETY FOR THE COUNTY OF BUCKINGHAM.

Hon. Secs.—Rev. C. Lowndes, Hartwell Rectory, Aylesbury; Rev. W. J. Burgess, Lacy-Green, Princes Risborough; and Rev. W. H. Kelke, Drayton Beauchamp.

Society's Room—Silver-street, Aylesbury.

Two numbers of the "Records of Buckinghamshire" are published annually.

PENITENTIARIES.

CLEWER.

THIS house was opened June, 1849, in a lent house. In 1850 a freehold estate of 15 acres was purchased as a permanent site. In November, 1855, an additional set of new buildings on this site were opened, which have since been enlarged, and are now completed.

In St. John's Home, situated near the House of Mercy, girls are taken in from twelve years old to be trained. They do all the work of the house, make their own clothes, and take in needlework, and will hereafter, in the new building, also take washing; and they assist in the care of the younger children. The new building will accommodate 20 orphans, and 16 industrial training girls.

St. John's Home is in no way connected with the House of Mercy, except that the orphanage, training servants, and infirmary are carried on by members of the same sisterhood.

WANTAGE.

AT Wantage, since the establishment of the Home in Feb. 1850, to Feb. 1858, no less than 98 penitents have been received. 20 of these are now in the Home, and of those who have left it, 30 are known to be doing absolutely well. The annual expense of the institution, borne hitherto mainly by subscriptions, has been about £600. Ground has been secured and buildings erected at a cost of £3,000; a chapel and infirmary are still urgently needed; and when these additions shall have been made, nothing more will remain to set the institution in perfect working order.

Subscriptions or donations, either to the current expenses, or for the Building Fund, will be received by

THE RIGHT REV. THE LORD BISHOP OF OXFORD.

The REV. WILLIAM JOHN BUTLER, the Vicar, ⎫
The REV. THOMAS VINCENT, the Chaplain, ⎬ Wantage.
Messrs. BARNES, MEDLEY, and ANSELL, Bankers, ⎭
Messrs. PARSONS and Co., the Old Bank, Oxford.
Messrs. H. and J. JOHNSTON and Co., 28, Cannon-street, London.

Friends intending their donations to aid the Building Fund, will be kind enough to specify this.

OXFORD.

Secretaries—Rev. R. M. Benson, Ch. Ch., and Rev. H. E. Moberly, New College. *Treasurers*—Messrs. Parsons and Co.

Situation—Holywell Manor House, Oxford.

At the beginning of 1857 there were 19 inmates, 36 more were admitted during the year, making in all 55. Of these, 20 are now in the house, 9 sent to other penitentiaries, 2 ran away, of whom 1 is at home, 7 dismissed, 14 left by their own desire, of whom 3 are with their parents, and 2 doing well in service.

The accounts for 1857 shew the receipts to be £796 16s.; of which, donations amount to £517 10s., and subscriptions to £167 14s. Receipts for work to £111 11s.

The expenses amount to £796 16s., including £170 deficient last year, £100 to Wantage, and the remainder for rent, house expenses, salaries, &c.

OTHER SOCIETIES, NOT DIOCESAN, BUT WHICH ARE MORE OR LESS REPRESENTED IN THE DIOCESE.

THE SOCIETY FOR PROMOTING CHRISTIAN KNOWLEDGE. FOUNDED 1698.

Chairman of Committee—Ven. C. C. Clerke, D.D.
Secretary—Rev. J. Rigaud, B.D.
Society's Depository, 42, Queen-st., Oxford. Manager—Mr. H. Spackman.

From the Report of the Oxford Diocesan Committee of the Society, we learn that for the past year the following has been the sale in the Oxford diocese; to which is appended the corresponding list of the parent Society from the current Annual Report :—

	Oxford Society.	By parent Society.
Bibles	1,246	151,235
New Testaments	499	72,416
Common Prayer-books	2,731	310,846
Books and Tracts	23,328	3,974,469
Totals	27,804	4,508,966

The value of the stock at the close of the year was £151 19s. 6d.; the amount of subscriptions £110 7s.

Charges :— 1st. To Members of the Society who are subscribers to the Depôt, books are sold at *Members' prices*, without any additional charge.

2nd.—To Members of the Society who are not subscribers to the local Depôt, or to subscribers to the Depôt who are not Members of the Society, books are sold at *Members'* prices, but with the additional charge of 1*d.* in the shilling, for the expense of carriage, &c.

3rd.—To those who are neither Members of the Society, nor subscribers to the Depôt, books are sold at *Non-Members'* or trade prices.

THE SOCIETY FOR THE PROPAGATION OF THE GOSPEL IN FOREIGN PARTS.

President—The Abp. of Canterbury.
Secretary—The Rev. Ernest Hawkins, B.D.

THE Society for the Propagation of the Gospel in Foreign Parts was incorporated by charter, granted by King William the Third, in 1701, for the receiving, managing, and disposing of such funds as might be contributed for the religious instruction of her Majesty's subjects beyond the seas; for the maintenance of clergymen in the plantations, colonies, and factories of Great Britain; and for the propagation of the Gospel in those parts.

There are now in thirty colonial dioceses 406 ordained missionaries, maintained wholly or in part by the Society.

The Office of the Society is at 79, Pall Mall, London, S.W. Quarterly Papers and other gratuitous publications may be had on application at the Office.

The Society's total receipts in 1857 amounted to £92,488, exclusive of sums raised and spent in the missions.

ASSOCIATIONS in behalf of the Society for the Propagation of the Gospel have been established in several *parishes* of the city of Oxford for many years past. The "Oxford District Association" seems to have been formed in 1823. In which year the gross receipts were £917 0s. 5d.

In the year 1848, in seventeen of the colleges and one of the halls, associations of undergraduates were formed spontaneously, and have continued ever since. The contributions may be seen in the Annual Report of the Society. The Secretaries for the University are the Rev. E. C. Woollcombe and the Rev. J. Rigaud.

OXFORD ORGANIZING SECRETARIES,

Appointed for the purpose of assisting in making local arrangements for meetings in aid of the Society, and with whom Parochial Secretaries living in the same archdeaconry are requested to communicate.

Berks.—Rev. H. H. Swinny, Wargrave, Henley-on-Thames.
Rev. R. Milman, Lamborne.

Buckingham—Rev. C. Lloyd, Hampden, Great Missenden.
Oxford—Rev. J. C. Blomfield, Launton, Bicester.

CONTRIBUTIONS FROM THE DIOCESE OF OXFORD:—

	No. of Churches.	Churches remitting.	Collections.		
			£	*s.*	*d.*
Archdeaconry of Oxford	263	116	1,410	10	5
———————— Berks	203	102	1,179	2	0
———————— Buckingham	220	92	931	12	2
Totals	686	310	3,521	4	7

The Society is still anxiously inquiring for well-qualified clergymen to send into the great mission-field of India; and the following letter on the subject has been addressed by the Archbishop of CANTERBURY to the Bishops, many of the principal persons in our Universities, and other active friends of the Society throughout the country:—

"Lambeth, June, 1858.

"It has recently been brought to my knowledge, as President of the Society for the Propagation of the Gospel, that, although a considerable fund has been already raised for the extension of the Indian Missions, the Society experiences great difficulty in finding properly qualified clergymen to occupy them.

"I venture, therefore, to request your good offices in making this fact known amongst the younger clergy, and to ask your co-operation in supplying an urgent want of our Church at this particular crisis.

"The Society could at once offer promising stations to six or eight additional Missionaries: and it is to be earnestly hoped that the missionary work of the Church will not be permitted to languish for want of men ready to devote themselves to the important object of preaching the Gospel amongst the heathen.

"I am, your faithful Servant,
"J. B. CANTUAR."

THE NATIONAL SOCIETY

FOR PROMOTING THE EDUCATION OF THE POOR IN THE PRINCIPLES OF THE ESTABLISHED CHURCH THROUGHOUT ENGLAND AND WALES.

Patron.—Her Majesty the Queen.
President.—His Grace the Archbishop of Canterbury.
Vice-Presidents.—His Grace the Archbishop of York, the Bishops, and ten Peers of the United Kingdom or Members of the Privy Council.
Secretary.—Rev. John G. Lonsdale, M.A.
Travelling Secretary.—F. S. Warren, Esq.
Depository Secretary.—Rev. A. Wilson, M.A.
Offices.—Broad Sanctuary, Westminster.

The following Grants have, at different periods, been voted by the NATIONAL
SOCIETY *towards building and fitting-up Schoolrooms and Teachers'
Residences, &c. in the Diocese of Oxford.*

DIOCESAN TRAINING INSTITUTION, CULHAM, ABINGDON .	£1,270
OXFORD BOARD—Book Grant	25
———— Teachers' Aid Fund . . .	50
HENLEY-ON-THAMES DEPÔT	5

OXFORD.		OXFORD (cont.)		BERKS (cont.)		BUCKINGHAM(cont.)	
Aston Rowant	£50	Warborough	£154	Longworth .	£20	Farnham Royal	£40
Bampton . .	25	Watlington . .	85	Lyford . . .	10	Grandborough .	15
Banbury . . .	50	Wendlebury .	15	Maidenhead .	150	Hampden . .	15
Benson . .	45	Westwell . .	20	Morton, South .	20	Hughenden Prest-	
Broughton Pogis	5	Wheatley . .	80	Oakley Green .	80	wood . . .	85
Charlton-on-Ot-		Wiggington . .	20	Reading, St.Mary	80	Hulcott . . .	20
moor . .	25	Witney . . .	55	Ruscombe and		Iver . . .	50
Chipping-Norton	75	Woodcote . .	80	Hurst . .	55	Kimble, Great .	10
Cottesford . .	12	Woodstock . .	20	Sandhurst and		Langley Marsh	25
Cropredy . .	85	Woolvercot . .	85	Newtown . .	100	Lavendon . .	50
Cuddesdon . .	70			Stanford in Vale	50	Leckhampstead	10
Culham . .	40			Steventon . .	10	Linsdale . . .	70
Deddington . .	50	BERKS.		Sunningdale .	80	Loudwater . .	70
Ducklington .	27	Abingdon . .	200	Swallowfield .	45	Ludgershall . .	25
Ensham . . .	160	Appleton . .	10	Thatcham . .	215	Marsh Gibbon	115
Enstone . . .	10	Arborfield . .	10	Uffington . .	25	Marston, North	40
Handborough .	60	Arlesley . .	84	Waltham, White	80	Marsworth . .	30
Harpsden . .	5	Ascot Heath . .	10	Wantage . .	80	Monk's Risboro'	10
Hendred, West	80	Aston Tirrold .	85	Wargrave . .	50	Nash . . .	30
Henley - on -		Beenham . .	18	Windsor, New .	100	Newport Pagnell	60
Thames . .	165	Bray . . .	85	Old . . .	40	Olney . . .	120
Hethe . . .	15	Brightwell . .	80	Trinity Church	80	Padbury . .	40
Hincksey, North	15	Buckland . .	88	Wittenham, Long	55	Penn	50
Horley . . .	20	Burghfield . .	60	Wokingham .	180	Preston Bisset .	20
Hornton . .	40	Burnham . .	20	Wootton . .	15	Prince's Risboro'	120
Ibstone . . .	25	Challow . .	28			Quainton . .	140
Kidlington . .	100	Charlton . .	7	BUCKINGHAM.		Skirmett . .	11
Launton . . .	50	Cookham . .	85			Stantonbury .	80
Leafield . . .	82	Cookham Deane	40	Aston Clinton .	30	Stoke-Goldington	78
Marston . . .	25	Crowmarsh . .	20	Aylesbury . .	125	Stoke-Hammond	80
Mapledurham .	75	Denchworth . .	25	Bierton . . .	10	Stoke-Poges .	40
Merton . . .	35	Drayton . . .	85	Bletchley . .	55	Stratford, Fenny	30
Milton, Great .	60	Faringdon . .	125	Boarstall . .	25	Stratford, Stony	82
Northleigh . .	86	Fulmer . . .	15	Brickhill, Little	25	Swanbourne .	60
Oxford, St. Ebbe's	55	Greenham . .	20	Brill . . .	12	Taplow . . .	15
St. Paul	105	Grove . . .	80	Buckingham .	115	Thornborough .	88
St. Thomas	25	Hampstead Norris	15	Burnham Taplow	100	Towersey . .	20
Summertown	30	Hanney . . .	40	Cadmore End .	25	Turvey . . .	80
Rollright, Great	20	Harwell . . .	20	Chalfont St.Giles	75	Upton . . .	30
Rotherfield Greys	25	Hatford . . .	5	Cheddington .	30	Upton & Chalvey	75
Sandford . .	20	Hermitage . .	15	Chesham . .	120	Waddesdon . .	50
Southstoke . .	25	Hungerford . .	100	Coleshill . .	20	Weston Under-	
Standlake . .	80	Hurst and Rus-		Colnbrook . .	65	wood . .	20
Stonesfield . .	25	combe . .	80	St. Thomas .	35	Whaddon . .	12
Swalcliffe . .	25	Ilsley, East . .	50	Crendon, Long .	15	Winslow . .	40
Sydenham . .	15	Knowle Hill .	50	Cuddington .	50	Wooburn . .	80
Tackley . .	25	Lamborne . .	80	Dinton . . .	10	Woughton . .	25
Tetsworth . .	40	Langford . .	70	Drayton Beau-		Wycombe, West	70
Tew, Little . .	10	Letcombe Regis	20	champ . . .	20	High . .	150
Thame . . .	80	Littlewall . .	10	Dunton . . .	15		

· *Places where the Society's Publications may be purchased.*

Banbury.—Mr. Rusher, High-street.
Bicester.—Mrs. Watkins.
Buckingham.—Mrs. Harris.
Oxford.—Mr. H. Spackman, Queen-street.
Thame.—Rev. J. Prosser, *Secretary.*

LOCAL TREASURERS.

OXFORD	{ Old Bank. F. J. Morrell, Esq.	Newbury . . .	Rev. C. Whittle.
Oxford Univ. Ch. Aid Assoc. .	{ Rev. E. Palin, *St.* *John's College.*	Olney	Rev. J. P. Langley.
		Shrivenham . .	Rev. C. B. Calley.
Amersham Deanery	Rev. T. Evetts.	Windsor	Rev. W. Bromehead.
Fenny Stratford .	Rev. H. Burney.	„ (Ch. Union)	Rev. J. Ellison.
Henley-on-Thames (district) . . .	{ Rev. H. H. Swinny, *Wargrave.*	READING	{ Rev. J. B. Colvill. H. B. Blandy, Esq.
Henley-on-Thames	Rev. Henry Benson.	Mortimore & Ufton	Rev. J. A. Clarke.
Hungerford . . .	Rev. W. J. Baron.	Aldermaston, &c. .	Rev. I. B. Burne.
Lamborne . . .	Rev. H. R. Hayward.	Nash, Winslow .	Rev. H. S. Templar.
Maidenhead . .	Rev. G. H. Hodson.	Wallingford . .	Rev. J. M. Collyns.
		Wantage	Rev. W. G. Sawyer.

For Diocesan Board in connection with the National Society, *vide* p. 76.

GOVERNMENT INSPECTORS,

(Appointed by the Committee of Council on Education.)

Inspectors of Church Schools for the County of Oxford.—REV. H. W. BELLAIRS.

Assistants.—REV. J. W. D. HERNAMAN, and REV. H. M. CAPEL.

Inspector for the County of Berks.—REV. W. P. WARBURTON.

Assistant.—REV. R. HUGHES.

Inspector for the County of Bucks.—REV. J. D. STEWARD.

INCORPORATED SOCIETY FOR PROMOTING THE ENLARGEMENT, BUILDING, AND REPAIRING OF CHURCHES AND CHAPELS. *Office in London*—7, Whitehall.

(Established 1818. Incorporated by Act of Parliament 1828.)

THE total number of applications made for aid since the formation of the Society in the year 1818, is 5,233. To 3,900 cases, grants have been made in aid of the erection of 1,127 additional Churches and Chapels, and the rebuilding, enlarging, or otherwise increasing the accommodation in 2,773 existing Churches and Chapels; by which means 1,032,781 additional seats have been obtained, 798,608 of which are set apart for the use of the poorer inhabitants; the sum contributed by the Society towards carrying these works into execution being £560,731. This amount has called forth a further expenditure on the part of the public of not less than £3,760,977.

The grants made last year amounted to £13,290; the additional seats will be 26,910, of which 22,935 will be free.

Of this sum £1,150 was voted to the Oxford diocese to obtain additional accommodation for 1,538 persons, and 1,787 additional free seats.

Windsor and Eton Church Union—Rev. H. J. Ellison (amount remitted since last Report) . . .	£29	16	0
Henley Deanery—Sec., Rev. D. Rawnsley ditto .	7	16	6
Oxford Church Aid Association . . .	73	16	7
Collection after sermons from places assisted . .	43	15	0
Total received from Oxford diocese .	£155	4	1

Secretary for Oxford—Rev. P. G. Medd, University College.

SOCIETY FOR PROMOTING THE EMPLOYMENT OF ADDITIONAL CURATES IN POPULOUS PLACES.

THE object of this Society is to increase the means of pastoral instruction and superintendence now possessed by the Church, working for the Church, and strictly in accordance with her rules.

The contributions of the past year to this Society amount in all to £26,713 11s. 11d.

Secretary for the Diocese of Oxford—Rev. R. GRESWELL.

Grants made to the Diocese of £130.

Shipton . . . £30 to meet £120 subscription.
Windsor, Holy Trinity 20 ,, . 80 ,,
Wooburn . . 80 met by 20 ,,

	£	s.	d.
Amount of subscriptions received from diocese	£113	19	9
Oxford University and City Association .	298	18	8
Annual subscriptions in diocese paid direct .	270	4	0
Total receipts . . .	£683	2	5

CHURCH MISSIONARY SOCIETY.

Office—Salisbury-square, London. Open daily from nine till six, Saturday excepted, when the office closes at 2 o'clock.

According to the Annual Report, the income of the Society during the past year amounted in all to £123,174, including £1,719 for the fund for disabled missionaries.

The returns of the contributions received from the diocese during the past year were not received from the Secretaries at the time of going to press.

Secretaries for Oxford and its vicinity — { Rev. E. A. Litton.
{ Rev. R. Gandell.

LONDON SOCIETY FOR PROMOTING CHRISTIANITY AMONGST THE JEWS.

(Instituted 1809.) *Office*—16, Lincoln's-Inn-Fields, London, W.C.
Oxford Association President—Rt. Rev. Lord Bishop of Oxford.
,, ,, *Secretaries*—Rev. J. West; Rev. G. T. Cameron.

The income of the Society for the year ending March 31, 1858, was—

	£	s.	d.
For general purposes	£28,795	18	8
Special purposes and Special Endowments . .	1,724	10	10
Dividends of Widows' and disabled Missionaries' Fund .	454	16	10
Total . . .	£31,368	4	0
Temporary Relief Fund	680	8	6

Remittances from this Diocese, 1857-8 :—

	£	s.	d.
Archdeaconry of Berks.	£522	13	11
Archdeaconry of Bucks.	95	9	8
Archdeaconry of Oxford	176	19	4
Total	£795	2	11

THE FRIEND OF THE CLERGY CORPORATION,

For allowing permanent pensions of not less than £30, and not exceeding £40 per annum, to the widows and orphan unmarried daughters of Clergymen of the Established Church.

For further particulars, vide Advertisement.

CLERGY ORPHAN SOCIETY.

(Founded 1749.)

ʀOR clothing, maintaining, and educating poor orphans of Clergymen of the Established Church in England and Wales, until of age to be put apprentice.

There are five orphans from the Diocese of Oxford at present in the Schools.

For further particulars, vide Advertisement, p. xxvii.

CHURCH PENITENTIARY ASSOCIATION.

Office—35, Lincoln's-Inn-Fields, London.

THE object of this Association is to promote the establishment, and assist in the maintenance, of Houses of Refuge and Penitentiaries for the reception and reformation of Fallen Women, Penitents; and, when desirable, to facilitate the emigration of such women.

Donations, Subscriptions, &c. received during the year £1,041 9 8
Special Donations, &c. 65 14 6

From the last Report, 1857-8, we learn that a grant was made to

House of Mercy at Clewer, of . . . £400
St. Mary's Home, Wantage, of . . . 100
House of Refuge at Oxford, of . . . 150

SCOTTISH EPISCOPAL CHURCH SOCIETY.

1. To provide a fund for the aged and infirm Clergymen, or salaries for their assistants.
2. To assist candidates for the ministry in completing their Theological Studies.
3. To provide Episcopal Schoolmasters, books, and tracts for the poor.
4. To assist in the formation or enlargement of Diocesan Libraries.

London Auxiliary Committee. Office—79, Pall-Mall.

District Secretaries, Diocese of Oxford— { Rev. H. W. Majendie, Speen.
{ Rev. W. D. Macray, Oxford.

The preceding Societies appear to be under the sanction, &c. of the Lord Bishop of the Diocese. The following do not.

CHURCH PASTORAL AID SOCIETY.

Plan.—To provide means for maintaining Curates and Lay-agents in largely-peopled districts.

Operations.—Grants for 376 Clergymen and 163 Lay-agents are made to 425 parishes or districts, with a total population of upwards of THREE MILLIONS AND A QUARTER, or about 7,600 souls to each incumbent.

Receipts for the past year, £41,109 9s. 8d. Expenditure, 42,677 18s. 9d. Amounts received from Auxiliary Associations, (with names of Secretaries, &c.):—

BERKSHIRE.

	£	s.	d.
FARINGDON—E. Thompson	49	2	1
NEWBURY—P. A. Longmore	38	4	7
READING—Revs. J. Field, W. Payne, and Lt.-Col. Bazett	170	2	2
SHALBOURNE—Rev. J. Gore	9	15	8
WALLINGFORD—E. Wells, Esq.	13	15	8
WINDSOR and ETON—Rev. H. J. Ellison	40	5	6

BUCKINGHAMSHIRE.

	£	s.	d.
AYLESBURY—Rev. F. Young	11	4	9

	£	s.	d.
IVER—Rev. W. S. Ward	22	14	1
GREAT MISSENDEN—Rev. J. Greaves	5	2	4

OXFORDSHIRE.

	£	s.	d.
OXFORD and OXFORDSHIRE—Rev. W. S. Bricknell, Rev. G. Cameron, and Rev. R. Gandell	68	12	8
BICESTER—Rev. J. W. Watts	23	9	6
THAME—Rev. J. Prosser and W. Toovey, Esq.	19	4	10

GRANTS MADE TO THE OXFORD DIOCESE, 1856 :—

BICESTER—For curate	.	.	£100
FARINGDON—For curate	.	.	60

THE RELIGIOUS TRACT SOCIETY.

THE object of this Society is the circulation of small religious books and treatises, in foreign countries as well as throughout the British dominions.

CONSTITUTION OF COMMITTEES.—The Auxiliaries combine on their committees Evangelical Churchmen and Dissenters. The object of the Society is to disseminate saving truth, leaving all topics of secondary moment to other channels. By a fundamental law, the Committee of the Parent Society consists—one-half of members of the Church of England, and one-half of Evangelical Nonconformists.—*Report*, 1858.

All orders for publications and remittances to be addressed to Mr. William Tarn, 56, Paternoster-row, E. C.

Total receipts for the year, including sales, &c., £88,730 9s.

Contributions from Auxiliaries in Diocese of Oxford :—

	£	s.	d.
HUNGERFORD	6	2	6
READING	12	4	0
NEWBURY	3	8	0
	21	14	6

	£	s.	d.
AMERSHAM	2	0	0
NEWPORT PAGNELL	1	10	9
	3	10	9

THE BRITISH AND FOREIGN BIBLE SOCIETY.

ESTABLISHED MARCH 7, 1804.

ITS sole object is the circulation of the Holy Scriptures, without note or comment, at home and abroad. There are now 156 languages or dialects in which the Society has promoted the distribution, printing, or translation of the Scriptures.

The issues of the Society both at home and abroad for the year ending March 31, 1858, amounted to 1,602,187 copies.

The year's receipts, for general purposes	.	.	£79,040
„ „ for special funds	.	.	3,265
„ „ for Bibles and Testaments	.	.	70,267

London Office—10, Earl-street, Blackfriars, E.C.

President—The Right Hon. the Earl of Shaftesbury. *Secretaries*—Rev. J. Mee and Rev. S. B. Bergne.

DIOCESAN AUXILIARY AND BRANCH SOCIETIES.

OXFORDSHIRE.

Secretaries.

County Society, at Oxford	J. D. Macbride, D.C.L. Rev. W. Hayward Cox, Rev. G. Cameron.
Bicester Ladies'	Mrs. Josiah Smith.
Chipping Norton	W. Fowler.
Deddington	Rev. H. D. Harington, J. Philpotts.
Thame	James Marsh.
Witney	Rev. G. C. Rolfe, J. Early, T. Skinner.
Banbury	J. G. Rusher, H. Beesley, T. Hunt.
Brailes	Rev. T. Smith.
Southam Branch	Rev. J. B. Bishop.
Benson	Mrs. H. Corsellis, Mrs. J. Burgis.
Henley	Rev. W. T. Hopkins, Rev. Jas. Rowland.
Watlington	Mr. Bracey.

BERKSHIRE.

Windsor & Eton	Rev. John Gore, Rev. S. Lillycrop, J. W. Caley.
Egham	Rev. W. Knight, H. C. Paice.
Abingdon	Rev. S. V. Lervis, Rev. S. Lepine.
Faringdon	Rev. E. Thompson, Rev. A. Major.
Shrivenham, Watchfield, &c.	G. Ferris, E. W. Moore, Rev. J. P. Larkin.

Secretaries.

Maidenhead	B. Cail, J. Poulton.
Cookham	T. Cahusac.
Newbury	Rev. H. March.
Hungerford Branch	A. Lanfear, T. Lanfear.
Reading	Rev. W. Legg, Rev. H. Hole.
Wallingford	Rev. J. Langley.
Wantage	John Lewis, T. Bennett.
Wokingham	Rev. C. H. Harcourt.

BUCKINGHAMSHIRE.

Aylesbury	Rev. F. Young, Rev. W. J. Gates.
Brill	Rev. F. C. Fairfax.
Waddesdon	Rev. W. Walton.
Wendover	Z. Phillips.
Chesham Ladies'	Mrs. Aylward.
Great Missenden	Rev. J. Greaves.
Marlow	E. Taylor.
North Bucks	Rev. E. L. Smith, Rev. S. Bellamy.
Brackley	Mrs. J. Green.
Fenny Stratford	Rev. Mr. Carter, Mr. Whitelock.
Newport Pagnell	Rev. Josiah Bull.
Slough Ladies'	Miss Griffith.
Stony Stratford, Wolverton, and Potterspury	Rev. J. Ashby.
Winslow	Rev. S. M. White.
Wycombe and South Bucks	Rev. H. Paddon, Rev. J. Hayden, W. Butler.
Beaconsfield Branch	Rev. J. Harsant, James Russell.

COLONIAL CHURCH AND SCHOOL SOCIETY.

THE Principles of the Society are Evangelical and Protestant, and special care is taken that its missionaries and agents should be persons of decided piety, intelligent acquaintance with the truth, and earnest devotion to the missionary work,—combining a cordial attachment to the United Church of England and Ireland, with the exercise of a spirit of love towards Protestants of other communions.

Treasurer—R. C. L. Bevan, Esq.

Secretary—Rev. Mesac Thomas, M.A.

Offices—9, Serjeants' Inn, Fleet-street, London.

For further particulars, vide Advertisement, p. xxvi.

IRISH CHURCH MISSIONS TO THE ROMAN CATHOLICS.

Office—11, Buckingham-street, Adelphi.

According to the last report the income amounted to £27,164.

Secretary for Oxford—Rev. G. W. Langstaff.

Hon. Secretaries for Oxfordshire—Rev. J. G. Browne, Kiddington; Rev. H. A. Tyndale, Holton.

Hon Sec. for Buckinghamshire—Rev. J. Greaves, Great Missenden.

EDUCATIONAL FOUNDATIONS AND INSTITUTIONS IN THE DIOCESE.

For the "UNIVERSITY OF OXFORD," *vide* p. 40 of this Calendar.

ETON COLLEGE.

Founded by Henry VI., 1441.

Visitor for Final Appeal—The Archbishop of Canterbury.
Visitor—The Bishop of Lincoln.
Provost—Rev. E. C. Hawtrey, D.D. 1853.

Fellows.

Vice-Provost—Rev. Thos. Carter. 1857.

Rev. J. F. Plumptre, M.A.	1822	Rev. J. Wilder, M.A.	1840
Rev. G. R. Green, M.A.	1833	Rev. C. Luxmoore, M.A.	1853
Rev. G. J. Dupuis, M.A.	1838	Rev. E. Coleridge, M.A.	1857

Conducts.

Rev. C. K. Paul, B.A.　　T. H. Roper, M.A.　　H. S. Eyre, M.A.

Head Master—Rev. Charles O. Goodford, D.D.
Lower Master—Rev. W. A. Carter, M.A.

Assistants, Upper School.

Rev. F. Durnford, M.A.	Rev. C. Wolley, M.A.	Rev. C. C. James, M.A.
Rev. E. Balston, M.A.	Russell Day, M.A.	E. D. Stone, M.A.
Rev. J. E. Yonge, M.A.	A. F. Birch, M.A.	Rev. F. St. John Thackeray, M.A.
W. Johnson, Esq., M.A.	Rev. W. B. Marriott, M.A.	
Rev. J. Leigh Joynes, M.A.	Rev. W. Wayte, M.A.	H. Snow, B.A.

Assistants, Lower School.

Rev. W. L. Eliot, M.A.	Rev. W. L. Hardisty, M.A.
Rev. J. W. Hawtrey, M.A.	R. G. Dupuis, B.A.

Mathematical Assistants.

Rev. S. T. Hawtrey, M.A.	Rev. F. J. Ottley, M.A.	F. G. Crump, M.A.
Rev. G. Frewer, M.A.	Rev. J. Grainger, M.A.	R. Hudson, B.A.
	Rev. E. Hale, M.A.	

St. PETER'S COLLEGE, RADLEY.

Warden—The Rev. W. Sewell, D.D., Fellow of Exeter Coll., Oxford.
Sub-Warden—The Rev. W. Wood, M.A., Fellow of Trinity Coll., Oxford.
Precentor—E. G. Monk, Mus. Doc., Oxford.

Fellows.

Capt. W. Haskoll, R.N., *Bursar*.	Rev. W. H. Ranken, M.A.
Rev. R. Gibbings, M.A.	William Barber, B.A.
Rev. H. T. T. West, M.A.	Rev. R. W. Norman, M.A.
Hon. H. C. Forbes, M.A.	Rev. S. Andrews, M.A.
Rev. R. S. Wilson, M.A.	W. G. G. Austin, M.A.

Honorary Fellows.

Rev. Sir F. G. Ouseley, Bart., M.A.　　Hon. Arthur Gordon, M.A.
Rev. J. W. Burgon, B.D.

Drawing and Design—W. H. F. Hutchesson, Esq.
French—Mons. Bué, Professor in the Taylor Institution, Oxford.
Treasurer—Robert Burleigh Sewell.

Students limited to 150.

ST. ANDREW'S COLLEGE, BRADFIELD, BERKS.

Visitor—The Lord Bishop of the Diocese.
Warden—The Rev. T. Stevens, M.A., Oriel College, Oxford.
Sub-Warden—Rev. J. Marriott, M.A., Oriel College, Oxford.
Head Master—Rev. R. E. Sanderson, M.A., Lincoln Coll., Oxford.
Second Master—Mr. J. G. Gresson, M.A., Exeter College, Oxford.
Assistant Masters.

Composition Rev. G. B. Morley, M.A.	*Mathematics* Rev. G. R. Roberts, M.A.
Classics—Mr. T. J. Nunns, B.A.	„ Mr. Tapsfield.
„ Rev. R. Hammond, M.A.	*Modern Languages* } Mr. W. C. Ingram, B.A.

Music—Mr. R. L. Binfield.

Terms—One hundred guineas a-year.

Scholarships.—Two Scholarships, value twenty guineas a-year, to be held with good conduct for five years, are open, on the 18th of August every year, to boys of St. Andrew's College, who are under 12 years of age.

Exhibitions.—Thirty pounds a-year are to be given (for the three years of undergraduate residence) to any boys of St. Andrew's College who shall be elected, by merit, to open Scholarships in the University of Oxford, or of Cambridge.

COWLEY SCHOOL,

(OXFORD DIOCESAN CENTRAL).

Established 1841.   Number limited to 100 Boarders.
Head Master—Mr. Robert Hurman.

The Terms are £27 per annum, without any additional charge for School-books, Stationery, or Tuition.

Grammar Schools, &c.

ABINGDON.

Free Grammar-School. 1563.

Patrons—The Corporation.

Free to sixty-three boys of the town or neighbourhood.

Income from endowment, £140.

Exhibitions—Five Scholarships to Pembroke College, Oxford. Of these, one will be filled up annually: each is of the value of £50 per annum, or more, with rooms rent free, and is tenable for five years. Any boy educated in the school may be a candidate for its Scholarships after a residence of two years.

Head Master—Rev. W. A. Strange, D.D.

Second Master—Rev. E. T. H. Harper, M.A.

Mathematical—F. G. Howell, Esq.

French Master—M. de Briou.

Scholars in 1858—Sixty-eight.

AMERSHAM, Buckinghamshire.

Dr. Challoner's Grammar-School. 1622.

Patrons—Trustees.

Free to youths of the parish under 18 years of age, in Latin and Greek only. Every pupil pays one guinea per quarter.

Income from endowment, £66, and house rent free.

Head Master—Rev. E. Luce, M.A.

Scholars in 1858—Sixteen.

AYLESBURY, Buckinghamshire.

Free Grammar-School. 1620. Foundation increased 1714.

Patrons—Fourteen trustees.

Free to a limited number of the sons of inhabitants.

Income from endowment, £600.

Head Master—Rev. T. Gwynn, M.A.

Second „ Mr. Hen. C. Barber.

Third „ Mr. Wm. Crasler.

Scholars in 1858—120 on the foundation, 1 not free.

BAMPTON, Oxfordshire.
Free Grammar-School. 1670.
Patrons — The three Vicars of Bampton.
For the sons of inhabitants of Bampton, and of the surrounding hamlets.
Income from endowment, £20.
Head Master—Mr. E. R. Farbrother.
Scholars in 1858 — The present number of boys, twenty-two; all day-pupils.

BURFORD, Oxfordshire.
Grammar-School. 1571.
Patrons—Alderman, Steward, Bailiffs, and Burgesses of the borough.
Free to grammar-scholars.
Income from endowment, £85.
Master—Mr. William Young.
Scholars in 1858—Sixty.

CHIPPING-NORTON, Oxon.
Free Grammar-School. 1547.
Patrons—The Corporation.
Free to four sons of poor tradesmen.
Income—About £17, with house.
Head Master—Mr. Ed. R. Hartley.
Scholars in 1858—Four free, seventy private.

DORCHESTER.
Free Grammar-School, 1632.
Income, £10.
Head Master—
The old Grammar-School now used as a Parochial School.

EWELME, Oxfordshire.
Hospital School. 1436.
The Hospital School building has been since Michaelmas, 1830, used for the purposes of a parochial school. It is now under Government inspection.

HENLEY-ON-THAMES, Oxon.
Royal Free Grammar-School of James I. 1605.
Patrons—Trustees.
Visitor, The Lord Bishop of Oxford.

All scholars pay £6 per annum.
Income from endowment, portion of £362.
Head Master—Rev. C. H. S. Godby, D.C.L.
Second ,, L. Clarkson, Esq.
Math. ,, J. Froysell, Esq., M.A.
Scholars in 1858—Fifty-four.

HIGH WYCOMBE. Bucks.
Royal Grammar-School, 1562.
Patrons—Trustees.
Free to fifteen boys of the borough.
Anticipated value of the endowment for school and almshouses, £600.
Head Master—Rev. James Poulter, M.A. Salary, £150; house, rates, and tax free, with half cap. fees.
Second Master—Mr. Edw. Coombes. Salary, £70, and quarter cap. fees, &c.
See Advertisement.

HUNGERFORD. Berkshire.
Free Grammar-School. 1653.
Patrons — Vicar, Churchwardens, and Burgesses.
Free to nine boys, sons of the inhabitants.
Income, £20, and house.
Head Master—Mr. Hives.
Scholars in 1858—Nine free; total, forty-eight.

MARLOW. Buckinghamshire.
Free School. Founded 1624.
Governors—Sir Geo. E. Nugent, Bart., and twelve feoffees.
Free to twenty-four boys of the parishes of Great Marlow, Little Marlow, and Medmenham; and twenty-four girls, to be taught to make bone-lace.
Income, from endowment.
Master—Mr. E. Segrave.
Scholars in 1858—Twenty-four.

NEWBURY. Berkshire.
Free Grammar-School. From time immemorial forming part of the Hospital of St. Bartholomew, to

which a charter was granted by King John in 1216.

Patrons—The Municipal Trustees.

Free, by the new scheme, to twenty boys; numbers to be increased as the funds admit.

Income from endowment, £100, with £12 from the Exchequer, and a house, free of all expenses.

Head Master—Rev. W. Cole.

Second Master—Mr. C. H. Sanders.

French and Drawing-Master—Mr. G. R. Oldham.

Scholars in 1858—Forty-one.

OXFORD. New College School.

Patron—The Warden.

Free to sixteen choristers, on payment of £10 per annum.

Head Master—Rev. W. Tuckwell, M.A.

Terms for Boarders not on the Foundation, are sixty guineas; for Day-scholars, the sons of gentlemen living in Oxford, twenty pounds a-year.

OXFORD. Magdalen College School. 1480.

Patron—President of Magdalen College.

Free to sixteen choristers on the Foundation of the College.

Exhibitions—The Shepherd Exhibitions, viz. one of £40 a-year, tenable for four years, and one of £10 and two of £5, which are competed for annually, two of £35 per ann. for ex-choristers, and the Greene and Ellerton Exhibitions of £5 confined to choristers.

Head Master—Rev. J. E. Millard, B.D., Fellow of Magd. Coll.

Usher—Rev. W. J. Sawell, M.A.

Assist.-Masters—Rev. H. H. Minchin, M.A.; Rev. H. E. Garnsey, B.D., C. Griffith, B.A.

Scholars in 1857—Fifty-eight.

OXFORD. Christ Church School. 1546.

Patrons—The Dean and Chapter.

Head Master—Rev. J. Baker, M.A.

Second „ —Rev. T. Evans, M.A.

Number of Pupils—Forty-one.

READING. Berkshire.

Grammar-School. 1486.

Patrons—The Mayor and Town Council.

Sons of residents admitted on payment of ten guineas per annum.

Income from endowment, about £50.

Exhibitions—Two Fellowships at St. John's College, Oxford, founded by Sir Thomas White, were attached to the school, which the University Commissioners are about to commute into two Scholarships of £100 per annum each, tenable for five years.

Four Scholarships of £10 10s. per annum, for boys of fourteen years of age and upwards, tenable for four years at the school, are in the course of foundation. Two of these are now in operation.

Head Master—Rev. Robert Appleton, M.A., Pembroke College, Oxford.

Second Master—Rev. J. H. Appleton, B.A.

Assistant—Vacant.

German and French—Dr. Lehfeldt.

Drawing-Master—Mr. Streater.

Scholars in 1858—Twenty-five.

STEEPLE ASTON. Oxon.

Free Grammar-School. 1640.

Patrons—Brasenose College.

Head Master—

THAME. Oxfordshire.

Free Grammar-School. 1558.

Patrons—New College, Oxford, and Earl of Abingdon.

Head Master—Rev. T. B. Fooks, D.C.L.

WALLINGFORD. Berkshire.

Free Grammar-School. 1659.

Patrons—The Trustees.

Free to six boys.

Income from endowment, £26 per annum.

Master—

Scholars in 1858—Forty-five.

WANTAGE. Berkshire.
Free Grammar-School.
Patrons — The Governors of the Town-lands.
Head Master—Rev. C. H. Crooke, B.A.
Scholars in 1857—Thirty.
The present schools were built in 1850, in commemoration of the one thousandth anniversary of King Alfred's birth, but the foundation dates from Queen Elizabeth. The education is commercial and classical.
See Advertisement.

WITNEY. Oxfordshire.
Grammar-School. 1660.
Patrons·—The Grocers' Company.
Visitor—The Provost, &c. of Oriel College.

Free to ten scholars whose parents are not assessed to the poor's rate. The National and other schools now absorb this class.
Income from endowment, £63.
Head Master—Rev. H. Gregory, M.A.
Assistant Master—Mr. C. Collier.
Scholars in 1858—Twenty-nine.

WOODSTOCK. Oxfordshire.
Free Grammar-School. 1585.
Trustees—The Corporation.
Free to all boys in the borough, on the payment of one guinea per quarter.
Income from endowment, about £50, besides a residence.
Master—Rev. E. Reddall.

A LIST OF OTHER SCHOOLS.

AYLESBURY, (Temple-square).— Mr. J. E. H. Bingle, assisted by resident English and Foreign masters. Established to give a good sound education on Church-of-England principles.

BANBURY, (Parade). — Mr. W. Hartley. Classical and commercial education.

CAVERSHAM House Academy, Reading.—The course of instruction embraces every branch of a sound commercial education. Boarders at present, 100.
See Advertisement.

LANGLEY-HOUSE, near Slough, Bucks. — Rev. Henry Thomas Attkins, M.A. For classical and general education.

MAIDENHEAD, (Craufurd College). —The instruction founded on the requirements of the Oxford regulations for the examination of non-members of the University. *Principal*—J. D. M. Pearce, M.A. *First Master*—J. Eagleston, Esq., B.A. *Second Master*—J. Skinner, A.M. Pupils, 100.

NEWBURY: Woodspeen Academy. —Mr. C. E. Johnstone, M. C. P. Church of England School for the middle classes.

OXFORD, (New-Inn-Hall-street). —Mr. Andrews. Classical and Commercial School. Scholars, 40. *Diocesan.*

SOULBURY SCHOOL, Bucks., near Leighton Buzzard.—Mr. William Blundy, L.R.C.P. For the education of the children of the neighbourhood according to the principles of the Established Church. Scholars, 40.

SPEEN Hill, Newbury.—Mr. W. H. Bew. Classical, Mathematical, and Commercial Boarding-School. Pupils, average, 60 Boarders.

STOKE POGES.—Rev. J. Culling Evans, M.A. Classical Preparatory School, especially for Eton and Winchester. From 20 to 30 Pupils.

THAME, Howard-house Academy. —Mr. Jas. Marsh. Adapted especially for preparing youths for mercantile pursuits.
See Advertisement.

UXBRIDGE, (Cave-house).—Mr. J. Hunt, M.C.P. Classical, Commercial, and Scientific. 50 Pupils.

WALLINGFORD, (South-bridge-house). Mr. John Webb. To educate in the principles of the Established Church, and to impart such instruction as is necessary for the ordinary duties of life.

WANTAGE Church School for young ladies, under Mrs. Dynham, assisted by resident French and German governesses. For Terms apply to Mrs. Dynham.

WENDOVER, (Chiltern-house).— Mr. C. H. Fuller. Commercial School. Terms 32 guineas. Limited to 26 Scholars.

WINDSOR, (Peascod-st.).—Mr. H. J. Frowd, L.C.P. Classical and Commercial School. 60 Scholars.

WOKINGHAM.—Mr. W. C. Beechey and Sons. Classical, Mathematical, and Commercial School, conducted strictly in accordance with the principles of the Established Church. Number of pupils, 38.

THE RECORD OF THE DIOCESE DURING THE PAST YEAR.

This " Record " has been compiled chiefly from information rendered by the Incumbents of the various parishes. It has a twofold object ; the one to exhibit the energy and activity which prevails in the diocese, and the progress of the Church generally ; the other, to afford a source of reference for dates and events which, as years roll on, will become of historical and practical value. The list, it is feared, is not quite complete. No pains have been spared on the part of the Editor to render it so, but it is hoped that when the object is understood, all the clergy in the diocese will send notice of what takes place of importance in their respective parishes, so that a complete Annual Register may be thus supplied, accessible to every one. The numbers are the same as in the Clergy List, pp. 94—127.

For the Confirmations, Ordinations, &c., vide pp. 104—106.

19. Thame. An acre of land has been added to the burying-ground.
25. Bicester. July 6. Foundation-stone of parish school laid by the Rev. J. W. Watts. The school, which will accommodate ahout 400 children, will be opened on Lady-day next. The expense met by a public subscription and a government grant.
28. Cottisford. A teacher's house has been attached to the schoolroom.
29. Finmere. The nave of the church has been restored, and a new aisle added on the north side.
30. Fringford. The south aisle and porch rebuilt, and church and chancel restored. Omitted in *Record* for 1857.
34. Hethe. This church is undergoing restoration and enlargement. It will provide accommodation for 240.
43. Piddington. A school and master's house is in process of erection.
47. Stratton. Oct. 4. The Parochial and Commercial School re-opened.
70. Baldon. In November, 1857, the late rector, the Rev. Hugh Willoughby, was succeeded by the present rector, the Rev. H. S. M. Hubert.
75. Cuddesdon. On June 1 the fourth anniversary of the Cuddesdon Theological College was celebrated, when a very large assemblage met in the Bishop's Palace in honour of the occasion. The sermon was preached by Dr. Jelf, Canon of Christ Church, and Principal of King's College, London. After the service, about 400 ladies and

gentlemen sat down to a most hospitable entertainment provided for them in a tent in the grounds. Among these were the Bishops of Sodor and Man, Guiana, and Capetown; Sir Wm. Heathcote, Bart., Sir S. Glynn, Bart., Canon Wordsworth, and most of the principal clergy of the diocese, together with a large number of members of the University.

76. Culham. On Thursday and Friday, the 29th and 30th of August, the third yearly meeting of the Oxford Diocesan Schoolmasters' Association was held, and was fully as successful as its predecessors. On Thursday the Prize Essay, On the best Method of influencing Pupil-teachers, was read; a Lecture on London in the 16th century was delivered by the Rev. J. Lawrell, and the Rev. T. Jackson gave some reminiscences of schools in Holland, France, and Germany. On Friday there was a discussion on evening schools and an excursion to Nuneham, and the routine business of the Association was transacted. The papers read were extremely valuable. The Prize Essay was gained by Mr. Hughes, of the Blue-coat School, Oxford, and the Bishop's prize was presented to him. The Essay gave rise to a very long and interesting discussion, in the course of which several cases of pupil-teachers' difficulties which had actually happened were mentioned, and the mode of treatment in each discussed with great ability. The Bishop was present at Mr. Lawrell's lecture on Thursday, and at the meeting on Friday morning, which resulted in several rules for the conducting of evening schools, and a plan, which will be forwarded to Government, for the supply of masters to take charge of evening classes in certain cases.

85. Milton. Five windows in the church have been filled with stained glass from the works of Messrs. Clayton and Bell.

87. Newington. The schoolroom, with a school-house attached, has been completed at the expense of the rector.

92. Waterstock. The church of St. Leonard has been restored, and the number of the sittings increased; the cost defrayed entirely by the Ashhurst family.

93. Wheatley. May 5. The school was this day opened. It has been erected by subscription, and contains two large class-rooms and a teacher's residence.

108. Milcomb. The chancel is in process of re-building by Eton College and its lessees.

121. Harpsden. Feb. 6. A new school-house, with teacher's residence, opened.

123. Kidmore-End. A parsonage-house has been built on the glebe land at a cost of £1,400.

135. Hambleden. The church is undergoing restoration. When completed the accommodation will be, in the parish church 500, in Frieth Chapel 150, and in Skirmett School Chapel 60.

140. Charlton-on-Otmoor. The church has been completely restored, the chancel partially so.

163. South Stoke. April 13. The church re-opened after careful restoration.

166. Whitchurch. Nov. 4. This church was re-opened, having, during the last fourteen months, been almost entirely rebuilt. The old structure consisted of a nave and chancel, wooden tower and spire, of not very mediæval design. The very meagre accommodation for the poor was the immediate cause of the alteration, which has been most happily carried out. The seats of the church are all open, low, equally commodious and uniform.

170. Oxford. St. Clement's. July 5. Died at Southampton, aged 37, the Rev. James Nicholas Moody, the rector of this parish.

171. St. Ebbe's. The Lenten Sermons preached at this church were as follows :—

Feb. 17, *The Repentance of David*, by the Rev. H. B. W. Churton.
   „ 19, *The Repentance of Esau*, by the Rev. J. L. Hoskyns.
   „ 24, *The Repentance of Judas*, by the Rev. Canon Heurtley.
   „ 26, *The Repentance of Ahab*, by the Rev. Henry Mackenzie.
March 3, *The Convictions of Balaam*, by the Ven. Archdeacon Bickersteth.
   „   5, *The Goodness of King Joash*, by the Rev. D. Moore.
   „ 10, *The Convictions of Pilate*, by the Rev. Wm. Fremantle.
   „ 12, *The Convictions of Felix*, by the Lord Bishop of Antigua.
   „ 17, *The Convictions of Agrippa*, by the Lord Bishop of Ripon.
   „ 19, *The Change of Saul into St. Paul*, by the Rev. H. Linton.
   „ 24, *The Repentance and Despair of King Saul*, by the Rev. G. T. Cameron.
   „ 26, *The Repentance of St. Peter*, by the Rev. A. W. Thorold.
   „ 31, *The Penitent Thief*, by the Lord Bishop of Capetown.

172. St. Giles'. The Lenten Sermons preached at this church were as follows :—

Feb. 17, *The Repentance of David*, by the Rev. Canon Stanley.
   „ 19, *The Repentance of Esau*, by the Lord Bishop of Oxford.
   „ 24, *The Repentance of Judas*, by the Rev. Dr. Goulburn.
   „ 26, *The Repentance of Ahab*, by the Rev. R. P. Liddon.
March 3, *The Convictions of Balaam*, by the Rev. John Lawrell.
   „   5, *The Goodness of King Joash*, by the Rev. R. Drury.
   „ 10, *The Convictions of Pilate*, by the Rev. R. R. Swinny.
   „ 12, *The Convictions of Felix*, by the Rev. F. K. Leighton.
   „ 17, *The Convictions of Agrippa*, by the Rev. the Provost of Queen's College.
   „ 19, *The Change of Saul into St. Paul*, by the Rev. W. Butler.
   „ 24, *The Repentance and Despair of King Saul*, by the Rev. Dr. Hook.
   „ 26, *The Repentance of St. Peter*, by the Rev. T. T. Carter.
   „ 31, *The Penitent Thief*, by the Rev. T. B. Morrell.

176. Oxford. St. Mary Magdalen. May 18. On the departure of the late esteemed vicar (the Rev. Jacob Ley,) a handsome testimonial of plate was presented to him. He had been vicar of the parish for more than twelve years.

177. St. Mary's-the-Virgin. The Lenten Sermons preached at this church were as follows :—

Feb. 17, *The Repentance of David*, by the Lord Bishop of Oxford.
   „ 19, *The Repentance of Esau*, by the Lord Bishop of Lincoln.
   „ 24, *The Repentance of Judas*, by the Lord Bishop of Salisbury.
   „ 26, *The Repentance of Ahab*, by the Rev. J. M. Woodford.
March 3, *The Convictions of Balaam*, by the Rev. Dr. Moberly.
   „   5, *The Goodness of King Joash*, by the Rev. Jas. Randall.
   „ 10, *The Convictions of Pilate*, by the Rev. Canon Champneys.
   „ 12, *The Convictions of Felix*, by the Very Rev. the Dean of Westminster.
   „ 17, *The Convictious of Agrippa*, by the Rev. Canon Pusey.
   „ 19, *The Change of Saul into St. Paul*, by the Rev. Canon Wordsworth.
   „ 24, *The Repentance and Despair of King Saul*, by the Lord Bishop of London.
   „ 26, *The Repentance of St. Peter*, by the Rev. Dr. Hook.
   „ 31, *The Penitent Thief*, by the Rev. T. L. Claughton.

177. Oxford. St. Mary's. Sept. 15. At the residence of his brother, at Bradfield, died the Rev. Charles Marriott, vicar of this parish. The following is partly extracted from an account of his life which appeared in the "Literary Churchman" for Oct. 1, a journal of which he was one of the original promoters, and sole editor up to the time of his illness.

"The Church of England and theological literature have sustained a heavy loss in the death of the Rev. Charles Marriott, who died on Sept. 15, having been entirely prostrated for the last three years by an attack of paralysis, which seized him in the very prime of manhood, and in the full career of those useful labours in which he was so actively engaged, and under which at last he sank.

"Mr. Marriott was distinguished from his youth by his earnest, conscientious, and thoughtful character. Even trivial matters, which many do not consider worth thinking about, but on which much often depends, were duly weighed and considered by him. In society he was generally silent and thoughtful, but very observant of all that was going on around him, seldom speaking unless spoken to, and then often taking several minutes before he gave an answer to a question which had perhaps been asked heedlessly, but of which he saw all the bearings better than the person who had asked it, and would not give his answer until he had turned them all over in his mind; and then it would be so cautious and guarded, that it was sometimes difficult to fathom his meaning; but when the hearers had arrived at it, they found a depth in it which they had little anticipated. Such conversation was often remembered for years afterwards. It was easy then to see that this was no ordinary man, and as he advanced in years and his judgment ripened, he became more decided and positive in his views, and better estimated both by friends and opponents.

" As far as religious literature is concerned, although we must lament that a man of his extraordinary learning and thoughtful mind should have left so little of his own writings behind him, yet enough remains to shew in some degree what he would have done if leisure had been allowed him, and he had not given himself so much to the service of his friends."

Amongst the works he has left behind, and by which his name is best known, are the " Hints for Private Devotion," a small book, but for deep thoughtfulness and the suggestion of thoughts to others, this work is perhaps unrivalled. His *Analecta Christiana* consists of extracts from the Fathers, for the use of students in divinity. His " Reflections on a Lent Reading of the Epistle to the Romans" is intended to accompany the study of the whole Epistle distributed through a series of days. We have also two volumes of sermons from his pen, one consisting chiefly of University Sermons, the other of discourses delivered in the chapel of Bradfield College. In addition he published numerous single sermons. Amongst these should be especially mentioned " Five Sermons on the Principles of Faith," the Sermon on the death of the Duke of Wellington, entitled " Singleness of Purpose the secret of Success," and in 1854, on the occasion of the Patriotic Fund, " The Unity of the Spirit," all of which were preached at St. Mary's Church, Oxford. Besides the " Hints for Private Devotion," he published a " Selection of Prayers," and edited a small volume of " Preces Privatæ," &c., which had originally been printed in 1567. He contributed articles to the " Christian Remembrancer," and assisted Dr. Pusey in translating and editing several volumes of the Library of the Fathers. He also superintended the publication of " The Life and Times of Hincmar," and a series of " Lectures on the History of England." His last undertaking was the editorship of the " Literary Churchman," to which he contributed several valuable papers.

178. Oxford, St. Michael's. June 12. The decision in the Consistory Court was this day delivered against the churchwardens. The facts of the case are simply these. A gentleman of the name of Elliott, on a rate of 2*d.* in the pound being proposed, moved as an amendment a ½*d.* rate; a show of hands was taken; the show of hands was against Mr. Elliott's proposition, but by an extremely slender majority. After the show of hands, Mr. Elliott demanded a poll, and not unnaturally, considering the small difference in numbers on the show of hands.

This demand was refused by the chairman, acting, no doubt, quite conscientiously. The original proposition for a 2d. rate was then put, and carried, also by an extremely slender majority. The churchwardens proceeded to assess the rate, and a gentleman of the name of Luff refused to pay it. It was decided that Mr. Elliott had by the canon law the right to demand and have a poll on the *amendment*, and this not having been allowed, the rate was declared invalid.

181. Oxford, St. Peter's-in-the-East. Sept. 29th (the Feast of St. Michael and all Angels). The Rev. Edmund Hobhouse, for some years vicar of this parish, was consecrated in Lambeth Church Bishop of Nelson. The sermon was preached on the occasion by the Lord Bishop of this Diocese. The consecrating prelates were the Archbishop of Canterbury, the Bishops of London, Lichfield, and Oxford.

On Wednesday, Oct. 27, a large number of persons, principally inhabitants of St. Peter's-in-the-East, assembled in the hall of Merton College for the purpose of witnessing the presentation of a testimonial to the newly consecrated Bishop of Nelson, in grateful recognition of his services as vicar of the above parish for a period of seventeen years. The testimonial was placed on the table at the head of the hall, and consisted of a silver-gilt Communion Service, of a large and handsome pattern, an alms-box made of oak, ornamented with elaborate iron scroll-work, bearing an appropriate inscription, the whole being accompanied with a list of the subscribers to the testimonial fund, beautifully engrossed on vellum. The Bishop took leave of his congregation at Oxford on Advent Sunday, using for the first time the very handsome Communion Service presented by them to him as a testimonial. Never did a bishop quit the shores of England for his distant diocese with more fervent prayers for his welfare here and hereafter than the Bishop of Nelson.

182. Summertown. The church was re-opened on June 11, having been furnished with new and open seats throughout, and a new chancel and vestry added. The weekly offertory has since been established with marked success.

191. Brizenorton. July 10. Died, at Bampton, aged 89, the Rev. John Penson, vicar of this parish.

196. Ducklington. A national school-room and teacher's residence were erected in the course of last year on an eligible spot contiguous to the church.

198. Holwell. The living is further indebted to the liberality of William Hervey, sen., Esq., of Bradwell Grove, for an addition of £25 per annum, secured on the rectorial tithes, by a deed dated Oct. 15, 1858, making a total of £60 per annum thus given by the above-named patron and benefactor, who also rebuilt the parish church, and endowed the school with £8 per annum.

199. Kencot. The church has been partly restored, and the chancel windows filled with stained glass as a memorial to the late Rev. James Thorold.

205. Swinbrook. The Rev. W. Raine, incumbent, died Jan. 5, 1858.

220. Eynsham. An excellent foreign organ has been erected at the expense of Mr. G. Pinfold, late Vicar's churchwarden, and a night-school opened in the national school-room, attended by fifty or sixty boys.

234. Yarnton. Oct. 26. Died, at Oxford, aged 83, the Rev. Vaughan Thomas. He was promoted to the vicarage of Yarnton in 1803, by the patron, Sir George Dashwood, Bart. He held other livings in different

dioceses. He obtained his degree of B.A. in 1796, M.A. in 1800, and B.D. in 1809.

240. North Hincksey. The foundation-stone of a school-room and master's residence was laid on June 20, 1857. The school was opened on New Year's Day, 1858.

248. Radley. On Trinity Monday the Bishop of Oxford held his annual confirmation in the chapel of St. Peter's College, Radley; and on the Sunday following his Lordship preached both in the chapel and in the parish church. The confirmation was held in the presence of the college, the parents of the candidates, and the Bishop of Sodor and Man, the Bishop of Guiana, and the Bishop of Capetown. After the ceremony the usual Latin speech was delivered by the senior prefect in the school; after which the company, about seventy in number, were entertained at luncheon in the college hall. In the course of the addresses allusion was made to the honours recently gained by students. There have been within nearly the last twelve months three open scholarships at Oxford, and two good-conduct swords—a very rare honour—at Woolwich; while five out of nine young officers in India have already been honourably mentioned in public despatches.

256. Buckland. A new school-room opened, Sept. 18, 1857. (Omitted in last record.)

268. Shrivenham. May 4. Watchfield Chapel, erected by subscription in the place of one pulled down in 1799, was this day consecrated.

274. Bray. A chapel-of-ease at Oakley Green, which serves also as a school-room, was opened in February, giving a third school to the parish, and affording an additional service every Sunday for 200 persons.

276. Cookham. Sept. 7. New schools, erected at a cost of £1500, were opened this day.

276*. Boyne Hill. The Church of All Saints, Boyne Hill, was consecrated on Dec. 8, 1857. The buildings, which are wholly of brick, together form three sides of a quadrangle, on the north being the church, on the east the parsonage, and on the south a spacious school. The west side is bounded by the road, and in the centre stands a cross. The church consists of a nave, with two aisles divided by clustered columns, and a magnificent chancel separated by a screen. The columns are of stone, the arches being of stone and brick, serrated at the edges, and placed in alternate courses. The walls are of red brick, interspersed with black; the chancel presents a magnificent combination of colours by the use of bricks and stone of various hues; and the east end is resplendent with alabaster and inlaid marbles, of which the prevailing colour is white, which shone most brilliantly when the church was lighted with gas. We should add that the church was designed and mainly built at the cost of Miss Emily Hulme, a daughter of the Rev. W. Hulme, a clergyman well known and most highly respected at Reading; and when this lady was relieved of some considerable portion of the expense by the voluntary offerings of members of Mr. Gresley's (now vicar of the parish) former congregation at St. Paul's, Brighton, she nobly devoted what was so saved to her to the building of a handsome school chapel at another end of the parish of Bray, which is now nearly completed.

Oct. 1, 1858. This day, a commission issued by the Bishop of Oxford, under the Church Discipline Act, on the requisition of the Vicar and certain inhabitants of the parish of Stoke, to investigate the charges alleged against the Rev. R. T. West, curate of the district church of

Randall, archdeacon of Berkshire; the Rev. J. Austen Leigh, vicar of Bray, and rural dean; Mr. Charles Sawyer, of Heywood-lodge; and Mr. J. Hibbert, of Braywick-lodge. The Deputy-Registrar of the diocese, Mr. John Davenport, acted as secretary to the Commission. The following was the judgment:—

"The Commissioners, having paid the best attention in their power to the evidence of the witnesses and the arguments of counsel, were unanimously of opinion that the charge against Mr. West, that in the performance of his ministerial duty on the occasion of visiting a certain sick woman, he put improper questions to her with a view of leading her to make confession to him, has not been substantiated by the evidence. The charge rested upon the sole testimony of Anne Arnold, unsupported by that of any other witness, but contradicted in various material points by witnesses whose testimony has not been impugned.

"They therefore now, in compliance with the requirements of the statute, openly and publicly declare that there is not sufficient ground for instituting further proceedings against Mr. West, and they will advise the Bishop to that effect."

The Archdeacon of Berks, in common with the other Commissioners, afterwards received the following letter from the Bishop of Oxford:—

"Lavington-house, Petworth, Sept. 30.

"Gentlemen,—I have received the report of your Commission of Inquiry into the charges brought against Mr. West, and heartily accept as my own the decision at which, after a full examination of the matter, you have arrived.

"In thus formally adopting your decision, I wish, for the sake of my diocese at large, to add a few words on the general subject of confession.

"As I have already stated in writing to Mr. Shaw, I hold it to be a part of the wisdom and tenderness of the Church of England that she provides for any parishioner who in sickness shall 'feel his conscience troubled with any weighty matter,' being 'moved to make special confession of his sins;' and that she also provides for those who before Holy Communion 'cannot quiet their own consciences' being invited to 'open their grief to the minister of God's Word.'

"In making this special and limited provision for troubled souls, I hold that the Church of England discountenances any attempt on the part of her clergy to introduce a system of habitual confession, or, in order to carry out such a system, to require men and women to submit themselves to the questioning and examination of the priest. Such a system of inquiry into the secrets of hearts must. in my judgment, lead to innumerable evils. God forbid that our clergy should administer or that our wives and daughters should be subjected to it. I am sure that any attempt to introduce it would throw grievous difficulties in the way of that free ministerial intercourse with our people which, for their sakes and for the efficiency of our ministry, it is all-important to maintain open and unsuspected.

"I am, &c.
"S. OXON.

"The Commissioners of the Boyne-hill Inquiry."

278. Cookham. Sept. 7. New schools, erected at a cost of £1500, were opened this day.

285. Sandhurst. The Wellington College, situated in this parish, is nearly completed, and will be opened with 100 scholars, the children of officers of limited means, in January next. An asylum for the reception of 600 convict lunatics has been recently commenced within the parish.

289. Waltham. Oct. 24. Surlock-street district chapel was opened on this day.

293. Windsor. The national schools have been rebuilt by subscription. Rev. G. I. Sherwood, lay impropriator, died Sept. 30.

294. Windsor. March 26. The new cemetery was consecrated. The Bishop was met at the gate of the cemetery by the Mayor and Corporation in their robes, the clergy of the neighbouring parishes, and a con-

siderable number of the parishioners of Windsor. A procession being formed, headed by the choir of the parish church, those assembled walked round the enclosures of the cemetery, chanting the Psalm from the Consecration Service. The Bishop then delivered a very impressive address, and the service, with Holy Communion, was then concluded in the chapel. The Bishop and clergy were afterwards entertained by the Mayor and Corporation at a luncheon in the Town-hall.

Windsor Prize Scheme in connection with the Church Union.—The second annual examination of boys from schools in union was held at Windsor, and prizes, in books and money, to the amount of £15, were awarded. The masters from the neighbouring schools had borne unanimous testimony, at a meeting of the Schoolmasters' Associates, to the usefulness of the previous year's examination in keeping boys longer at school, and tending to raise the tone of their schools generally.

302. Brimpton. On Nov. 18, 1857, the Rev. Edmund Golding, vicar of this parish, died.

314. Ilsley. The church has been repewed and thoroughly repaired.

329. Thatcham. Oct. 5. The church was re-opened, having been closed for fifteen months, and undergone thorough restoration, at a cost of about £3,000. All the old pews and galleries have been removed, and new open pews substituted, by which means additional sittings for fifty persons have been obtained; the south aisle has been lengthened, the nave new roofed, several stained glass windows put in, including one (placed in the tower) as a memorial to the Bailey family; a very fine organ, by Gray and Davidson, erected at the east end of the north aisle, the Fuller Chapel restored at the expense of R. Tull, Esq., and the chancel again restored by the lay-rector, W. Mount, Esq. More than half the sittings are free. A vestry has also been built, and a piece of land has been munificently given by J. F. Winterbottom, Esq., for the enlargement of the churchyard.

337. Bradfield. Sept. 15. Died at his brother's house, the Rev. C. Marriott, (vide No. 177).

363. Aldworth. Oct. 16. At the vicarage, died the Rev. George Bullock, vicar of the parish. He took his degree of B.A. at Cambridge in 1834, M.A. in 1837, and B.D. in 1844. He was elected a Fellow of St. John's College in that University, and appointed to Aldworth in 1848.

366. Basildon. An elegant and expensive school-room, commenced by the late Jas. Morrison, Esq., has been completed by his widow, and opened to the parish.

368. Brightwell. The church is now undergoing restoration.

374. North Moreton. On Nov. 11 the church was re-opened after a thorough restoration, which has been effected with the heartiest co-operation of the parishioners. The proceedings at the re-opening were of the most satisfactory nature; the benches in the church were filled to overflowing. The Bishop preached most eloquently, and at the dinner, afterwards, at which 200 sat down, the Bishop's health was drunk with such manifestations of esteem as if they were determined to shew that his labours in his diocese were at least appreciated by the rustic inhabitants of North Moreton. It should be added that, though the greatest praise is due to the parish for the very handsome and liberal manner in which they came forward to effect the restoration of the church, yet its being carried out in its present perfect form is mainly attributable to the munificence and readiness with which the large landowners and

other subscribers responded to the appeals made to them by the late vicar, the Rev. W. Hollinsed, who with untiring zeal and energy devoted himself, even to death, to the sacred task.

385. Challow. June 4. The church at West Challow, which has been entirely restored, was re-opened, and a piece of ground consecrated for burial-ground, the gift of C. C. Ferard, Esq., who has also given a rent-charge of £80 per annum as an endowment for the united parishes, and is now building a handsome parsonage at his own cost.

393. Hanney. April 26. The new chapel of St. James-the-Less, in the hamlet of East Hanney, was consecrated and opened for divine service. The Bishop preached in the morning, taking for his text Rev. xxii. 3, 4. The Archdeacon of Bucks. preached in the evening on the Lord's Prayer. The church was crowded on both occasions. The collections amounted to £71 9s. 6½d. Between the services a cold collation was provided in the national schoolroom by the Vicar, liberally assisted by his parishioners, for the friends of the undertaking.

399. East Lockinge. Feb. 21. Mr. Sneyd, the Vicar of the parish, died.

416. Prestwood. Harvest-home has been kept for the last two years by the parish as a parish festival; divine service, and afterwards a general dinner among the parishioners.

421. Buckingham. The pews in the south gallery have been removed and replaced by open seats, and the churchyard fenced off from the public footpath and planted with flowers and shrubs.

428. Water Stratford. April 15. Died, the Rev. George Coleman, rector of the parish.

436. Calverton. July 26. Died, at the rectory, the Hon. and Rev. C. G. Perceval, heir-presumptive to the earldom of Egmont. The deceased gentleman was born at the Admiralty in Whitehall, in 1796, and in 1820 was admitted into holy orders by Dr. Pelham, then Bishop of Lincoln. Two years afterwards he was nominated by his brother, the Earl of Egmont, to the rectory of Calverton, which benefice he held up to the time of his death.

445. Stony Stratford. A font has been presented to the church by the late Hon. and Rev. C.G. Perceval. A handsome altar-cloth, with carpet for the chancel, and kneeling cushions for the communicants, have been purchased by subscription, and the aisles furnished throughout with matting by the same means. New schools have been erected for boys and girls, with master's house, on the site of the boys' old school, originally founded by Michael Hipwell, in the reign of James I. A District Visiting Society has been formed and a Penny Savings' Bank established.

448. Nash. May 10. A new church and churchyard for this parish consecrated this day.

451. Beaconsfield. The churchyard has been improved and somewhat enlarged.

453. Colnbrook. On Sept. 5 a stained glass window was opened at the east end of St. Thomas' church, erected as a memorial to the late John Goldie, Esq., of St. Marylebone, London, who endowed this church before its consecration. It is erected by his family, and consists of five medallions. In the centre compartment is the Entombment and Resurrection of Christ; and above this, in the tracery, the Saviour. On the right hand, in form of a vesica piscis, is the Raising of Lazarus, representing the *works* of Christ; on the left, the Sermon on the Mount, representing His *teaching*. Beneath, on slate, are the words, " In memory of John Goldie, Esq., deceased, June 11, 1855, aged 88."

457. **Farnham-Royal.** School-room, built by subscription on a site given by Eton College, was opened in October.

471. **East Claydon.** May 15. The Rev. Henry A. Hammond, who was about to leave the charge of East Claydon parish for that of South-borough, in Kent, was presented by his parishioners with a silver ink-stand, bearing the device of a wreath of forget-me-nots on the top, and an appropriate inscription.

491. **Hardwicke.** A new girls' school has been built and the boys' school much enlarged.

547. **Wavendon.** The schoolroom has been licensed for Divine Service at Woburnsands, a hamlet in the parish of Wavendon, giving accommodation for about 120 of the population.

549. **Wolston.** Mr. W. Smith, Churchwarden of Wolston, has been presented, at a public dinner held in his honour, with a service of plate, value 100 guineas, in testimony of the services to agriculture rendered by him in his discovery of a new and successful process of cultivation by steam.

565. **Aston-Clinton.** An obituary window has been inserted at the east end of the chancel to the memory of the Rev. Geo. Walter Wrangham.

569. **Ellesborough.** Oct. 6. Died, at Milan, the Rev. W. Henry England, rector of this parish.

574. **Missenden.** A new vicarage has been built at a cost of £1,685.

577. **Aylesbury.** The second anniversary of the Vale of Aylesbury Church Choral Association was attended with increasing success. The choirs of ten parishes attended divine service at the parish church, where an excellent sermon was preached by the Rev. H. H. Swinny, Rector of Wargrave, and they afterwards dined together, the Ven. the Archdeacon and many of the neighbouring clergy and their friends joining the repast, in all about 300. A short practice in the church occupied the time before Evening Service, after which the proceedings terminated. The musical portions of the service, which were well selected, and had been practised over a short time previously, were joined in with great breadth and harmony, shewing a marked improvement over last year, and giving promise of a successful future, and increasing benefits to a society whose influence is becoming widely felt and acknowledged. The new burial-ground was opened March 31.

583. **Hulcot.** Rev. W. Morgan, rector, died March 26.

594. **Lacey-Green.** The parsonage house was completed in 1857, and the ecclesiastical district legally constituted.

600. **Monk's Risborough.** Aug. 24. The foundation-stone of a school-room was laid.

605. **High Wycombe.** Sept. 23. The foundation-stone of chapel-of-ease was laid for Wycombe Marsh, to contain eighty-two persons.

Number of Confirmations in the Diocese of Oxford during the year, 82.

Persons Confirmed, Males	.	.	.	3,305
„ Females	.	.	.	3,383
				6,688

Ordinations.

ALL CANDIDATES FOR DEACON'S ORDERS must have attended the several Lectures at Oxford, or passed the Voluntary Theological Examination at Cambridge, or kept a year's residence at the Theological College at Wells, Chichester, or Cuddesdon, or obtained the Divinity Certificate from King's College, London. The Bishop requires six months' notice from all Candidates of their intention of applying to him for Deacon's, and three months' notice for Priest's Orders. In the notice for Deacon's Orders the Candidates are desired to state what their Title is, if they are provided with one, or, if not, their need of one. The requisite papers to be sent to the Bishop's Secretary, John M. Davenport, Esq., Oxford, fourteen days before the day of Ordination.

On Sunday, December 20, 1857, by the Lord Bishop of Oxford, in the Cathedral of Christ Church.

Priests.—R. W. Allsopp, S.C.L., Emmanuel College, Cambridge; Lewis Campbell, M.A., Queen's College, Oxford; Robert Cholmeley, M.A., Magdalen College, Oxford; Robert H. Codrington, M.A., Wadham College, Oxford; David Alexander Court, B.A., and John Edwards, M.A., St. Mary Hall, Oxford; Henry Furneux, M.A., Corpus Christi College, Oxford; James Black Gray, B.A., St. John's College, Oxford; Clifford Malden, B.A., Trinity College, Cambridge; William Morrison, B.A., Christ Church. Oxford; James Oakley, B.A., Jesus College, Oxford; John Carne Pocock, Theological College, Cuddesdon; S. Slocock, B.A., Gonville and Caius College, Cambridge; Charles Smith, B.A., Trinity College, Dublin.

Deacons.—Henry Alexander Barclay, M.A., Christ Church, Oxford; Ambrose Sneyd Cave-Brown-Cave, B.A., Corpus Christi College, Oxford; Philip Reginald Egerton, B.C.L., New College, Oxford; Richard Elliott, M.A., Christ Church, Oxford; Charles Henry Everett, B A., Balliol College, Oxford; Charles Henry Faithfull, B.A., Lincoln College, Oxford; Wilfred Fisher, B.A., Christ Church, Oxford; Vernon Thomas Green, B.A., Trinity College, Cambridge; Henry Houseman, T.A., King's College. London; Compton Reade, B A., and William Sandars, M.A., Magdalen College, Oxford; George Steele, B.A., Worcester College, Oxford; Henry Aston Walker, B.A., Oriel College, Oxford; Frederick Peers Wickham, S.C.L.. New College, Oxford; William Francis Wilberforce, B.A., University College, Oxford.

On Trinity Sunday, May 30, 1858, in the Parish Church of Cuddesdon.

Priests. — Revs. C. Alabaster, B.A., Lincoln College, Oxford; J. Aldworth, B.A., Worcester College, Oxford; A. Blomfield, M.A., All Souls' College, Oxford; H. R. Bramley, B.A., Magdalen College, Oxford; G. J. Brown. M.A., Christ Church, Oxford; V. C. B. Cave, B.A., Exeter College, Oxford; J. P. Kane, B.A.. Trinity College, Oxford; R. C. Kempe, M.A.. Magdalen College. Oxford; L. J. Lee, B.A., New College. Oxford; G. F. Le Mesurier, M.A., Exeter College, Oxford; W. P. Michell, B.A., Emmanuel College, Cambridge; G. T. Palmer, B.A., St. Peter's College, Cambridge; H. A. Pickard. M.A., Christ Church, Oxford; W. H. Ranken, M.A., Corpus Christi College, Oxford; H. Robeson, M.A., Balliol College, Oxford; G. G. Ross, B.C.L., St. Mary Hall, Oxford; O. Shipley, M.A., Jesus College, Cambridge; H. M. Smyth, B.A., St. Catherine's College, Cambridge; J. Squire, Literate; W. Tuckwell, M.A., New College, Oxford; T. J. Williams, M.A., University College, Oxford.

Deacons.—G. F. Browne, B.A., St. Catherine's College, Cambridge; W. J. Few, B.A., Christ Church, Oxford; A. Goalen, B.A., New Inn Hall, Oxford; J. G. Greason, M.A., Exeter College, Oxford; G. E. Jelf, B.A., Christ Church, Oxford; H. E. Suckling, Student of the Theological College, Cuddesdon; S. Thornton, M.A., Queen's College, Oxford; H. B. Wilder, B.A., Balliol College, Oxford; C. L. Wingfield, M.A., All Souls' College, Oxford.

On Sunday, Sept. 19, at Cuddesdon Church.

Priests.—Rev. C. H. Everett, B.A., Balliol College, Oxford ; Hon. E. F. Nelson, M.A., Trinity College, Cambridge; R. M. Rowe, M.A., Exeter College, Oxford ; G. E. O. Watts, B.A., Lincoln College, Oxford.

Deacons.—E. Cooper, B.A., Trinity College, Cambridge ; A. Cumberlege, Theological College, Cuddesdon, for the Bishop of Exeter ; J. Daubeny, M.A., Exeter College, Oxford ; R. Faussett, M.A., Student of Christ Church, Oxford ; F. Harrison, M.A., Oriel College, Oxford ; F. H. Joyce, M.A., Student of Christ Church, Oxford ; J. C. Pearson, B.A., St. Catherine's College, Cambridge ; W. J. Pickard, Oxford Diocesan Training College, Culham ; W. C. Risley, M.A., and R I. Salmon, B.A., Exeter College, Oxford ; T. R. R. Stebbing, B.A., Worcester College. Oxford ; W. H. Young, M.A., Pembroke College, Oxford.

𝕮𝖔𝖓𝖋𝖎𝖗𝖒𝖆𝖙𝖎𝖔𝖓𝖘 𝖍𝖊𝖑𝖉 𝖉𝖚𝖗𝖎𝖓𝖌 1858,
BY THE LORD BISHOP OF THE DIOCESE.

6. Chalgrove, April 11, for Chalgrove, Easington, Berwick.
12. Lewknor, March 28, for Lewknor, Adwell, Aston Rowant, South Weston, Stoke-Talmage, Wheatfield.
16. Stokenchurch, March 27, for Stokenchurch, Pyrton, Shirburn, Watlington.
17. Sydenham, March 29, for Sydenham, Chinnor, Crowell, Emmington.
19. Thame, March 29, for Thame and Tetsworth.
26. Rousham, March 8, for Rousham, Steeple Aston, Lower and Upper Heyford.
27. Chesterton, March 5, for Chesterton, Ambrosden, Bucknell, Middleton-Stoney, Wendlebury.
30. Fringford, March 7, for Fringford and Newton-Purcell.
37. Kirtlington, March 5, for Kirtlington, Bletchingdon, Tackley, Weston-on-the Green.
38. Launton, March 6, for Launton, Bicester, Piddington, Stratton-Audley.
41. Mixbury, March 7, for Mixbury and Finmere.
44. Somerton, March 8, for Somerton, Dunstew, North Aston, Souldern, Fritwell.
46. Stoke-Lyne, March 6, for Stoke Lyne with Caversfield, Ardley, Cottisford, Goddington, Hardwick, Hethe.
51. Charlbury, March 19, for Charlbury, Chadlington and Chilson, Finstock, Shorthampton, Spelsbury, Stonesfield.
53. Chipping-Norton, March 16, for Chipping-Norton, Chastleton, Heythrop, Little Rollright, Salford.
58. Hooknorton, March 18, for Hooknorton, Great Rollright, Swerford with Shoel.
60. Kingham, March 16, for Kingham, Churchill, Cornwell, Sarsden.
64. Deddington, March 10, for Deddington, Clifton, Hempton.
66. Milton-under-Wychwood, March 18, for Milton-under-Wychwood, Lyneham, Ascott, Idbury, Ramsden, Shipton-under-Wychwood, Fifield, Leafield.
72. Stadhampton, March 27, for Stadhampton, Chiselhampton, Newington, Marsh and Toot Baldon.
75. Cuddesdon, March 28, for Cuddesdon, Horspath, Garsington.
76. Culham, March 3, for Culham, Clifton-Hampden, Nuneham-Courtenay.
77. Dorchester, March 2, for Dorchester, Drayton, Warborough.
84. Littlemore, April 12, for Littlemore, Sandford, Iffley.
85. Great Milton, March 30, for Great and Little Milton, Great Haseley.
89. Sandford, March 9, for Sandford, Steeple and Westcot Barton, Great and Little Tew, Upper and Lower Worton.
92. Waterstock, March 29, for Waterstock, Albury, Waterperry.
93. Wheatley, April 10, for Wheatley, Forest-Hill, Holton, Stanton St. John.

97. South Banbury, March 12, for South Banbury, Neithrep, Banbury.
102. Mollington, March 11, for Mollington with Claydon.
103. Cropredy, March 11, for Cropredy and Wardington.
107. Horley, March 12, for Horley with Hornton, Alkerton, Balscot, Drayton, Hanwell, Wroxton.
109. South Newington, March 15, for South Newington, Bloxham, Milcomb, Wigginton.
111. Swalcliffe, March 13, for Swalcliffe, Broughton with North Newington, Epwell, Shutford, Sibford, Tadmarton.
120. Caversham, Feb. 22, for the parishes of Caversham and Kidmore-End.
121. Harpsden, Feb. 23, for Harpsden, Rotherfield-Greys, Rotherfield-Peppard.
122. Henley, Feb. 21, for Henley and Bix.
124. Mapledurham, Feb. 22. Sermons preached during Lent by clergy of the Henley Mission.
129. Early, Feb. 24, for Early.
131. Sonning, Feb. 24, for Sonning and its Chapelries.
133. Wargrave, Feb. 26, for Wargrave.
141. Elsfield, April 6, for Elsfield, Beckley, Headington, Headington Quarry, Marston, Noke, Woodeaton.
161. Nuffield, March 1, for Nuffield, Checkendon, Ipsden, Woodcote, Nettlebed, Stoke-Row, Goring.
165. Swyncombe, March 1, for Swyncombe and Pishill.
174. Oxford, St. John's, March 28.
181. Oxford, St. Peter's-in-the-East, Oct. 3, *By the Right Rev. the Lord Bishop of Nelson.*
188. Bampton, March 20, for Bampton, Blackbourton, Bampton Low and Aston, Clanfield, Brizenorton, Shifford.
192. Filkins, March 20, for Filkins, Alvescot, Bradwell with Kelmscott, Shilton, Broughton Pogis, Langford with Little Faringdon.
193. Burford, March 19, for Burford with Fulbrook, Asthall, Taynton, Swinbrook, Widford, Westwell.
196. Ducklington, March 21, for Ducklington.
202. Northmoor, March 22, for Northmoor and Standlake.
209. Witney, March 22, at the Church of Holy Trinity, Woodgreen, for Witney with Curbridge, Coggs, Minster-Lovell, and St. John's, Hailey, with Crawley.
216. Woodstock, March 23, for Bladon with Woodstock.
217. Cassington, March 23, for Cassington, Eynsham, Yarnton.
221. Glympton, March 9, for Glympton, Enstone, Kiddington, Wootton.
224. Kidlington, April 5, for Kidlington with Watereaton, Begbrook, Hampton-Gay, Hampton-Poyle, Shipton-on-Cherwell.
225. Northleigh, March 23, for Northleigh, Combe, Handborough.
229. Stanton-Harcourt, March 21, for Stanton-Harcourt and Southleigh.
247. Milton, March 10, for Adderbury, Milton, Barford St. John, Barford St. Michael, Boddicot with Banbury.

Diocese of Oxford.

A LIST OF THE
PARISHES AND PLACES
IN THE SEVERAL
RURAL DEANERIES. 1858.

THE following list of Parishes, and statistics of Church Accommodation, &c., have been corrected chiefly from information obtained direct from the Incumbent of each parish. In some cases the Church Accommodation has not been returned, consequently it is impossible to give the statistic which was intended and which is still much desired. In this edition the names of the Chaplains to Institutions, Masters of Grammar-Schools, &c., have been incorporated.

R., signifies Rector; V., Vicar; P.C., Perpetual Curate; C., Curate; CC., Curates. S. (after a name) Surrogate. The Population is chiefly from the last Census, and the Church accommodation, as a rule. omits room set apart for children only. Suff. signifies that the room has been returned as "sufficient." No R. is placed in those cases where the Incumbents have not made any return on our application.

Archdeaconry of Oxford.
DEANERY OF ASTON.
RURAL DEAN—The Rev. George Marshall, Pyrton.

	Population.	Church Accom.
1. Adwell, *Tetsworth*, R., W. L. Buckle; C., C. V. Spencer .	56	70
2. Aston-Rowant, *Tetsworth*, V., Robert Williams . .	901	280
3. Baldwin-Brightwell, *Tetsworth*, R., George Day . .	294	Suff.
4. Britwell-Salome, *Wallingford*, R., James T. Johnson .	240	100
5. Cadmore End [a], *High Wycombe*, P. C., F. R. Perry .	327	150
6. Chalgrove, *Tetsworth*, V., R. F. Lawrence, . .	600	387
With Berwick-Salome	160	137
7. Chinnor, *Tetsworth*, R., W. A. Musgrave ; CC., A. S. Latter, F. Buttanshaw	1257	No R.
8. Crowell, *Tetsworth*, R., James Beauchamp . .	160	120
9. Cuxham, *Tetsworth*, R., John D. Piggott . .	149	130
10. Easington, *Tetsworth*, R., Isaac Fidler . . .	25	100
11. Emmington, *Thame*, R., W. A. Musgrave . .	104	No R.
12. Lewknor, *Tetsworth*, V., W. H. Fremantle . .	650	230
13. Pyrton, *Tetsworth*, V., George Marshall . .	400	350
14. Shirburn, *Tetsworth*, V., J. Beauchamp; C., C. Nursey .	250	200
15. Stoke-Talmage, *Tetsworth*, R., Hon. W. Byron .	107	No R.
16. Stokenchurch [b], *Tetsworth*, P. C., Job Mayo . .	1500	450
17. Sydenham, *Tetsworth*, V., W. D. Littlejohn .	390	240
18. TETSWORTH, V., J. W. Peers	1390	No R.
19. THAME, V., James Prosser, S. . . . Chaplain to the Union, A. Hayton.	3250	1000
20. WATLINGTON, V., W. J. A. Langford, S. .	1884	No R.
21. Weston, South, *Tetsworth*, R., George Hayton . .	102	Suff.
22. Wheatfield, *Tetsworth*, R., Charles Vere Spencer .	78	100

[a] Cadmore End has now been transferred to the Wycombe Deanery.
[b] Part of parish now joined to Cadmore End.

DEANERY OF BICESTER.

RURAL DEAN—The Rev. James Charles Blomfield, Launton.

	Population.	Church Accom.
23. Ambrosden[a], *Bicester, V.,* L. G. Dryden	900	350
24. Ardley, *Bicester, R.,* John Lowe	155	100
25. BICESTER, *V.,* John W. Watts, ♋; *C.,* T. J. Lingwood .	3200	1500
Chaplain to the Union, J. W. Watts.		
26. Bucknell, *Bicester, R.,* William Master . . .	283	250
27. Chesterton, *Bicester, V.,* W. F. Fortescue . . .	435	300
28. Cottisford, *Bicester, R.,* C. S. Harrison . . .	263	120
29. Finmere, *Buckingham, R.,* Frederic J. Walker . .	390	200
30. Fringford, *Bicester, R.,* H. J. A. F. De Salis, ♋. . .	390	230
31. Fritwell, *Bicester, V.,* Rev. W. Rawlings, ♋.; *C.,* E. Gordon	500	200
32. Goddington, *Bicester, R.,* T. T. Haverfield; *C.,* W. Perkins	82	70
33. Hardwick, *Bicester, R.,*(vide 491); *C.* M.Style; with Tusmore	66	No R.
34. Hethe, *Bicester, R.,* Frederick Salter	418	128
35. Heyford, Lower, *Woodstock, R.,* George D. Faithfull .	605	Suff.
36. Heyford, Upper, *Bicester, R.,* W. J. Baker; *C.,* T. Brown	400	No R.
37. Kirtlington, *Oxford, V.,* T. K. Chittenden; *C.,* J. H. Eld .	c 650	348
38. Launton, *Bicester, R.,* James C. Blomfield . . .	703	260
39. Merton, *Bicester, V.,* G. T. Stupart; *C.,* C. Tudor . .	200	Suff.
40. Middleton-Stoney, *Bicester, R.,* R. Pretyman; *C.,* D. Dewar	300	200
41. Mixbury, *Buckingham, R.,* G. H. Palmer	360	180
42. Newton Purcell with Shelswell, *Bicester, R.,* J. Meade .	160	80
43. Piddington, *Bicester, P. C.,* Charles Hill; *C.,* W. Gilbert	420	Suff.
44. Somerton, *Deddington, R.,* R. C. Clifton; *C.,* J. Aldworth	342	250
45. Souldern, *Brackley, R.,* Lawrence Stephenson, D.D. .	600	274
46. Stoke-Lyne with Caversfield, *Bicester, V.,* C. Marsham .	630	No R.
47. Stratton-Audley, *Bicester, P. C.,* J. E. Tweed . . .	350	Suff.
48. Wendlebury, *Bicester, R.,* Walter L. Brown . . .	226	120
49. Weston-on-the-Green, *Bicester, V.,* W. J. Dry, ♋. . .	500	230

DEANERY OF CHIPPING - NORTON.

RURAL DEAN—Rev. Charles Barter, Sarsden.

	Population.	Church Accom.
50. Ascott-under-Wychwood [d], *Charlbury, P. C.,* A. C. Tarbutt	500	Suff.
51. Charlbury, *Enstone, V.,* S. H. Russell, ♋. . . .	1500	540
With Finstock and Fawler hamlets, *C.,* J. Cross . .	676	350
" Shorthampton, Chadlington and Chilson,*C.,* T. L. Griffith	1000	400
52. Chastleton, *Moreton-in-Marsh, R.,* Horatio Westmacott .	160	150
53. CHIPPING-NORTON, *V.,* Alex. Whishaw, ♋.; *C.,* J. Edwards		
With Over-Norton	3400	1185
Chaplain to the Union, J. Samuel.		
54. Cornwell, *Chipping-Norton, R.,* Charles Barter . .	100	No R.
55. Enstone, *R.,* J. Jordan	1250	No R.
56. Fifield, *Chipping-Norton, P. C.,* M. Talmage . . .	210	190
57. Heythrop, *Chipping-Norton, R.,* J. Samuel . . .	e 116	140
58. Hooknorton, *Chipping-Norton, P. C.,* John C. Rushton, ♋.	1495	745
59. Idbury[f], *Chipping-Norton, P. C.,* M. Talmage . . .	214	160

   a With hamlets of Arncot and Blackthorne.
   d Till recently held with Leafield.
   e Roman Catholics, 49; Protestants, 67.
   f The living held with that of Fifield, and the services interchanged, but parishes distinct. With hamlets of Bowld and Forscote.

		Popu-lation.	Church Accom.
60.	Kingham, *Chipping-Norton*, R., John W. Lockwood . .	600	300
61.	Leafield, *Witney*, P.C., John H. Worsley . . .	827	250
62.	Rollright, Great, *Chipping-Norton*, R., Henry Rendall .	450	236
63.	Rollright, Little, *Chipping-Norton*, R., W. E. Stevens .	26	30
64.	Salford, *Chipping-Norton*, R., W. E. Stevens . .	350	209
65.	Sarsden, *Chipping-Norton*, R., Chas. Barter . .	200	120
	With Churchill	600	500
66.	Shipton-under-Wychwood, *Chipping-Norton*, V., W. E. Dickson Carter, ♨.; C., George Carpenter		
	With Lyneham, Milton-under-Wychwood, Ramsden, and Langley	616	348
67.	Spelsbury, *Enstone*, V., T. C. Barker . . .	580	No R.
68.	Swerford with Shoel, *Enstone*, R., Thomas Harris .	369	245

DEANERY OF CUDDESDON.

	RURAL DEAN—	Popu-lation.	Church Accom.
69.	Albury, *Tetsworth*, R., Hon. F. Bertie . . .	230	No R.
70.	Baldon, Marsh, *Oxford*, R., H. S. M. Hubert . .	380	Suff.
71.	Baldon, Toot, *Oxford*, P. C.; C., W. B. Clarke .	260	Suff.
72.	Chiselhampton with Stadhampton, *Wallingford*, P. C., Wm. P. Perry	553	320
73.	Clifton-Hampden, *Abingdon*, P. C., Joseph Gibbs; C., H. L. Fanshawe	369	150
74.	Cowley, *Oxford*, P. C., R. M. Benson; C., J. P. Kane .	1057	250
	Chaplain to Industrial School, R. H. Charsley.		
75.	Cuddesdon [g], *Wheatley*, V., ; C., David A. Court	520	250
	Chaplain to the Theological College, A. Barff.		
76.	Culham, *Abingdon*, V., Robert Walker, ♨. . .	410 [h]	250
	Principal of the Training College, A. R. Ashwell.		
77.	Dorchester, *Wallingford*, P. C., W. C. Macfarlane, ♨.		
	With Burcote	1100	578
78.	Drayton, *Wallingford*, P.C., A. J. Williams, ♨. .	327	160
79.	Garsington, *Oxford*, R., J. Wilson, D.D.; C., G. F. Wilgress	630	350
80.	Haseley, Great, *Tetsworth*, R., W. Birkett . .	750	No R.
81.	Holton, *Wheatley*, R., Henry A. Tyndale . .	280	150
82.	Horspath, *Wheatley*, P.C., H. Cholmeley . .	333	189
83.	Iffley [i], *Oxford*, P. C., Thomas A. Warburton, D.C.L. .	482	250
84.	Littlemore, *Oxford*, P. C., Geo. W. Huntingford .	570	250
	Chaplain to the Pauper Lunatic Asylum, E. W. R. Pulling.		
85.	Milton, Great, *Tetsworth*, V., Henry M. Turton; C., A. M. Morgan	733	400
86.	Milton, Little, *Tetsworth*, P. C., H. Shute; C., W. Young	400	256
87.	Newington, *Wallingford*, R., S. Cotes . . .	400	No R.
	With Britwell Prior	50	,,
88.	Nuneham-Courtenay, *Oxford*, R., H. P. Cooke. .	356	150
89.	Sandford, *Littlemore*, C., John Slatter, ♨. . .	320	120
90.	Warborough, *Wallingford*, P. C., H. White; C., F. Reyroux	730	312
91.	Waterperry, *Wheatley*, V., Francis Henley . .	240	Suff.
92.	Waterstock, *Wheatley*, R., James H. Ashhurst, ♨. .	134	150
93.	Wheatley [k], P.C., Edward Elton.	1037	511

g The Theological College is in this parish, *q. v.*
h Exclusive of the Training College, which is in this parish.
i A portion of the parish situate in Cowley, of about 280 population.
k Was formerly under Cuddesdon; but now independent. Church rebuilt in June, 1857.

DEANERY OF DEDDINGTON.

RURAL DEAN—Rev. Edward Payne, Swalcliffe.

	Popu-lation.	Church Accom.
94. Adderbury, *Woodstock*, *V.*, R. R. Stephens ; *C.*, J. Marshall With Barford St. John's Chapelry, and Milton Hamlet.	1400	650
95. Alkerton, *Banbury*, *R.*, Robert E. Hughes	190	120
96. BANBURY, *V.*, W. Wilson, &.; *CC.*, J. D. Fish, W. H. Hewitt, W. Best	5500	1750
With St. Paul's, Neithrop		430
97. BANBURY, South, *V.*, Charles Forbes Chaplain to the Union, C. Forbes.	3500	944
98. Barford St. Michael's, *Banbury*, *V.*, P. Hookins	392	170
99. Bloxham, *Banbury*, *V.*, James Hodgson	1335	624
100. Bodicote, *Banbury*, *P. C.*, J. A. Gould	673	No R.
101. Broughton, *Banbury*, *R.*, C. F. Wyatt; *C.*, C. N. Bradford With North Newington	590	350
102. Claydon, *Banbury*, *P. C.*, Thomas H. Tait	350	89
With Mollington	360	210
103. Cropredy, *Banbury*, *V.*, A. W. Noel; *C.*, C. Knipe	1161	363
104. Deddington, *Woodstock*, *V.*[1], J. Brogden; *C.*, J. H. Burgess	2178	1500
With Clifton, *C.*, W. C. Risley, &.	250	200
And Hempton, *C.*, H. D. Harington	200	150
105. Drayton, *Banbury*, *R.*, William Lloyd	245	160
106. Hanwell, *Banbury*, *R.*, Wm. Pearse; *C.*, R. McD. Caunter	300	400
107. Horley, *Banbury*, *V.*, W. J. Pinwill; *C.*, P. Russell	392	325
With Hornton	591	250
108. Milcomb, *Banbury*, *P. C.*, Philip Hookins	242	80
109. Newington, South, *Banbury*, *V.*, Henry D. Harington	400	391
110. Sibford-Gower, *Banbury*, *P.C.*, W. S. Miller; *C.*, W. B. Smith	899	500
111. Swalcliffe, *Banbury*, *V.*, E. Payne, &.; *CC.*, W. Butcher, G. Montague	759	No R.
With Epwell and Shutford	350	Suff.
112. Tadmarton, *Banbury*, *R.*, Thomas Lea	451	250
113. Tew, Great, *Enstone*, *V.*, John J. Campbell, &.	510	571
113*. Tew, Little, *Enstone*, *P. C.*, C. F. Garratt	240	140
114. Wardington, *Banbury*, *P. C.*, Charles Walters With Coton and Williamscote	862	520
115. Wigginton, *Banbury*, *R.*, J. Williams; *C.*, J. Squire	314	Suff.
116. Worton, Nether, *Woodstock*, *P. C.*, F. G. Wilson; *CC.*, V. Blake, W. Best	67	200
117. Worton, Over, *Woodstock*, *R.*, T. W. Lancaster; *C.*, Wm. Wilson, D.D.	93	120
118. Wroxton, *Banbury*, *V.*, John Murray	600	Suff.
With Balscot	220	Suff.

DEANERY OF HENLEY.

RURAL DEAN—Rev. T. B. Morrell, Henley-on-Thames.

Portion in Archdeaconry of Oxford.

	Popu-lation.	Church Accom.
119. Bix, *Henley-on-Thames*, *R.*, Horace R. Pechell	367	150
120. Caversham[m], *Reading*, *P. C.*, Joshua Bennett, &.	1751	480

[1] Non-resident.   [m] 500 of the population are attached to Kidmore-End.

	Popu-lation.	Church Accom.
121. Harpsden, *Henley-on-Thames, R.,* F. K. Leighton, D.D., 𝔖. With Bolney, J. H. Appleton	215	163
122. HENLEY-ON-THAMES, *R.,* T. B. Morrell, 𝔖.; *CC.,* H. Benson, John F. Fixsen . . . . . . Chaplain to the Union, T. B. Morrell.	3800	1500
123. Kidmore-End, St. John Baptist's, *Henley-on-Thames, P.C.,* F. Fleming	670	240
124. Mapledurham [n], *Reading, V.,* E. C. Hawtrey, D.D., Provost of Eton; *C.,* C. E. Powys	500	170 [o]
125. Rotherfield-Greys, *Henley-on-Thames, R.,* Joseph Smith; *C.,* W. M. Shewell	640	Suff.
126. Rotherfield, Holy Trinity Church, *Henley-on-Thames, P.C.,* W. P. Pinckney; *C.,* C. P. Longland . .	551	No R.
127. Rotherfield-Peppard, *Henley-on-Thames, R.,* H. Reynolds	1146	400
128. Shiplake, *Reading, V.,* R. D. B. Rawnsley, 𝔖. . .	529	230
Portion in the Archdeaconry of Berks.		
129. Early [p], *Reading, P.C.,* John Horne . . .	700	350
130. Remenham, *Henley-on-Thames, R.,* B. Owen . .	486	No R.
131. Sonning, *Reading, V.,* Hugh Pearson; *C.,* F. A. Powys .	1855	600
132. Sonning [q], All Saints' Chapel-of-ease, *Reading, V.,* Hugh Pearson; *C.,* W. O. P. Wilson	650	215
133. Wargrave, *Henley-on-Thames, V.,* Henry H. Swinny; *CC.,* Alan B. Cheales, J. Monkhouse	1636	546
Portion in the Archdeaconry of Buckingham.		
134. Fawley, *Henley-on-Thames, R.,* H. Almack, D.D. . .	c 280	150
135. Hambleden, *Henley-on-Thames, R.,* W. H. Ridley; *CC.,* J. Pooley, W. C. Risley	1366	500
136. Hambleden, St. John's-Frieth, *Henley-on-Thames, P. C.,* W. H. Ridley; *C.,* James Pooley . . .	1304	150 [r]
137. Medmenham, *Marlow, V.,* Frederick W. Harris . .	401	170

DEANERY OF ISLIP.

RURAL DEAN—Rev. Richard Gordon, Elsfield, Oxford.

	Popu-lation.	Church Accom.
138. Beckley [s], *Oxford, P.C.,* George T. Cooke With Studley and Horton	800	Suff.
139. Bletchingdon, *Oxford, R.,* F. Dand, 𝔖. . .	673	No R.
140. Charlton-on-Otmoor, *Islip, R.,* Henry Gough .	651	300
141. Elsfield, *Oxford, V.,* Richard Gordon, 𝔖. .	168	105
142. Forest-Hill, *Wheatley, P.C.,* Charles F. Wyatt .	160	Suff.
143. Hampton-Gay, *Woodstock, P.C.,* .	69	100

[a] A corruption of Maplederham, or Maple-deer-ham.
[o] Including children.—There is an aisle attached to this church, which has been considered the property of the possessor of Mapledurham House. There were, not many years since, several pews in this aisle of early date, one of which was occupied by the tenant of the house, and others by several of the poor. These pews have been taken down, and the aisle has been closed for all purposes of worship by the proprietor. The change had the full sanction of the late Dr. Phillimore, then Chancellor of the diocese, whose opinion was asked on the occasion, on the part of the Vicar, Lord A. Fitzclarence, and the Churchwardens.
[p] Originally a district of Sonning. Made an incumbency in 1855.
[q] In county of Oxford.
[r] Besides room for 150 in Frieth Chapel, and sixty in Skirmett School Chapel.
[s] A private chapel also at Studley which the parishioners are permitted to attend.

	Population.	Church Accom.
144. Hampton-Poyle, *Kidlington*, R., Joseph Dodd . .	132	200
145. Headington, *Oxford*, V., J. C. Pring; C., J. E. T. Rogers	1082	No R.
Chaplain to the Union, J. C. Pring.		
„　　to the Warneford Asylum, the Rev. R. G. Orchard.		
146. Headington Quarry, *Oxford*, P. C., S. W. Mangin . .	510	Suff.
147. Islip, *Oxford*, R., F. Trench	774	300
148. Marston, *Oxford*, V., R. Gordon; C., C. P. Golightly .	471	300
149. Noke, *Oxford*, R., John Carlyle	140	75
150. Oddington, *Oxford*, R., George Petch . . .	150	118
151. Stanton-St.-John, *Oxford*, R., H. Stonhouse . .	555	No R.
152. Woodeaton, *Oxford*, R., Thomas Clarke . . .	89	70

DEANERY OF NETTLEBED.

RURAL DEAN—Rev. William Toovey Hopkins, Nuffield.

	Population.	Church Accom.
153. Benson, *Wallingford*, P. C., J. M. Collyns . .	1231	270
154. Checkendon, *Henley-on-Thames*, R., William Crabtree;		
C., A. H. Birkett	360	250
155. Crowmarsh-Gifford, *Wallingford*, R., John Trollope, ♉. .	325	200
156. Ewelme, *Wallingford*, R., W. Jacobson, D.D.; C., H. T.		
Gillam	673	No R.
157. Goring, *Reading*, V., W. H. Stokes . . .	993	No R.
Chaplain to the Almshouses, R. T. Powys.		
158. Mongewell, *Wallingford*, R., Thomas V. Durell . .	133	100
159. Nettlebed, *Henley-on-Thames*, P. C., J. Hazel, ♉. .	754	320
160. North Stoke, *Wallingford*, V., R. Twopeny . .	160	No R.
With Ipsden	331	„
And Newnham Murren . . .	162	„
161. Nuffield, *Henley-on-Thames*, R., William T. Hopkins .	250	200
162. Pishill with Assendon, *Henley-on-Thames*, P.C., W. Prince	450	180
163. South Stoke with Woodcote, *Henley-on-Thames*, V., Philip		
H. Nind, ♉.; C., J. A. S. Hilliard . . .	800	500
164. Stoke-Row (District Church), *Henley-on-Thames*, P. C.,		
James Arrowsmith	390	190
165. Swyncombe, *Henley-on-Thames*, R., Hon. H. A. Napier .	427	243
166. Whitchurch, *Reading*, R., Edward Moore . . .	893	400

DEANERY OF OXFORD.

RURAL DEAN—Rev. F. K. Leighton, D.D., Warden of All Souls.

	Population.	Church Accom.
167. OXFORD.—All Saints, P. C., W. West	600	No R.
168. St. Aldate, R., T. C. L. Layton	1830	500
169. Binsey, P. C., Thomas J. Prout	60	Suff.
170. St. Clement, R., E. A. Litton	2400	1060
171. St. Ebbe, R., W. Hanbury; C., G. T. Cameron .	2300	700
172. St. Giles[a], V., G. M. Bullock; CC., J. Barmby, R.		
Cholmeley	2588	620
173. Holywell[x], otherwise St. Cross, P. C., H. B. Walton;		
C., H. Joscelyne	1000	500

[a] The district of St. John, Summertown, has been taken out of this parish, or the population would be 4,591.

[x] The Oxford Penitentiary is in this parish, also one of the three Oxford Cemeteries.

	Popu-lation.	Church Accom.
174. *Oxford*—St. John Baptist, *P. C.,* H. W. Sargent	107	250
Chaplain to the Union & Radcliffe Infirmary, G. R. P. Tiddeman.		
„ to the City Prison, E. A. Litton.		
„ to the County Prison, J. Thorpe.		
175. St. Martin, otherwise Carfax, *R.,* R. C. Hales	449	900
Oxford City Lecturers, W. S. Bricknell, H. O. Coxe, R. Gandell, R. C. Hales.		
176. St. Mary Magdalen, with St. Geo. the Mart., Chapel-of-E., *V.,* R. St. John Tyrwhitt; *CC.,* E. Marshall, W. D. Macray, F. Cooper	2476	1250
177. St. Mary-the-Virgin, *V.,* D. P. Chase; *C.,* H. Anstey	ʸ400	1000
178. St. Michael, *P. C.,* F. Metcalfe, ⚭.	1100	420
179. St. Paul, *P. C.,* Alfred Hackman, ⚭.; *C.C.,* A. R. P. Venables, C. Anderson	2700	700
180. St. Peter-le-Bailey, *R.,* Henry Linton; *C.,* A. Hoskins	1500	450
181. St. Peter-in-the-East, *V.,* E. C. Cure; *C.,* — Minchen	1140	650
182. Summertown, *P. C.,* Edward Palin	1450	380
183. St. Thomas, *P. C.,* T. Chamberlain; *CC.,* J. H. Blunt, W. W. Walter	2296	No R.
Chaplain of the Boatmen's Chapel, T. Chamberlain.		
184. The Holy Trinity, *P. C.,* J. West	2358	800
185. Wolvercot, *P. C.,* S. Edwardes; *C.,* J. B. Gray	640	200 ᶻ

DEANERY OF WITNEY.

Rural Dean—Rev. Dacres Adams, Bampton.

	Popu-lation.	Church Accom.
186. Alvescot, *Faringdon, R.,* A. Neate	375	No R.
187. Asthall, *Burford, V.,* Henry Gregory, ⚭.	372	170
188. Bampton Proper, *Witney, V.,* D. Adams, ⚭.	1677	Suff.
Bampton Aston, *Witney, V.,* R. Barnes, *C.,* G. S. Griffith	968	Suff.
Bampton, Low, *Witney, V.,* F. E. Lott	195	Suff.
189. Blackbourton, *Witney, V.,* J. Lupton, ⚭.; *C.,* W. Dry	278	No R.
190. Bradwell, *Lechlade, V.,* F. T. Woodman	150	Suff.
With Kelmscott, *P. C.*	150	Suff.
191. Brizenorton, *Witney, V.,*	720	No R.
192. Broughton-Pogis-cum-Filkins ᵃ, *Lechlade, R.,* Thos. W. Goodlake, ⚭.	783	246
193. Burford, *V.,* D. W. Goddard	1819	900
With Fulbrook, *P. C.,*	406	160
194. Clanfield, *Lechlade, V.,* J. P. Penson	591	No R.
195. Coggs, *Witney, P. C.,* James Bandinel	814	No R.
196. Ducklington, *Witney, R.,* T. Farley, D.D.; *C.,* G.E.O. Watts	447	Suff.
With Cokethorpe	137	Suff.
197. Hailey, with Crawley, *Witney, P.C.,* George C. Rolfe	600	300
198. Holwell, *Burford, P. C.,* Cunningham Boothby	170	140
199. Kencot, *Lechlade, R.,* Edward Sturges	207	120
200. Langford, *Lechlade, V.,* F. G. Lemann; *C.,* F. Pocock	800	c. 400
With Little Faringdon, Grafton, and Radcot		150
201. Minster-Lovell, *Witney, V.,* R. Earle; *C.,* J. Slade	450	180

ʸ Exclusive of residents in College.
ᶻ A collection is now being made for repairing and enlarging the Church.
ᵃ Formerly part of Bradwell parish, but joined to Broughton in 1855.

		Popu-lation.	Church Accom.
202. Northmoor, *Witney*, P.C., E. Coupland	. . .	375	150
203. Shilton, *Burford*, V., A. Neate	. . .	319	No R.
204. Standlake, *Witney*, R., H. Biddulph; C., A. H. Nourse	.	800	350
205. Swinbrook [b], *Burford*, P.C., G. D. T. Layton	. .	180	Suff.
206. Taynton, *Burford*, V., T. Lewes	. . .	379	No R.
207. Westwell, *Burford*, R., J. E. Bode, ℥.	. . .	183	Suff.
208. Widford [c], *Burford*, R., G. D. T. Layton	. .	20	Suff.
209. WITNEY, R. & V., R. Sankey; CC., W. Mills, W. A. Harrison			
With Curbridge		4300	1600
Chaplain to the Union, W. Mills.			
210. Yelford, *Witney*, R., George Hough	. . .	17	No R.

DEANERY OF WOODSTOCK.

RURAL DEAN—Rev. William Blackstone Lee, Rector of Wootton.

		Popu-lation.	Church Accom.
211. Aston, North, *Deddington*, V., Chas. R. Clifton	. .	307	150
212. Aston, Steeple, *Woodstock*, R., J. Burrows; C., A. W. Mills		702	300
213. Barton, Steeple, *Woodstock*, V., Wm. Green	. .	820	300
214. Barton, Westcott [d], *Woodstock*, R., Edmund L. Lockyer .		270	130
215. Begbrooke, *Oxford*, R., Ellis Ashton; C., Charles Fort .		88	100
216. Bladon [e] with Woodstock, *Woodstock*, R., G. W. St. John; CC., Edward Geare, George Steele . . . Master of the Grammar-School, and Chaplain to the Union, E. Reddall.		2000	1100
217. Cassington with Worton, *Eynsham*, V., Thomas Forster, ℥.		454	Suff.
218. Combe, Long, *Woodstock*, P.C., William Barrett .	.	600	250
219. Dunstew, *Deddington*, V., Archibald Malcolm	.	454	200
220. Eynsham, *Oxford*, V., William Simcox Bricknell, ℥.	.	1941	600
221. Glympton, *Woodstock*, R., C. W. M. Bartholomew .		148	90
222. Handborough, *Oxford*, R., R. W. Higgs, D.C.L. .	.	1153	No R.
223. Kiddington, *Woodstock*, R., J. G. Browne	. .	303	No R.
224. Kidlington [f], *Oxford*, V., J. P. Lightfoot, D.D.; CC., T. Whitehead, Henry Newby.—With Water-Eaton .	.	1491	750
225. Northleigh, *Witney*, V., Cyrus Morrall	. . .	725	350
226. Rousham, *Woodstock*, R.,	. . . .	134	120
227. Sandford, *Woodstock*, V., Thomas Curme	. .	515	300
228. Shipton-on-Cherwell, *Kidlington*, R., Henry J. Passand .		125	100
229. Stanton-Harcourt, *Witney*, V., William P. Walsh .	.	699	385
With Southleigh		360	290
230. Stonesfield, *Woodstock*, R., F. Robinson, ℥.	. .	g 632	250
231. Tackley, *Oxford*, R., L. A. Sharpe, ℥. . .	.	558	Suff.
232. Wilcot, *Witney*, R., J. Buck; C., G. Carpenter	.	10	No R.
233. Wootton, *Woodstock*, R., W. B. Lee; C., John Hurst	.	1150	350
234. Yarnton, *Oxford*, V., P. Maurice, D.D.; C., W. Price	.	317	No R.

[b] This parish is united with Widford in respect of many of its charities, which are very numerous, having been founded by the members of the now extinct family of the Fettyplaces.

[c] The Church in a miserable condition ; the chancel in ruins.

[d] The church re-opened for divine service, after complete restoration, Jan. 2, 1856.

[e] Bladon is the mother parish to the Chapelry of Woodstock.

[f] Vicarage annexed to Exeter College, which society are Rectors.

[g] 316 males and 316 females.

Archdeaconry of Berks.,

Including the County of Berks., and insulated places in the County of Wilts., was annexed and united to the Diocese of Oxford by virtue of an Order in Council of the fifth of October, 1836, and the union took effect from the publication of the Order in the "London Gazette" on the seventh day of October, 1836.

DEANERY OF ABINGDON. (*First Portion.*)

RURAL DEAN—Rev. Nathaniel Dodson, St. Helen's, Abingdon.

	Population.	Church Accom.
235. Abingdon, St. Helen, *V.*, N. Dodson, ✠; *CC.*, W. A. Strange, D.D., H. A. Pickard, T. D. Mortimer, H. O. Crawley .	6152	No R.
With Drayton, Sandford, Shippon	505	
Master of the Grammar-School, W. A. Strange, D D.		
Chaplain to Gaol and Union, G. M. Walkem.		
236. Abingdon, St. Nicholas, *R.*, N. Dodson, ✠; *CC.*, T. Short, E. T. H. Harper	696	No R.
237. Appleton, *Abingdon, R.*, W. James Butler, ✠. . .	540	450
238. Besselsleigh, *Abingdon, R.* ; *C.*, C. D. Everett	93	No R.
239. Cumnor, *Abingdon, V.*, C. F. O. Spencer; *C.*, R. Ley .	1100	220
240. Hincksey, North, *Oxford, P. C.*, R. P. G. Tiddeman, ✠. .	488	112
241. Hincksey, South, *P. C.*, Hon. F. Bertie; *C.*, W. Morrison	300	No R.
With Wootton, *Abingdon, P. C.*, ...	370	No R.
242. Fyfield, *Abingdon, P. C.*, F. Burges	428	No R.
243. Hinton Waldrich, *Faringdon, R.*, Wm. Jephson .	389	150
244. Kingston Bagpuze, *Abingdon, R.*, James F. Jowett .	290	200
245. Longworth, *Faringdon, R.*, O. Jenkyns; *CC.*, M. W. Currie, H. Crook		
With Charney	1119	No R.
246. Marcham with Garford, *Abingdon, V.*, H. Randolph; *C.*, T. J. Williams	1197	No R.
247. Milton, *Abingdon, R.*, Ven. C. C. Clerke . . .	445	250
248. Radley, *Abingdon, P. C.*, R. Gibbings . . .	556	No R.
Warden of St. Peter's College, W. Sewell; Subwarden, W. Wood.		
249. Steventon, *Abingdon, V.*. William Harley . . .	1000	360
250. Sunningwell with Kennington.*Abingdon, R.*, G. H. Sawyer	266	205
251. Sutton-Courtney, *Abingdon, V.*, R. J. H. Rice		
With Appleford and Sutton-Wick	1600	700
252. Tubney, *Abingdon, R.*, W. J. Butler, ✠. . . .	233	150
253. Wytham, *Oxford, R.*, Hon. F. Bertie; *C.*, H. O. Coxe .	200	Suff.

DEANERY OF ABINGDON. (*Second Portion.*)

254. Ashbury, *Faringdon, V.*, Wm. Chambers; *C.*, H. Lee .	800	500
255. Balking, *Faringdon, P. C.*, Francis Rose, D.D. . .	210	Suff.
With Woolstone	290	Suff.
256. Buckland[h], *Faringdon, V.*, Joseph Moore . .	1000	350
257. Buscott, *Faringdon, R.*, F. A. Dawson . . .	438	100
258. Coleshill, *Faringdon, V.*. E. Bouverie; *C.*, R. H. Hooper	391	No R.
259. Compton-Beauchamp, *Great Faringdon, R.*, G. Carter .	138	No R.
260. Coxwell, Great, *Great Faringdon, V.*, J. F. Cleaver .	365	No R.
261. Eaton-Hastings, *Faringdon, R.*, Richard Rice .	140	70
262. Faringdon, *V.*, Henry Barne, ✠; *C.*, Edmund Thompson	3122	800
With Little Coxwell	286	150
Chaplain to the Union, R. H. Hooper.		

	Popu-lation.	Church Accom.
263. Hatford, *Faringdon, R.*, James Hearn	140	100
264. Littleworth, *Faringdon, P. C.*, J. Moore ; *C.*, J. Budd .	380	240
265. Longcot, *Faringdon, P. C.*, J. Hughes	696	No R.
266. Pusey, *Faringdon, R.*, William Evans, ⚥. . . .	157	140
267. Shellingford, *Faringdon, R.*, H. R. Dupré . . .	293	No R.
268. Shrivenham, *Faringdon, V.*, E. Berens ; *C.*, C. B. Calley,		
H. Suckling	1469	600
With Watchfield Chapel		168
And Bourton Chapel		100
269. Stanford-in-the-Vale with Goosey, *Faringdon, V.*, *C.*		
Wordsworth ; *CC.*, E. H. Lloyd, M. A. Camilleri, D.D.	1150	500
270. Uffington, *Faringdon, V.*, Henry P. Gurney . .	650	650
271. Wittenham, Long, *Abingdon, V.*, J. C. Clutterbuck .	608	300
272. ———— Little, *Abingdon, R.*, Fred. Thos. Hilliard .	125	250

DEANERY OF MAIDENHEAD.

RURAL DEAN—Rev. James Edward Austen Leigh, Bray, Maidenhead.

	Popu-lation.	Church Accom.
273. Binfield, *Bracknell, R.*, James Randall ; *C.*, E. Savory .	1280	550
274. Bisham, *Maidenhead, V.*, T. E. Powell ; *C.*, C. F. Porter	530	330
275. BRACKNELL [k], *P. C.*, E. H. Linzee ; *C.*, P. B. Collings .	950	300
276. Bray, *Maidenhead, V.*, J. Edward A. Leigh, ⚥.; *C.*,		
Hemming Robeson	2250	800
Chapel of Ease at Oakley Green		200
276.*Boyne Hill, *Maidenhead, P. C.*, W. Gresley, *C.*, R. West	NoR	No R.
277. Clewer [l], *Windsor, R.*, T. T. Carter ; *CC.*, W. Cowper,		
John C. Pocock, Henry Lanphier . . .	1800	600
Chaplain to St. Mary's Home, T. Vincent.		
278. Cookham, *Maidenhead, V.*, Joseph T. Brown . .	1089	No R.
Chaplain to the Union, J. B. Smith.		
279. Cookham-Dean, *Maidenhead, P. C.*, Geo. H. Hodson, ⚥.;		
C., H. T. Howes	750	320
Chaplain to the Union, A. H. Pearse.		
280. Cranborne St. Peter's, *Windsor, P. C.*, Conyngham Ellis .	1141	424
281. Hampstead, East, *Bracknell, R.*, A. B. Townsend ; *C.*, F.		
G. Sturgis	[m]650	350
282. Hurley, *Maidenhead, V.*, F. J. Wethered, ⚥. . .	642	308
283. Knowle Hill [n], *Maidenhead, P. C.*, Simon Sturges .	750	300
284. Maidenhead, *P. C.*, J. Knollis ; *C.*, J. L. Roberts .	3600	800
285. Sandhurst [o], *Wokingham, P. C.*, Henry Parsons .	570	212
286. Stubbings, *Maidenhead, P. C.*, W. H. Skrine . .	370	170
287. Sunningdale [p], *Chertsey, P. C.*, Wm. C. R. Flint .	610	340
288. Sunninghill, *Windsor, V.*, A. M. Wale . . .	1228	No R.

[k] Formed out of parts of parishes of Warfield and Winkfield.

[l] In the parish, a House of Mercy for penitents, and St. John's Home for orphans and training servants.

[m] Exclusive of the Workhouse situated in the parish.

[n] Ecclesiastical district taken out of the parishes of Hurley and Wargrave.

[o] Exclusive of the Royal Military College (*circa* 300) in this parish, which has its separate chaplain.

[p] A district church formed out of five parishes ; i. e., Old Windsor, Egham, Chobham, Sunninghill, and Windleshall.

No.	Parish	Population.	Church Accom.
289.	Waltham-St.-Lawrence, *Reading*, *V.*, Edwin J. Parker, 𝔖.; *C.*, Edward Gunner	760	376
290.	White-Waltham, *Maidenhead*, *V.*, Wm. W. Yonge; *C.*, N. L. Shuldham	1100	250
	With Shottesbrooke		150
291.	Warfield, *Bracknell*, *V.*, C. J. Furlong; *C.*, W. A. Newman	930	No R.
292.	WINDSOR, New, *V.*, H. J. Ellison, 𝔖.; *CC.*, W. C. Bromehead, Joseph A. Miller, C. J. Robinson	7500	1800
293.	WINDSOR[q], Holy Trinity, *P. C.*, H. C. Hawtrey; *CC.*, S. W. Lloyd, F. Sterry	2862	1300
	Chaplain to the Chapel Royal, J. St. John Blunt.		
	,, to the Union, G. A. Hopkins.		
294.	WINDSOR, Old, *V.*, A. A. Cornish, 𝔖.		
	With Park Chapel, *P. C.*, J. S. Blunt	[r]850	460
295.	Winkfield, *Windsor*, *V.*, Charles J. Elliott	700	500
296.	WOKINGHAM, *P. C.*, T. Morres, 𝔖.; *C.*, W. Hirst	3658	900
	Chaplain to the Union, W. Hirst.		

DEANERY OF NEWBURY.

RURAL DEAN—Rev. Henry William Majendie, Speen.

No.	Parish	Population.	Church Accom.
297.	Aldermaston, *Reading*, *P. C.*, J. P. Burne	730	250
298.	Avington, *Hungerford*, *R.*, John James, 𝔖.	101	70
299.	Beedon, *Newbury*, *V.*, David R. Murray; *C.*, T. J. Heard	308	Suff.
300.	Beenham-Vallance, *Reading*, *V.*, Thomas H. Bushnell	430	140
301.	Boxford, *Newbury*, *R.*, George Wells	581	270
302.	Brimpton, *Newbury*, *V.*, G. B. Caffin	531	182
303.	Bucklebury with Marlestone, *Reading*, *V.*, G. Valpy; *C.*, R. L. Armstrong	1219	No R.
304.	Catmere, *Wantage*, *R.*, T. G. Onslow	127	100
305.	Chaddleworth, *Wantage*, *V.*, Edward Thompson, 𝔖.	520	400
306.	Chieveley, *Newbury*, *V.*, John E. Robinson, 𝔖.; *CC.*, Edward Salter, F. P. Wickham, with Leckhampstead, Oare, and Winterbourne	2100	Suff.[s]
307.	Enborne, *Newbury*, *R.*, C. A. Johnson; *C.*, B. G. Goodrich	407	250
308.	Garston, East, *Hungerford*, *V.*, Leveson Randolph	660	200
309.	Greenham, *Newbury*, *R.*, John H. Milne; *C.*, C. Whittle	1280	300
310.	Hampstead-Marshall, *Newbury*, *R.*, C. A. Johnson; *C.*, B. G. Goodrich	345	230
311.	Hermitage[t], *Newbury*, *P. C.*, Philip A. Longmore	410	145
312.	HUNGERFORD, *V.*, Wm. Cookson; *CC.*, Robert Chilton, Wm. J. Baron	2852	800
	Chaplain to the Union, W. J. Baron.		
313.	Ilsley, East, *Newbury*, *R.*, Thomas Loveday, 𝔖.	750	450
314.	Ilsley, West, *Newbury*, *R.*, Edward G. Moore; *C.*, Thos. Cox	406	160

[q] Holy Trinity parish, constituted in 1844, comprises that portion of the former parish of Clewer situated within the borough of Windsor. There is no parsonage-house:—right of burial at Clewer.

[r] This includes 300 in the Union, and the students (50) of the Jesuits' College at Beaumont.

[s] In the four churches.

[t] A district of Hampstead-Norris.

	Popu-lation.	Church Accom.
315. Inkpen, *Hungerford*, R., John Butler	760	300
316. Kintbury, *Hungerford*, V., J. W. D. Dundas . . .	1600	600
With Denford Chapel, P. C., F. Alderman. . .		100
317. LAMBORNE, V., R. Milman		
With Eastbury, C., H. R. Hayward	2222	No R.
318. Lamborne-Woodlands, *Lamborne*, R., J. Bacon ; C., H. Walker	355	No R.
Chaplain to the Union, H. T. White.		
319. Midgham, *Newbury*, P. C., T. Barton . . .	250	200
320. NEWBURY, R., James L. Randall, S.; CC., W. F. Norris, E. C. Oldfield	6000	1500
321. Peasemore, *Newbury*, R., F. A. Houblon . . .	360	240
322. Shalbourn, *Hungerford*, V., J. Gore ; C., R. G. Bryan .	1023	No R.
323. Shaw with Donnington, *Hungerford*, R. . . .	700	400
324. Shefford, East, *Hungerford*, R., S. Brown . . .	60	90
325. Shefford, West, *Hungerford*, R., T. T. Churton . .	523	200
326. Speen, *Newbury*, V., H. W. Majendie, S.; C., F. W. Harnett	750	400
327. Speenhamland, St. Mary's, *Newbury*, P.C., J.A.D.Meakin ;		
Lecturer, F. W. Harnett	1500	1000
328. Stockcross, St John's, *Newbury*, C. P., John Adams .	1150	350
329. Thatcham [x], *Newbury*, V., John H. Milne; CC., C. Whittle, H. B. Stevens	2600	682
330. Wasing, *Reading*, R., Samuel George Rees . . .	80	161
331. Welford with Wickham, *Newbury*, R., W. Nicholson ; CC., W. R. Dickson, G. F. Le Mesurier . .	1160	c 500
332. Woodhay, West, *Newbury*, R, Geo. A. Moullin . .	130	150
333. Woolhampton, *Newbury*, R., L. M. Hatton ; C., D. C. Gill	602	No R.

DEANERY OF READING.

RURAL DEAN—Rev. John Wilder, Sulham.

	Popu-lation.	Church Accom.
334. Arborfield, *Reading*, R., J. W. Hayes, Bt. ; C., A. Buchanan	300	130
335. Barkham, *Wokingham*, R., E. St. John ; C, A. Roberts .	200	160
336. Bearwood, *Wokingham*, P. C., R. E. A. Willmott . .	500	No R.
337. Bradfield, *Reading*, R., T. Stevens ; CC., J. Marriott, J. Reeves	1216	500
With Holy Trinity, ...		150
St. Simon and St. Jude, for the workhouse, C., J. Robinson		200
338. Burghfield, *Reading*, R., H. C. Cherry . . .	1193	608
339. Englefield, *Reading*, R., F. J. Eyre . . .	375	180
340. Finchampstead, *Wokingham*, R., E. St. John ; C., S. Slocock	600	260
341. Hurst, *Reading*, P. C., A. A. Cameron ; C., E. P. Wellings	1238	480
Twyford, St. Mary, C., L. H. Rudd . . .	560	280
342. Lambwood-hill Common [y], *Reading*, P. C., F. H. Bishop	600	230
343. Padworth, *Reading*, R., George W. Curtis . . .	290	90
344. Pangbourne, *Reading*, R., Robert Finch . . .	800	300
345. Purley, *Reading*, R., Richard Palmer	178	Suff.

[x] Originally comprising Midgham and Greenham, now each a perpetual curacy.
[y] The hamlet of Graizley is within the district, with a population of 64.

	Popu-lation.	Church Accom.
346. READING.—St. Giles', *V.*, T. V. Fosbery, ☒; *CC.*, Wm. F. Addison, John Fletcher	6250	870
Chaplain of the Royal Berkshire Hospital, J. B. Colvill.		
347. St. John, *P. C.*, W. Payne; *C.*, F. B. Blenkin . .	2750	730
348. St. Lawrence, *V.*, J. Ball, ☒.; *C.*, W. B. Drawbridge .	4571	No R.
349. St. Mary-the-Virgin, *V.*, S. W. Yates; *CC.*, H. C. Calverly, W. Romanis	9148	No R.
350. St. Mary, Castle-st., *P. C.*, G. I. Tubbs; *C.*, C. Sterling		No R.
351. Holy Trinity[a], *P. C.*, W. W. Phelps; *C.*, H. H. Phelps	2000	1100
Master of the Royal Grammar-School, R. Appleton.		
Chaplain of the Berks County Prison, R. Mant.		
Chaplain to the Union, C. Hole.		
352. Ruscombe, *Reading*, *P. C.*, L. H. Rudd	c 280	160
353. Shinfield, *Reading*, *V.*, B. Bayfield	657	Suff.
354. Stratfield-Mortimer, *Reading*, *V.*, John A. Clarke .	900	500
With Chapel-of-ease, *R.*, A. L. White . . .		300
355. Sulham, *Reading*, *R.*, John Wilder; *C*, H. B. Wilder .	131	110
356. Sulhamstead-Abbots, *Reading*, *R.*, Robert Coulthard, with Sulhamstead-Banister	620	Suff.
357. Swallowfield, *Reading*, *P. C*, J. Kitcat . . .	1213	411
358. Theale, *Reading*, *R.*, Thomas Butler . . .	650	300
359. Tidmarsh, *Reading*, *R.*, Henry H. Woods . . .	172	115
360. Tilehurst[b], *Reading*, *R.*, John William Routh .	1200	340
361. Twyford. *See Hurst*, 341.		
362. Ufton-Nervet, *Reading*, *R.*, John F. Christie . .	421	120

DEANERY OF WALLINGFORD.

RURAL DEAN—Rev. Robert Sumner, Brightwell.

	Popu-lation.	Church Accom.
363. Aldworth, *Reading*, *V*[b]	817	250
364. Ashampstead, *Reading*, *P. C*, John Holding . .	439	200
365. Aston-Tirrold, *Wallingford*, *R.*, J. L. Hoskyns .	363	260
366. Basildon, *Reading*, *V.*, R. B. Fisher; *C.*, W. G. Baxter .	798	350
367. Blewbury, *Wallingford*, *V.*, J. Macdonald, ☒, with Aston Upthorpe and Upton . . .	650	Suff.
368. Brightwell, *Wallingford*, *R.*, R. Sumner; *C.*, R. S. Gubbins	678	250
369. Cholsey, *Wallingford*, *V.*, H. W. Lloyd, ☒. . . .	1200	380
370. Didcot, *Abingdon*, *R.*, J. A. Ashworth . . .	241	No R.
371. Frilsham, *Newbury*, *R.*, J. Flory Howard . .	184	No R.
372. Hagbourne, *Wallingford*, *V.*, Richard Meredith .	905	300
373. Hampstead-Norris, with Langley, *Newbury*, *V.*, J. Blissard	913	c. 300
374. Moreton, North, *Wallingford*, *V.*, Albert Barff . .	830	,, ,,[c]
375. Moreton, South, *Wallingford*, *R.*, R. Michell; *C.*, J. Frith	435	250
376. Moulsford, *Wallingford*, *P. C.*, G. K. Morrell, D.C.L., ☒.	170	125
377. Stanford-Dingley, *Reading*, *R.*, Chas. Holloway; *C.*, T. W. Cockell	178	185
378. Streatley, *Reading*, *V.*, J. R. Burgess . . .	584	No R.

[a] A district by courtesy of the parish of St. Mary.
[a] Joined to Theale as far as rates, &c., are concerned.
[b] Parish under the charge of the Rev. W. B. Young, formerly Surrogate in this diocese.
[c] The church is in process of restoration.

	Population.	Church Accom.
379. WALLINGFORD, St. Leonard, *R.*, J. Langley . . .	929	No R.
With Sotwell . . .	133	
380. ——— St. Mary-the-More, *R.*, J. Langley, *S.* . .	1304	No R.
381. ——— St. Peter, *R.*, William Hazel . . .	600	180
Chaplain to the Union, F. Reyroux.		
382. Yattendon, *Newbury*, *R.*, J. H. Howard . . .	260	No R.

DEANERY OF WANTAGE.

RURAL DEAN—Rev. William John Butler, Wantage.

	Population.	Church Accom.
383. Ardington, *Wantage*, *V.*, Ralph Barnes	397	230
384. Brightwaltham, *Wantage*, *R.*, Richard Marter; *C.*, J. T. Woodcock	460	200
385. Challow, East and West, *Wantage*, *P. C.*, Geo. Purdue; *C.*, J. C. Pearson	550	300
386. Childrey, *Wantage*, *R.*, Samuel Whittingham, D.D. .	553	446
387. Chilton, *East Ilsley*, *R.*, E. M. Chaplin . . .	282	`o R.
388. Compton, *Newbury*, *V.*, J. S. Wasey . . .	587	150
389. Denchworth, *Wantage*, *V.*, T. S. F. Rawlins . .	278	160
390. Farnborough, *Wantage*, *R.*, Wm. Price; *C.*, W. H. Price	225	200
391. Fawley, *Wantage*, *Don.*, H. Hayward . . .	250	220
392. Grove, *Wantage*, *P. C.*, W. S. Bricknell; *C.*, Rev. J. S. G. Cranmer	530	300
393. Hanney[e], *Wantage*, *V.*, J. Macdougall; *C.*, A. Goalin	1040	420
394. HARWELL, *V.*, S. M. Smith	800	400
395. Hendred, East, *Wantage*, *R.*, A. Pott, *S.* . . .	900	No R.
396. Hendred, West, *Wantage*, *V.*, J. Tucker . . .	335	180
397. Letcombe-Basset, *Wantage*, *R.*, Charles F. Willis .	292	No R.
398. Letcombe-Regis, *Wantage*, *V.*, E. S. James . .	480	300
399. Lockinge, East, *Wantage*, *R.*, F. K. Leighton, D.D., *S.*; *C.*, J. F. Collins . . , . . .	295	Suff.
400. Lyford[f], *Wantage*, *P. C.*, Walton G. Wilkinson .	143	100
401. Sparsholt with Kingston-Lisle, *Wantage*, *V.*, H. A. Dodd, *S.*; *C.*, R. Z. Walker	517	No R.
402. WANTAGE with Charlton, *V.*, W. J. Butler; *CC.*, W. G. Sawyer, E. F. Nelson	3300	1100
Master of the Grammar-School, C. R. Crooke.		
Chaplain of St. Mary's Home, T. Vincent.		
Chaplain to the Union, W. J. Butler.		

The Archdeaconry of Buckingham,

Being the whole County of Buckingham, was annexed and united to the Diocese of Oxford by virtue of an Order in Council of the nineteenth of July, 1837, and the union took effect on the first avoidance of the See of Oxford, namely, on the thirtieth of November, 1845.

e The parish consists of two distinct townships, East and West Hanney. The church is situated in the latter, but a new chapel has been erected in the former.
f Originally a hamlet of Hanney, but made a separate parish since 1840.

DEANERY OF AMERSHAM.

RURAL DEAN—Rev. Thomas Evetts, Prestwood.

	Population.	Church Accom.
403. AMERSHAM, *R.*, J. T. Drake, ℈., *C.*, R. H. Kingdon . Chaplain to the Union, E. J. Luce.	3662	No R.
404. Chalfont St. Giles, *Slough*, *R.*, G. T. Pretyman ; *C.*, J. Clark	1160	500
405. Chalfont St. Peter, *Gerrard's Cross*, *V.*, G. Gleed ; *C.*, H. W. Ferrier	1482	No R.
406. Chenies, *Amersham*, *R.*, Lord W. Russell ; *C.*, J. Matthews	565	No R.
407. CHESHAM, *V.*, A. F. Aylward ; *C.*, C. T. Binns . .	6093	800
408. Chesham-Bois, *Chesham*, *R.*, Charles Blackman . .	185	150
409. Denham, *Uxbridge*, *R.*, C. A. Hall ; *C.*, C. Joyce .	1062	No R.
410. Fulmer, *Slough*, *R.*, H. Butterfield . . .	330	200
411. Hazlemere, *High Wycombe*, *P. C.*, George Allan . .	1106	350
412. Latimer*g*, *Chesham*, *R.*, Bryant Burgess, ℈. . .	271	210
413. Missenden, Little, *Amersham*. *V.*, T. W. Hanmer ; *C.*, T. S. Pepper	656	No R.
414. Penn, *Amersham*, *V.*, J. Knollis ; *C.*, Thos. Owen Hall .	725	Suff.
415. Penn-Street, *Amersham*, *P. C.*, A. S. Butler . .	782	400
416. Prestwood, *Gt. Missenden*, *P. C.*, T. Evetts, ℈. ; *C.*, G. R. Scobell	900	300
417. Seer-Green, *Beaconsfield*, *P. C.*, H. Herbert . .	317	188
418. Tyler's-Green, *Amersham*, *P. C.*, Walter Gibbs . .	500	250

DEANERY OF BUCKINGHAM. (*First Portion.*)

RURAL DEAN—Rev. James Cockerton, Turweston.

	Population.	Church Accom.
419. Barton-Hartshorn, *Buckingham*, *C.*, E. L. Smith, with Chetwode	137	140
420. Biddlesden, *Brackley*, *P. C.*, Hugh W. Smith . .	123	140
421. BUCKINGHAM, *V.*, H. Roundell, ℈. ; *CC.*, W. B. Kenna-way, C. H. Travers . . . . . . Chaplain to the Union, D. Watkins. Chaplain to the Bucks. Lunatic Asylum, J. B. Reade.	4020	1320
422. Gawcott, *Buckingham*, *P. C.*, T. C. Whitehead . .	630	400
423. Hillesden, *Buckingham*, *P. C.*, William T. Eyre, ℈. .	250	250
424. Padbury, *Buckingham*, *V.*, William T. Eyre, ℈. .	600	400
425. Preston-Bisset, *Buckingham*, *R.*, John E. Sabin, with Cowley hamlet	450	c300
426. Radcliffe, *Buckingham*, *R.*, John Coker ; *C.*, T. Walters, with Chackmore	350	140
427. Shalstone, *Buckingham*, *R.*, Cadwallader Coker .	210	140
428. Stratford-Water, *Buckingham*, *R.*, Jos. Bosworth, D.D. .	179	No R.
429. Tingewick, *Buckingham*, *R.*, John Coker . .	850	430
430. Turweston, *Brackley*, *R.*, James Cockerton . .	322	250
431. Twyford, *Bicester*, *R.*, William Perkins, ℈. .	727	500
432. Westbury, *Buckingham*, *V.*, W. Gurden ; *C.*, C. E. Thompson	458	230

g A hamlet of Chesham.

DEANERY OF BUCKINGHAM. (*Second Portion.*)
RURAL DEAN—The Rev. Richard Norris Russell, Beachampton.

	Popu-lation.	Church Accom.
433. Akeley, *Buckingham*, R., J. H. Risley	370	200
434. Beachampton, *Stony Stratford*, R., R. N. Russell, 🎓. .	245	200
435. Bradwell, *Stony Stratford*, V., W. Drake; C., J. Randolph	386	120
436. Balverton, *Stony Stratford*	505	300
437. Foscote, *Buckingham*, R., E. A. Uthwatt . . .	90	150
438. Leckhampstead, *Buckingham*, R., H. Drummond .	518	298
439. Lillingstone-Darrell, *Buckingham*, R., W. Bell .	207	No R.
440. Lillinstone-Lovell [h], *Buckingham*, R., William Lloyd .	149	200
441. Loughton, *Stony Stratford*, R., John Athawes .	325	195
442. Maids' Moreton, *Buckingham*, R., W. Uthwatt; C., W. Davies	573	250
443. Shenley, *Stony Stratford*, R., R. W. Scurr . .	493	No R.
444. Stantonbury [i], *Stony Stratford*, V., Charles P. Cotter, with Newbradwell	800	No R.
445. STONY STRATFORD, P. C., J. B. Ansted, 🎓. . .	1751	700
446. Stowe, *Buckingham*, V., W. Uthwatt . . .	342	No R.
447. Thornborough, *Buckingham*, V., D. Watkins . .	700	No R.
448. Thornton, with Nash, *Winslow*, R., H. S. Templer .	534	120
449. Wolverton, New [k], *Stony Stratford*, P.C., Geo. Weight .	1666	Suff.
450. Wolverton, Old, *Stony Stratford*, V., W. P. Trevelyan .	540	150

DEANERY OF BURNHAM.
RURAL DEAN—Rev. Charles Whately, Taplow.

	Popu-lation.	Chur h Accom.
451. BEACONSFIELD, R., John Gould, 🎓.: C., S. E. Major .	1686	c 370
452. Burnham with Boveney, *Maidenhead*, V., T. Carter, 🎓.; C., R. P. Bent	2301	c 500
453. COLNBROOK, P. C., C. D. Goldie; C., F. S. Sykes · .	1400	350
454. Datchet, *Slough*, V., H. F. U. Hall; C., C. Maldon .	898	No R.
455. Dorney, *Windsor*, V., L. Campbell Edwards . .	4.0	200
456. Eton [l], St. John the Evangelist, *Windsor*, *Provost*, E. C. Hawtrey; *Conducts*, C. C. Paul, Henry Roper, H. S. Eyre Chaplain to the Union, R. F. Holt.	3000	1200
457. Farnham-Royal, *Eton*, R., S. F. Marshall . .	983	Insuf.
458. Hedgerley, *Gerrard's Cross*, R., Edward Baylis .	140	235
459. Hedsor, *Great Marlow*, R., A. Youldon; C., J. B. Smith	183	No R.
460. Hitcham, *Maidenhead*, R., Henry M. Groves . .	170	100
461. Horton, *Slough*, R., Richard G. Foot . . .	330	130
462. Iver, *Uxbridge*, P. C., W. S. Ward; C., H. Housman .	1985	678
463. Langley-Marsh, *Colnbrook*, P. C., W. D. Scoone .	1394	No R.
464. Stoke-Poges [m], *Slough*, V., John Shaw . . . c.	1400	700

[h] Returned as in the Deanery of Bicester.

[i] The foundation-stone of a parish church was laid May 24, 1853, by the most noble the Marquess of Chandos, at Stantonbury, which name was given on the occasion to the village situated in the district of Newbradwell united to Stantonbury parish by order in council dated July 16, 1857.

[k] A district of the old parish. Church consecrated 1844.

[l] The College and parish of Eton are excluded by statutes confirmed by Act of Parliament from the Archdeaconry of Burnham. The Archdeacon receives a yearly payment as compensation. The archidiaconal authority over the parish is vested in the Provost.

[m] Greater part of the population in the hamlet of Ditton, five miles from the church. Very few houses within a mile of the church.

	Population.	Church Accom.
465. Taplow, *Maidenhead*, *R.*, Charles Whately . . .	704	400
466. Upton-with-Chalvey, *Slough*, *V.*, E. T. Champnes; *C.*, J. A. Cree	3573	No R.
467. Wenham, *Slough*, *R.*, A. A. Kempe; *C.*, F. F. Fawkes .	190	80
468. Wyrardisbury, or Wraysbury, *Staines*, *V.*, S. Neville .	701	No R.

DEANERY OF CLAYDON.
RURAL DEAN—Rev. William Robert Fremantle, Claydon.

	Population.	Church Accom.
469 Addington, *Winslow*, *R.*, R. W. Scurr; *C.*, T. W. Perry .	72	ᵃ 84
470. Adstock, *Winslow*, *R.*, A. Baynes; *C.*, W. H. Plummer .	393	No R.
471. Claydon, East, *Winslow*, *V.*, W. R. Fremantle, S.; *C.*, H. Hammond	350	300
472. Claydon, Middle, *Winslow*, *R.*, W. R. Fremantle, S.; *C.*, H. Lloyd	150	250
473. Claydon, Steeple, *Winslow*, *V.*, W. R. Fremantle, S.; *C.*, R. Burges	900	400
474. Edgcot, *Bicester*, *R.*, David E. Dewar; *C.*, C. M. de P. Gillam	193	100
475. Granborough, *Winslow*, *V.*, John W. Hayward; *C.*, G. O. Corbett	355	300
476. Grendon-Underwood, *Bicester*, *R.*, W. J. Marshall .	427	No R.
477. Ludgershall, *Thame*, *R.*, T. Martyn; *C.*, Cl. Martyn .	514	No R.
478. Marsh-Gibbon, *Bicester*, *R.*, Thomas H. Greene . .	944	378
479. Marston, Fleet, *Aylesbury*, *R.*, H. Wanklyn . . .	30	70
480. Marston, North, *Winslow*, *P. C.*, Richard Knight .	692	280
481. Oving, *Aylesbury*, *R.*, J. H. Thelwall; *C.*, H. Le Grand Boyce	442	157
482. Pitchcott, *Aylesbury*, *R.*, William Noble . . .	48	80
483. Quainton, *Winslow*, *R.*, Edward N. Young . . .	947	500
484. Waddesdon, *Aylesbury*, *RR.*, first and second portions, E. W. F. Latimer°; third portion, Rev. J. Lowry°; *CC.*, W. W. Walton, J. E. Weddell . . .	1800	550
485. WINSLOW, *V.*, W. W. McCreight, S.; *C.*, S. M. White Chaplain to the Union, W. W. McCreight.	1889	No R.
486. Wotton-Underwood, *Aylesbury*, *P. C.*, J. C. Addison .	253	No R.

DEANERY OF MURSLEY. (*First Portion.*)
RURAL DEAN—Rev. A. P. Cust, Cheddington.

	Population.	Church Accom.
487. Aston-Abbots, *Aylesbury*, *V.*, John Thornton . . .	320	100
488. Cublington, *Aylesbury*, *R.*, William Bousfield . .	285	120
489. Drayton-Parslow, *Bletchley*, *R.*, Benjamin Spurrell .	480	180
490. Dunton, *Winslow*, *R.*, E. Q. Ashby; *C.*, E. H. Hoare .	98	126
491. Hardwicke, *Aylesbury*, *R.*, Christopher Erle; *C.*, H. Rich	645	Suff.
492. Hogston, *Winslow*, *R.*, John G. Villar . . .	220	186
493. Horwood, Great, *Winslow*, *R*, Simon T. Adams . .	831	550
494. ———— Little, *Winslow*, *V.*, T. B. Holt . . .	400	200
495. Mursley, *Winslow*, *R.*, T. K. W. Harries; *C.*, R. Holt .	553	c 200

ᵃ Number of fixed seats in the church (now being restored), but space enough for 120.
° Non-resident.

	Population.	Church Accom.
496. Stewkley, *Winslow*, *V.*, R. Roberts	1432	No R.
497. Swanbourne, *Winslow*, *V.*, J. Niven	646	No R.
498. Tattenhoe, *Stony Stratford*, P. C., John Randolph	50	40
499. Whaddon, *Stony Stratford*, *V.*, William Pigott	458	300
500. Whitchurch, *Aylesbury*, *V.*, Alfred Turner	925	500

DEANERY OF MURSLEY. (*Second Portion.*)
RURAL DEAN—Rev. Arthur P. Cust, Cheddington.

	Population.	Church Accom.
501. Cheddington, *Tring*, *R.*, Arthur P. Cust	507	300
502. Drayton-Beauchamp, *Tring*, *R.*, W. H. Kelke	260	250
503. Eddlesborough, *Ivinghoe*, *V.*, W. B. Wroth; *C.*, R. Spoonley	1838	No R.
504. Grove, *Leighton-Buzzard*, *R.*, H. Matthew; *C.*, A. Morice	38	No R.
505. IVINGHOE, *V.*, William J. Hamilton	2023	425
506. Linslade, *Leighton-Buzzard*, P. C., W. E. Richardson	1309	600
507. Marsworth, *Tring*, *V.*, Isaac B. Turner	431	210
508. Mentmore, *Leighton-Buzzard*, *V.*, J. N. O. North, with Ledburn hamlet	361	250
509. Nettleden, *Hemel-Hempstead*, P. C., G. S. Cautley	108	160
With St. Margaret's hamlet	70	
510. Pightlesthorne, or Pitstone, *Tring*, P. C., C. R. Hutchinson	460	200
511. Slapton, *Leighton-Buzzard*, *R.*, T. B. Ludlow	298	122
512. Soulbury, *Leighton-Buzzard*, P. C., John Hart	600	250
513. Wing, *Leighton-Buzzard*, *V.*, Peter T. Ouvry	1400	300
514. Wingrave, *Aylesbury*, *V.*, J. M. Butt	813	No R.

DEANERY OF NEWPORT. (*First Portion.*)
RURAL DEAN—Rev. Henry Bull, Lathbury.

	Population.	Church Accom.
515. Astwood, *Newport-Pagnell*, *V.*, Charles Cumberlege	258	130
516. Chicheley, *Newport-Pagnell*, *V.*, Charles F. Partridge; *C.*, William Jeudwine	250	200
517. Clifton-Reynes, *Newport-Pagnell*, *R.*, Har y A. Small; *C.*, Henry Burgess, LL.D., Ph. D.	220	Suff.
518. Crawley, North, *Newport-Pagnell*, *R.*, C. L. Lowndes	914	No R.
519. Emberton, *Newport-Pagnell*, *R.*, T. Fry; *C.*, C. G. Hulton	600	500
520. Gayhurst, *Newport-Pagnell*, *R.*, F. S. Trotman	88	No R.
With Stoke-Goldington, *Newport-Pagnell*, *R.*	902	
521. Hanslope, *Stony Stratford*, *V.* and *R.*, M. A. Nicholson	1604	800
With Castlethorp	346	
522. Hardmead, *Newport-Pagnell*, *R.*, Bartlett G. Goodrich; *C.*, James H. Talbot	75	300
523. Haversham, *Newport-Pagnell*, *R.*, Arthur B. Frazer	275	c 300
524. Lathbury, *Newport-Pagnell*, P. C., H. Bull	147	No R.
525. Lavendon, *Olney*, *V.*, W. Tomkins	769	No R.
With Cold Brayfield	80	
526. Linford, Great, *Newport-Pagnell*, *R.*, F. Litchfield; *C.*, J. M. Webb	486	342
527. Linford, Little, *Newport-Pagnell*, P. C., L. Spencer; *C.*, J. W. Irving	57	No R.
528. NEWPORT-PAGNELL, *V.*, George Morley, S.	3651	1500
Chaplain to the Union, G. Morley.		

	Popu-lation.	Church Accom.
529. Newton-Blossomville, *Olney, R.*, James H. Talbot . .	270	350
530. OLNEY, *V.*, J. P. Langley, S.	2350	900
With Warrington hamlet	50	
531. Ravenstone, *Newport-Pagnell, V.*, William Godfrey .	446	300
532. Sherrington, *Newport-Pagnell, R.*, Alexander King .	900	280
533. Tyringham with Filgrove, *Newport-Pagnell, R.*, J. Tarver	180	Suff.
534. Weston-Underwood, *Newport-Pagnell, P. C.*, W. Godfrey;		
C., James C. Farmbrough	405	300

DEANERY OF NEWPORT. (*Second Portion.*)
RURAL DEAN—Rev. G. Wingram Pierce, Walton.

	Popu-lation.	Church Accom.
535. BLETCHLEY, with Water-Eaton hamlet, *R.*, T. D. Broughton	460	1000
536. Brickhill, Bow, *Bletchley, R.*, J. M. Jackson .	591	No R.
537. Brickhill, Great, *Bletchley, R.*, Sir Henry Foulis, Bart.;		
C., Frederick Veasey	729	400
538. Brickhill, Little, *Fenny Stratford, P. C.*, J. C. L. Court .	420	200
539. Broughton, *Newport-Pagnell, R.*, J. W. Irving .	182	Suff.
540. Milton-Keynes, *Newport-Pagnell, R.*, John N. Dalton .	320	180
541. Moulsoe, *Newport-Pagnell, R.*, Walter Drake .	240	160
542. Newnton-Longville, *Bletchley Station, R.*, J. R. Hughes	565	397
543. Simpson, *Fenny Stratford, R.*, T. W. Hanmer; *C.*, G.		
W. Pearse	300	No R.
544. Stoke-Hammond, *Bletchley, R* , Theodore Bouwens .	429	200
545. Stratford, Fenny^P, *Bletchley, P. C.*, Th. Pym Williamson	1000	250
546. Walton, *Bletchley, R.*, G. W. Pearse . .	90	No R.
547. Wavendon, *Woburn, Beds., R.*, H. Burney; *C.*, C. Mayor	970	400
548. Willen, *Newport-Pagnell, V.*, John Benthall, S. .	85	Suff.
549. Wolston, Great, *Bletchley Station, R.*, Edward Hill, with		
Wolston, Little	180	200
550. Woughton-on-the-Green, *Fenny Stratford, R.*, M. Farrell		
C., H. T. Sneppe	330	300

DEANERY OF WADDESDON.
RURAL DEAN—Rev. William Frederick Cartwright, Oakley.

	Popu-lation.	Church Accom.
551. Ashenden, *Thame, P. C.*, T. W. Gardner . .	290	No R.
With Dorton	139	
552. Brill with Boarstall, *Thame, P. C.*, John S. Baron, S. .	1311	500
553. Chearsley, *Thame, P. C.*, Amos Hayton; *C.*, Wm. Borrows	298	160
554. Chilton, *Thame, P. C.*, G. Chetwode . .	398	No R.
555. Crendon, Long, *Thame, P. C.*, Thomas Hayton .	1710	500
556. Ickford, *Wheatley, R.*, Richard Townsend . .	409	180
557. Ilmer, *Risborough, V.*, W. E. Partridge . .	84	Suff.
558. Kingsey, *Thame, V.*, William N. Jackson . .	210	160
559. Oakley, *Thame, V.*, Frederick W. Cartwright, S. .	420	390
560. Shabbingdon, *Wheatley, V.*, Benjamin Morland .	321	130
561. Towersey, *Thame, V.*, S. W. Barnett . .	450	220
562. Winchendon, Lower, *Waddesdon, P. C.*, Thomas Hayton	280	Suff.
563. Winchendon, Upper, *Aylesbury, P. C.*, F. Cox; *C.*, J. E.		
Weddell	230	80
564. Worminghall, *Wheatley, V.*, James Statter . .	375	200

^P A part of the parish of Simpson forms an integral portion of the town of Fenny Stratford.

DEANERY OF WENDOVER. *(First Portion.)*

RURAL DEAN—Rev. Arthur Isham, Weston-Turville.

	Population.	Church Accom.
565. Aston-Clinton, *Tring*, R., C. W. W. Eyton . . .	928	418
566. ———— St. Leonard's, P. C., Robt. Sutton . .	166	250
567. Cholesbury, *Tring*, P. C., H. P. Jeston ; CC., J. Hedges, J. S. Hill	113	60
568. Dinton, *Aylesbury*, V., J. Harrison ; C., C. S. Grubb .	859	523
569. Ellesborough, *Wendover*, R., ...	782	No R.
570. Halton, *Wendover*, R., G. A. Cuxson ; C., J. Browne .	170	200
571. Hawridge, *Tring*, R., Alfred C. Richings . . .	284	180
572. Kimble, Little, *Wendover*, R., J. Ormond . . .	180	100
573. Lee, *Tring*, P. C., S. S. Crutch	126	No R.
574. MISSENDEN, GREAT, V., Joshua Greaves ; C., F. W. Young	1700	700
575. Wendover, *Tring*, V., C. F. Champneys ; C., J. B. Watson	1950	640

DEANERY OF WENDOVER. *(Second Portion.)*

RURAL DEAN—Ven. Archdeacon Edward Bickersteth, Aylesbury.

	Population.	Church Accom.
576. Aston-Sandford, *Thame*, R., G. Alford . . .	88	No R.
577. AYLESBURY q, V., Ven. E. Bickersteth ; CC., W. Rawson, John Wood, John Daubeny . . . . Chaplain to the Gaol, G. A. Cuxson.	5081	1023
578. Bierton, *Aylesbury*, V., J. Crane Wharton . .	680	300
579. Cuddington, *Aylesbury*, P. C., James M. Price . .	650	256
580. Haddenham, *Thame*, V., Henry Meeres . .	1706	No R.
581. Hartwell, *Aylesbury*, R., Charles Lowndes . .	97	200
With Little Hampden	52	40
582. Horsenden, *Tring*, R., W. E. Partridge . . .	36	Suff.
583. Hulcot, *Aylesbury*, R., G. R. Ferris . . .	150	140
584. Quarrendon r, *Aylesbury*, V., ...	42	
584.*Stoke Mandeville with Buckland, *Aylesbury*, P. C., C. E. Partington	538	No R.
585. Stone, *Aylesbury*, V., J. B. Reade	800	265
586. Walton, *Aylesbury*, P. C., F. Young . . .	1200	600
587. Weston-Turville, *Wendover*, R., Arthur Isham, S. .	749	407

DEANERY OF WYCOMBE.

RURAL DEAN—Rev. Charles Lloyd, Great Hampden.

	Population.	Church Accom.
588. Bledlow, *Prince's Risborough*, V., W. Stephen ; C., O. J. Grace	1250	750
With Bledlow Ridge hamlet		250
589. Bradenham, *High Wycombe*, R., Isaac King . .	c 160	80
590. Fingest, *High Wycombe*, R., George A. Baker . .	330	120
With Ibstone		100
591. Hampden, Great, *Great Missenden*, R., Charles Lloyd .	300	250
592. Hughenden, *High Wycombe*, V., Charles W. Clubbe, S.	700	250
593. Kimble, Great, *Wendover*, V., J. Ormond . .	501	300
594. Lacey-Green, *Prince's Risborough*, P. C., W. J. Burgess	1000	504
595. Lane-End, *High Wycombe*, P. C., F. Ashpitel . .	955	No R.
596. Loudwater Chapel, *High Wycombe*, P. C., E. Arnold .	s	400
597. MARLOW, GREAT, V., Fred. Bussell ; C., G. Taylor .	t 4457	1600

q Aylesbury Schoolmasters' and Church Choral Association, (pp. 77, 78); Endowed School, (p. 90); and Infirmary, in the parish.
r Church in ruins. See Bierton.
s No district ; but lies at the south extremity of High Wycombe parish.
t A portion of this population taken off in the district of Lane-End.

	Population.	Church Accom.
598. Marlow, Little, *Great Marlow, C.*, R. Cattermole; *C.*, William Milton	891	350
599. Radnage, *Stokenchurch, R.*, G. Phillimore . .	433	No R.
600. Risborough, Monk's, *Prince's Risborough, R.*, H. W. J. Beauchamp	1064	400
601. RISBOROUGH, PRINCE'S, *P. C.*, C. E. Gray, S. . .	1407	No R.
602. Saunderton, *Tring, R*, F. A. Faber; *C.*, C. H. Phillips	232	130
603. Turville, *Henley-on-Thames, V.*, E. Scobell; *C.*, P. H. Boissier	450	350
604. Wooburn, *Beaconsfield, V.*, F. B. Ashley: T. Foulkes	2300	360
605. WYCOMBE, HIGH, *V.*, T. H. Paddon; *C.*, J. J. Ellis .	7300	1200
Chaplain to the Union, W. J. Burgess.		
606. Wycombe, West, *High Wycombe, V.*, G. Broadhead .	1645	No R.

ANNUAL CHARITIES IN THE DIOCESE.

SUMMARY.

Archdeaconry of OXFORD—	Poor.			Schools.			Other Charities.			Total.		
ASTON.	497	3	0	59	3	6	106	15	2	699	1	8
BICESTER.	311	14	2	44	4	0	45	6	3	401	4	5
CHIPPING-NORTON.	351	10	1	72	18	9	143	13	2	568	2	0
CUDDESDON.	307	0	7	246	7	8	129	1	8	682	9	11
DEDDINGTON.	1055	10	3	245	9	7	351	8	10	1652	8	8
HENLEY.	384	14	5	423	0	6	455	1	4	1262	16	3
Portion in Berks.	39	16	0	262	9	6	17	12	2	319	17	8
Portion in Bucks.	18	12	0	4	16	0				23	8	0
ISLIP.	101	11	11	176	10	0	25	1	8	303	3	7
NETTLEBED.	488	5	0	25	0	0	283	14	4	1796	19	4
OXFORD.	2041	14	4	110	0	0	1395	5	11	3547	0	3
WITNEY.	1028	7	0	540	17	2	374	10	0	1943	14	2
WOODSTOCK.	506	8	1	194	3	6	137	4	1	837	15	8
BERKS.—												
ABINGDON.	1800	19	7	528	12	3	291	5	9	2620	17	7
Second Portion.	295	4	3	123	5	9	173	5	9	591	15	9
MAIDENHEAD.	2477	12	0	1150	12	0	441	15	0	4069	19	0
NEWBURY.	3223	16	8	999	11	7	436	6	2	4659	14	5
READING.	2259	19	2	1583	17	6	938	16	2	4782	12	10
WALLINGFORD.	449	5	0	929	3	0	254	16	10	1633	4	10
WANTAGE.	945	10	4	148	16	0	425	10	10	1519	17	2
BUCKS.—												
AMERSHAM.	534	3	8	242	7	6	14	11	8	791	2	10
BUCKINGHAM.	200	8	8	49	12	6	74	3	9	324	14	11
Second Portion.	240	0	4	146	11	6	497	5	0	883	16	10
BURNHAM.	1027	14	9	257	17	3	566	18	0	1852	10	0
CLAYDON.	387	0	4	52	10	0	147	4	3	586	14	7
MURSLEY	78	12	6	25	0	0	21	10	0	125	2	6
Second Portion.	201	8	11	82	0	0	153	2	4	436	11	3
NEWPORT.	1143	12	1	130	0	0	401	17	7	1675	9	8
Second Portion.	324	10	10	54	18	4	198	12	10	578	2	0
WADDESDON.	415	6	0	123	5	9	94	5	0	632	16	9
WENDOVER.	208	13	4	16	12	0	430	13	0	655	18	4
Second Portion.	338	19	8	542	8	8	828	17	5	1710	5	9
WYCOMBE.	782	1	0	181	6	8	199	15	6	1163	3	2

As the chief items in these annual charities were given with the last issue of the DIOCESAN CALENDAR, and as they do not vary, it is not thought necessary to repeat them.

INDEX OF PARISHES IN THE DIOCESE.

INDEX OF THE NAMES OF THE CLERGY IN THE DIOCESE.

NOTES RELATING TO THE DIOCESE.

Documents in the Registry of the Diocese at Oxford:—

WILLS from the date of the Reformation till the present time.

ADMINISTRATIVE PAPERS and BONDS of the same dates.

PRESENTATIONS to Livings.

PARISH REGISTERS.

CONSECRATION ACTS.

DEEDS OF ENDOWMENT.

CONVEYANCE OF SITES.

Mortgage of Livings.

FACULTY PAPERS.

MARRIAGE BONDS and AFFIDAVITS.

TERRIERS.

ORDERS of the Queen in Council.

VISITATION Books.

INSTITUTION Books.

FACULTY Books.

COURT Books.

CURACY LICENCE Books.

ORDINATION and SUBSCRIPTION Books.

ORDINATION Papers.

TITHE COMMUTATION Plans, and CERTIFICATES of Redemption.

VISITATION Papers.

PRESENTMENTS, &c.

The Registry of the Diocese is situated in the New-road, close to the County Court. Hours of attendance from

Communications to be addressed to J. M. Davenport, Esq.

ARMS OF THE SEE.—Sable, a fesse argent, in chief three ladies' heads crowned or, arrayed and veiled of the second: in van an ox of the last passant over a ford proper.

THE BISHOP'S JURISDICTION.

THE Ecclesiastical Jurisdiction of the Bishop of Oxford is co-extensive with the Diocese, which consists of the Counties of Oxford, Berks., and Buckingham, including, as to Oxfordshire, the insulated parish of Widford, and, as to Berkshire, certain insulated parishes of Wiltshire.

PECULIARS.

BY order of the Queen in Council, based upon the statute 6th and 7th Wm. IV. cap. 77, §. 10, all Peculiars in the Diocese of Oxford were made subject to the Jurisdiction of the Bishop of that Diocese, and constituted a part thereof.

MISCELLANEOUS.

THE Diocese consists of OXFORDSHIRE, BERKSHIRE, and BUCKING-HAMSHIRE.

OXFORDSHIRE.

Lord-Lieutenant of the County—His Grace the Duke of Marlborough.

OXFORDSHIRE lies along the north bank of the Thames, the windings of which it follows, so that whereas in some places it is only seven miles across, in the north it is as much as twenty-eight miles across. Its greatest length is reckoned at about fifty miles.

The POPULATION in 1841 was returned at 161,571, and in 1851 at 170,439; while its EXTENT may be calculated at about 450,000 acres, or 750 square miles.

The RIVERS are numerous; the chief being the Thames, which for some distance bears the name of the Isis. There is the Windrush, which rises in the Cotswold Hills, and falls into the Thames near Standlake, passing Burford and Witney in its course. The Cherwell, rising in Northamptonshire, and joining the Thames at Oxford. The Thame, rising in Hertfordshire, and falling into the Thames at Dorchester, passing through Thame. The Evenlode, rising in Worcestershire, and falling into the Thames near Ensham. Besides these there are many smaller streams.

For RAILWAYS, *vide* p. 144. The chief line is the Great Western, an important branch from which runs from Didcot to Birmingham, passing through Oxford. The Worcester and Wolverhampton line branches off at Oxford, as well as the branch of the North-Western line from Oxford to Bletchley. There remains to be mentioned a small junction line between Banbury and Winslow.

There are in Oxfordshire fourteen HUNDREDS, including about 275 parishes. The names of the Hundreds are as follows:—

Bampton, s.w.	Chadlington, s.w.	Pyrton.
Banbury, n.	Dorchester, s.mid.	Ploughley.
Binfield, s.e.	Ewelme.	Thame.
Bloxnam, s.w.	Langtree.	Wootton.
Bullington.	Lewknor.	

Oxfordshire sends three MEMBERS TO PARLIAMENT; viz., Lieut.-Col. J. S. North; G. Granville Harcourt; Rt. Hon. J. W. Henley.

The City of Oxford, population 27,843[a], sends two Members; viz., J. H. Langston, D.C.L.; Rt. Hon. Edward Cardwell.

The University of Oxford, also two Members; viz., Sir William Heathcote, Bart., D.C.L.; Rt. Hon. William Ewart Gladstone, D.C.L.

Woodstock, 7,983[b] inhabitants, one; viz., Lord A. S. Churchill.

Banbury, 8,715 inhabitants, one; viz., Henry William Tancred, Q.C.

The chief MARKET TOWNS, with the Population and Acreage of the Parish, are as follows:—

	Population.	Acreage.		Population.	Acreage.
Bampton	1,708	10,250	Henley	3,773	
Bicester	3,054	2,600	Thame	3,060	5,100
Burford	1,819		Watlington	1,884	2,901
Chipping-Norton	2,932	2,079	Witney	3,099	7,084
Deddington	1,543	4,150	Woodstock	1,262.	

[a] This return includes the University, the resident members of which may be reckoned at sixteen hundred.

[b] The populations of the parliamentary boroughs are given throughout.

The Magistrates of the County of Oxford are as follows:—

Abingdon, Right Hon. Montague, Earl of *Wytham*
Adams, Rev. Dacres *Bampton*
Arnould, Joseph, Esq. *Whitecross*
Ashhurst, J. H., Esq. *Waterstock*
Barker, Thos. R., Esq. *Hambledon*
Barnett, G. H., Esq. *Glympton-park*
Barnett, Henry, Esq. *Glympton-park*
Baskerville, H., Esq. *Crowsley-park*
Bertie, Hon. and Rev. Fred. *Albury*
Birch, Wm. John, Esq. *Pudlicot*
Blackstone, W. Seymour, Esq. *Howberry*
Blount, M. H., Esq. *Mapledurham*
Bowles, Col. C. Oldfield *North Aston*
Bricknell, Rev. W. S. *Vicarg., Eynsham*
Brown, John, Esq. *Kingston-grove*
Brown, A. H. C., Esq. *Kingston-grove*
Camoys, Rt. Hon. T., Lord *Stonor-pk.*
Chandos, R. Plantagenet Campbell Grenville, Marquess of *Wotton-house*
Carter, Rev. William Edward Dickson, *Vicarage, Shipton-under-Wychwood*
Cartwright, R. Aubrey, Esq. *Edgcot*
Chetwode, Rev. George *Chilton-house*
Churchill, Right Hon. Francis G., Lord *Cornbury-park*
Churchill, Lord A. Spencer, M.P., 27, *Chapel-st., Grosvenor-sq., London* (W.)
Clarke, G. Rochfort, Esq. *Chesterton-lodge*
Clifton, Rev. R. Cox *Somerton Rectory*
Curme, Rev. T. *Sandford Vicarage*
Dashwood, Sir G., Bart. *Kirtlington-park*
Dashwood, Hen. Wm., Esq. *Dunstew*
Dillon, Right Hon. C. H. Viscount *Dytchley*
Dormer, Ch. Cottrell, Esq. *Rousham*
Dormer, Cottrell, Esq. *Rousham*
Duff, Adam, Esq. *Heath-End*
Evans, Tho. Brown, Esq. *Dean-house*
Fane, Lieut-Col. J. Wm. *Wormsley*
Fane, John Augustus, Esq. *Wormsley*
Fiennes, Hon. John Fiennes Twisleton Wykeham *Broughton-castle*
Forbes, Alex. Clark, Esq. *Whitchurch*
Gammie, George, Esq. *Shotover-park*
Gaskell, H. L., Esq. *Kiddington-hall*
Goddard, Rev. Dan. Ward *Vic., Burford*
Goddard, Hor. Nelson, Esq. *Adderbury*
Grisewood, Harman, Esq. *Daylesford*
Guest, Edwin, Esq., LL.D. *Sand ord-pk.*
Hall, Henry, Esq. *Barton*
Hamersley, H., Esq., (*Vice-Chairman of Quart. Sess.,*) *Pyrton-manor*
Hamilton, C. J. B., Esq. *Thame-park*
Harcourt, G. Granville, Esq., M.P., *Nuneham-park*
Harris, Rev. Thomas *Swerford*
Henley, Rt. Hon. J. Warner, M.P., (*Chairm. of Quart. Sess.*) *Waterperry*
Henley, Jos. J., Esq. *Shirburn-lodge*
Hippisley, Hen., Esq. *Lambourn-place*
Hodges, J. Fowden, Esq. *Bolney-court*
Jersey, Rt. Hon. G. Earl of *Middleton-pk.*

Jones, W. Whitmore, Esq. *Chastleton*
Keene, Rev. C. Ed. Ruck *Swyncombe*
Keene, Major Edm. R. *Swyncombe*
Knollys, Lieut.-Gen. William Thomas *The Camp, Aldershot*
Lambert, Sir H. J., Bart. *Aston-house*
Lambert, H. E. F., Esq. *Aston-house*
Lane, Charles. Esq. *Badgemore*
Langston, J. H. Esq., M.P. *Sarsden*
Lechmere, John, Esq. *Hill-house*
Lloyd, Rev. Wm. *Drayton Rectory*
Loveday, John, Esq. *Williamscot*
Lowe, Rev. John *Ardley Rectory*
Macclesfield, Rt. Hon. T. A. Wolstenholme, Earl of *Shirburn-castle*
☞ Marlborough, Most Noble John Winston, Duke of (*Lord-Lieutenant*), *Blenheim-palace*
Marsham, R. Bullock, Esq., D.C.L. *Merton College, Oxford*
Montagu, G. H., Esq. *Caversham-hill*
Morrell, J., Esq. *Headington-hill*
Musgrave, Rev. Wm. Aug. *Chinnor*
Neate, Rev. Arthur *Alverscot*
Norris, Henry, Esq. *Swa'cliffe-park*
North, Lieut.-Col. John Sidney, M.P. *Wroxton-abbey*
Parry, J. Billingsley, Esq., Q.C. *Oxford*
Passand, Rev. H. J. *Shipton Rectory*
Peyton, Sir H., Bart. *Swift's-house*
Peyton, Alg. Wm., Esq. *Swift's-house*
Phillips, J. S., Esq. *Culham-house*
Pickering, L., Esq. *Wilcot-grove*
Pierrepont, Hon. P. S. *Evenley-hall*
Powys, H. P., Esq. *Hardwick-house*
Pretyman, Rev. R. *Middleton-S'oney*
Reade, Wm. Bar., Esq. *Dogmore-End*
Risley, Rev. Wm. Cotton *Deddington*
Sivewright, J., Esq. *Shinfield Manor*
Spencer, Col. Hon. R. C. H. *Combe*
Spencer, Rev. Chas. Vere *Wheatfield*
Stevens, Rev. Thos. *Bradfield Rectory*
Stone, W. H., Esq. *Streatley-house*
Stonor, Hon. Thos. Edw. *Stonor-park*
Strickland, W., Esq. *Cokethorpe-park*
Style, Cap. Wm., R.N. *Bicester-house*
Taunton, W. E., Esq. *Freeland-lodge*
Thomson, Guy, Esq. *Baldon-house*
Vanderstegen, Wm. Hen., Esq. *Cane-end-house, Caversham*
Rev. Vice-Chancellor of the University of *Oxford.*
Villiers, G. A. F., Viscount *Upton-house*
Viret, F. E. S., Esq. *Watlington*
Weyland, R., Esq. *Woodrising-hall*
Weyland, John, Esq. *Woodeaton*
Whippy, Ben. John, Esq. *Lee-place, Charlbury,*
Willes, Wm., Esq. *Astrop-house*
Wilson, Jos. Hen., Esq. *Gillots*
Wyatt, Rev. C. F. *Broughton Rectory*
Wynter, Rev. Philip, D.D. *St. John's College, Oxford*
Yeates, Wm. Willson, Esq. 11, *Norfolk-crescent, Hyde-park, London* (W.)

Sessions—County........Tuesday, Jan. 3   April 6   June 29   Oct. 19
Oxford City...Monday, Jan. 11   April 12   July 5   Oct. 25

The FAIRS in OXFORDSHIRE are as follows:—

BAMPTON, March 26, pigs, Aug. 26, horses.

BANBURY (Th.) 1st aft. Jan. 18, horse-fair on preceding M., 3rd Th. in Feb., 3rd Th. in March, statute, 3rd Th. in April, Holy Thursday, 3rd Th. in June, July 2, wool, 3rd Th. in July, Aug., and Sept., 1s and 3rd Th. aft. Oct. 11, 3rd Th. in Nov., 2nd bef. Christmas.

BICESTER, grt. market 1st Friday in each month, 1st F. in June, Aug. 5, 6, 1st F. in July, wool, F. bef and 1st and 2nd F. aft. Oct. 11, F. aft. Dec. 11.

BURFORD (S.) last S. in April, sheep, July 5, cherry, Sept. 25, cat., cheese.

CHARLBURY, Jan. 1, 2nd F. in Lent, 2nd F. aft. May 13, 1st F. in Oct.

CHIPPING-NORTON (W.) W. aft. Jan. 1, cat., corn, &c., monthly great market the last W. in every month but Dec., W. aft. Dec. 11.

DEDDINGTON, Oct. 12, pl., Nov. 22, cat., pl.

DORCHESTER, Easter-Tu., 3rd W. in July.

HENLEY-ON-THAMES (Th.) March 7, Holy Th., Th. aft. Trin. Sun., cat., Tu. aft. 21st Sept., statute.

HOOKNORTON, 2nd Tu. aft. May 12, June 29, Nov. 28, cat., pigs.

NETTLEBED, M. bef. Oct. 29, statute, Tu. se'nnight aft. Whitsuntide.

OXFORD (W.S.) May 3, M. aft. Sept. 1, Th. bef. Michaelmas-day.

STOKENCHURCH, July 10, cat., Whit-Tu., pl.

THAME (Th.) Oct. 11, 12, 13, cat., stat., pl., Tu. in Easter-week, Tu. bef. Whit-Sun., Aug. 3, cat.

WATLINGTON (S.) April, S. bef. & aft. Oct. 11.

WHEATLEY, Sept. 30, pl.

WITNEY (Th.) Tu. in Easter-week, Holy Thursday, July 10, M. Tu. and Th. aft. Sept. 8, Th. bef. Oct. 10, Dec. 4.

WOODCOT, Aug. 2, M. aft. Nov. 16.

WOODSTOCK, First Tu. in Feb., Nov., and Dec., cat., 1st Tu. in Ap., Aug., Oct., cheese and stat., Whit-Tu., pl.

BERKSHIRE.

Lord-Lieutenant of the County—The Earl of Abingdon.

BERKSHIRE lies upon the south bank of the Thames, and is of irregular shape. Its greatest length from east to west is 43 miles, and its greatest breadth from north to south 30 miles.

The POPULATION in 1831 was returned at 146,234. In 1841 at 161,759, and at the last census 170,065. Its area is 752 square miles, or 481,280 acres.

There are in Berkshire twenty Hundreds.

SESSIONS—Abingdon ...Monday, Jan. 4   June 28
            Reading......Monday, April 5   Oct. 18

Berkshire sends three Members to Parliament, viz., Robert Palmer, Esq., Hon. P. P. Bouverie, G. H. Vansittart, Esq.

Reading, 21,456, returns two Members; viz., Francis Pigott, Esq., Sir H. S. Keating, Q.C.

Windsor, 9,596, returns two Members; viz., Charles William Greenfel, Esq., William Vansittart, Esq.

Abingdon, 5,954, returns one Member; viz., John T. Norris, Esq.

Wallingford, 8,064, also one Member; viz., Richard Malins, Esq. Q.C.

The MAGISTRATES in the County of Berks. are:—

Abingdon, Rt. Hn. Earl of *Wytham-abb.*
Allfrey, Robert, Esq.   *Wokefield-park*
Arbuthnot, J. A., Esq.   *Coworth-park*
Arnould, Joseph, Esq.   *White-cross*
Ashley, Hon. H. *Clewer-park, Windsor*
Atkins, E. M., Esq.   *Kingston-Lisle*
Barrington, Rt. Hon. Visc. *Becket-house*
Barrington, Hon. Geo. W. *Becket-house*
Braybrooke, Rt. Hon. Lord *Audley-End*
Barker, G., Esq. *Stanlake-pk., Twyford*
Barker, Geo. Wm., Esq. *Stanlake-park*
Barrett, Jno. B., Esq. *Milton, Abingdon*
Beauchamp, G. E., Esq.   *Beech-hill*
Bennett, Dem., Esq. *Faringdon-house*
Benyon, Rich., Esq. *Englefield-house*
Berens, Ven. Edw., D.D. *Shrivenham*
Best, H. P., Esq. *Donnington, Newbury*
Blackstone, Wm. Seym., Esq. *Howberry*

Blagrave, J., Esq. *Calcot-park, Reading*
Blandy, William, Esq.   *Reading*
Boldero, H.G., Esq. *Hurst-gro., Twyford*
Bouverie, Rt. Hon. Ed. Pleydell, M.P. *Coleshill-house, Faringdon*
Bouverie, Hon.P.P.M.P.*Hill-st., London*
Bouverie, Rev. Ed. *Coleshill, Faringdon*
Bowles, J. S., Esq. *Milton-hill, Abingdon*
Bowyer, Sir George, Bart.
Bowyer, Geo., Esq., M.P. *King's-bench-walk, Temple, London*
Bros, Thomas, Esq.   *Upper Clapton*
Bulkeley, John Jesse, Esq.   *Linden-hill*
Bulkeley, T., Esq. *Clewer-villa, Windsor*
Bunbury, H. Mill, Esq. *Malstone-house*
Bunny, E. B., Esq., *Speen-hill, Newbury*
Butler, Geo., Esq. *Woolstone, Faringdon*
Burr, D. H. D., Esq. *Aldermaston-park*

Challoner, C. B., Esq. *Portnall-park*
Chatteris, W. P. B., Esq. *Sandleford*
Cherry, Rev. H. C. *Burghfield Rectory*
Cherry, Geo. Chas., Esq. *Denford-house*
Cleaver, Rev. J. F. *Great Coxwell*
Cobham, Alex. Cobham, Esq. *Shinfield*
Collins, Rev. John Ferd. *Betterton*
Compton, Richard, Esq. *Eddington*
Coney, John J., Esq. *Braywick-grove*
Conroy, Sir Edward, Bart. *Arborfield*
Cooper, Leonard Morse, Esq.
Court, Major Henry, Esq. *Castlemans*
Coxe, F. L., Esq. *Wormstall*
Craven, F., Esq. *Brockhampton-park*
Croft, Archer J., Esq. *Greenham-lodge*
Crowdy, Francis, Esq. *Chieveley*
Crutchley, P. H., Esq. *Sunninghill-park*
Currie, E., Esq. *Adbury-house, Newbury*
Dalzell, John, Esq. *Wallingford*
Dawson, George Pelsant, Esq.
Dodson, Rev. Nathaniel *Abingdon*
Downshire, Marq. of *Easthampstead-pk.*
Doyne, Bury, Esq. *White Waltham*
Duffield, C. P., Esq. *Marcham-park*
Dundas, Adm. Sir J. W. D. *Barton-court*
East, Sir G. E. G., Bart. *Hall-pl., Hurley*
Elliot, Geo. Hen., Esq. *Binfield-park*
Elwes, Henry, Esq. *Marcham-park*
Eyre, C., Esq. *Welford-park, Newbury*
Eyre, H. R., Esq. *Shaw-place, Newbury*
Eyston, C. J., Esq. *East Hendred-house*
Ferard, C. C., Esq. *Ascot-place, Windsor*
Fitz-Gerald, Gerald, Esq. *Pope's-lodge*
Fitz-Roy, C. W. H. G., Esq. *Woolstone*
Folkestone, Viscount *Longford-castle*
Forbes, John, Esq. *Winkfield-plain*
Foster, Edmund, Esq. *Clewer, Windsor*
Fowke, Tho. Thorpe, Esq. *Midgham*
Fowler, Adm. Rob. Merrick *Walliscote*
Freemantle, Sir William Henry
Garth, Thos. Colleton, Esq. *Haines-hill*
Gibson, Robert, Esq. *Sandhurst-lodge*
Goodlake, Tho. M., Esq. *Wadley-house*
Goodlake, Tho. Leinster, Esq. *Buckland*
Gower, J. L., Esq. *Bill-hill, Wokingham*
Gower, John Ed. Lev., Esq. *Bill-hill*
Greenway, Henry, Esq. *Reading*
Gregson, Rev. J. *Wallingford*
Griffith, C. D., Esq. *Padworth-house*
Hall, T. J., Esq. *Police-office, Bow-st.,*
Hamilton, C J. B., Esq. *Thame-park*
Hanmer, H., Esq. *Bear-pl., Wargrave*
Hayter, Right Hon. Wm. Goodenough
South-hill-house, Easthampstead
Hercy, John, Esq. *Hawthorn-hill*
Hibbert, John, Esq. *Braywick*
Hilliard, Rev. F. J. *Long-Wittenham*
Hippisley, Henry, Esq. *Lamborne*
Honywood, Wm., Esq. *Chilton-lodge*
Hopkins, John, Esq. *Tidmarsh*
Hopkins, Rob. John, Esq. *Tidmarsh*
Hoskyns, Rev. J. Leigh *Aston Tirrold*
Hughes, John, Esq. *Donnington*
Hunter, Sir C. S. P., Bt. *Mortimer*
Huntley, Rev. J.W. *Vicarage, Kirkland*
Hunter, Hen. Lannoy, Esq. *Mortimer*
King, Wm. Charles, Esq. *Warfield-hall*
Lancaster, B., Esq. *Englemere, Chertsey*
Lenthall, Ed. Kyffin, Esq. *Besselsleigh*
Maitland, E. Fuller, Esq. *Park-place*
Maitland, Wm. Fuller, Esq. *Park-place*
Maitland, John F., Esq. *Park-place*

Maitland, Thos. F., Esq. *Wargrave*
Matthews, John, Esq. *Newbury*
Merry, Wm., Esq. *Highlands, Reading*
Milman, H. H., D.D. *Deanery, St. Paul's*
Monck, J. B., Esq. *Coley-park, Reading*
Morland, E. H., Esq. *West Ilsley*
Morrell, James, Esq. *Oxford*
Morrison, J., Esq. *Basildon-pk., Reading*
Morshead, Sir W. C., Bart. *Forest-lodge*
Mount, W., Esq. *Wasing-pl., Reading*
Mount, W. G., Esq. *Wasing-pl., Reading*
Mowbray, Rt. Hon. J. R. *Mortimer*
Neate, Rev. Thomas.
Norreys, Lord *Wytham-abbey, Oxford*
Norris, J.T., Esq., M.P. *Sutton-Courtney*
Nicholls, Solomon, Esq.
Orkney, Rt. Hon. Earl of *Taplow, Bucks*
Oliver, John, Esq. *Buckland*
Palmer, Robt., Esq., M.P. *Holme-park*
Parker, K. Steph., Esq., Q.C. *Stockcross*
Parry, John B., Esq., Q.C. *Oxford*
Phillips, John S., Esq. *Culham-house*
Pigott, Fr., Esq., M.P. *Heckfield*
Powys, Henry Philip, Esq. *Hardwick*
Radnor, Rt. Hon. Earl of *Coleshill-house*
Ramsbottom, James, Esq.
Reade, W. B., Esq. *Ipsden*
Ricardo, Samson, Esq. *Sunninghill*
Riley, Wm. Felix, Esq. *Clewer, Windsor*
Roe, Sir Fred. Adair *Worthing, Sussex*
Rooke, Gen. Sir Henry Willoughby
Russell, Sir Charles, Bart. *Swallowfield*
Saunders, Robert, Esq. *Remenham*
Sawyer, Charles, Esq. *Heywood-lodge*
Sawyer, Her., Esq. *Bray, Maidenhead*
Scott, G. D., Esq. *Lovel-hill, Winkfield*
Seymour, H., Esq. *Park-pl., Windsor*
Seymour, Hen. Richm., Esq. *Inholmes*
Simonds, Henry, Esq. *Reading*
Sivewright, John, Esq. *Hartley-court*
Slocock, Charles, Esq. *Donnington*
Smith, Thos. H., Esq. *Forberry-grove*
Spencer, Hon. Rev. C. F. O. *Cumnor*
Standish, R. E. W. P., Esq. *Farley-hill*
Stephens, Chas., Esq. *Early, Reading*
Stevens, Rev. Thos. *Bradfield, Reading*
Stevens, Wm., Esq. *Binfield, Reading*
Stone, Wm. Hen., Esq. *Streatley-house*
Storer, A. M., Esq. *Purley-pk., Reading*
Sumner, Rev. Robert *Brightwell*
Thelluson, Hon. Arthur
Theobald, Theob., Esq. *Sutton-Courtney*
Thomas, Le M., Esq. *Sea-View, I. of W.*
Thomson, Thomas James, Esq.
Thoyts, M. G., Esq. *Sulhamstead-house*
Throckmorton, Sir Robert George, Bart.
Buckland-house, Faringdon
Tucker, H., Esq. *Bourton, Faringdon*
Tull, Edw., Esq. *Peasemore, Newbury*
Tull, Richard, Esq. *Crookham, Newbury*
Valpy, R. H., Esq. *Enborne, Newbury*
Vansittart, G.H., Esq., M.P. *Bisham-abbey*
Vansittart, Robert, Esq. *Braywick*
Vernon, L. V., Esq. *Ardington*
Vizard, W. jun., Esq. *Little Faringdon-ho.*
Walsh, Sir John B., Bart. *Warfield-park*
Walter, J., Esq. *Bear-wood, Wokingham*
Ward, T. R., Esq. *Upton-park, Slough*
West, Adm. Sir J. *99, Eaton-sq., Pimlico*
Whately, Rev. T. *Chetwynd Rly., Salop*
Wheble, Jam. J., Esq. *Bullmershe-court*
Wilder, Fred., Esq. *Purley, Reading*

Willes, George, Esq. *Hungerford-park*
Williams, Rev. Sir Erasmus Henry Griffies, Bart. *Marlborough, Wilts.*
Williams, T. P., Esq. *Temple-ho., Hurley*
Wroughton, P., Esq. *Ibstone-hou., Oxon*
Wynn, Sir William *Woolley-park*
Wynter, Rev. Philip, D.D. *St. John's College, Oxford*

The FAIRS in BERKSHIRE are as follows :—

ABINGDON (M.F.) 1st M. in Lent, May 6, June 20, lambs, 1st M. in July, wool, Aug. 5, lambs, Sept. 19, Dec. 11, cat. M. bef. Oct. 11, statute.

ALDERMASTON, May 6, July 7, cat., Oct. 13, statute.

BLEWBURY, Th. aft. Sep. 29, pl.

BRACKNELL, Ap. 25, Aug. 22, stat., hogs, Oct. 1, stat.

CHAPELROW, M. after July 26, cat., stat.

COOKHAM, May 16, Oct. 11, general.

FARINGDON (T.) Feb. 13, Ap. 6, Whit-Tu. cat., Tu. bef. & aft. Oct. 11, stat., Oct. 29, cat.

HENDRED, EAST, Oct. 14, statute.

HUNGERFORD (W.) last W. in April, W. bef. and aft. Oct. 11. Aug. 11, statute, sheep, last Tu. in April, Aug. 17, & Nov. 10.

ILSLEY (M.) W. in Easter-week, every fortnight after till last in June, 1st W. in July, Aug. 1, 26, sheep, W. aft. Sept. 19, Oct. 17, Nov. 12.

LAMBOURN (F.), May 12, pl., 1st Fr. aft. Oct. 12, statute, Dec. 4. eat.

MAIDENHEAD (W.) Whit-Wed., Mich.-day, Nov. 30, cat.

MORTIMER, Ap. 27, cat., Nov. 7, ponies.

NEWBRIDGE, Mar. 31, Sep. 28.

NEWBURY (Th.) 1st Tu. in Feb., wool, Holy Thurs., horses, July 5, eat., Sept. 4, Nov. 8, cat., statute, cheese, 1st Th. aft. Oct. 11, statute.

OAKINGHAM (Tu.) April 23, June 11, Oct. 11, statute, Nov. 2, cat.

READING (W.S.) Feb. 2, May 1, July 25, cat., Sept. 21, cat. stat. pl.

SWALLOWFIELD, June 9, pl.

THATCHAM, 2nd Tu. after East., Tu. pl., Tu. after Sept. 29, statute.

TWYFORD, July 26, Oct. 11, horses.

WALLINGFORD (F.) Th. in East.-week, Sept. 29, statute, cat.

WANTAGE (S.) 1st S. in March & May, cat., July 18, cherry, Oct. 18, stat.

WINDSOR (W.S.) Easter-Tuesday, July 5, October 24, cat., pigs.

BUCKINGHAMSHIRE.

Lord-Lieutenant of the County—Lord Carrington.

BUCKINGHAMSHIRE lies in the centre of England, as nearly midway as possible between the North Sea and the Bristol Channel.

Its area is computed at 738 square miles, or 472,320 acres, being rather below the average. Its greatest breadth from east to west is 27 miles, but its length from north to south is as much as 53 miles.

The Chiltern Hills run right across the county, dividing it into two parts, the upper portion being watered by the Thame and the Ouse, the lower by the Thames.

The POPULATION of the County in 1831 was returned at 130,982; in 1841 at 138,248, and in 1851, 163,723.

There are eight HUNDREDS in the County, viz.—

Ashenden, W.
Aylesbury, MID.
Buckingham, N.W.

Burnham, S.E.
Cottesloe, E.
Desborough, S.W.

Newport-Pagnell, N.
Stoke, S.

The County returns three Members to Parliament; viz., Caledon Geo. Du Pré, Esq., Rt. Hon. Benjamin Disraeli, and W. G. Cavendish, Esq.

Aylesbury, population 26,794, returns two Members; viz., Sir Richard Bethell, Q.C., Thos. T. Bernard, Esq.

Buckingham, population 8,064, returns two Members; viz., Sir Harry Verney, Bart., Maj.-Gen. John Hall.

High Wycombe, population 7,179, returns two Members; viz., Sir G. H. Dashwood, Bart., Martin Tucker Smith, Esq.

Great Marlow, population 6,523, also two Members; viz., Thos. Peers Williams, Esq., Lieut.-Col. B. W. Knox.

The JUSTICES residing within the County of Buckingham are :—

Allen, T. Newland, Esq. *The Vache*
Athawes, Rev. John *Loughton*
Atkinson, Benj., Esq. *Great Marlow*
Barker, T. Raymond, Esq. *Hambledon*
Baron, Rev. John Samuel *Brill*
Bartlett, John Edw., Esq. *Buckingham*
Baynes, Rev. Adam *Adstock*
Bell, Rev. Wm. *Lillingstone Darrell*
Bent, J., Esq. *Wexham-lodge, Slough*
Bernard, T. Tyringham, Esq., M.P. *Winchendon Priory*
Boston, Rt. Hon, Geo. Ives, Lord, 4, *Belgrave-square, s.w.*
Broughton, Rev. T. Delves *Bletchley*
Barrington, Hon. Percy *Westbury*
Carrington, Rt. Hon. R. J., Lord, (*Lord-Lieut.,*) *The Abbey, High Wycombe*
Carrington, George, Esq. *G. Missenden*
Carter, Rev. Thomas *Burnham*
Cavendish, Hon. Wm. George *Latimer*
Cavendish, Hon. Richard *Thornton-hall*
Chandos, R. P. C. Grenville, Marq. of, M.P. *Wotton-house*
Chesham, Rt. Hon. the Lord *Latimer*
Chester, Rev. Anthony *Chicheley-hall*
Chetwode, Rev. George *Chilton-house*
Clayton, Sir W. R., Bart. *Harleyford*
Clayton, Rice Rd., Esq. *Hedgerley-pk.*
Clowes, C., Esq. *Delaford-park*
Coker, Rev. John *Radcliffe*
Connel, Abraham J. Nisbet, Esq. *Lilies, Aylesbury*
Crewe, Randolph H., Esq. *Loakes Hill*
Curzon, Rt. Hon. G. A. P. L., Viscount *Penn-house, Beaconsfield*
Cust, Rev A. Perceval *Cheddington*
Darby, Abraham, Esq. *Stoke Poges*
Dashwood, Sir G. H., Bart., M.P. *West Wycombe-park*
Dauncey, Philip, Esq. *Little Horwood*
Dayrell, E. F., Esq. *Lillingstone Dayrell*
De Rothschild, M. A., Esq. *Mentmore*
Dewes, Edward, Esq. *Buckingham*
Disraeli, Rt. Hon. B., M.P. *Hughenden*
Drake, Rev. John Tyrwhitt *Amersham*
Drake, T. Tyrwhitt, Esq. *Shardeloes*
Drake, Rev. Walter *Moulsoe*
Drake, Admiral John *Castle Thorp*
Drummond, H., Esq. *Fishery, Denham*
Duncan, Wm. Geo., Esq. *Bradwell*
Duncombe, P. D. P., Esq. *Gt. Brickhill*
Du Pre, James, Esq. *Wilton-park*
Du Pre, Caledon G., Esq. *Wilton-park*
Erle, Rev. Christopher *Hardwick*
Eyre, Rev. Wm. Thomas *Padbury*
Eyton, Rev. C. W. W. *Aston Clinton*
Fitzgerald, Thomas, Esq. *Shalstone*
Foulis, Rev. Sir H., Bart. *Gt. Brickhill*
Freeman, R. M., Esq. *Stony Stratford*
Fremantle, Rt. Hon. Sir Thos. F., Bart. *Swanbourne*
Fremantle, T. F., Esq. *Swanbourne*
Fuller, Benjamin, Esq. *Chesham*
Gleed, Rev. George *Chalfont St. Peter*
Gray, Rev. C. E. *Prince's Risborough*
Gregory, W. J., Esq. *Castle-hill, Chepping Chesham*
Hale, John, Esq.

Hall, Lawrence Robert, Esq. *Foscott*
Hanmer, Henry, Esq. *Stockgrove*
Harrison, Rev. John *Dinton*
Harvey, R., Esq. *Langley-pk., Slough*
Harvey, R. B., Esq. *Langley-park*
Hibbert, J. N., Esq. *Chalfont-house*
Hibbert, F. D., Esq., *Chalfont-house*
Higginson, Lt.-Gen. G. P. *Gt. Marlow*
Hubbard, John G., Esq. *Addington*
Jenney, W., Esq. *Drayton-lodge, Tring*
Jeston, Rev. H. Playsted *Cholesbury*
Kaye, J., Esq. *Fulmer-grove, Slough*
King, Rev. Isaac *Bradenham*
Knapp, Matthew, Esq. *Little Linford*
Lane, John, Esq. *Culverton-ho., Stony Stratford*
Langley, Rev. Dan. B., D.C.L. *Olney*
Lee, J., Esq., LL.D. *Hartwell-house*
Lloyd, Rev. Chas. *Hampden Rectory*
Lowndes, W., Esq. *The Bury, Chesham*
Lowndes, Wm. S., Esq. *Whaddon-hall*
Lowndes, E. W. S., Esq. *Winslow*
Lowndes, R. W. S., Esq. *Bletchley*
Lowndes, Rev. C. W. S. *North Crawley*
Lucas, Geo., Esq. *Newport Pagnell*
Martyn, Rev. Thomas *Ludgershall*
Martyn, Rev. Claudius *Ludgershall*
Maul, J. C., Esq. *Newport Pagnell*
Morland, Sir F. B., Bt. *Monk's Risbro'*
Murray, C. R. S. S., Esq. *Danesfield*
Musgrave, H. M., Esq. *Beech Hill*
Newman, John, Esq. *Brand's-house*
Ouvry, Rev. Peter Thomas *Wing*
Owen, Rev. Edward *St. Leonard's*
Owen, Rev. Edw., jun. *St. Leonard's*
Palmer, C. J., Esq. *Dorney-crt., Slough*
Parkinson, Jas. B., Esq. *Cholesbury*
Partridge, Rev. W. E. *Horsendon-ho.*
Pennington, Wm., Esq. *Fernacres*
Phillimore, Rev. G. *Radnage Rectory*
Pigott, Geo. G., Esq. *Doddershall-park*
Pratt, Walter Caulfield, Esq.
Price, T. E., Esq. *Abbey, Little Missenden*
Praed, W. B., Esq. *Tyringham*
Ricketts, C. S., Esq. *Dorton-ho., Thame*
Rose, Rev. F., D.D.
Russell, Rev. R. N. *Beachampton*
Rudyerd, Henry, Esq. *Iver*
Sandars, Joseph, Esq. *Taplow-house*
Senior, J. T., Esq. *Broughton-house*
Small, Rev. Harry Alex. *Haversham*
Smith, M. T. Esq. *Chepping-Wycombe*
Stratton, J. Locke, Esq. *Turweston*
Swabey, M. Esq. *Langley-Marsh*
Tower, C, Esq. *Huntsmore-park*
Townsend, Rev. Richd. *Ickford Rectory*
Uthwatt, Rev. W. A. *Moreton-house*
Verney, Sir Harry, Bt. *Claydon-house*
Walpole, R. R. *Haslope-park*
Wanklyn, Edw., Esq. *Fulmer*
Ward, Thos. Rawdon, Esq. *Upton*
Wroth, Rev. W. Bruton *Edlesborough*
Wroughton, P., Esq. *Ibstone-house*
Wykeham, P. T. H., Esq. *Tythrop-ho.*
Young, Rev. Edw. Newton *Quainton*
Young, G. A., Esq. *The Grove, Fingest*

The JUSTICES not residing within the County of Buckingham are :—

Alves, Nathaniel, Esq. *Jersey*
Apthorp, Rev. W. H.   *Blackford*
Ashfield, Rev. C. R.   *Burgate, Scole*
Baily, William James, Esq.
Barnes, John, Esq.   *Chorley Wood,*
          Rickmansworth
Barton, Rev. H. J. *Wicken, Stony Strat.*
Beard, Rev. James.
Brandreth, H., Esq.   *Dunstable*
Brown, A. H. C., Esq.   *Kingston*
Buckingham & Chandos, Richard Plan-
     tagenet, Duke of, K.G. *Carlton-club*
Creaton, J. J. A. L., Esq. 7, *Sydney-pl.,*
          Onslow-square, London
Calvert, F., Esq.   8, *New-sq., Lincoln's*
          Inn, London
Cartwright, W., Esq. *Floore-ho., Weedon*
Chapman, T. S., Esq. 14, *Southampton*
     Buildings, Lincoln's Inn, London
Cooper, Sir A. P., Bt. *Gadebridge, Hemel*
          Hempstead
Croke, George, Esq.   *Studley Priory*
Drummond, J., Esq. *Redenham, Andover*
Edgell, H., Esq. *Cadogan-place, Chelsea*
Fitzmaurice, Hon. W. E. *Vanburgh-ho.,*
          Blackheath
Freeman, Wm. P. W., Esq.   *Arniston*
     Fushie Bridge, Edinburgh
Gilpin, R. T., Esq.   *Hockliffe Grange,*
          Leighton Buzzard
Grafton, Duke of,   *Stony Stratford*
Hall, Major Gen. J., M.P. *1st Life Guards*
Hamilton. Charles John Baillie, Esq.
Hanmer, W., Esq.   *Rushmere-lodge*
Harcourt, G. S., Esq.   *Great Yarmouth*
Henley, Rt. Hon. J. W., M P. *Waterperry*
Higgins, T. C., Esq. *Turvey-ho., Olney*
Higgins, Colonel W. B. *Picts Hill, Olney*

Jenks, Rev. David, *Little Gaddesden*
Koe, J. H., Esq. 19, *Old-sq., Lincoln's Inn*
Lambert, H. E F., Esq. *Aston Rowant*
Lacy, Rev. C. 25, *Finsbury-sq., London*
Mansell, John C., Esq.   *Cosgrove-hall,*
          Stony Stratford
Melvill, Rev. E. *St. David's, Haverford-*
          west
Moore, Frank J., Esq. *Berkhampstead*
Nugent, Sir Geo. Edm., Bart. *Norfolk*
Osborne, Hon. & Rev. S. G. *Blandford*
Peyton, Sir H. Bart. *Swift's-ho., Bicester*
Pierrepont, Hon. P. S.   *Evenly-hall,*
Price, T. E.. Esq.   *[Brackley*
Raper, H. Esq. 6, *Prince's-ter., Brompton*
Rich, Rev. J. *Newtimber Recty., Sussex*
Robarts, Abraham Geo., Esq. *Towcester*
Roe, Sir Frederick Adair, Bart.
Ryder, Hon. G. D *Westbrook, St. Alban's*
Scobell, Rev. E.   14, *Blandford-street,*
          Portman-sq., London
Smith, A., Esq.   *Ashlyn's-hall, Great*
          Berkhampstead
Stone, J., Esq. 28, *Westbourne-terrace,*
          Hyde-park, London
Sullivan, John Augustus, Esq.
Sutton, Robert, Esq. 79, *Hamilton-ter.,*
          St. John's Wood, London
Thornton, H., Esq.   *Newport Pagnell*
Vansittart, G. H., Esq. *Bisham Abbey,*
          Great Marlow
Vincent, Rev. F.   *Slinfold Rectory*
Wentworth, T. F. C. V., Esq. *Stoke-pk.*
Williams, Rev. James   *Tring-park*
Williams, T. P., Esq. *Temple-ho., Gt.*
Worley, Henry Thomas, Esq. *[Marlow.*
Young, Rev. H. T.   *Purleigh, Maldon*

SESSIONS, Aylesbury, Tuesday, Jan. 3, April 6, June 29, Oct. 19.
The FAIRS in BUCKINGHAMSHIRE are as follows :—

AMERSHAM (Tu.) Whit.-M. Sept. 19, cat.,
     stat.
AYLESBURY (W.S.) 1st F. aft. Jan. 18,
     Palm-Sat., May 8, June 14, Sept. 25,
     Oct. 12, cat. stat. 2nd M. in Dec , fat
     cat.
BEACONSFIELD (W.) Feb. 13, Holy-
     Thursday, cat.
BRILL, 2nd W. in May, cat., 1st W. aft.
     Oct. 11, statute.
BUCKINGHAM (M.S.) Jan. 12, last M. in
     Jan., March 7, 2nd M. in April, May 6,
     Whit-Th., July 10, wool and cat., 2nd
     W. in Aug., Sept. 4, Oct. 2, Sat. aft.
     Oct. 11, Nov. 8, Dec. 13, cat.
BURNHAM, May 1, Oct. 2, stat. pl.
CHESHAM (W.) Ap. 21, July 22, 2nd W.
     in Nov. cat., Sep. 28, cat., stat.
COLNBROOK, April 5, May 3, Oct. 16, cat.
ELTON, Ash-Wed., pigs.
FENNY STRATFORD, April 19, July 18,
     Oct. 11, stat., Nov. 28, cat.
GREAT MARLOW, (S.) May 1, 2, 3, cheese,
     hops, butter, Oct. 29, cat. stat.
HANSLOPE, Holy-Th., cat.

HIGH WYCOMBE (F.) 3rd M. in Ap., Oct.
     28, cat., last W. in June, wool, M.
     bef. Sept. 29, stat.
IVER, May 10, pl.
IVINGHOE (S.) May 6, Oct. 17, cat , pigs.
LAVENDON (M.) 2 Tu. bef. East., pl.
LITTLE BRICKHILL, May 12, pl., Oct. 29,
     cat.
NEWPORT PAGNELL (S.) Feb. 22, Mar.
     21, Aug. 29, Oct. 22, Dec. 22, cat., Ap.
     22, June 22, cat., pl.
OLNEY (Th.) Easter-M. June 29, 30, pl.,
     stat., Oct. 13.
PRINCE'S RISBOROUGH (Th.) May 6, cat.,
     Oct. 21, pl.
STONY STRATFORD (F.) 2nd F. in Feb.,
     1 F. in May, 3 F. in Sept., 1 F. in
     Nov. cat., Aug. 2, cat., pl., F. aft. Oct.
     11, cat., pl., stat.
WENDOVER (M.) May 13, Oct. 2, cat.
WINSLOW (W.) Feb. 18, March 20, April
     20, 8 W. in May, Aug. 21, Sept. 22,
     Nov. 26, 2 W. in Dec., cat., Wed. bef.
     & Wed. aft. Oct. 11, stat.
WOOBURN, May 4, Nov. 12, cat.

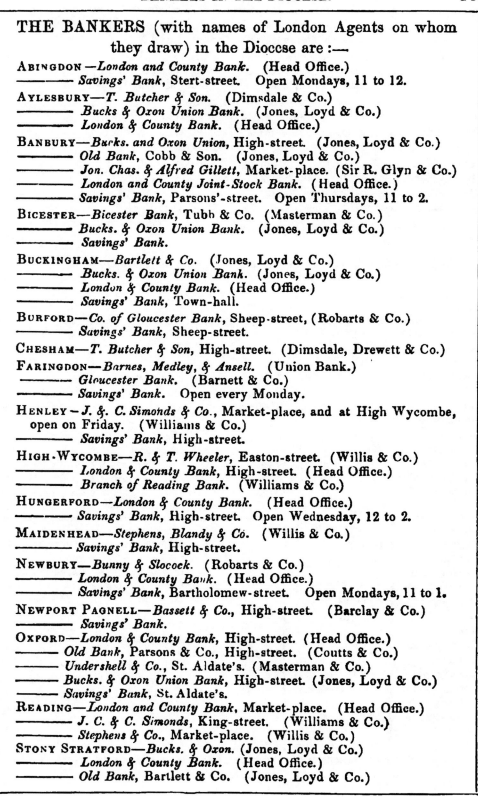

THE BANKERS (with names of London Agents on whom they draw) in the Diocese are :—

ABINGDON —*London and County Bank.* (Head Office.)
———— *Savings' Bank*, Stert-street. Open Mondays, 11 to 12.

AYLESBURY—*T. Butcher & Son.* (Dimsdale & Co.)
———— *Bucks & Oxon Union Bank.* (Jones, Loyd & Co.)
———— *London & County Bank.* (Head Office.)

BANBURY—*Bucks. and Oxon Union*, High-street. (Jones, Loyd & Co.)
———— *Old Bank*, Cobb & Son. (Jones, Loyd & Co.)
———— *Jon. Chas. & Alfred Gillett*, Market-place. (Sir R. Glyn & Co.)
———— *London and County Joint-Stock Bank.* (Head Office.)
———— *Savings' Bank*, Parsons'-street. Open Thursdays, 11 to 2.

BICESTER—*Bicester Bank*, Tubb & Co. (Masterman & Co.)
———— *Bucks. & Oxon Union Bank.* (Jones, Loyd & Co.)
———— *Savings' Bank.*

BUCKINGHAM—*Bartlett & Co.* (Jones, Loyd & Co.)
———— *Bucks. & Oxon Union Bank.* (Jones, Loyd & Co.)
———— *London & County Bank.* (Head Office.)
———— *Savings' Bank*, Town-hall.

BURFORD—*Co. of Gloucester Bank*, Sheep-street, (Robarts & Co.)
———— *Savings' Bank*, Sheep-street.

CHESHAM—*T. Butcher & Son*, High-street. (Dimsdale, Drewett & Co.)

FARINGDON—*Barnes, Medley, & Ansell.* (Union Bank.)
———— *Gloucester Bank.* (Barnett & Co.)
———— *Savings' Bank.* Open every Monday.

HENLEY—*J. & C. Simonds & Co.*, Market-place, and at High Wycombe, open on Friday. (Williams & Co.)
———— *Savings' Bank*, High-street.

HIGH-WYCOMBE—*R. & T. Wheeler*, Easton-street. (Willis & Co.)
———— *London & County Bank*, High-street. (Head Office.)
———— *Branch of Reading Bank.* (Williams & Co.)

HUNGERFORD—*London & County Bank.* (Head Office.)
———— *Savings' Bank*, High-street. Open Wednesday, 12 to 2.

MAIDENHEAD—*Stephens, Blandy & Co.* (Willis & Co.)
———— *Savings' Bank*, High-street.

NEWBURY—*Bunny & Slocock.* (Robarts & Co.)
———— *London & County Bank.* (Head Office.)
———— *Savings' Bank*, Bartholomew-street. Open Mondays, 11 to 1.

NEWPORT PAGNELL—*Bassett & Co.*, High-street. (Barclay & Co.)
———— *Savings' Bank.*

OXFORD—*London & County Bank*, High-street. (Head Office.)
———— *Old Bank*, Parsons & Co., High-street. (Coutts & Co.)
———— *Undershell & Co.*, St. Aldate's. (Masterman & Co.)
———— *Bucks. & Oxon Union Bank*, High-street. (Jones, Loyd & Co.)
———— *Savings' Bank*, St. Aldate's.

READING—*London and County Bank*, Market-place. (Head Office.)
———— *J. C. & C. Simonds*, King-street. (Williams & Co.)
———— *Stephens & Co.*, Market-place. (Willis & Co.)

STONY STRATFORD—*Bucks. & Oxon.* (Jones, Loyd & Co.)
———— *London & County Bank.* (Head Office.)
———— *Old Bank*, Bartlett & Co. (Jones, Loyd & Co.)

THAME—*London & County Joint-Stock Bank*, High-street, (Head Office.)
———— *Bucks. and Oxon Union Bank.* (Jones, Loyd & Co.)
WANTAGE—*Barns & Co.*, Newbury-street. (Union Bank.)
———— *London & County Bank*, Market-place. (Head Office.)
———— *Savings' Bank*, Town-hall. Open Wednesdays, 12 to 1.
WINDSOR—*Neville, Reid, & Co.* (Williams & Co.)
———— *London and County Joint-Stock Bank.* (Head Office.)
WINSLOW—*Bucks. & Oxon Union Bank.* (Jones, Loyd. & Co.)
———— *Bartlett & Co*, Old Bank. (Jones, Loyd & Co.)
WITNEY, *J. W. Clinch & Co.*, High-street. (Masterman & Co.)
———— *London & County Bank*, Market-place. (Head Office.)
WOKINGHAM—*Simonds & Co.*, Roebuck Inn, Tuesday. (Williams & Co.)
———— *Savings' Bank*, Town-hall. Open Mondays, 12 to 1.
WOODSTOCK—*Gillett & Co.* (Glyn & Co.)
———— *Savings' Bank.*

The RAILWAY STATIONS in the Diocese are as follows :—

G. W. R.

LONDON.)
Langley.
SLOUGH, *with branch to* WINDSOR.
MAIDENHEAD, *with branch to* Taplow.

N.B. From Windsor there is also a line to London [per S.W.R.

TWYFORD, *with branch to* Henley.

G. W. R.

L. & S.W. R.

READING.		READING.	READING.	READING.
Pangbourne.		Mortimer.	Theale.	Wokingham,
Goring.		(BASINGSTOKE).	Aldermaston.	*with branch to*
Wallingford.			Woolhampton.	(REIGATE).
DIDCOT.	DIDCOT.		Thatcham.	Bracknell.
Steventon.	Culham,		NEWBURY.	Ascot.
Wantage Road.	*with branch*		Kintbury.	Sunningdale.
Faringdon Road.	to Abingdon.		HUNGERFORD.	Virginia Water.
Shrivenham.				(STAINES.)
BRISTOL.)				

O. W. & W. R. / **G. W. R.** *continued.* / **L. & N.W.** / *Continued.*

O. W. & W.R.	G. W. R. *continued.*		L. & N.W.	*Continued.*
OXFORD.	OXFORD.		OXFORD.	LONDON.
Handborough,	WoodstockRoad.		Islip.	(TRING.)
(*with* Blen-	Kirtlington.		Bicester.	Cheddington,
heim).	Heyford.		Launton.	*with branch*
Charlbury.	Somerton.		Claydon.	*to* Aylesbury.
Ascott.	Aynho.	WINSLOW.	WINSLOW.	Leighton-Buz-
Shipton.	BANBURY.	Buckingham.	Swanbourn.	zard, *with*
Chipping-Nor-	Cropredy.	Brackley.	BLETCHLEY.	*branch to*
ton.	(BIRMINGHAM.)	Farthinghoe.		(DUNSTABLE).
Addlestrop.		BANBURY.	BLETCHLEY.	BLETCHLEY.
Moreton-in-the			Fenny Stratford.	Wolverton.
Marsh.			Wavendon, (*for*	(RUGBY.)
(WORCESTER.)			Woburn).	(BIRMINGHAM.)
(WOLVERHAMP-			BEDFORD.	
TON.)				

N.B. Those Stations printed within a parenthesis are not in the Diocese.

Oxford Diocesan Calendar
ADVERTISEMENTS.

S. MARY'S COLLEGE, HARLOW.

WAS founded in the Year 1851, with the special object, under the blessing of Almighty God, of affording to the Sons of Gentlemen, in addition to the ordinary course of instruction pursued at the Public Schools, a careful and definite training in the Principles of the Church of England.

The ordinary course of instruction includes Divinity, Latin, Greek, French, Arithmetic, Algebra, Euclid, Trigonometry, Mechanics, and other branches of Natural Philosophy; Mensuration, Ancient and Modern History and Geography, English Grammar, Writing from Dictation, Composition, Book-keeping, Music, Theoretical and Practical, and Gymnastic Exercises.

German, Italian, Fortification, Drawing and Surveying, Navigation, Drilling, and Instrumental Music, may also be studied on the payment of extra fees.

Students who may be called to serve God in the Holy Order of the Priesthood are at liberty, after they have passed the lower school, at the special request of their parents, to attend the elementary lectures of the Ecclesiastical Department instead of proceeding further in Mathematical Science.

Students whose vocation it is to enter the Army, Navy, or to undertake any Civil Appointment, can any time be specially prepared by competent masters for Public Examinations. The course for such students will vary according to the vocation of each, or the nature of the examination he will be required to undergo.

A Report of each student's conduct and progress is sent to the Parents or Guardians at the close of each Term.

The Terms are as follows:—Lent commences on Feb. 2; Easter the third week after Easter-day; Michaelmas, the third week in August; Christmas, October 18th.

Besides the ordinary Examination at the close of each Term, there is a special Annual Examination by Graduates of the Universities of Oxford and Cambridge, who award the Prizes, which are distributed on the Annual Commemoration-day, July 2, when Parents and other friends of the College are particularly invited to attend.

Parents living abroad can leave the entire care of their sons to the President for any lengthened period.

A boy is not considered eligible for admission till he can read and write. Each Student has a separate Dormitory.

College Fees, £13 per Term. Entrance Fee, 3 Guineas.

For any further particulars and references, application must be made to the President, the Rev. CHARLES J. GOULDEN, at the College.

Books Published by John and Charles Mozley,
6, Paternoster Row, London.

SUNSHINE IN SICKNESS. By the Author of "Pictures of the Heavens." Foolscap 8vo., cloth, 1s. 6d.

THE CHRISTMAS MUMMERS. By the Author of "The Heir of Redclyffe." Second Edition, demy 18mo., price 1s.; cloth, 1s. 6d.

MY THREE AUNTS; or, LOWMINSTER. By the Author of "Long, Long, Ago." Fcap. 8vo., 2s. 6d.

ROYAL ROSE-BUDS; or, Historical Sketches of Illustrious Children. Demy 8vo., 1s.; cloth, 1s. 6d.

LANDMARKS OF HISTORY: A Summary of Ancient History. By the Author of "The Heir of Redclyffe." Third Edition, fcap. 8vo., cloth, 2s. 6d.

By the same Author.

LANDMARKS OF HISTORY. Middle Ages. Second Edition, fcap. 8vo., cloth, 3s.

LANDMARKS OF HISTORY. Modern History: from the Reformation to the Fall of Napoleon. Fcap. 8vo., cloth, 5s. 6d.

KINGS OF ENGLAND: A History for the Young. Fifth Edition, with the addition of a Table of the Contemporary Sovereigns of Europe, a Genealogical Table of the Kings of England, and a list of the Royal Families of England. Fcap. 8vo., cloth, 3s.

ALSO, A CHEAP SCHOOL EDITION, slightly abridged, demy 18mo. price 1s.; and with Questions for Examination, price 1s. 2d. in cloth.

MEDIÆVAL PREACHERS AND MEDIÆVAL PREACHING. A Series of Extracts, translated from the Sermons of the Middle Ages, Chronologically Arranged; with Notes and an Introduction. By the Rev. J. M. NEALE, M.A. Post 8vo., cloth, price 7s.

A CONCORDANCE OF THE PRAYER-BOOK VERSION OF THE PSALMS. Demy 18mo., price 2s. cloth.

Three volumes, post 8vo., price 15s. cloth.

THE SEASONS OF THE CHURCH, WHAT THEY TEACH. Edited by the Rev. HENRY NEWLAND.
Vol. I. Advent to Lent. 5s.
Vol. II. Easter to Whitsuntide. 5s.
Vol. III. The Sundays after Trinity. 5s.

Demy 18mo., price 6d. each, or in limp cloth, 8d.

NEW SERIES OF BOOKS FOR SERVANTS,

By the Author of "Stories and Lessons on the Catechism," &c. Edited by the Rev. W. JACKSON, Vicar of Heathfield, Sussex.
1. Emily the Nursemaid.
2. Emily in her New Place.
3. The Under Housemaid. Part I.
4. The Under Housemaid. Part II.
5. Grave and Gay. Part I.
6. Grave and Gay. Part II.

London: J. and C. MOZLEY, 6, Paternoster Row.

Works by the Lord Bishop of Oxford.

HALF-REPENTANCE.

A SERMON PREACHED IN THE CHURCH OF ST. MARY-THE-VIRGIN, OXFORD, on Ash-Wednesday, 1857. 8vo. 1s.

THE REPENTANCE OF DAVID.

A SERMON PREACHED IN THE CHURCH OF ST. MARY-THE-VIRGIN, OXFORD, on Ash-Wednesday, 1858. 8vo. 6d.

THE REPENTANCE OF ESAU.

A SERMON PREACHED IN THE CHURCH OF ST. GILES, OXFORD, on Friday, Feb. 19, 1858. 8vo. 6d.

ROME—HER NEW DOGMA AND OUR DUTIES.

A SERMON PREACHED BEFORE THE UNIVERSITY, AT ST. MARY'S CHURCH, OXFORD, on the Feast of the Annunciation of the Blessed Virgin Mary, 1855. 8vo. 1s.

THE ENGLISH REFORMATION.

A SERMON PREACHED BEFORE THE UNIVERSITY. Nov. 5, 1855. 8vo. 1s.

SERMONS PREACHED AND PUBLISHED ON SEVERAL OCCASIONS. 1854. 8vo. 10s. 6d.

CHRIST, THE HEALER: A SERMON PREACHED AT CLEWER, 1855. 8vo. 1s.

SIX SERMONS PREACHED BEFORE THE UNIVERSITY OF OXFORD. Fcap. 8vo. *Second Edition.* 4s. 6d.

SERMONS PREACHED BEFORE THE QUEEN. Fcp. 8vo. 7s.

FOUR SERMONS PREACHED BEFORE THE QUEEN IN 1841 AND 1842. Fcap. 8vo. 4s.

HISTORY OF THE EPISCOPAL CHURCH IN AMERICA. Fcap. 8vo. 5s.

THE REBUILDING OF THE TEMPLE A TIME OF REVIVAL;
BEING
A SERMON PREACHED AT THE RE-OPENING OF THE CATHEDRAL OF LLANDAFF, April 16, 1857. 8vo. 1s.

A PRIMARY CHARGE, DELIVERED IN 1845, 1s. 6d.

A CHARGE DELIVERED IN 1857, 1s.

JOHN HENRY and JAMES PARKER, Broad-street, Oxford.

Recent Publications of the Eton Press.

WORKS BY THE RT. REV. THE BISHOP OF WELLINGTON, NEW ZEALAND.

READINGS, MEDITATIONS, and PRAYERS on the HOLY COMMUNION, in accordance with the Church of England's Teaching. 12mo., cloth, 2s.; morocco, 5s.

THE SERMON Preached in Eton College Chapel on Election Sunday, July 24th, 1858, on "PERSONAL RELIGION AND CATHOLIC MEMBERSHIP, AS APPLIED TO PUBLIC SCHOOLS" [Published at the request of the REV. THE PROVOST OF ETON.] Small 8vo., Fourpence.

LESSONS on the CHURCH CATECHISM. 12mo., cloth, 1s. 6d.

FAMILY PRAYERS, selected from the PRAYER-BOOK; With Psalms adapted to Family Reading. 12mo., cloth, 1s. 6d.

AN ACCIDENCE OF THE LATIN TONGUE, in accordance with ARNOLD'S Exercise Books. 12mo., bound, 2s.

LECTURES on ANCIENT and MODERN HISTORY, on Church of England Principles. Illustrated with Maps, &c. 8vo., cloth, 5s.

ETON SELECTIONS FROM GREEK AND LATIN AUTHORS.

POETÆ GRÆCI; PARS I.
Homero (Odyss.) Hesiodo, Mimnermo, Bione, Moscho, Meleagro, et Musæo; cum Notis a COOKESLEY. 8vo., cloth, 4s.

POETÆ GRÆCI; PARS II.
Ex Homero (Hymn.), Theocrito, Callimacho, Apollonio, Tyrtæo, Sapphone, et aliis; cum Notis a COOKESLEY. 8vo., cloth, 8s.

SCRIPTORES GRÆCI;
Ex Herodoto, Thucydide, Xenophonte, Platone, et Luciano; cum Notis. 8vo., bound, 9s.

SCRIPTORES ROMANI,
Ex Cicerone, Livio, Tacito, Paterculo, Quintiliano, et Plinio. 8vo., half calf, 7s. 6d.

Eton: E. P. WILLIAMS; and at 1, Bride-court, Bridge-street, Blackfriars, London, E.C.

Books at Reduced Prices,

(a) Printed at the University Press; (b) Published by Messrs. Parker, Oxford.

	Published at			Offered at		
ANDREWES' (BP.) Complete Works, 11 vols. 8vo.	5	18	6	3	6	0
———— English Theological Works, 7 vols.	3	18	0	2	5	0
———— Opera Theologica Latina, 4 vols.	2	0	0	1	1	0
———— Sermons, 5 vols. *second edition*	2	16	0	1	15	0
Aquinas' Catena Aurea, translated. 8 vols.	3	17	0	1	18	6
Beveridge's Complete Works, 12 vols.	6	3	0	4	4	0
———— English Theological Works, 10 vols. 8vo.	5	5	0	3	10	6
———— Codex Canonum, &c. 2 vols. 8vo.	0	18	0	0	14	0
Bradley's Miscellaneous Works, with Supplement, 1832, 4to.	1	12	0	0	17	0
———— Observations, by Busch, 1838, 4to.	0	4	6	0	3	0
———— Astronomical Observations, 2 vols. folio	5	5	0	1	1	0
Bramhall's (Abp.) Works, 5 vols. 8vo.	3	3	0	1	15	0
Bull's Harmony of the Apostles St. Paul and St. James on Justification, 2 vols.	0	18	0	0	10	0
——— Defence of the Nicene Creed, 2 vols.	1	0	0	0	10	0
——— Judgment of the Catholic Church, 8vo.	0	10	0	0	5	0
Burton's Testimonies, 1829, 8vo.	0	13	6	0	7	0
———————— vol. 2, 1831, 8vo.	0	5	6	0	3	6
Butler's (Bp.) Analogy, 1833, 12mo.	0	4	6	0	2	6
Calendar of the Saints of the Anglican Church, fcap. 8vo. *with numerous woodcuts*	0	10	0	0	7	6
Catalogue of the Bodleian Library, 3 vols. folio, 1843	5	10	0	3	10	0
—————————— vol. 4, folio, 1850	1	16	0	1	3	0
Catenæ Græcorum Patrum in Novum Testamentum, ed. Cramer, 8 vols. 8vo.	4	4	0	2	4	0
Chœrobosci Grammat. dictata in Theodosii Canones, ed. T. Gaisford, 3 vols. 8vo.	1	6	6	0	15	0
Clarendon's Life, 3 vols. 1827, 8vo	1	11	6	0	16	6
Comber's Works, 7 vols. 1841, 8vo.	2	3	0	0	11	6
Cosin's (Bp.) Works, 5 vols. 8vo.	2	13	0	1	10	0
Cramer's Asia Minor, 2 vols. 8vo.	1	1	0	1	11	0
———— Ancient Greece, 3 vols. 8vo. 1828	1	11	6	0	16	6
Cranmer's Works, by Jenkyns, 1834, 4 vols. 8vo.	3	0	0	1	10	0
———— Catechism, with cuts, 1829, 8vo	0	14	0	0	7	6

Books at Reduced Prices.

	Published at			Offered at		
Cutts' Ancient Gravestones, 8vo. (300 Examples)	0	12	0	0	6	0
Ebert's Bibliographical Dict., 1837, 4 vols.	3	0	0	1	10	0
Etymologicon Magnum, Gaisford, folio, 1848	3	6	0	1	10	0
Euripides, Dindorfii, 1834, 2 vols. 8vo.	0	14	0	0	10	0
———— Annot., 2 vols. 8vo. 1840	1	10	0	0	10	0
———— textus, Matthiæ, 2 vols. 8vo.	0	16	0	0	4	0
Eusebii, Preparatio Evangelica, 4 vols. 1843	2	10	0	1	16	0
———— Demonstratio Evangelica, 2 vols. 1852	1	1	0	0	15	0
———— Contra Hieroclem, 8vo. 1852	0	10	6	0	7	0
———— Annotationes, Burton, 2 vols. 8vo. 1842	1	10	0	0	17	0
Fleury's Ecclesiastical History, 3 vols. 8vo.	1	11	6	0	15	0
Forbes' Considerationes Modestæ, 2 vols. 8vo.	1	5	0	0	12	0
Frank's Sermons, 2 vols. 8vo.	1	1	0	0	10	0
Fuller's Church History, 6 vols. 8vo. 1845	3	3	0	1	19	0
Gothic Architecture, an Introduction to the Study of, 16mo.	0	4	6	0	3	0
Gunning on the Paschal, or Lent Fast, 8vo.	0	9	0	0	6	0
Hammond's Sermons, 2 parts, 8vo.	0	16	0	0	10	0
Hickes's Treatises on the Christian Priesthood, 3 vols.	1	8	6	0	15	0
Homeri Opera, Porsoni, 1800, 4 vols. 4to.	2	4	0	0	16	0
Jackson's Works, 12 vols. 8vo. 1844	4	16	0	3	6	0
Jewel's (Bp.) Works, by Jelf, 8 vols. 8vo.	3	12	0	2	10	0
Johnson's (John) Unbloody Sacrifice, 2 vols. 8vo.	1	1	0	0	10	0
———— English Canons, 2 vols. 8vo.	1	4	0	0	12	0
Jones's Canonical Authority, 1827, 3 vols.	1	1	6	0	15	0
Keble (J.) Prælectiones Academicæ, 2 vols. 8vo.	1	1	0	0	10	6
Kennett's Parochial Antiquities, 1818, 2 vols. 4to.	6	6	0	1	14	0
Laud's (Archbishop) Works, 8 vols. 8vo.	3	4	6	2	10	0
Leslie's (C.) Works, 1832, 7 vols. 8vo.	2	16	0	2	0	0
Marshall's Penitential Discipline, 8vo.	0	6	0	0	4	0
Morgan's Doctrine and Law of Marriage, Adultery, and Divorce, 2 vols. 8vo.	1	1	0	0	10	0
Novum Test. Copticum, Wilkins, 1716, 4to.	1	2	6	0	12	6
———— Syriac, ed. White, 1778, 4 vols. 4to.	3	8	0	1	8	0
———— editio Hellenistica, et Scholia, ed. Grinfield, 4 vols. 8vo.	3	12	0	1	16	0
Ormulum, The, by White, 2 vols. 8vo. 1852	1	16	0	1	1	0
Oxford, Ingram's Memorials of, 3 vols. 4to.	5	5	0	3	3	0
Parœmiographi Græci, Gaisford, 1836, 8vo.	0	11	0	0	5	6
Pauli's Analecta Hebraica, with a Key, 8vo.	0	10	6	0	5	0

Books at Reduced Prices.

	Published at			Offered at		
Pearson's Minor Works, by Churton, 2 vols.	1	8	0	0	14	0
———— Vindiciæ Epistolarum S. Ignatii, by Churton, 2 vols. 8vo. . .	0	16	0	0	10	0
Polybius Schweighæuser, 5 vols. 8vo. .	2	12	6	1	8	0
Potter's (Abp.) Works, 3 vols. 8vo. 1753 .	1	1	0	0	15	0
Prideaux's Connection, 2 vols. 8vo. 1851 .	0	14	0	0	10	0
Primers, Three, of Henry VIII., 1848, 8vo.	0	9	0	0	5	0
Ralegh's (Sir W.) Works, 1829, 8 vols. 8vo.	4	4	0	2	12	0
Rigaud's Correspondence of Scientific Men, 2 vols. 8vo. 1841 . . .	1	4	0	0	16	0
Scapulæ Lexicon, Gr. et Lat., folio .	3	15	0	0	10	0
Scheller's Latin Lexicon, *translated by Riddle*, 1835, folio, *in strong cloth boards* .	4	10	0	1	1	0
In quires for binding . .				0	12	0
Scott's Christian Life, &c., 1826, 6 vols. 8vo.	2	8	0	1	7	0
Scriptores Rei Metricæ, Gaisford, 1857, 8vo.	0	12	0	0	5	0
Sharp's (Abp.) Works, 1829, 5 vols. 8vo. .	1	16	0	1	2	6
Shuckford's Connection, 1848, 2 vols. 8vo.	0	16	0	0	10	0
Spanheim's Ecclesiastical Annals, 8vo. .	0	12	0	0	6	0
Stillingfleet's Origines Britannicæ, 1841, 2 vols. 8vo.	1	1	0	0	13	0
———————— Sacræ, 1837, 2 vols. 8vo.	0	15	0	0	9	0
——————— Vindication of Laud, 1844, 2 vols. 8vo.	0	17	0	0	10	0
Stobæi Florilegium, Gaisford, 1822, 4 vols.	2	10	0	1	0	0
——— Eclogæ, Gaisford, 2 vols. 8vo. 1850	1	1	0	0	11	0
Strype's Works, with a general Index, 27 vols. 8vo. . . .	14	0	0	7	13	0
Suidæ Lexicon, Gaisford, 1834, 3 vols. fol.	7	10	0	3	10	0
Taverner's Postils, 1841, 8vo. . .	0	10	0	0	5	6
Theodoreti Græcarum Affectionum Curatio, ed. Gaisford, 1840, 8vo. . .	0	14	0	0	7	6
——— Hist. Eccles., ed. Gaisford, 1854 .	0	10	6	0	7	6
Thorndike's Theological Works, 10 vols. 8vo.	5	2	0	2	10	0
Vetus Testamentum Græcum, Holmes et Parsons, 1798—1827, 5 vols. folio, *quires*	15	0	0	10	0	0
Wells's Geography of Palestine, 2 vols. .	0	15	0	0	7	6

A complete Catalogue to be had on application to Messrs. Parker, 377, Strand, London.

For University School and the Oxford and Cambridge Middle-Class
Examinations, and Professional and Popular Use.

BLACKSTONE'S COMMENTARIES,

Systematically abridged, and adapted to Existing Law, with many New
Chapters, containing great and important additions on the subject of Consti-
tutional Law, Rights of Persons and of Property, and Criminal Law. Second
Edition. By Samuel Warren, Esq., M.P., D.C.L., one of Her Majesty's
Counsel. In one thick volume, post 8vo., price 18s. cloth. This work now
forms a permanent text-book in the new legal curriculum at the University
of Cambridge.

In One Vol., 12mo., price 5s. 6d. cloth,

THE NEW PARISHES ACTS, 1843, 1844, and 1856.

Being Sir Robert Peel's Acts, and Lord Blandford's Act for making
provision for the Spiritual Care of Populous Parishes. With Introduction,
Explanatory Notes, and copious Index, adapted as a Manual for all Clergymen. By James Christie Traill, M.A., of the Inner Temple, Barrister-
at-Law.

Second Edition, 12mo., price 6s., cloth,

BAKER'S LAW OF BURIALS.

The Law relating to Burials; with Notes, Forms, and Practical In-
structions. By Thomas Baker, Esq., of the Inner Temple, Barrister-at-
Law, (of the Burial Acts Office). Second Edition, including the Statutes of
the present Session, and the Scotch and Irish Acts.

"This is a most useful digest of the laws passed during the last five years relative to
burials."—*Record.*

Also,

BAKER'S BURIAL FORMS.

Forms for Books of Account, Registers, Table of Fees, and Regulations, &c.,
for the use of Burial Boards, Managers of Cemeteries, Clergymen, &c.;
drawn up by Thomas Baker, Esq., of the Burial Acts Office, Author of the
"Laws relating to Burials."

*A Specimen Set of the above Forms, containing a single sheet of each, can be
forwarded Post Free, on receipt of stamps, or a Post Office Order for 2s.*

In One Vol., 8vo., price 7s. 6d., cloth,

PROFESSOR GREENLEAF'S EXAMINATION OF THE TESTIMONY OF THE FOUR EVANGELISTS,

By the Rules of Evidence administered in Courts of Law; with
the Harmony of the Four Gospels, arranged in four parallel columns, and a
Synopsis of their Contents. To which is added,

M. DUPIN'S REFUTATION OF JOSEPH SALVADOR'S TRIAL AND CONDEMNATION OF OUR SAVIOUR.

Translated from the French by Dr. Pickering.

In One Vol., fcap. 8vo., price 7s. 6d., extra cloth, (with numerous
Woodcut Illustrations),

CRABB'S TECHNICAL DICTIONARY.

A Technical Dictionary; or, A Dictionary explaining all Terms of Art
and Science. By George Crabb, Esq., M.A., Author of the "Universal
Technological Dictionary," the "Dictionary of Synonymes," &c.

London: Wm. Maxwell, 32, Bell-yard, Lincoln's Inn.

The Parish Magazine.

Monthly Medium of Communication with Parishioners.

In January, 1859, will be Published No. I.
OF AN ILLUSTRATED MONTHLY PENNY MAGAZINE,

EDITED BY

REV. J. ERSKINE CLARKE,
Vicar of St. Michael's, Derby;

Which, besides giving more matter than existing religious magazines, will offer a new feature, likely to make it useful to active Clergymen.

The *inside* of this Magazine will be printed separate from the *cover*, so that any clergyman, who wishes it, can be supplied with the *inside* alone, by the 20th of the preceding month. He can then have a cover provided by his local printer, and can call the Magazine after the name of his own parish, e. g.

"St. Michael's Derby Parish Magazine,"

and can have printed on the three pages of cover any matters of local or parochial interest, e. g.

> Hours of Church Services.
> Lectures, or Missionary Associations.
> Statements of Accounts, Clothing Clubs, &c.
> Hours and Regulations of Schools.
> Additions to Parish Libraries.
> Extracts from Sermons, &c.

The whole or part of this local matter might, for a very trifling sum, when the types were set up, be struck off in the form of *parochial hand-bills*, and distributed through the parish; so that the Clergyman might relieve his conscience by feeling that he had brought his *mind* before the eyes of those who would not come to hear his voice.

The "Parish Magazine," while distinctly Church of England, will be written and compiled rather with the hope of fostering the home affections, and promoting social improvement, than with the wish to enforce any technicalities of doctrine. It will be arranged with special thought for the tastes of children and of the handicraft classes.

Price 8d. per dozen of 13, without Covers.
,, 9d. per dozen of 13, with "Parish Magazine" Covers.

So that any Schoolmaster selling six dozen per month, would raise £1 per annum for the Schools—equal to one new subscriber—while the expense of not a few handbills would be saved.

Clergymen or others wishing to adapt the Magazine to their own parishes, are requested to apply, without delay, in the first instance to the Editor,

ST. MICHAEL'S VICARAGE, DERBY.

Publisher, H. G. HEALD, Ludgate-hill, London.

BY J. ERSKINE CLARKE, M.A.,
VICAR OF ST. MICHAEL'S, DERBY.

What the Children ought to know about Lichfield.

Price 6d.

✝

Lichfield: LOMAX.

Children at Church.

First and Second Series.

1s. 6d. cloth gilt.
1s. paper.

✝

London: NISBET.

Price 1s. 6d. cloth gilt,
OUR HAPPY HOME UNION.
BEING THE YEAR'S NUMBERS OF A PAROCHIAL MAGAZINE.
London: NISBET.

Price 2s. cloth gilt ; 1s. 6d. cloth limp ; 1s. paper,
HEART-MUSIC:
A POETRY-BOOK FOR WORKING PEOPLE.
London: PARTRIDGE.

Price 4d., same size as "Harland's Hymnal."
HEARTY STAVES:
A SONG-BOOK FOR WORKING PEOPLE.
London: G. ROUTLEDGE.

Price 6d. each,
Plain Papers on the Social Economy of the People.
No. 1.—RECREATIONS OF THE PEOPLE: Real and Imaginary.
No. 2.—PENNY BANKS: with all details necessary to establish them.
No. 3.—WORKING MEN'S REFRESHMENT ROOMS AND LABOURERS' CLUBS— (Preparing.)

London: BELL and DALDY. Derby: R. KEENE.

REWARD BOOKS, &c.

COXE'S CHRISTIAN BALLADS. 1d. each.

Dreamland.	Churchyards.
Hymn of Boyhood.	Little Woodmere.
England.	Matin Bells and Curfew.
Lenten Season.	St. Silvan's Bell.
Chronicles.	Daily Services.
Chimes of England.	The Calendar, and I love the Church.

TALES FROM THE PAROCHIAL TRACTS, *Illustrated*, 2d. each.

26. Alice Grant.	11. Joseph and his Brethren.
152. Bye and Bye.	5. The Village Shop.
19. Complaints and their Cure.	139. Jane Smith's Marriage.
66. The Curate's Daughter, or, Sacredness of Churchyards.	149. Little Geoffrey.
83. The Day that never came.	48. Mary Fisher.
135. Edward Elford ; or, Who's afraid ?	63. Mr. Sharpley.
18. Edwin Forth ; or, The Emigrant.	6. Who Pays the Poor-rate !
25. The Fair on Whit-Monday.	141. The Modern Martyr.
2. Keeping Poultry no Loss.	84. Nothing lost in the Telling.
90. Hannah Dean.	89. The Prodigal.
10. Harry Fulton.	88. The Promised Estate.
1. The Cottage Pig-Stye.	118. Richard Reveley's Legacy.
101. The Hop Picker.	12. The Rock and the Sand.
3. Mrs. Martin's Bee-hive.	85. Too old to be questioned.
78. Her Sun has gone down while it was yet Day.	148. Two-pence for the Clothing Club.
80. It might have been Worse.	9. "Thou shalt not Steal ;" or, The School Feast.
4. The Honest Widow.	82. Tony Dilke.
86. Mrs. Morton's Walk.	159. The Widower. 2d.
	81. The Cloud upon the Mountain. 3d.

Seléne ; or, The Queen of the Fairy Cross. 4d.

The Loaves and Fishes. 4d.

SEVEN FAIRY TALES, with Illustrations, 4d. each.

1. Little Ino C. and his Companions.	4. Rose and the Fairy Helpful.
2. Ulric and Laura.	5. The Fairy Devoirgilla.
3. Sholto and his Little Dog Bowowsky.	6. Sansouci and his Sister Soigneuse.
	7. Bonnatura.

Old Christmas. 6d.

Mount Gars ; or, Marie's Christmas-Eve. Adapted from the German of STIFTER. Fcap. 8vo., 6d ; by post, 7d.

Little Footprints on the old Church Path. Third Edition. 8d.

Fairton Village ; or, Wesleyan Beginnings. 8d.

Smyttan's Florum Sacra. 16mo. 1s.

Messrs. J. H. and J. PARKER, Broad-street, Oxford.

Reward Books, from 4d. to 6s.

The Matin Bell. 1s.
The Village Choristers. 1s.
The Garden of Life ; an Allegory. 1s.
THE CHILD'S CHRISTIAN YEAR, *New and Cheaper Edition*, 1s.
The Christian Year, cheap edition. 1s. 6d.
The Lyra Innocentium, cheap edition. 1s. 6d.
The Penny Post. Vols. 1, 2, 3, and 4. Cloth, each 1s. 6d. The Set, 5s.
————— *The New Series*, 8vo. Vols. I. II. and III. in Ornamental
    Wrapper, 1s. each ; cloth, 1s. 8d. each.
Woodleigh ; or, Life and Death. 2s.
The Christian Year, cheap roan. 2s.
The Lyra Innocentium, cheap roan. 2s.
Tracts for Cottagers, (from the Parochial Tracts). 2s.
Ann Ash. 2s.
The Pastor of Wellbourn. 2s.
*Storm and Sunshine ; or, The Boyhood of Herbert Falconer. Fcap.
    8vo., cloth, 2s.
Angels' Work. 2s.
Seven Fairy Tales, *with Illustrations.* Cloth, 2s. 6d.
Ada's Thoughts ; or, The Poetry of Youth. 2s. 6d.
The History of our Lord in Easy Verse. 2s. 6d. Coloured, 3s. 6d.
The Singers of the Sanctuary. 2s. 6d.
Parochial Tales, (from the Parochial Tracts). 2s. 6d.
*The Two Homes, by the Author of " Amy Grant." 2s. 6d.
Chronicles of Camber Castle. Cloth, 3s.
Coxe's Christian Ballads, complete. 3s.
The Christian Year. 32mo. 3s. 6d.
The Lyra Innocentium. 32mo. 3s. 6d.
The Californian Crusoe. A Mormon Tale. 2s. 6d.
Amy Grant ; or, The One Motive. 3s. 6d.
Tales and Allegories, (from the Parochial Tracts). 3s. 6d.
PILGRIM'S PROGRESS, (for the use of Children of the Church of
    England). Best Edition. 3s. 6d.
*————————— Cheap Edition, *with eight Illustrations.* 2s. 6d.
Rodolph the Voyager. First Voyage. 4s. 6d.
————————————— Second Voyage. 6s.
Mant's Reginald Vere. 6s.
Kenneth ; or, The Rear-Guard of the Grand Army. Illustrated, 5s.
Speculation ; a Tale. 2s. 6d.

Messrs. J. H. and J. PARKER, Broad-street, Oxford.

THE PENNY POST.

A Monthly Magazine for the Middle Classes, and better educated of the Poorer Classes.

THE attention of the Clergy is respectfully drawn to the following extract from a Circular which was issued last year :—

A Periodical with a large circulation obtains an influence in these days which can scarcely be equalled by any other means. Both personal intercourse and pulpit eloquence often fail to reach the homes and hearts that the printed tract will find a way to ; but the Tract is read and placed aside—its impression may be obliterated by some fresh influence—while the Periodical is ever awakening ; what it tells in one number it enforces in the next, and so the principles it advocates take root : and again, the Tract, on some minds, will produce no impression at all ; it is only by constant repetition of the same truths under different forms, and on different occasions, that such minds are influenced. Hence the great use that the "Dissenters" from the Church have made of these engines of warfare ; hence it is that so much stress is laid upon the advantages of their Periodicals, that the Baptists, and Wesleyans, and Independents have each their Penny Periodical,—circulated noiselessly, but insidiously, throughout the whole kingdom.

The neglect of an otherwise most useful adjunct to the pulpit is not only negative in its effects, but produces positive evil, by allowing other periodicals to unteach the lessons taught in the Church. Little will the teaching from the pulpit be listened to, little will the words of warning be attended to, when the seed of false doctrine in the shape of schismatic Tracts, dissenting Magazines, or semi-infidel journals, has been sown in the parish. The Church has not kept the supply equal to the demand. Of doctrinal tracts there may be many ; of devotional works also ; but not entertaining reading—reading that men, and women, and children, will read with pleasure, and not only from a sense of duty. It may now well be said with Sir WALTER SCOTT, "To make boys learn to read, and then to place no good books within their reach, is to give them an appetite and leave nothing in the pantry save unwholesome and poisonous food, which, depend upon it, they will eat rather than starve."

A Prospectus, such as can be issued in a parish, has been drawn up and printed. To those who cannot otherwise obtain any copies, a letter, addressed to the "Publishers of the PENNY POST," enclosing a penny stamp, will meet with prompt attention.

From fifty to one hundred Prospectuses can be sent free by Post for one Penny.

Address to   THE OFFICE OF THE "PENNY POST,"

377, STRAND,

LONDON,   (W. C.)

Or to MESSRS. PARKER, BROAD-STREET, OXFORD.

THE AIM AND OBJECT OF THE "PENNY POST."

In the first place it is not a "Party Magazine." It *does not* consider itself to be the organ of any one section of the Church, or bound to support any particular set of opinions. In a word, it abides by the "Prayer-book;" and a certain latitude, allowed wisely by those great and learned compilers, must be allowed where minds and temperaments so widely differ.

But the PENNY POST *does* aim at stirring up a livelier interest, so to speak, in religious matters—a love and respect for the Church, her teaching and her ordinances. To do battle with irreligion, indifference, and dissent, not so much by attacks, as by raising up strong bulwarks in a knowledge and understanding of her doctrines, a devotion to her cause, a faith in her integrity; which, while repelling assaults of enemies, will confirm and strengthen the Churchman in his position.

And yet, in doing this, religion should not appear too prominently upon the surface; rather in the tale, or the allegory, or the essay on some scientific or historical subject, the mind must be drawn gradually to contemplate the affairs of every-day life from a higher and better point of view. Slowly the work must be done, as month after month some one point must be brought forward, corroborating others which have been insisted on before. One number may do little, but the year's series may do much.

In TALES and ALLEGORIES, and lighter reading, Entertainment will be found which will leave behind agreeable reminiscences when the reading is over;— Lessons which may benefit old as well as young, rich as well as poor, in rendering their lives more holy and more happy;—Thoughts which may lead to the consideration of an Ever-watching Providence, of a Life after this life, and of an Eternity of joy or misery.

In more directly RELIGIOUS ARTICLES, whether doctrinal or practical, the truth and reality of the Church's System are brought home to the reader's mind, and principles explained and enforced, not in an angry and controversial spirit, but in a spirit of peace and love.

In MISCELLANEOUS ARTICLES, various scientific or historical subjects are presented in a popular form, providing wholesome material for thought and conversation.

Finally, in the shorter NOTES and CORRESPONDENCE will be found clear and concise information on the numerous and varied matters which possess an interest, and oftentimes are of importance for Churchmen to be acquainted with, and which could only otherwise be gleaned from long research, or reference to ponderous volumes.

P.S. It is suggested that teachers in schools, with the clergyman's approval, could assist materially, if they would, in increasing the circulation of the PENNY POST by distributing Prospectuses, or other means which might be found convenient.

Messrs. J. H. and J. PARKER, Broad-street, Oxford.

BOOKS PUBLISHED BY MR. VAN VOORST.

Instrumenta Ecclesiastica; a Series of Working Designs, engraved on 72 Plates, for the Furniture, Fittings, and Decorations of Churches and their Precincts. Edited by the Ecclesiological, late Cambridge Camden Society. 4to., £1 11s. 6d.

The Second Series contains a Cemetery Chapel, with Sick-house and Gateway Tower—A Wooden Church—A Chapel School—Schools and School-houses— A Village Hospital—An Iron Church—and Designs for Funeral Fittings, for Timber Belfries, and for a Variety of Works in Metal, Wood, and Stone. Price also £1 11s. 6d.

Manual of Gothic Architecture. By F. A. PALEY, M.A. With a full Account of Monumental Brasses and Ecclesiastical Costume. Fcap. 8vo., with 70 Illustrations, 6s. 6d.

"To the student of the architecture of old English churches this beautiful little volume will prove a most acceptable manual. The two chapters on . . . . form an epitome of the whole subject, so lucid, concise, and complete, that it may be regarded as a model of succinct and clear exposition. Both in description and analysis, Mr. Paley is remarkable for neatness and perspicuity; his style is terse and precise, yet withal easy and elegant. The examples, engraved by Thurston Thompson, are the perfection of wood engraving, as applied to architecture: exact in detail, picturesque in effect, and cut with equal firmness and delicacy."—*Spectator.*

Baptismal Fonts. A Series of 125 Engravings, examples of the different periods, accompanied with Descriptions; and with an Introductory Essay. By F. A. PALEY, M.A., Honorary Secretary of the Cambridge Camden Society. 8vo., One Guinea.

Treatise on the Rise and Progress of Decorated Window Tracery in England. By EDMUND SHARPE, M.A., Architect. 8vo., Illustrated with Ninety-seven Woodcuts and Six Engravings on Steel, 10s. 6d. And—

A Series of Illustrations of the Window Tracery of the Deco-rated Style of Ecclesiastical Architecture. Edited, with descriptions, by Mr. SHARPE. Sixty Engravings on Steel. 8vo., 21s.

Manual of Gothic Mouldings. A Practical Treatise on their formations, gradual development, combinations, and varieties; with full directions for copying them, and for determining their dates. Illustrated by nearly 600 examples. By F. A. PALEY, M.A. Second Edition, 8vo., 7s. 6d.

"Mouldings are the scholarship of architecture. The present is a most learned work, and displays an amount of practical knowledge which those who know the difficulties of the subject alone can appreciate."—*Christian Remembrancer.*

Heraldry of Fish. By THOMAS MOULE. The Engravings, 205 in number, are from Stained Glass, Tombs, Sculpture and Carving, Medals and Coins, Rolls of Arms, and Pedigrees. 8vo., 21s. A few on large paper (royal 8vo.) for colouring, £2 2s.

London: JOHN VAN VOORST, 1, Paternoster-row.

SACRED PRINTS FOR PAROCHIAL USE.

PRINTED IN SEPIA, WITH ORNAMENTAL BORDERS.

Price One Penny each; or the set in an ornamental envelope,

One Shilling.

1. The Nativity.	7. The Tribute-Money.
2. St. John Preaching.	8. The Preparation for the Cross.
3. The Baptism of Christ.	9. The Crucifixion.
4. Jacob's Dream.	10. Leading to Crucifixion.
5. The Transfiguration.	11. Healing the Sick.
6. The Good Shepherd.	12. The Return of the Prodigal.

They are also kept mounted and varnished, 3d.

N.B.—Upwards of Eighty Thousand of these Prints have already been sold.

COTTAGE PICTURES FROM THE OLD TESTAMENT.

A Series of Twenty-eight large folio Engravings, brilliantly coloured by hand.   The set, 7s. 6d.

Also, uniform with the above,

COTTAGE PICTURES FROM THE NEW TESTAMENT.

A Series of Twenty-eight large folio Engravings, brilliantly coloured. The set, 7s. 6d.

TALES FOR THE YOUNG MEN AND WOMEN OF ENGLAND.

	s.	d.		s.	d.
1. MOTHER AND SON	1	0	12. THE TENANTS AT		
2. THE RECRUIT	1	0	TINKERS' END	1	0
3. THE STRIKE	1	0	13. WINDYCOTE HALL	1	0
4. JAMES BRIGHT, THE			14. FALSE HONOUR	1	0
SHOPMAN	1	0	15. OLD JARVIS'S WILL	1	0
5. JONAS CLINT	1	0	16. THE TWO COTTAGES	1	0
6. THE SISTERS	1	0	17. SQUITCH	1	0
7. SERVANTS' INFLUENCE	0	6	18. THE POLITICIAN	1	0
8. CAROLINE ELTON; or,			19. TWO TO ONE	1	0
Vanity and Jealousy	0	6	20. HOBSON'S CHOICE	0	6
9. THE RAILWAY ACCIDENT	1	0	21. SUSAN	0	4
10. WANTED, A WIFE	1	0	22. MARY THOMAS; OR,		
11. IRREVOCABLE	1	0	DISSENT AT EVENLY	0	4

Messrs. J. H. and J. PARKER, Broad-street Oxford.

M

THE CLERGY MUTUAL ASSURANCE SOCIETY.
Established in 1829.
OFFICE, No. 3, BROAD SANCTUARY, WESTMINSTER.
(REMOVED FROM 41, PARLIAMENT-STREET.)

Patrons.—The Archbishops of Canterbury and York.

DIRECTORS.

Chairman.—The Archdeacon of London.

Deputy Chairman.—F. L. Wollaston, Esq., M.A.

Sir E. Antrobus, Bart., M.A.
B. G. Babington, Esq., M.D.
Charles John Baker, Esq.
Rev. G. B. Blomfield, M.A.
The Dean of Bristol.
Rev. R. W. Browne, M.A.
Rev. A. M. Campbell, M.A.
The Dean of Chichester.
Richard Clarke, Esq.
Rev. C. B. Dalton, M.A.

Rev. W. H. Dickinson, M.A.
The Archdeacon of Essex.
Robert Few, Esq.
Rev. Temple Frere, M.A.
Rev. J. D. Glennie, M.A.
Chris. Hodgson, Esq., M.A.
Rev. John Jennings, M.A.
The Dean of Lincoln.
Rev. Henry Mackenzie, M.A.
The Dean of Manchester.

Rev. Charles Marshall, M.A.
The Archdeacon of Maidstone.
Rev. Evan Nepean, M.A.
Rev. William Stone, M.A.
Charles Sumner, Esq., M.A.
Rev. William Webster, M.A.
The Archdeac. of Winchester.
Rev. S. C. Wilks, M.A.

Treasurers.—Sir E. Antrobus, Bart., M.A.; The Archdeacon of London.

Counsel.—Thomas Bourdillon, Esq., M.A.   *Solicitors.*—Messrs. Lee and Bolton.

Physician.—Dr. Babington.

Consulting Actuary.—C. Ansell, Esq., F.R.S., Actuary to the Atlas Assurance Office.

Secretary.—Rev. J. Hodgson, M.A.   *Bankers.*—Messrs. Coutts and Co.

Auditors.—John Cotton, Esq.; William Robinson White, Esq.; Thomas Keen, Esq.; George Aston, Esq.

Assistant Secretary.—Frank Webb, Esq.

LIFE ASSURANCE.—RATES TO BE PAID ANNUALLY.

Age next Birthday	£100 due at Death. £. s. d.	Age next Birthday	£100 due at Death. £. s. d.	Age next Birthday	£100 due at Death. £. s. d.	Age next Birthday	£100 due at Death. £. s. d.
14	1 10 4	26	2 1 4	38	2 18 4	50	4 7 4
15	1 11 0	27	2 2 6	39	3 0 2	51	4 11 4
16	1 11 8	28	2 3 10	40	3 2 2	52	4 15 8
17	1 12 6	29	2 5 0	41	3 4 0	53	5 0 2
18	1 13 4	30	2 6 4	42	3 6 0	54	5 5 0
19	1 14 2	31	2 7 6	43	3 8 0	55	5 10 4
20	1 15 0	32	2 8 8	44	3 10 0	56	5 16 0
21	1 16 0	33	2 10 0	45	3 12 4	57	6 2 2
22	1 17 0	34	2 11 6	46	3 14 10	58	6 8 6
23	1 18 0	35	2 13 0	47	3 17 6	59	6 15 0
24	1 19 0	36	2 14 8	48	4 0 4	60	7 1 6
25	2 0 2	37	2 16 6	49	4 3 8		

ASSURANCES may be effected on Lives, Survivorships, &c., &c., as stated in the Society's Prospectus, to any amount not exceeding £5,000.

The whole available Bonus is the sole property of Life Assurers, no part whatever is taken from it to be shared amongst proprietors. The greatest advantage to Life Assurers necessarily results from this principle of Mutual Assurance, that at the end of every fifth year return is made to every Assurer of that which is then found to be an excess of payment made by him, beyond that which the circumstances of the case required, as proved by experience.

The Fee to the Medical Referees is paid by the Society.

N.B.—Assurances may be made upon payment of Two-Thirds of the Annual Premium, as above, *upon special conditions.*

Applications for Prospectuses, or further information, to be made at the Office, 3, BROAD SANCTUARY, WESTMINSTER.

"This Society is strictly confined to the Clergy of the Church of England and of the Episcopal Church of Scotland, their wives and families, and the near relations of themselves and wives, and is distinguished from other institutions by the title of

"THE CLERGY MUTUAL ASSURANCE SOCIETY."

COLONIAL CHURCH AND SCHOOL SOCIETY.

Patron—HER MOST GRACIOUS MAJESTY THE QUEEN.

Vice-Patrons—{ His Grace the Archbishop of Canterbury.
His Grace the Archbishop of York.

President—The Right Honourable the Marquis of Cholmondeley.

Vice-Presidents.

His Grace the Duke of Marlborough.	Right Rev. the Bishop of Calcutta.
Right Hon. the Earl of Chichester.	Right Rev. the Bishop of Madras.
Right Hon. the Earl of Effingham.	Right Rev. the Bishop of Bombay.
Right Hon. the Earl of Gainsborough.	Right Rev. the Bishop of Sydney.
Right Hon. the Earl of Harrowby.	Right Rev. the Bishop of Melbourne.
Right Hon. the Earl of Mountcashel.	Right Rev. the Bishop of Montreal.
Right Hon. the Earl of Shaftesbury.	Right Rev. the Bishop of Victoria.
Right Hon. the Earl Waldegrave, C.B.	Right Rev. the Bishop of Nova Scotia.
Right Hon. Viscount Hill.	Right Rev. the Bishop of Rupert's Land.
Rev. Lord Wriothesley Russell.	Right Rev. the English Bishop in Jerusalem.
Right Hon. and Right Rev. the Lord Bishop of London.	Right Rev. the Bishop of Mauritius.
	Right Rev. the Bishop of Grahamstown.
Right Rev. the Lord Bishop of Winchester.	Right Rev. the Bishop of Sierra Leone.
Right Rev. the Lord Bishop of Peterborough.	Right Rev. the Bishop of Perth.
Right Rev. the Lord Bishop of Manchester.	Right Rev. the Bishop of Huron.
Right Rev. the Lord Bishop of Carlisle.	Right Rev. the Bishop of Kingston.
Right Rev. the Lord Bishop of Gloucester and Bristol.	Right Rev. Bishop Carr, D.D.
	Right Hon. Lord Calthorpe.
Right Rev. the Lord Bishop of Ripon.	Lieut.-General Lord Seaton, G.C.B.
Right Rev. the Lord Bishop of Norwich.	Right Hon. Lord Teignmouth.
Right Hon. and Most Rev. the Lord Bishop of Meath.	Hon. Arthur Kinnaird, M.P.
	Right Hon. Frederick Shaw.

Treasurer—R. C. L. BEVAN, Esq.   **Secretary**—Rev. MESAC THOMAS, M.A.

Assistant-Secretary—WILLIAM H. A. HART, Esq.

GENERAL OBJECTS OF THE SOCIETY.

THE leading object of the Society is to send Clergymen, Catechists, and Teachers of the Church of England and Ireland to the Colonies of Great Britain, and to British subjects in other parts of the world.

Its PRINCIPLES are Evangelical and Protestant, and special care is taken that its missionaries should be persons of intelligent acquaintance with the truth, and earnest devotion to the missionary work—uniting a cordial attachment to the United Church of England and Ireland, with the exercise of a spirit of love towards Christians of other Protestant communities.

Its AGENCY is as follows:—

Clergymen	54
Catechists and Schoolmasters	86
Female Teachers	46
	186

The income of the Society for the year ending 31st March, 1858, was £19,327 4s. 6d.

The Clergymen employed by the Society are subject to the ecclesiastical jurisdiction of their Diocesans, precisely as in this country.

The Mission to BRITISH SAILORS in Colonial and Foreign Ports is an important branch of labour which the providence of God has opened to the Society, and deserves more earnest attention than it has yet received from the Christian public.

Colonial populations are rapidly increasing. The number of emigrants in 1856 to the North American Colonies was 17,554, and to Australia 44,584.

Special Missions to FUGITIVE SLAVES and FRENCH HABITANS in Canada, and to NATIVES OF MALTA, are other interesting features of the Society's operations.

Besides its work in the Colonies, the Society aims to promote the spiritual welfare of our countrymen in Foreign Lands, and assists in procuring faithful Clergymen to act as Chaplains to British travellers and residents on THE CONTINENT.

Thus, both in the Colonies and in Foreign Lands, the Society's work appeals to the sympathy of every Christian patriot, and especially of the Evangelical members of the United Church of England and Ireland. The Committee will not believe that such a cause can fail to command earnest and liberal support.

Contributions for the Society are earnestly requested, and will be thankfully received at the Office, 9, SERJEANTS'-INN, FLEET-STREET, London, and at the Bank of Messrs. BARCLAY, BEVAN, & Co., 54, LOMBARD-STREET. Post Office Orders are payable to WILLIAM HART, Esq.

Clergy Orphan Society,

For Clothing, Maintaining, and Educating Poor Orphans of Clergymen, of the Established Church, in England and Wales, until of age to be put Apprentice.

FOUNDED 1749.

Incorporated at the expense of the Hon. and Rev. Shute Barrington, Lord Bishop of Durham, 1809.

BOYS' SCHOOL, ST. THOMAS'S HILL, CANTERBURY.
GIRLS' SCHOOL, ST. JOHN'S WOOD, MARYLEBONE, LONDON.

Patron—Her Most Gracious MAJESTY THE QUEEN.

President—His Grace the LORD ARCHBISHOP OF CANTERBURY.

Vice-President—Vice-Chancellor Sir W. PAGE WOOD.

Treasurer—Rev. JOHN RUSSELL, D.D.

Secretary—Rev. J. D. GLENNIE, M.A.

Collector—Mr. HENRY STRETTON.

Bankers—Messrs. DRUMMOND, Charing Cross, London.

OFFICE, 67, Lincoln's-Inn-Fields, London.

THE handsome and commodious building recently erected on St. Thomas's Hill, Canterbury, by means of funds collected for the purpose, together with a munificent donation from the late Rev. Dr. Warneford, and an outlay of about £6,000 from the capital property of the Corporation, is fitted up for the reception of 100 Boys, while the school at St. John's Wood is capable of accommodating 100 Girls. But at present the funds of the Corporation do not allow of the admission of more than about two-thirds of those numbers. Hence is furnished an urgent plea for effective and increased support. The arrangements for receiving more Orphans being now complete, *every increase of Annual Contributions will directly and immediately have the effect of extending the benefits of this charity to fresh objects deserving of aid and sympathy.*

There are five Orphans from the Diocese of Oxford at present in the Schools, viz.—

A son of the Rev. John Weighell, late Rector of Cheddington, Bucks.

A son and a daughter of the Rev. Henry John Whitfield, late Vicar of Granborough, Bucks.

A son and a daughter of the Rev. George Thomas Spring, late Perpetual Curate of Hampton Gay, Oxfordshire.

The Elections, which are by Polling-papers, take place twice in the Year, in May and in November.

Forms of Petition may be obtained from the Secretary, 67, Lincoln's-Inn-Fields, London, W.C.

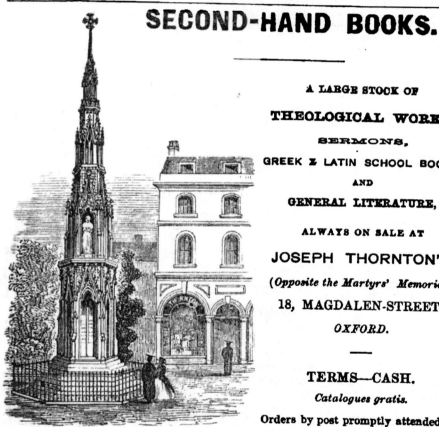

Electro-plated Table Cutlery,

Of warranted quality, from the best Makers, at

SPIERS AND SON'S WAREHOUSES,

102 and 103, HIGH-ST., and 45 and 46, CORNMARKET-ST., OXFORD.

Table forks or spoons,	24s., 36s., 48s.	per doz.	net prices.
Dessert ,, ,,	18s., 27s., 36s.	,,	,,
Tea spoons	9s., 15s., 21s.	,,	,,

Salt, egg, mustard, and gravy spoons; sauce and soup ladles; sugar-tongs and spoons, and sifters; caddy-shells; butter-knives, cheese-knives; cruet-frames, pickle-frames, spirit-stands, &c.; tea and coffee pots, cream-jugs and sugar-basins, toast-racks, &c., &c.

Orders by post promptly attended to, and patterns forwarded for selection.

DOUBLE CARBONATED SODA-WATER,

3s. 6d. PER DOZEN.

BRIGHTON SELTZER,

4s. PER DOZEN.

IN THE HIGHEST STATE OF PERFECTION.

FOREIGN MINERAL WATERS,

VICHY, PULLNA, MARIENBAD, and others, direct from their several Springs.

HENRY BROWN,

PHARMACEUTICAL, DISPENSING, AND FAMILY CHYMIST,

101, HIGH-STREET, OXFORD.

Established 1812.

The Dispensing Department is entrusted only to Competent Assistants, under Mr. Brown's immediate supervision.

Prescriptions are correctly copied into a Book kept for that purpose, and may be found at any distant period, should the original be lost.

FREDERICK TELFER,

PHARMACEUTICAL & DISPENSING CHEMIST,

No. 11, Cornmarket-street,

(*Opposite the Star Gateway,*)

Respectfully informs Gentlemen of the University, and the Public generally, that he has always on Sale

PURE CHEMICALS FOR ANALYSIS, PHOTOGRAPHY, &c.,

Also Chemical Apparatus and Utensils in great variety,

AT THE LOWEST POSSIBLE PRICE FOR CASH.

SCHWEPPE'S SELTZER AND SODA-WATER, LEMONADE, &c.

The greatest attention paid to the preparation of Physicians' Prescriptions, &c.

SPIERS AND SON'S TABLE CUTLERY,

MARKED with their name, maintains an unrivalled reputation for excellence of quality, combined with moderate prices. Their stock is very large, and includes balance ivory-handled, of various sizes ; also in handles of silver, bone, and black horn. Their long ivory-handled knives are much admired for their elegance and convenience.

Net prices of ivory-handled cutlery, warranted quality :—

Table-knives, 15s., 20s., 25s., 31s. 6d., 38s. per dozen.
Dessert-knives, 11s. 10d., 15s., 19s., 27s. 6d., 28s. „

Silver-handled table-knives, 72s., Dessert, 60s. per dozen.

Black horn and bone-handled knives and forks at various prices.

Carving knives and forks. Ditto for Game, Poultry, and Venison. Bread-knives, knife sharpeners, steels, &c. Electro-plated forks, spoons, etc.

Kent's knife-cleaning machines, £4 15s., and upwards, saving much time, preserving the cutlery, and keeping the polish equal to new.

SPIERS AND SON,

102 & 103, HIGH-ST. ; 45 & 46, CORNMARKET-ST., OXFORD.

Orders by post promptly attended to, and patterns forwarded for selection.

Cocoa Fibre Mats and Matting.

S. L. EVANS & COMPANY have been appointed SOLE AGENTS in the OXFORD DISTRICT for the sale of the MATS and MATTINGS manufactured at the Wakefield House of Correction.

The MATTINGS are manufactured in six widths, commencing at 18 inches, advancing to 2 yards wide.

There are ten different makes of Mats, measuring from 2 feet to 4 feet long, widths in proportion ; or made to any dimensions, and charged per square foot.

N.B. These MATS and MATTINGS are made by the Prisoners, and the trifling cost for labour enables them to produce Articles hitherto unequalled for durability and cheapness.

S. L. EVANS and COMPANY,

MERCERY, DRAPERY, AND HOSIERY WAREHOUSE,

12, *High-street*, (*late Morley and Evans*).

OXFORD: 23, CORNMARKET-STREET.

FISKE AND SON'S

Academical and Clerical Warehouse for Robes and Clothing.

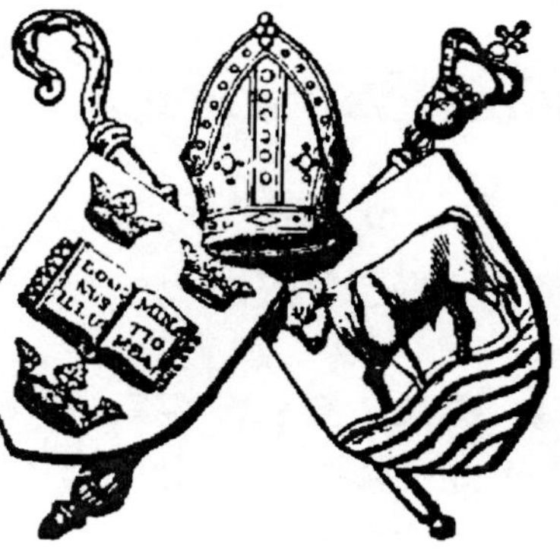

M.A. Gowns of Anti-fraying Silk, 5 to 7½ Guineas. Cassocks, ditto, 3 to 4½ Guineas. Gowns of Ribbed Stuff, 30s. to 50s. Surplices, improved make, 25s. to 60s. Undergraduates' Gowns, from 12s. 6d. Literates', M.A., B.A. Hoods, from 10s. to 28s. Black Wool-dyed Cloth Suits from 4 Guineas.

ROBES FOR PRESENTATION ACCURATELY SUPPLIED.

Caps and Gowns for Collegiate Schools.

F. and S. continue their principle, which has insured to them public patronage, of supplying first-rate articles at fair and moderate prices.

Orders by post promptly attended to.

C. P. PIKE,

CLERICAL TAILOR & ROBE-MAKER,

SHIRT-MAKER, GLOVER, HATTER, HOSIER, ETC.,

TURL-STREET, OXFORD.

THE most correct and cheapest House in the Trade.—CLERICAL COATS, from 50s. to 70s.; VESTS, 13s. to 15s.; TROWSERS, 23s. to 30s.; SURPLICES, 21s. to 42s.; CASSOCKS, 21s. to 30s.; CINCTURES, 4s. 6d. to 7s. 6d.; STOLES, 7s. 6d. to 14s. 6d., work extra; OVER COATS, various shapes, from 25s. to 60s. Altar-Cloths, Linen for Altars, Veils, Alms'-bags, Maniples, Chasubles, Albs, Palls, Damask Hangings, Lace, Caps, Gowns, &c., at equally low prices.

Pianoforte and Harmonium Warehouse.

H. HOUGHTON,

(OF THE CHOIRS OF MAGDALEN AND ST. JOHN'S COLLEGES,)

116, HIGH-STREET, OXFORD.

Pianofortes, Harmoniums, Concertinas, &c., sent out on Hire, and if purchased after a sufficient time for a fair trial of the Instrument, the hire not charged.

J. S. BROWNING,

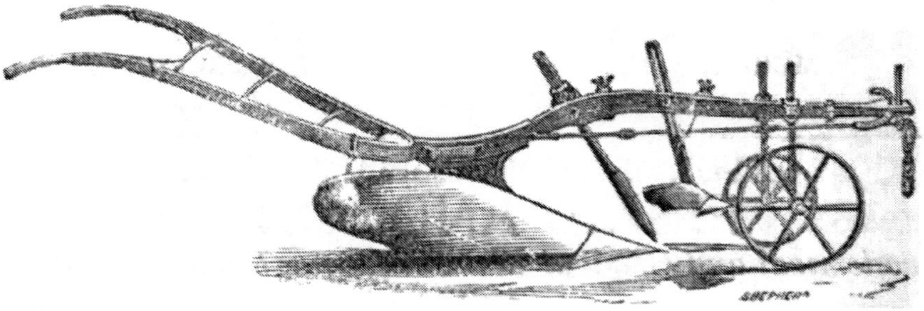

General Agent for Agricultural Implements,

Furnishing Ironmonger and Manufacturer,

57, CORNMARKET-STREET, OXFORD.

FLAVELL'S CLOSE AND OPEN FIRE-RANGES,

TO SUPPLY HOT WATER AND BATHS.

MILNER'S FIRE-PROOF SAFES.

OXFORD UNIVERSITY
Ecclesiastical and Academical Warehouse.

C. FOSTER & Co.

Respectfully solicit the attention of the Clergy to their Extensive Assortment of

ECCLESIASTICAL VESTMENTS, ACADEMICAL ROBES, &c.

prepared with great care, in the most correct forms and style. They have a great number of designs and patterns for

ALTAR VESTMENTS, FRONTALS, SURPLICES, STOLES, SERMON-CASES, CHASUBLES, &c.,

and request the Clergy and others to visit their Extensive Establishment.

The annexed List of Prices has been prepared with scrupulous attention to Durability of Material and Good Workmanship, and will be found strictly Moderate :—

	£	s.	d.		£	s.	d.
Commoner's Gown ... from	0	10	6	to	1	1	0
B.A. and M.A. Mohair ditto ...	1	1	0		2	10	0
Ditto ditto Silk ditto ...	4	10	0		7	10	0
Mohair Cassock	1	10	0		2	10	0
Silk Preaching Gown, full sleeves	5	0	0		7	10	0
B.A. Silk Hood	0	10	6		0	18	6
M.A. ditto	0	16	6		1	5	6
Academic Cap	0	6	6		0	8	6
Chorister's Cap	0	4	6				
Ditto Gowns and Surplices ...	0	12	6		0	16	6
Lay Clerk's ditto	0	16	6		1	1	0

Foster's Oxford Surplice.

The pattern of this celebrated Surplice is taken from an ancient specimen, and is by far the most approved shape on sale, made in Fine Linen or Lawn from 30s. to 63s.

A SUIT OF SUPERFINE BLACK CLOTHES, 5 Guineas ;
Ditto of the very best Cloth, 6 Guineas.

₄ *Special attention is requested to their Black and Oxford Mixed Scotch Tweeds, which are very durable, and well adapted for the morning wear of Clergymen. Price £3 10s. to £4 4s. the entire Suit.*

AN ILLUSTRATED CATALOGUE FORWARDED ON APPLICATION, AND PROMPT ATTENTION PAID TO ORDERS BY POST.

C. FOSTER & Co., 123 & 124, High-street, Oxford.

NEW SERIES OF
HISTORICAL TALES

TO BE PUBLISHED BY

JOHN HENRY AND JAMES PARKER,

Illustrating the chief events in Ecclesiastical History, British & Foreign,

ADAPTED FOR GENERAL READING, PAROCHIAL LIBRARIES, &c.

THOSE who know the Church to be God's appointed instrument for the regeneration of mankind, and, regarding it as such, have tried to impress her claims upon others, in opposition to the sectarianism of the day, are well aware of the difficulty they have to encounter in the almost universal ignorance, even amongst persons supposed to be well educated, of the facts of Ecclesiastical History. This is not surprising, considering how dry and uninteresting to all but the divinity student are most treatises upon this subject. Yet the moment we turn aside from the beaten track that connects one great epoch with another, we find incidents of the most exciting, attractive, and instructive kind, crowding together with a truth more strange than fiction, and wonderfully illustrative of the progress of the faith and of the inner and outer life of the Church. * * * * * . * . * The Series of Tales now announced will embrace the most important periods and transactions connected with the progress of the Church in ancient and modern times. They will be written by authors of acknowledged merit, in a popular style, upon sound Church principles, and with a single eye to the inculcation of a true estimate of the circumstances to which they relate, and the bearing of those circumstances upon the history of the Church. By this means it is hoped that many, who now regard Church history with indifference, will be led to the perusal of its singularly interesting and instructive episodes.

The series is to be conducted by a responsible editor, and it is intended that, when complete, it shall illustrate not only portions of the history of the Church in Great Britain, but also in her Colonies, in the different countries of Europe, and in the East. The extent of the series must, of course, greatly depend upon the favour and support accorded to it by the public.

Each tale, although forming a link of the entire series, will be complete in itself, enabling persons to subscribe to portions only, or to purchase any single tale separately.

It is intended to issue a volume on the first of each month, at the uniform price of One Shilling.

Subscribers' Names received by all Booksellers.

CONTENTS OF THE ADVERTISEMENT SHEET.

As it is intended next year to issue the Diocesan Calendar earlier, ADVERTISEMENTS *for next year's issue must be sent to the* PUBLISHERS, BROAD-STREET, OXFORD, *by October 20th, 1859.*

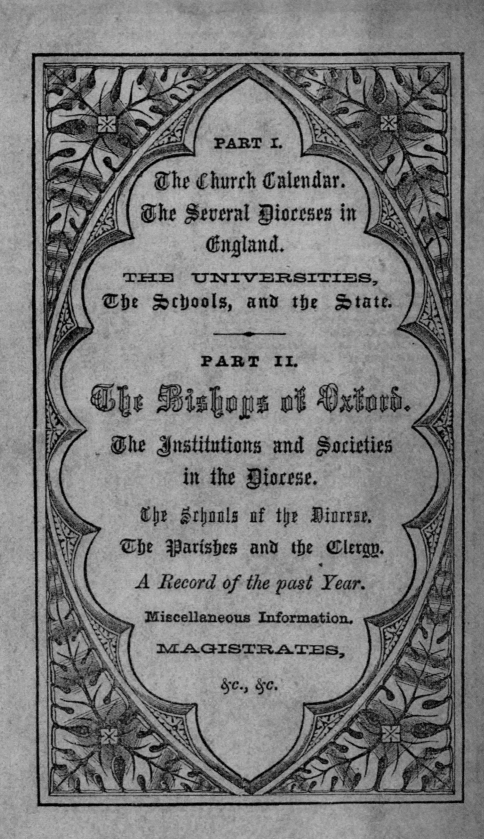

PART I.

The Church Calendar.
The Several Dioceses in
England.

THE UNIVERSITIES,
The Schools, and the State.

PART II.

The Bishops of Oxford.

The Institutions and Societies
in the Diocese.

The Schools of the Diocese.
The Parishes and the Clergy.

A Record of the past Year.

Miscellaneous Information.

MAGISTRATES,

&c., &c.

CPSIA information can be obtained at www.ICGtesting.com
Printed in the USA
BVOW07s1430240314

348598BV00009B/441/P